Fodor's

VENICE

Welcome to Venice

Venice is a city unlike any other. No matter how often you've seen it in photos and films, the real thing is more dreamlike than you could imagine. With canals where streets should be, water shimmers everywhere. The fabulous palaces and churches reflect centuries of history in what was a wealthy trading center between Europe and Asia. Getting lost in the narrow alleyways is a quintessential part of exploring Venice, but at some point you'll almost surely end up in Piazza San Marco, where tourists and locals congregate for a coffee or an aperitif.

TOP REASONS TO GO

★ **Landmarks:** The Rialto Bridge and Palazzo Ducale are simply unforgettable.

★ **Festivals:** Carnevale and the Biennale are celebrations of art, film, music, and dance.

★ **Art:** Titian, Tintoretto, and Tiepolo, as well as contemporary artists, are represented.

★ **Seafood:** Fish so fresh many restaurants boast they don't even own a refrigerator.

★ **Churches:** The Basilica di San Marco and Santa Maria della Salute are two of many.

★ **Shopping:** Spectacular masks, candy-color glass, paper goods, lace, and linens.

Contents

Fodor's Features

MAPS

Chapter 1

EXPERIENCE VENICE

18 ULTIMATE EXPERIENCES

Venice offers terrific experiences that should be on every traveler's list. Here are Fodor's top picks for a memorable trip.

1 Piazza San Marco

Perhaps nowhere else in the world gathers together so many of humankind's noblest artistic creations. The centerpiece of the piazza is the Basilica di San Marco, the most beautiful Byzantine church in the West. Next door is the magnificent Palazzo Ducale.

2 Grand Canal by Vaporetto

No one ever forgets a first trip down the Grand Canal. It's one of any world traveler's great experiences, and it can all be had via Venice's public vaporetti boats.

3 Art Museums

The Gallerie dell'Accademia, the greatest art museum in northern Italy, is a treasure trove of Venetian masters: Titian, Veronese, Tintoretto, Tiepolo, Bellini, and more.

4 Biennale

This international festival showcases the best art, film, music, dance, theater, and architecture April through November, alternating focuses each year. The city's palaces, churches, and more host exhibits.

5 Gelato

During warmer months, gelato—the Italian equivalent of ice cream—is a national obsession. It is the only food that is socially acceptable to eat while walking on the street and not at a table.

6 Gondola Ride

Sure, a gondola ride is the obvious tourist experience, but being rowed through Venice's narrow back canals allows you to see the most beautiful facades in the city up close.

7 Wine at a Bacaro

The Venetian hinterland and adjacent provinces comprise one of the major wine-producing areas in Europe. A visit to one of the city's *bacari*, or wine bars, will allow you to savor the Veneto's wines.

8 Rialto Bridge and Market

Come for the markets, stay for the views at this picturesque bridge, the oldest of the four that cross the Grand Canal.

9 Scuola Grande di San Rocco

Although this elegant example of Venetian Renaissance architecture is bold and dramatic outside, its contents are even more so—more than 60 Tintoretto paintings.

10 La Passeggiata

A favorite Italian pastime is *la passeggiata* (literally, strolling), and in Venice, the favorite place for the ritual is the Zattere, the southern walkway of the city, facing the Giudecca.

11 L'Aperitivo

A late afternoon or early evening ritual is to meet friends at a bar or café for an aperitif, either a spritz or a glass of prosecco. It's supplemented with *cicheti*, or Venetian tapas.

12 Opera at La Fenice

Attending an opera at Venice's historic, restored 18th-century opera house allows you to hear some of the best music the city has to offer and brings you into contact with all walks of Venetian society.

13 Caffè

The Venetian day begins and ends with coffee, and more cups of caffè punctuate the time in between. To live like the Venetians, drink as they drink, standing at the counter or sitting at an outdoor table.

14 Il Dolce Far Niente

"The sweetness of doing nothing" has long been an art form in Italy. It means doing things differently: lingering over a glass of wine, strolling, or savoring a sunset.

15 Churches

In Venice, churches like Santa Maria Gloriosa dei Frari were built as a way of demonstrating wealth and power; hence, the proliferation of splendid religious buildings.

16 Palaces

When in Venice, you must see at least two of its stunning palaces: the Doge's Palace and Ca' Rezzonico, which once hosted some of the grandest parties in the city's history.

17 Islands of the Lagoon

See strikingly colorful homes on Burano, shop for Venetian glass on Murano, and visit the spectacular cathedral on Torcello with a visit to the islands surrounding Venice.

18 Carnevale

The days leading up to Lent draw many visitors to Venice for festivities, including masquerade balls, fashion shows, street performances, and all sorts of revelry.

WHAT'S WHERE

1 San Marco. Monument-filled Piazza San Marco famously houses the Basilica di San Marco, the Doge's Palace, and other museums and architectural treasures.

2 Dorsoduro. Visitors head here for top sights like Santa Maria della Salute, the Gallerie dell'Accademia, and the Peggy Guggenheim Collection; Venetians relax in lively Campo San Margherita and stroll the Zattere promenade.

3 San Polo. Two of Venice's great treasure houses, the Frari church and the Scuola di San Rocco, rise above bustling streets near the Rialto fish and produce markets.

4 Santa Croce. The main attractions of this residential district are the Baroque church of San Stae and the leafy and peaceful Campo San Giacomo dall'Orio.

5 Cannaregio. The sunny Fondamenta della Misericordia is a hub of restaurants and cafés; the Jewish Ghetto reveals a fascinating history.

6 Castello. This workaday district is home to the church of Santi Giovanni e Paolo, Carpaccio's paintings

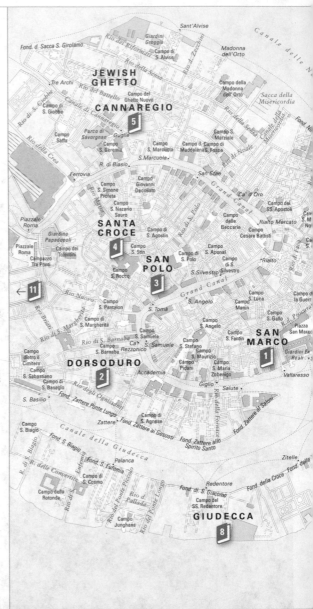

in the Scuola di San Giorgio, and the Querini Stampalia museum.

7 San Giorgio Maggiore. This island across from Piazza San Marco is home to the Cini Foundation.

8 The Giudecca. Palladio's elegant Redentore church is the major landmark on this large island where the main attractions are serene isolation and wonderful views of Venice.

9 The Lido. This barrier island closes the Venetian Lagoon off from the Adriatic and is Venice's beach.

10 Islands of the Lagoon. Torcello, even older than Venice, has a mosaic-rich cathedral; Murano is known for its glass industry; colorful Burano is the center of lace production; and San Michele is the cemetery island.

11 Side Trips. To the west of Venice are three great art cities: Padua, noted for the Cappella degli Scrovegni; Vicenza, known for its Palladian architecture; and Verona, one of Italy's oldest and most beautiful cities. The Friuli–Venezia Giulia area bears the mark of the Romans (in Aquileia), the 18th-century painter Gianbattista Tiepolo (in Udine), and Habsburg nobility (in Trieste).

Venice Today

While Venice spends a great deal of energy preserving its past, this city is also entrenched in the here and now and modern Venetian life has many fascinating facets. Specifically, Venice. . .

...FEELS THE INFLUENCE OF IMMIGRATION, BUT STILL RETAINS ITS CULTURAL INTEGRITY

Venice, like the rest of Italy, has recently experienced an influx of immigrants, and Venetians are fairly open to these newcomers. The city has a proud cosmopolitan tradition. Renaissance Venice had one of the largest, and richest, Jewish communities in Europe, and the Greek, Turkish, Armenian, German, Albanian, and Slavic communities have given their names to important streets and buildings. Pressure upon immigrants to assimilate culturally is much less intense here than it is in other Italian cities. They are hired and befriended, and some even learn Venetian dialect, but they are not expected to become Venetians. Local Venetian culture has, overall, maintained itself pretty well. The local dialect is spoken by all levels of society. Venetians still enjoy the 18th-century dialect comedies of Goldoni, and it's not uncommon to hear dialect spoken by elegant operagoers at La Fenice. Local festivals, such as the Redentore, Salute, and la Sensa, are celebrated with enthusiasm.

...IS A CITY OF PISCIVORES

As is to be expected in a maritime republic, fish plays the starring role on the traditional Venetian table. Certain fish, such as sardines, are plentiful and always fresh, and working class neighborhoods are frequently pungent with the perfume of grilled sardines, which you can frequently also find in inexpensive restaurants. Or you can try the traditional Venetian classic, *sarde in saor,* fresh fried sardines marinated in olive oil, sautéed onions, vinegar, raisins, and pine nuts, an ancient recipe from Venice's time as part of the Byzantine Empire. Another classic and inexpensive fish dish is *seppie al nero,* cuttlefish stewed in a sauce made with its own ink, generally served with creamy polenta. The one classic Venetian pasta dish is *bigoli in salsa,* thick homemade whole wheat spaghetti, with a sauce featuring anchovies, fried onions, and cinnamon; the anchovies are totally transformed by the sweetness and pungency of the onions and cinnamon.

...GOES WILD FOR FRESH VEGETABLES

Venetians are passionate about vegetables from the islands in the Venetian Lagoon, especially from the island of Sant'Erasmo, and those from the adjacent mainland. In the spring Venetians wait anxiously for the *castraure,* the tiny white artichokes from Sant'Erasmo, with as much zeal as the Piemontesi wait for the white truffles of Alba in the fall. But the castraure are even rarer. Since they grow only one to a plant, their number is very limited, and each year's crop is consumed almost totally in Venice. Springtime also brings the plump, succulent white asparagus from Bassano, in the foothills of the Dolomites north of Venice, and in the fall there is the famous radicchio, a red and white endive, from Treviso, just a stone's throw from Venice on the mainland. *Pasta e fagioli,* bean soup with pasta, is enjoyed all over Italy, but in Venice it is frequently made with beans from the mainland Veneto town of Lamon, which have a delicate and complex taste and beat out other beans hands down.

...IS ONE WITH THE SEA

Venetians historically have taken great pleasure from rowing out into the lagoon to gaze back at their city. They are acutely aware of the beauty of Venice—they, just like the visitors, never tire of it—and there are few views more breathtaking than sunset on the lagoon with the domes and towers of the city in the background. Venetian youth take to the waters for fun. Although soccer, the Italian national passion, is widely followed in Venice, Venetian youths seem to prefer sailing and cruising in motorboats on the lagoon or duck hunting in the salt marshes, and Venetian couples often go out for a moonlit sail on the lagoon. Many young Venetians also join rowing clubs and learn how to row *alla veneta*, standing up in the stern, like a gondolier.

...DOES NOT LIVE BY TOURISM ALONE

Because of the hordes of tourists, many visitors get the false impression that Venice is simply a tourist attraction and is no longer a real city. In fact, Venice officials have announced they will limit the number of tourists allowed in per day, and cruise ships have been banned from docking in the lagoon. While tourism is obviously important for the economy, most visitors are unaware that Venice is also a major educational center, home to three major institutions of higher learning. The largest of the three, Ca' Foscari, has more than 17,000 students; the School of Architecture is one of the most prestigious in Italy; and Venice International University attracts students and scholars from all over the world. Venice also has thriving glass, fishing, shipbuilding, and petroleum-refining industries.

...BATTLES RISING WATERS

While Venice may be sinking slightly, it is rising water levels and seasonal high tides (*acqua alta*) that are the main problem. Industrial landfill in the lagoon and the channels dug to accommodate the oil tankers and cruise ships have increased the frequency and intensity of the floods, as have the rising sea levels

caused by worldwide climate change and an increase in the frequency of the sirocco winds from North Africa that force the waters of the Adriatic up into the Venetian Lagoon. The city is pinning hopes on a long-term solution: the MOSE system. Its four defense barriers at the lagoon inlets by the Lido, Malamocco, and Chioggia were first tested during an acqua alta event in October 2020.

...STRIVES TO COMBINE THE NEW WITH THE OLD

Most visitors to Venice enter into a world of the past, and the city seems more suited to life in the 18th century than to the exigencies of modern life. Nevertheless, Venice is also a center of contemporary artistic creativity. There are, of course, the Biennale Arte, Venice's biannual international festival of contemporary art, its annual festival of cinema on the Lido, and the Biennale Architettura. Even more significant for everyday life in Venice, however, is one of the first things visitors see when they enter the city: the elegant and graceful bridge crossing the Grand Canal and linking the bus station at Piazzale Roma with the train station, by noted Spanish contemporary architect Santiago Calatrava. At the other end of the Grand Canal is Japanese architect Tadao Ando's inventive remodeling of the 17th-century customs depot to house contemporary art. But modernity in Venice has its limits: protests prohibited the construction of two concrete obelisks at Ando's entrance to the Pinault Collection, and Charles Ray's contemporary statue of a nude boy holding a frog, which had become an icon of the collection, was removed and replaced with a traditional lantern at the well-loved Venetian meeting spot on the point.

Best Museums in Venice

PEGGY GUGGENHEIM COLLECTION

Wealthy art collector and dealer and socialite Peggy Guggenheim turned Palazzo Venier dei Leoni, an unfinished but upscale bungalow on the Canal Grande, into a modern art gallery in 1951. It contains the most stunning collection of surrealist, cubist, and abstract expressionist art in Italy.

MUSEO CORRER

Abbot Teodore Correr's bequest to Venice has some gorgeous artworks from Bellini, Canova, Carpaccio, and da Messina. The exhibition spaces were remodeled in an understated contemporary style by influential 20th-century architect Carlo Scarpa. Seek out *The Two Venetian Ladies* (aka *The Courtesans*).

CA' PESARO INTERNATIONAL

The imposing Baroque palazzo Ca' Pesaro on the Canal Grande houses the International Gallery of Modern Art, a captivating collection of 19th- and 20th-century paintings and sculptures. In addition to work by Matisse, Kandinsky, and Klimt, there's a wealth of Italian art.

GALLERIE DELL'ACCADEMIA

One of the top fine art galleries in the world and *the* best for Venetian paintings, this art haven consists of three handsome religious buildings that sit by the Grand Canal and Accademia Bridge. Originally created by the Venetian Senate in 1750 as a fine art school, L'Accademia moved to its present site in 1807. This is the place to soak up works by Venetian masters Bellini, Giorgione, Tintoretto, Carpaccio, and Veronese.

PALAZZO DUCALE (DOGE'S PALACE)

All the decisions that brought the rise and fall of the Venetian empire took place at this seat and expression of power. A comprehensive tour of the opulent Gothic palace of sorts lets you walk in the footsteps of 120 doges up the Scala dei Giganti. You'll stroll amid sumptuous chambers festooned with great artworks by the likes of Veronese and Tintoretto and creep around the doge's private apartments and secret passageways.

CA' REZZONICO

Built in 1648 and remodeled by Massari 107 years later for the Rezzonico family, the palazzo now houses the Museum of 18th Century Venice. Architectural marvels include the grand ballroom by Visconti, the Sala dell'Allegoria Nuziale with its chariot by Tiepolo, and Massari's grand staircase. Rooms are devoted to la crema della crema of 1700s art from Canaletto to Guardi.

SCUOLA GRANDE DI SAN ROCCO

Built in the 1500s as a charitable confraternity guild (the Venetian *scuole* were a kind of social worker mens' clubs), the real draw for visitors today are the stunning 60-plus paintings by Tintoretto. The commission took the maestro 23 years to complete; the scale and intensity of his vision is breathtaking.

LACE MUSEUM

A former governmental palace on Burano, which, from 1872 to 1970, housed the Lace School, is now dedicated to the island's famed craft. The museum tells the story of Venetian lacemaking from its origins in the 11th century, with needlepoint technique finessed from the Aegean during the Renaissance. Elaborate examples illustrate the 16th-century boom in the industry, renewal under Napoleonic rule, and present-day trends.

PUNTA DELLA DOGANA

Set in the old Sea Customs House (1682) at the western tip (*punta*) of Dorsoduro and the Canal Grande, this contemporary art gallery has one of Venice's most dramatic locations. The Pinault Collection displays changing artworks amid the stunningly revamped historic building. The real pull of this place is the view from the punta outside, with its water-level views of San Marco, Giudecca, and beyond.

GLASS MUSEUM

The compact yet illuminating collection of glass is worth visiting to get a feel for Murano glass styles before making any purchases. Displays and artifacts stretching back to the 3rd century tell the story of glassmaking and its various techniques, many of which are still in use today.

What to Eat and Drink in Venice

PASTA E FAGIOLI

Pasta e fasiòi veneziana is the Venetian version of the hearty Italian classic pasta e fagioli, a bean soup with pasta. Here, it's filled with ingredients like short dried pasta and Lamon beans. The dish packs in a ton of flavor and is usually enjoyed as a first course.

GELATO

This creamier, richer, more intensely flavored type of ice cream is ubiquitous in Venice, served in myriad flavors, like *nocciola* (hazelnut) and *fragola* (strawberry), either in a *coppa* (small tub) or a *cono* (cone). Eaten as a snack or a dessert, the best gelato is homemade, labeled *produzione propria* or *fatto in casa*.

CICHETI

You can sample regional wines and scrumptious cicheti (small snacks) in bacari (wine bars), a great Venetian tradition. Crostini and *polpette* (meat, fish, or vegetable croquettes) are popular cicheti, as are small sandwiches, seafood salads, *baccalà mantecato* (creamy, whipped salt cod), and toothpick-speared items like roasted peppers, marinated artichokes, and mozzarella balls.

WINE

Tre Venezie regional wines (from the Veneto, Trentino–Alto Adige, and Friuli–Venezia Giulia) go far beyond the famous Amarone and include some spectacular white varieties, such as the crisp Malvasia, the hearty Friulano, and the smooth Garganega (Soave) and Ribolla Gialla, along with the versatile, just-dry-enough bubbly prosecco. Reds are dry, flavorful, and relatively low in alcohol.

SPRITZ

The refreshing *aperitivo* (aperitif, or pre-meal drink) had all over the Veneto is two parts dry white wine or prosecco and one part Aperol (a bright-orange herb liquor) or Campari (for a more bitter punch), sometimes with a bit of soda water. Enjoy it on a hot summer day, lounging at tables on the Piazza San Marco and gabbing with friends over cicheti.

TIRAMISU

Famous the world over, this creamy coffee-flavor dessert was invented in the Veneto. The luscious concoction is made with layers of ladyfingers soaked in espresso and rum or brandy, plus heaps of mascarpone cream and dustings of cinnamon.

RISOTTO

Cooked with broth or wine and Parmesan cheese, this creamy northern Italian rice dish is a great first course, especially when loaded with local shellfish or mushrooms. Venetians favor it *al onda* ("undulating" as opposed to firm).

POLENTA

This cornmeal staple is often served with meaty sauces, either in the consistency of porridge or solidified and cooled into a block, then baked, grilled, or fried.

SARDE IN SAOR

In this classic Venetian dish, fresh pan-fried sardines are marinated with onions, raisins, and pine nuts.

LINGUINE AL NERO DI SEPPIA

Noodles covered in strikingly black squid-ink sauce make this dish a showstopper. Garlic and olive oil enhance the flavor.

BELLINI

Created at Venice institution Harry's Bar in the '40s, this cocktail made with prosecco and peach puree was invented by founder and barman Giuseppe Cipriani, who named it after a famous Italian painter.

FRITTURA MISTA

A summery dish of tempura-like fried seafood and vegetables is served with a lemon wedge to squeeze.

What to Buy in Venice

MASKS

The boom in Venetian mask shops started in the late 1970s when the Carnevale tradition was resurrected. There is now a dizzying array of masks for sale across Venice, in countless sizes, colors, designs, and materials, from cheap, mass-produced ceramics to the original white papier-mâché to more recent ornate designs and handcrafted leather inspired by the commedia dell'arte. Leather and gilded masks and expensive *pezzi da collezione* (collectors' items)—unique pieces whose casts are destroyed—can be sought too. For the best value, compare several producers.

GLASS

Colorful glass, much of it made on Murano, is Venice's trademark product. Bear in mind that the value of any piece—signature and shape apart—is also based on the number and quality of colors, the presence of gold, and, in the case of goblets, the thinness of the glass.

CERAMICS

Venice may be known for glass, but there is also lovely pottery to be found. Look for replicas of 19th-century chocolate cups, usually cream-white and delicately gilded (not for daily use); pottery from Bassano, typically decorated with reliefs of fruit and vegetables; and some modern, handmade plates and mugs.

LEATHER GOODS

In Venice you'll find a wide assortment of leather goods, especially shoes, gloves, and crossbody bags. There are plenty of boutiques selling upmarket designer articles; for less fancy items, explore the areas of Rialto and Campo San Polo.

LACE

Burano is the traditional home of Venetian lace-making and, although most of the lace sold in town is machine-made in China or Taiwan, you can still find the real thing in the best shops. Surprisingly, period lace (made between 1900 and 1940) is easier to find and less expensive than contemporary lace.

BOTTEGHE FASHIONS

Wandering around the *calli* (streets) you'll come across small, one-off *botteghe*: independent shops selling unusual clothing and accessories, such as handmade slippers, hats, and gloves, plus lavish fabrics from around the world. Some even have workshops out back where owners may tell you about their craft and the stories behind each item and design.

VENETIAN WOODWORK

The sculpted walnut-wood oarlocks (*fórcole*) used exclusively by Venetian rowers may be utilitarian, but they are beautiful, custom-made objects that make for uniquely Venetian gifts or souvenirs. Saverio Pastor in Dorsoduro is one of the few remaining oar and fórcola makers in Venice.

JEWELRY

Venetians have always liked gold, and the city is packed with top-of-the-line jewelry stores, as well as more modest shops found, most notably, around the Rialto district. A typical piece of inexpensive jewelry is the *murrina*, a thin, round slice of colored glass (imagine a bunch of colored spaghetti firmly held together and sliced) encircled with gold and sold as a pendant or earrings.

GOLDWORK

Venice's passion for glittering golden objects, which took off with the decoration in the Basilica di San Marco and later spread into the finest noble palaces, kept specialized gold artisans (called *doradori*) busy throughout the city's history. They still produce lovely cabinets, shelves, wall lamps, lanterns, candleholders, banisters, headboards, frames, and the like by applying gold leaf to wrought iron and carved wood.

PAPER GOODS

In 1482 Venice was the printing capital of the world, and nowadays you'll find dozens of *legatori* (bookbinderies) around town. Hand-printed paper and ornate leather-bound diaries make great souvenirs. Some shops are filled with more contemporary designs with lavish covers made of silk.

Architectural Wonders in Venice

PONTE DI RIALTO

The iconic Ponte di Rialto was completed in 1591. Its generous arch, central portal, and Renaissance arcade make it appear so beautifully balanced that Palladio himself would surely have approved.

SAN FRANCESCO DELLA VIGNA

The harmonious combination of architectural designs by two Renaissance maestri and the tranquil neighborhood setting make this church a wonderful place to escape the crowds.

MOLINO STUCKY

This behemoth, neo-Gothic warehouse-like building, formerly a flour mill and pasta factory, on the western end of the Giudecca certainly stands out on the Venetian skyline.

SANTA MARIA DELLA SALUTE

One of the city's most beloved and iconic churches, La Salute was built to mark the end of the 1630 plague that took almost 50,000 Venetian lives.

PUNTA DELLA DOGANA

There has been a Punta della Dogana (Sea Customs House) situated between the Grand and Giudecca Canals since the 15th century, although the building you see today was designed in the 1860s. Above the entrance tower, two Atlases lift a bronze sphere topped by the figure of Fortune.

ARSENALE

For centuries, the colossal Arsenale complex of shipyards, warehouses, and armories was Europe's largest military-industrial compound. Although many areas are still cordoned off as military zones, the southern side is open to the public during the Biennale Arte.

JEWISH GHETTO

Originally the site of a foundry (*geto* in the local dialect), both the atmosphere and the architecture set the Jewish Ghetto apart: palazzi and *case* (houses) are taller here than elsewhere, with story upon story piled on high in an effort to make the best use of limited space.

PALAZZO DUCALE

Adorned with a series of soaring Gothic arches topped by an ornately columned arcade, the labyrinthine Doge's Palace has a wedding-cake-like delicacy when viewed from the Piazza San Marco or the waterside Bacino di San Marco.

MADONNA DELL'ORTO

An alluring, redbrick Gothic church with ornate marble decoration, it was dedicated to St. Christopher, the patron saint of travelers, until a Madonna statue was found in a nearby *orto* (kitchen vegetable garden).

CA' DA MOSTO

As you drift along the Grand Canal, you'll see palazzi far more eye-catching than the Ca' da Mosto, but none more enduring—the crumbling Byzantine-style palace has been here since the 13th century. The ground and first floors are an example of a *casa fondaco*, a building that combined both a merchant's living space and office or warehouse.

Carnevale in Venice

Ever since its revival in the 18th century, the Venice Carnevale has been aimed at drawing visitors to the city. For the 12 days leading up to *quaresima* (Lent), the city celebrates, with more than half a million people attending masquerade balls, historical processions, concerts, plays, street performances, fashion shows, and all other manner of revelry.

The first record of Carnevale dates back to 1097, but it was in the 18th century that Venice earned its international reputation as the "city of Carnevale." During that era the partying began after Epiphany (January 6) and transformed the city for over a month into one ongoing masquerade. After the Republic's fall in 1797, Carnevale was periodically prohibited by the French and then the Austrian occupiers. After the departure of the Austrians in 1866, Venetians were slow to reinstate the festivities.

Carnevale was not revived again until 1979, when the municipality saw a way of converting the unruly antics of throwing water balloons in the days preceding Lent into a more pleasant celebration. It wasn't long before events became more elaborate, emulating their 18th-century predecessors.

Many of Carnevale's costume balls are open to the public—but they come with an extravagant price tag, and the most popular need to be booked well in advance. Balls start at roughly €295 per person, dinner included, and though you can rent a standard costume for €200–€400 (not including shoes or mask), the most elaborate attire can cost much more.

EVENTS TO WATCH FOR

The **Ballo del Doge** (☎ 041/2413802, 041/5224426) is one of the most exclusive (and expensive) events, held at Palazzo Pisani Moretta the last Saturday of Carnevale. Full participation in the ball, including dinner, costs €1,800 per person, but you can opt for admission after dinner, at €800 per person.

Those on a tighter budget should look into the **Ballo Tiepolo** (☎ 041/524668, 041/722285), which also takes place in the Tiepolo-frescoed ballroom of Pisani Moretta and costs €550 per person.

You don't have to blow the bank on a masquerade ball in order to take part in Carnevale—many people go simply for the exuberant street life. Be aware, though, that the crowds are enormous, and ball or no ball, prices for everything absolutely skyrocket.

Carnevale events and schedules change from year to year. If you want to attend, first check out these resources:

The official **Carnevale website** (⊕ www.carnevale.venezia.it) has listings and a blog with behind-the-scenes stories, as well as links to other official events.

The official **City of Venice website** (⊕ www.veneziaunica.it) and the tourist office at Santa Lucia railway station (☎ 041/5298711) have detailed information about daily events.

Uno Ospite di Venezia (⊕ www.unospitedivenezia.it/en) advertises public and private events for free, and as a result it's one of the most complete—if potentially overwhelming—Carnevale guides.

Venice's Biennale

The **Biennale Arte** originated in 1894 and, except for COVID-19 and World War interruptions, has taken place every two years since. In 1910 Klimt and Renoir had their own exhibition rooms, while Picasso was removed from the Spanish salon over concern his paintings were too shocking. Picasso's work was finally shown in 1948, the same year Peggy Guggenheim brought her collection to Venice at the Biennale's invitation. During the century-plus of its existence, it has become one of the world's major interdisciplinary art expositions. "Biennale" now refers to the group that coordinates festivals of art, film, music, dance, theater, and architecture.

WHERE TO GO
Traditionally, the Biennale Arte has taken place from mid-June to early November, but in recent years it has been extended to late April through late November. It is usually held in odd-numbered years. The Giardini della Biennale, in the sestiere Castello, was developed specifically for the event. In this park-like setting overlooking the lagoon, 30 countries have permanent pavilions to exhibit works by their sponsored artists. In the neighboring Arsenale's Corderie, a long, impressive former rope-works building otherwise off-limits to visitors has works by artists from smaller nations, as well as some more avant-garde installations. Numerous palaces, warehouses, and churches all over town also hold exhibits, often in buildings not normally open to the public.

MOVIES
The **Biennale Cinema** (also known as the Mostra Internazionale d'Arte Cinematografica, or Venice Film Festival) was first held in 1932 and soon became an annual event. Films are shown in several theaters at the **Palazzo del Cinema** (✉ *Lungomare Guglielmo Marconi 90, Lido*

☎ *041/5218711* 🚊 *Vaporetto: Lido Casinò or S.M. Elizabetta*), which is closed most of the year but comes to life in August with bright lights, movie stars, and thousands of fans.

Ten days of screenings include films vying for awards as well as retrospectives and debuts of mainstream releases. Advance tickets are recommended for the most eagerly awaited films (the tourist office has details). The night after major films play the Palazzo del Cinema, they're shown in Venice proper at Campo San Polo's open-air cinema and at the Giorgione Movie d'Essai. San Polo screens the winner of the Leone d'Oro (Golden Lion) prize the night following the awards ceremony.

MUSIC
Since its launch in 1930, the **Biennale Musica** has attracted world-famous composers and performers. Igor Stravinsky premiered *The Rake's Progress* during the 1951 festival, and four years later it was George Gershwin's turn with *Porgy and Bess*. The annual event stretches over several months, with performances in some of the city's smaller venues.

THEATER, ARCHITECTURE, AND MORE
The **Biennale Danza** and **Biennale Teatro** both stage performances during the year in the city's *campi* (squares) and in other venues. The Teatro Verde, an outdoor amphitheater on the island of San Giorgio, was restored for Biennale use, and you can't beat its lagoon backdrop. The **Biennale Architettura** began in 1980 and now exhibits in the Corderie in alternate years with the Biennale Arte.

INFORMATION
For information on all events, visit ⊕ *www.labiennale.org* or contact **La Biennale di Venezia** (✉ *Ca' Giustinian, San Marco 1364/A* ☎ *041/5218711*).

Speaking Venetian

Venice is one of the few Italian cities where the local dialect is still alive and well. Much of the language you hear in Venice is not Italian but rather Venetian, or Italian heavily laced with Venetian. *Veneziano* (in Italian) or locally *Venessian* has its own rich and widely respected literature. The Venetian dialect comedies of Goldoni, the great 18th-century playwright, are regularly performed in the city the natives call *Venessia*.

Even when speaking Italian, Venetians will use dialect terms to refer to certain common objects. Sometimes the term means something totally different in standard Italian.

Here are a few frequently used words:

■ *sestiere:* One of six neighborhoods in central Venice.

■ *rio:* A canal. Only the Grand Canal and a few other major waterways are called "canali." Everything else is a "rio."

■ *fondamenta:* A quay, a street running along a canal or a "rio."

■ *calle:* A street, what is elsewhere in Italy called a "via." "Via" is used in Venice, but it means "boulevard."

■ *campo:* A square—what is elsewhere in Italy called a piazza. (The only piazza in Venice is Piazza San Marco.)

■ *bacaro:* A traditional wine bar.

■ *cicheto* (pronounced chee-*kay*-toh): An hors d'oeuvre—roughly the Venetian equivalent of tapas—generally served at a bacaro and in many cafés.

■ *ombra:* A small glass of wine.

■ *focaccia:* A traditional Venetian raised sweet cake, similar to a panettone, but much lighter and without candied fruit or raisins. (Very different from the better-known Genoese focaccia, a dense slightly raised bread sometimes flavored with herbs or cheese.)

Venetians tend to use the informal second person form, *tu,* much more readily than people do in other parts of Italy. Venetians also frequently address each other with the term *amore* (love), as is done sometimes in England. But in Venice it is used even between members of the same sex, without any romantic connotation.

CRUISING THE GRAND CANAL

THE BEST INTRODUCTION TO VENICE IS A TRIP DOWN MAIN STREET

Venice's Grand Canal is one of the world's great thoroughfares. It winds its way from Piazzale Roma to Piazza San Marco, passing 200 palazzi built from the 13th to the 18th centuries by Venice's richest and most powerful families. There's a theatrical quality to a boat ride on the canal: it's as if each pink- or gold-tinted facade is trying to steal your attention from its rival across the way.

In medieval and Renaissance cities, wars and sieges required defense to be an element of design; but in rich, impregnable Venice, you could safely show off what you had. But more than being simply an item of conspicuous consumption, a Venetian's palazzo was an embodiment of his person—not only his wealth, but also his erudition and taste.

The easiest and cheapest way to see the Grand Canal is to take the Line 1 vaporetto (water bus) from Piazalle Roma to San Marco. The ride takes about 35 minutes. Invest in a day ticket and you can spend the better part of a day hopping on and off at the vaporetto's many stops, visiting the sights along the banks. Keep your eyes open for the highlights listed here; some have fuller descriptions later in this chapter.

FROM PIAZZALE ROMA TO RIALTO

Palazzo Labia

Tiepolo's masterpiece, the cycle of Antony and Cleopatra, graces the grand ballroom in this palazzo. The Labia family, infamous for their ostentation, commissioned the frescos to celebrate a marriage and had Tiepolo use the face of the family matriarch, Maria Labia, for that of Cleopatra. Luckily, Maria Labia was known not only for her money, but also for her intelligence and her beauty.

Santa Maria di Nazareth

Ponte di Scalzi

R. Di BIASIO

FERROVIA

Stazione Ferrovia Santa Lucia

SANTA CROCE

Ponte di Calatrava

After you pass the Ferrovia, the baroque church immediately to your left is the baroque **Santa Maria di Nazareth**, called the Chiesa degli Scalzi (Church of the Barefoot).

After passing beneath the Ponte di Scalzi, ahead to the left, where the Canale di Cannaregio meets the Grand Canal, you'll spy **Palazzo Labia**, an elaborate 18th-century palace built for the social-climbing Labia family.

Known for their ostentation even in this city where modesty was seldom a virtue, the Labias chose a location that required three facades instead of the usual one.

A bit farther down, across the canal, is the 13th-century **Fondaco dei Turchi**, an elegant residence that served as a combination commercial center and ghetto for the Turkish community. Try not to see the side towers and the crenellations; they were

added during a 19th-century restoration.

Beyond it is the obelisk-topped **Ca' Belloni-Battagia**, designed for the Belloni family by star architect Longhena. Look for the family crest he added prominently on the facade.

On the opposite bank is architect Mauro Codussi's magnificent **Palazzo Vendramin-Calergi**, designed just before 1500. Codussi ingeniously married the fortress-like Renaissance style of the Florentine Alberti's Palazzo Rucellai to the lacy delicacy of the Venetian Gothic, creating the prototype of the Venetian Renaissance palazzo. The palazzo is now Venice's casino.

Palazzo Vendramin-Calergi
Venice's first Renaissance palazzo. Immediately recognized as a masterpiece, it was so highly regarded that later, when its subsequent owners, the Calergi, were convicted of murder and their palace was to be torn down as punishment, the main building was spared.

Ca' d'Oro
Inspired by stories of Nero's Domus Aurea (Golden House) in Rome, the first owner had parts of the facade gilded with 20,000 sheets of gold leaf. The gold has long worn away, but the Ca' D'Oro is still Venice's most beautiful Gothic palazzo.

Ca' da Mosto
Venice's oldest surviving palazzo gives you an idea of Marco Polo's Venice. More than any other Byzantine palazzo in town, it maintains its original 13th-century appearance.

GHETTO

S. MARCUOLA

Church of San Marcuola

Ca' Belloni-Battagia

S. STAE

Ca' Pesaro

Fondaco dei Turchi

Depositi del Megio

San Stae Church

CA' D'ORO

SAN POLO

Ca' Corner della Regina

Rialto Mercato

Pescheria
Stop by in the morning to see the incredible variety of fish for sale. Produce stalls fill the adjacent fondamenta. Butchers and cheesemongers occupy the surrounding shops.

Fondaco dei Tedeschi

Ca' dei Camerlenghi

RIALTO

SAN MARCO

The whimsically Baroque church of **San Stae** on the right bank is distinguished by a host of marble saints on its facade.

Farther along the bank is one of Longhena's Baroque masterpieces, **Ca' Pesaro**. It is now the Museum of Modern Art.

Next up on the left is **Ca' d'Oro** (1421-1438), the canal's most spendid example of Venetian Gothic domestic design. Across from this palazzo is the loggia of the neo-Gothic *pescheria*, Venice's fish market.

Slightly farther down, on the bank opposite from the vegetable market, is the early 13th-century **Ca' da Mosto**, the oldest building on the Grand Canal. The upper two floors are later additions, but the ground floor and piano nobile give you a good idea of a rich merchant's house during the time of Marco Polo.

As you approach the Rialto Bridge, to the left, just before the bridge, is the

Fondaco dei Tedeschi. German merchants kept warehouses, offices, and residences here; its facade was originally frescoed by Titian and Giorgione.

FROM RIALTO TO THE PONTE DELL' ACCADEMIA

SAN POLO

Ponte di Rialto

RIALTO

Ca' Foscari
The canal's most imposing Gothic masterpiece, Ca' Foscari was built to blot out the memory of a traitor to the Republic.

Palazzo Barzizza

Ca' Loredan

S. SILVESTRO

Ca' Farsetti

Palazzo Pisani Moretta

Ca' Grimani

S. ANGELO

TOMA

Ca' Garzoni

Ca' Balbi

Palazzo Grassi

Ca' Rezzonico

REZZONICO

SAN MARCO

ACCADEMIA

Gallerie dell'Accademia

DORSODURO

The shop-lined **Ponte di Rialto** was built in stone after former wooden bridges had burned or collapsed. As you pass under the bridge, on your left stands star architect Sansovino's Palazzo Dolfin Manin. The white stone–clad Renaissance palace was built at huge expense and over the objections of its conservative neighbors.

A bit farther down stand **Ca' Loredan** and **Ca' Farsetti**, 13th-century Byzantine palaces that today make up Venice's city hall.

Along the same side is the **Ca' Grimani**, by the Veronese architect Sanmichele. Legend has it that the palazzo's oversized windows were demanded by the young Grimani's fiancée, who insisted that he build her a palazzo on the Canalè Grande with windows larger than the portal of her own house.

At the Sant'Angelo landing, the vaporetto passes close to Codussi's **Ca' Corner-Spinelli**. Back on the right bank, in a lovely salmon color, is the graceful **Palazzo Pisani Moretta**, built in the mid-15th century and typical of the Venetian Gothic palazzo of the generation after the Ca' D'Oro.

A bit farther down the right bank, crowned by obelisks, is **Ca' Balbi**. Niccolò Balbi built this elegant palazzo in order to upstage his former landlord, who had insulted him in public.

Farther down the right bank, where the Canale makes a sharp turn, is the imposing **Ca' Foscari**. Doge Francesco Foscari tore down an earlier palazzo on this spot and built this splendid palazzo to erase memory of the traitorous former owner. It is now the seat of the University of Venice.

Continuing down the right bank you'll find Longhena's **Ca' Rezzonico**, a magnificent baroque palace. Opposite stands the Grand Canal's youngest palace, Giorgio Massari's **Palazzo Grassi**, commissioned in 1749. It houses part of the François Pinot contemporary art collection.

Near the canal's fourth bridge, is the former church and monastery complex that houses the world-renowned **Gallerie dell'Accademia**, the world's largest and most distinguished collection of Venetian art.

ARCHITECTURAL STYLES ALONG THE GRAND CANAL

BYZANTINE: 13th century
Distinguishing characteristics: high, rounded arches, relief panels, multicolored marble.
Examples: Fondaco dei Turchi, Ca' Loredan, Ca' Farsetti, Ca' da Mosto

GOTHIC: 14th and 15th centuries
Distinguishing characteristics: pointed arches, high ceilings, and many windows.
Examples: Ca' d'Oro, Ca' Foscari, Palazzo Pisani Moretta, Ca' Barbaro (and, off the canal, Palazzo Ducale)

RENAISSANCE: 16th century
Distinguishing characteristics: classically influenced emphasis on harmony and motifs taken from classical antiquity.
Examples: Palazzo Vendramin-Calergi, Ca' Grimani, Ca' Corner-Spinelli, Ca' dei Camerlenghi, Ca' Balbi, Palazzo Corner della Ca' Granda, Palazzo Dolfin Manin, and, off the canal, Libreria, Sansoviniana on Piazza San Marco

BAROQUE: 17th century
Distinguishing characteristics: Renaissance order wedded with a more dynamic style, achieved through curving lines and complex decoration.
Examples: churches of Santa Maria di Nazareth, San Stae, and Santa Maris della Salute; Ca' Belloni Battaglia, Ca' Pesaro, Ca' Rezzonico

FROM THE PONTE DELL'ACCADEMIA TO SAN ZACCARIA

Ca' Barbaro
John Singer Sargent, Henry James, and Cole Porter are among the guests who have stayed at Ca' Barbaro. It was a center for elegant British and American society during the turn of the 20th century.

Santa Maria Della Salute
Baldessare Longhena was only 26 when he designed this church, which was to become one of Venice's major landmarks. Its rotunda form and dynamic Baroque decoration predate iconic Baroque churches in other Italian cities.

SAN MARCO

Ponte dell' Accademia

Ca' Pisani-Gritti

Palazzo Corner della Ca' Granda

ACCADEMIA

Casetta Rossa

S. M. DEL GIGLIO

DORSODURO

Ca' Barbarigo

SALUTE

Palazzo Salviati

Palazzo Venier dei Leoni
Eccentric art dealer Peggy Guggenheim's personal collection of modern art is here. At the Grand Canal entrance to the palazzo stands Marino Marini's sexually explicit equestrian sculpture, the Angel of the Citadel. Numerous entertaining stories have been spun around the statue and Ms. Guggenheim's overtly libertine ways.

S. Maria della Salute

Ca' Dario
Graceful and elegant Ca' Dario is reputed to carry a curse. Almost all its owners since the 15th century have met violent deaths or committed suicide. It was, nevertheless, a center for elegant French society at the turn of the 20th century.

Down from the Accademia Bridge, on the left bank next door to the fake Gothic Ca' Franchetti, is the beautiful **Ca' Barbaro**, designed by Giovanni Bon, who was also at work about that time on the Ca' D'Oro.

Farther along on the left bank Sansovino's first work in Venice, the **Palazzo Corner della Ca' Granda**, begun in 1533, still shows the influence of his Roman Renaissance contemporaries, Bramante and Giulio Romano. It faces the uncompleted **Palazzo Venier dei Leoni**, which holds the Peggy Guggenheim Collection, a good cross-section of the visual arts from 1940 to 1960.

Ca' Dario a bit farther down, was originally a Gothic palazzo, but in 1487 it was given an early Renaissance multicolored marble facade.

At this point on the canal the cupola of **Santa Maria della Salute** dominates the scene. The commission for the design of the church to celebrate the Virgin's rescuing Venice from the disastrous plague of 1630, was given to the 26-year-old Longhena. The young architect stressed the new and inventive aspects of his design, likening the rotunda shape to a crown for the Virgin.

Basilica di S. Marco

PIAZZA SAN MARCO

Palazzo Ducale

S. ZACCARIA

VALLARESSO

Palazzo Dandolo a San Moise

Punta della Dogana

The Grand Canal is 2½ miles long, has an average depth of 9 feet, and is 76 yards wide at its broadest point and 40 yards at its narrowest.

SAN GIORGIO MAGGIORE

Across from the Salute, enjoying the magnificent view across the canal, are a string of luxury hotels whose historic façades have either been radically modified or are modern neo-Gothic fantasies. The main interest here is the rather unimposing Hotel Monaco e Gran Canal, the former Palazzo Dandolo a San Moise, which contains Europe's first casino, the famous ridotto, founded in 1638. It was a stomping ground of Casanova, and was closed by the Republic in 1774 because too much money was being lost to foreigners.

At the **Punta della Dogana** on the tip of Dorsoduro, Japanese architect Tadao Ando, using Zen-inspired concepts of space, has transformed a 17th–century customs house into a museum for contemporary art. It is a fitting coda to the theme of Venice as living center for international artistic creativity, as set by Calatrava's bridge at the beginning of the Grand Canal.

At the Vallaresso vaporetto stop you've left the Grand Canal, but stay on board for a view of the **Palazzo Ducale**, with **Basilica di San Marco** behind it, then disembark at San Zaccaria.

What to Watch, Read, and Listen to

DON'T LOOK NOW (1973)
Donald Sutherland and Julie Christie play a grieving couple in this haunting Nicolas Roeg adaptation of a Daphne du Maurier thriller. Watch out for the church of San Nicolò dei Mendicanti, the Bauer Hotel, and San Stae.

BREAD AND TULIPS (2000)
Frustrated by her family life, a housewife stranded at a highway café hops on a bus to Venice and begins a life-changing adventure in this Italian film.

CASANOVA (1976 AND 2005)
The 18th-century Venetian adventurer's memoirs have many adaptations, but a few of the most memorable debuted in 1976 and 2005. The first is a meandering, esoteric romp by Fellini starring Donald Sutherland with a chilling Nino Rota score. The more recent BBC miniseries from Russell T. Davies features David Tennant hopping around the bedchambers and courts of Venice and Europe. The same year, Heath Ledger played the womanizer in a film by Lasse Hallström.

MERCHANT OF VENICE (2004)
Al Pacino plays Shylock, the embittered Jewish moneylender seeking his "pound of flesh" in Michael Radford's version of Shakespeare's classic.

SENSO (1954)
Venice is the backdrop of Visconti's tale in which a Venetian countess falls for an Austrian officer during the 1866 Italian-Austrian war.

THE VENICE GHETTO (2016)
In this BBC Radio podcast, historian and broadcaster Jerry Brotton visits Venice and talks to local experts to tell the story of the Ghetto, which became a safe haven for Jews across Europe.

A HISTORY OF ITALY (2017–)
Mike Corradi's 20-minute podcasts delve into the history of Italy from the fall of the Western Roman Empire to the present day. A handful of episodes concentrate on Venetian themes, including the birth of the city and its curious drive for independence in 1997.

VENETIAN LEGENDS AND GHOST STORIES (2004)
Descended from a family of Murano glassmakers, journalist Alberto Toso Fei interweaves history, legend, and topography in this series of captivating ghost walks around the city.

THE WINGS OF THE DOVE (1902 AND 1997)
Set in London and then Venice, Henry James's novel follows a rich, dying American heiress amid friends and hovering parasites. Iain Softley's 1997 film of Hossein Amini's screenplay adaptation is poignant and aesthetically gorgeous.

VIRGINS OF VENICE (2002)
This eye-opening work by Mary Laven examines Venice's 15th- and 16th-century convents, where hundreds of Venetian girls were sent when their fathers couldn't marry them off. Their real-life stories are both entertaining and shocking.

FRANCESCO'S VENICE (2007)
Broadcaster Francesco da Mosto's love letter to his native city is told through this television documentary in four parts. It's a visually rich outline of what he calls "the dramatic history of the world's most beautiful city."

THE FLOATING BOOK (2003)
In this novel by Michelle Lovric, two German brothers in a love triangle decide to publish the erotic verses of the Roman poet Catullus at the Fondaco dei Tedeschi printing press. Naturally, they rub up against Venetian authority.

Chapter 2

TRAVEL SMART

2

Updated by
Nick Bruno

★ **COUNTRY CAPITAL:**
Rome

☗ **POPULATION:**
59 million (Italy) 638,000
(Venice)

💬 **LANGUAGE:**
Italian

$ **CURRENCY:**
Euro

☏ **COUNTRY CODE:**
+39

⚠ **EMERGENCIES:**
112, 113

🚗 **DRIVING:**
On the right

⚡ **ELECTRICITY:**
220 volts, 50 cycles AC; two
or three round prong outlet

🕓 **TIME:**
CET; 6 hours ahead of
New York

🌐 **WEB RESOURCES:**
www.thelocal.it
www.lifeinitaly.com
www.italymagazine.com

Know Before You Go

Benvenuti a Venezia! Venice is an unusual city with a curious layout of islands and particular local customs and regulations, so there are many things to consider before your trip. We have a few tips and tricks to make sure your visit to La Serenissima ("the most serene," as the city is affectionately nicknamed) is as smooth as possible.

A NOTE ABOUT GREETINGS.

Upon meeting and leave-taking, both friends and strangers wish each other good day or good evening (*buongiorno, buona sera*); *ciao* isn't used between people who are not on very familiar terms with each other, or where there is a great age or status difference. Venetians who are friends greet each other with a kiss, usually first on the left cheek, then on the right. When you meet a new person, shake hands and give your name.

PREPARE FOR CHURCH VISITS.

Shorts, tank tops, and sleeveless garments are taboo in most churches throughout the country. To avoid being denied entrance, carry a shawl or other item of clothing to cover bare shoulders.

You should never bring food into a church, and don't sip from your water bottle inside. If you have a cell phone, turn it off before entering. Ask whether photographs are allowed—and *never use a flash.*

FOLLOW THESE DINING RULES.

When you've finished your meal and are ready to go, ask for the check (*il conto*); a waiter will not put a bill on your table until you've requested it.

It is considered uncivilized to eat or drink while walking—except when eating gelato—and especially rude when seated on the steps of a building or bridge. You may see some Italian tourists or students breaking such rules, but you can be sure that they are not from Venice.

BRUSH UP ON YOUR ITALIAN.

One of the best ways to connect with Italians is to learn a little of the local language. You need not strive for fluency; just mastering a few basic words and terms is bound to make interactions more rewarding. "Please" is *per favore,* "thank you" is *grazie,* "you're welcome" is *prego,* and "excuse me" is *scusi* (or *permesso* when you need to move past someone, as on a bus).

GONDOLAS AREN'T THE BEST WAY TO GET AROUND.

Hiring a gondola is fun but not a practical way to get around. The price of a 40-minute ride is €80 for up to six passengers, increasing to €100 between 7 pm and 8 am. You'll have better luck with Venice's primary public transportation, the vaporetto (water bus). A single ticket costs €7 and is good for 60 minutes one-way, but there are various ways to save, like the Travel Card. Tickets are available at main vaporetto stops. You must validate your ticket before riding; if you don't you may receive a hefty fine.

AVOID THE LINES.

Avoid lines and hassle with the online Venezia Unica City Pass (⊕ *www.veneziaunica. it*). This all-in-one pass can be used for public transportation and entry to museums, churches, and other attractions; you only pay for the services you wish to add.

Fifteen of Venice's most significant churches covered by the Venezia Unica City Pass are part of the Chorus Foundation umbrella group (⊕ *www.chorusvenezia.org*), which coordinates their administration, hours, and admission fees.

Some visitors may not wish or have time to visit all the attractions covered by the Venezia Unica City Pass. In this case save money and opt for one of the combined passes offered by Fondazione Musei Civici Venezia (⊕ *www.visitmuve.it/en/ tickets*). Their Museum Pass (€35) includes single entry to 12 Venice city museums for six months.

SKIP PEAK TOURIST HOURS.

The hordes of tourists here are legendary—there's really no "off-season" in Venice. A little bit of planning, however, will help you avoid the worst of the crowds.

Most tourists do little more than take the vaporetto down the Grand Canal to Piazza San Marco, see the piazza and the basilica, and walk up to the Rialto and back to the station. You'll want to visit these areas, too, but do so in the early morning, before most tourists have finished their breakfast cappuccinos. You can further decrease your competition for Venice's sights by choosing to visit the city on weekdays.

WALK OR VAPORETTO?

Save yourself a lot of money and time by carefully considering how to get around the city and before taking a vaporetto. Venice is very much a walking city, and unless your destination is on the other side of town, most places can be reached on foot. Of course, if you have mobility issues and/or heavy luggage, this is another consideration, as negotiating bridges can be very tiring. In spring, summer, and other busy periods like Carnevale, the vaporetti can be crammed and very problematic to use.

VENICE CAN BE ACCESSIBLE.

Those in wheelchairs may be intimated by the idea of negotiating Venice's transport and the city's bridges. However,

with advanced planning everyone can enjoy the city without undue stress. Vaporetto lines 1 and 2 along the Canale Grande and some larger boats are better equipped for taking wheelchairs.

The gondola station at Piazzale Roma is the only one currently fully equipped for wheelchair users. The major bridges, such as the Ponte degli Scalzi near Santa Lucia railway station, have a dedicated lane with ramp and rails. For more information and an English-language version of the Accessible Venice map, visit ⊕ *disabledaccessibletravel.com/ venice-as-a-wheelchair-user*.

CHECK FOR THE BEST ROUTE.

The curious layout of the city and the various vaporetto route options mean that the nearest vaporetto stop to your destination may not be the best to head to from your starting point. For anyone opting to travel by vaporetto, check out the handy app Che Bateo (⊕ *chebateo.it*), which helps you decide the quickest route: you input your starting point and destination, and it presents you with various route options in real time. Sometimes you may just need to get across the Grand Canal, so taking a *traghetto* (little gondola ride) near you for €2 may save you a sweaty schlep and exorbitant vaporetto fares.

YOU WILL PROBABLY GET LOST.

Finding your way around Venice is complicated. Street names are often duplicated; few roads follow a straight line; and addresses are given by *sestiere* (district, or neighborhood), meaning you may find yourself wandering aimlessly on a back street. It's all part of the joy of exploring here. The best method of navigation is to figure out which landmark your destination is near and then get directions from that point.

NEVER PASS A RESTROOM.

Public restrooms in train stations usually cost €1, and bars frown on the use of theirs without making a purchase, so before you leave the hotel, restaurant, or museum, use the facilities.

DRINK YOUR FILL.

Bottled water is available everywhere but often at an inflated price. Carry a refillable bottle and fill up for free at the strategically placed water fountains throughout the city. In restaurants you can ask for tap water (*acqua del rubinetto*), although you may have to insist.

FLOODING CAN OCCUR.

Venice's flooding (*acqua alta*) is most frequent, and severe, in late November, although the new MOSE flood defense system has lessened instances. Bring shoes you're willing to get wet.

Getting Here and Around

Air

Most nonstop flights between North America and Italy serve Rome and Milan, where connections to Venice are available, though the airport in Venice also now accommodates some nonstop flights from the United States. International flights land at Milan's Malpensa Airport, so make sure a connecting flight to Venice also leaves from there rather than Linate, Milan's other airport. It's also easy, and often more convenient, to connect to Venice via other European hubs, such as Paris or Amsterdam.

Flying time to Milan, Rome, or Venice is approximately 8–8½ hours from New York, 10–11 hours from Chicago, and 11½ hours from Los Angeles. Flight time from Rome or Milan to Venice is about an hour.

Labor strikes are not as frequent in Italy as they were some years ago, but when they do occur they can affect not only air travel, but also local public transit that serves airports. Your airline will usually have details about strikes affecting its flight schedules.

AIRPORTS
Venice is served by Aeroporto di Venezia Marco Polo (VCE). The airport is small but well equipped, with restaurants, snack bars, shopping, and Wi-Fi access.

AIRPORT TRANSFERS
WATER TRANSFER
From Marco Polo terminal it's a mostly covered seven-minute walk to the dock where Alilaguna ferries depart for Venice's historic center. The journey costs €15 and takes 120 minutes to San Marco. Unless your hotel is near one of the Alilaguna stops, taking the bus and vaporetto should be quicker, and the service is often more reliable. Another option is a *motoscafo* (water taxi), which carries up to four people and four bags

to the city center in a powerboat—with a base cost of €110 for the 25-minute trip. Each additional person over four people costs €10 extra. You can book in advance at ⊕ *www.motoscafivenezia.com*.

LAND TRANSFER
Depending on your hotel's location, the most convenient way to reach it may be by ATVO bus from the airport to Piazzale Roma (€8, 20 minutes) and vaporetto or a walk from there. The ACTV Aerobus (Bus No. 5) also makes the same journey for €8. Return fare is €15. Consult ⊕ *www. veneziaunica.it* for various combined tickets and passes and to buy in advance and therefore avoid lines.

Boat
GONDOLA
Hiring a gondola is fun but not a practical way to get around. The price of a 40-minute ride is €80 for up to six passengers, increasing to €100 between 7 pm and 8 am. Every 20 minutes extra is an additional €40. ■ TIP➡ **Agree with your gondolier on price and duration of the ride beforehand to avoid confusion and unexpected costs.**

TRAGHETTO
Traghettos are gondolas that cross the Grand Canal at strategic points along the waterway. A one-stop traghetto crossing takes just a few minutes—it's customary to stand—and can be a lot more convenient than using one of the few bridges. It's €2 for tourists and less for Venice residents. Take a traghetto for a much cheaper (if brief) alternative to the gondola ride experience.

VAPORETTO
Venice's primary public transportation is the vaporetto (water bus). ⇨ *For more information, see Public Transportation.*

Car

There are no cars in Venice, so plan to arrive by train or plane, or if you do drive, return your rental on the outskirts of the city as soon as you arrive. Several rental agencies have outlets in Piazzale Roma, the terminus of road access to Venice.

DRIVING TO VENICE

Venice is at the end of SR11, just off the east–west A4 autostrada. If for some reason you choose to keep a car while visiting Venice, you will have to park in one of the garages on the outskirts of the city around Piazzale Roma or on the island of Tronchetto. For long stays, consider leaving your car in Mestre.

PARKING IN VENICE

A warning: don't be waylaid by illegal touts, often wearing fake uniforms, who try to flag you down and offer to arrange parking and hotels; use one of the established garages, mainly clustered at Piazzale Roma. Consider reserving a space in advance. The **Autorimessa Comunale** (☎ 041/2722394) costs €26 for 24 hours. **Garage San Marco** (☎ 041/5232213) costs €15 from 5 pm to 5 am, and €39 for 24 hours with online reservations. For brief stays, opt for **Parcheggio Sant'Andrea** (☎ 041/2722384), where up to two hours costs €7. On its own island, **Isola del Tronchetto** (☎ 041/5207555) charges €22 for 24 hours. Watch for signs coming over the bridge—you turn right just before Piazzale Roma.

Many hotels and the casino have guest discounts with the San Marco or Tronchetto garages. A cheaper, and perfectly convenient, alternative is to park in Mestre, on the mainland, and take a train (10 minutes, €1) or bus into Venice. The garage across from the station and the Bus 2 stop costs €12 for up to 24 hours.

Public Transportation

Venice's primary public transportation is the vaporetto (water bus). The ACTV operates vaporetti on routes throughout the city. Departures are quite frequent; during the day, for example, Line 1 from Piazzale Roma along the Grand Canal to the Lido, departs every 10 minutes. The trip from Ferrovia to San Marco takes about 35 minutes. Most other lines depart frequently as well, at least every 20 minutes. During times of heavy traffic, ACTV sometimes puts on extra vaporetti, so that departures are even more frequent. Beginning at about 11:30 pm, there's limited, but fairly frequent, night service. Although most landings are well marked, the system takes some getting used to; check before boarding to make sure the boat is going in your desired direction.

There are seats reserved for pregnant, elderly, and disabled passengers, and other passengers are expected to surrender such seats if requested.

Individual Biglietto Navigazione tickets are €7.50 and are good for 75 minutes of travel one-way (*corsa semplice*). Children under the age of six travel free. People in wheelchairs pay €1.50 for a Biglietto Navigazione.

Check that the number and dimensions of your luggage conform to the latest regulations before boarding. At time of press one piece of luggage with total dimensions (length + width + depth) not exceeding 150cm is included per ticket. Ask for a *supplemento* (surcharge) for large and additional baggage.

Considerable savings are possible if you buy a pass: €20 for 24 hours, €30 for 48 hours, €40 for 72 hours, and €60 for a week of unlimited travel. Travelers ages 6–29 can opt for the €6 Rolling Venice card (available from the HelloVenezia booth at principal vaporetto stops and

Getting Here and Around

at ⊕ *www.veneziaunica.it/en/content/rolling-venice)*. A €22 3-day youth pass without Marco Polo Airport bus transfer, €28 3-day youth pass with airport transfer, and a €34 3-day youth pass with airport transfer return are available. Tickets are available at the airport, tobacco shops, and from machines or booths at some, but not all, vaporetto stops. Purchase in advance online at ⊕ *www.veneziaunica.it*.

Remember to validate your ticket at the scanner before boarding. Your ticket's duration starts at time of validation. Tickets are checked frequently, and fines for using the vaporetto without a validated ticket are substantial. If you get onboard without a ticket, you should go straight to the *marinaio* (vaporetto staff) to declare your mistake and avoid a hefty fine.

From—To	Time	Cost
Venice to Padua	25–30 minutes, up to 1 hour on a local train	€19 (express-Freccia) €4.60 (local or regionale)
Venice to Vicenza	45 minutes, up to 1 hour 30 minutes on a local train	€22 (express-Freccia) €6.70 (local or regionale)
Venice to Verona	1 hour 10 minutes, up to 2 hours, 20 minutes on a local train	€24.90 (express-Freccia) €9.70 (local or regionale)

🚆 Train

Venice has rail connections with many major cities in Italy and Europe. Note that Venice's train station is **Venezia Santa Lucia,** not to be confused with Venezia Mestre, which is the mainland stop prior to arriving in the city. Some trains do not continue beyond the Mestre station; in such cases you can catch the next Venice-bound train. Get a €1.40 ticket from the newsstand on the platform and validate it (in the yellow time-stamp machine) to avoid a fine.

Traveling by train in Italy is simple and efficient. Service between major cities is frequent, and trains usually arrive on schedule. The fastest trains on the Trenitalia Ferrovie dello Stato (FS)—the Italian State Railways—are Frecciarossa Alta Velocità. Ferrari mogul Montezemolo offers the competing Italo high-speed service. Bullet trains on both services run between all major cities from Venice, Milan, and Turin down through Florence and Rome to Naples and Salerno.

Seat reservations are mandatory, and you'll be assigned a specific seat; to avoid having to squeeze through narrow aisles, board only at your designated coach (the number on your ticket matches the one near the door of each coach). Reservations are also required for Eurostar and the slower Intercity (IC) trains; tickets for the latter are about half the price of the faster trains. If you miss your reserved train, go to the ticket counter within the hour and you may be able to move your reservation to a later one (this depends on the type of reservation, so check rules when booking). Note that you'll still need to reserve seats in advance if you're using a rail pass.

There are often significant discounts when you book well in advance. On the websites, you'll be presented with available promotional fares, such as Trenitalia's "Mini" (up to 60% off), "Famiglia" (a 20% discount for one adult and at least one child), and "A/R" (a round-trip in a day). Italo offers "Low Cost" and "Economy." The caveat is that the discounts come with restrictions on changes and cancellations; make sure you understand them before booking.

Reservations are not available on Inter-regionale trains, which are slower, make more stops, and are less expensive than high-speed and Intercity trains. Regionale and Espresso trains stop most frequently and are the most economical (many serve commuters). There are refreshments on long-distance trains, purchased from a mobile cart or a dining car, but not on the commuter trains.

All but commuter trains have first and second classes. On local trains a first-class fare ensures you a little more space; on long-distance trains you also get wider seats (three across as opposed to four) and a bit more legroom, but the difference is minimal. At peak travel times a first-class fare may be worth the additional cost, as the coaches may be less crowded. In Italian, *prima classe* is first class; *seconda classe* is second.

Many cities have more than one train station, **so be sure you get off at the right station.** In Venice, it is important to note that the Venezia Mestre station is not in Venice itself but is the stop for the mainland industrial city across the lagoon. You can purchase train tickets and review schedules online, at travel agencies, at train station ticket counters, and at automatic ticketing machines located in all but the smallest stations. If you'd like to board a train and don't have a ticket, seek out the conductor prior to getting on; he or she will tell you whether you may buy a ticket onboard and what the surcharge will be (usually €8). Fines for attempting to ride a train without a ticket are €50 plus the price of the ticket.

For trains without a reservation, **you must validate your ticket before boarding** by punching it at a wall- or pillar-mounted yellow or green box in that train station or at the track entrance of larger stations. If you forget, find a conductor immediately to avoid a hefty fine.

Train strikes of various kinds are not uncommon, so it's wise to confirm that your train is actually running. During a strike minimum service is guaranteed (especially for distance trains); ask at the station or search online to find out about your particular reservation.

Traveling by night can be a good deal—and somewhat of an adventure—because you'll pass a night without the need for a hotel room. Comfortable trains run on the longer routes (Sicily–Rome, Sicily–Milan, Rome–Turin, Lecce–Milan); request the good-value T3 (three single beds), Intercity Notte, and Carrozza Comfort. The Vagone Letto has private bathrooms and single-, double-, or twin-bed suites. Overnight trains also travel to international destinations like Paris, Vienna, Munich, and other cities.

TRAIN PASSES

Rail passes promise savings on train travel. Italy is one of 24 countries that accept the Eurail Pass, which provides unlimited first- and second-class travel. Check the website for the latest options (⊕ *www.eurail.com/en*).

The Eurail Italy Pass, available for non-European residents, allows a certain number of travel days within the country over the course of two months. Three to eight days of travel cost from $169 to $320 (1st class) or $127 to $240 (2nd class). All passes must be purchased before you leave for Europe. Keep in mind that even with a rail pass you still need to reserve seats on the trains that require them.

Essentials

◎ Addresses

Getting around Venice presents some unusual problems: the city's layout has few straight lines; house numbering seems nonsensical; and the six sestieri of San Marco, Cannaregio, Castello, Dorsoduro, Santa Croce, and San Polo all duplicate each other's street names. What's more, addresses in Venice are given by sestiere rather than street, making them of limited help in getting around. Venetians commonly give directions by pinpointing a major landmark, such as a church, and telling you where to go from there.

◎ Dining

Dining options in Venice range from the ultra-high end, where jackets and ties are a must, to the very casual.

Once staunchly traditional, many restaurants have renovated their menus along with their dining rooms, creating dishes that blend classic Venetian elements with ingredients less common to the lagoon environs. Midrange restaurants are often more willing to make the break, offering innovative options while keeping traditional dishes available as mainstays.

Restaurants are often quite small, with limited seating, so make sure to reserve ahead. It's not uncommon for restaurants to have two seatings per evening, one at 7 and one at 9.

Restaurant listings have been shortened. For full information, visit Fodors.com. Prices in the dining reviews are the average cost of a main course at dinner, or, if dinner is not served, at lunch.

WHAT IT COSTS in Euros

$	$$	$$$	$$$$
AT DINNER			
under €15	€15–€24	€25–€35	over €35

There's no getting around the fact that Venice has more than its share of overpriced, mediocre eateries that prey on tourists. Avoid places with cajoling waiters standing outside, and beware of restaurants that don't display their prices. At the other end of the spectrum, showy *menu turistico* (tourist menu) boards make offerings clear in a dozen languages, but for the same €15–€20 you'd spend at such places, you could do better at a *bacaro* (bar) making a meal of *cicheti* (savory snacks).

Budget-conscious travelers might want to take their main meal at lunch, when restaurant prices tend to be lower. Also keep an eye out for cafés and trattorias that offer meals prepared for *operai* (workers); they'll have daily specials designed for those who have to eat and run, in which anyone is welcome to partake. Bacari offer lighter fare, usually eaten at the bar (prices are higher if you sit at a table), and wine lists that offer myriad choices by the glass.

Although pizzerias are not hard to find, Venice is not much of a pizza town—standards aren't what they are elsewhere in Italy, and local laws impede the use of wood-burning ovens. Seek out recommended pizzerias, or opt for a bacaro snack instead of a soggy slice of pizza *al volo*, which is too commonly precooked and reheated. *Tramezzini*, the triangular white-bread sandwiches served in bars all over Italy, however, are almost an art form in Venice. The bread is white but doesn't at all resemble the "Wonder" of your youth; many bars here still make their own mayonnaise, and few skimp on the fillings.

BACARI (BARS)

The handiest places for a snack between sights are bars, cafés, and the quintessentially Venetian bacari. Bars are small cafés that can serve any sort of drink from coffee to grappa, along with cicheti, a quick *panino* (sandwich, often warmed on a griddle), or a tasty *tramezzino* (sandwich on untoasted white bread, usually with a mayonnaise-based filling).

A café is like a bar but usually with more seating, and it may serve a few additional food items. If you place your order at the counter, ask if you can sit down: many places charge considerably more for table service. In train stations and along the highway, you'll pay a cashier first, then give your *scontrino* (receipt) to the person at the counter who fills your order.

GELATERIE (ICE CREAM SHOPS)

According to Venetians, Marco Polo imported from China a dessert called *panna in ghiaccio* (literally, "cream on ice"), a brick of frozen cream between wafers. There's no documentation to support the claim, but the myth lives on. Several local *gelaterie* (gelato shops) sell panna in ghiaccio, the supposed "ancestor" of gelato, but you'll have to ask around for it, because it's almost never kept on display. On a hot summer day, nothing is better than a cup of fruity gelato to restore your energy: light and refreshing, it will help you go that extra mile before you call it a day.

Newer gelato enterprises, including some chains, are popping up almost daily, many right next to the less flamboyant artisan operations that have been producing their own gelato for decades. The new stuff may or may not be better—but you can almost guarantee it will cost more. Most gelaterie are open nonstop from midmorning to late evening; some keep longer business hours in summer.

MEALS AND MEALTIMES

What's the difference between a *ristorante* and a *trattoria*? Can you order food at an *enoteca* (wine bar)? Can you go to a restaurant just for a snack or order only salad at a pizzeria? The following definitions should help.

Not long ago, ristoranti tended to be more elegant and expensive than trattorie (which serve traditional, homestyle fare in an atmosphere to match) or osterie (which serve local wines and simple, regional dishes). But the distinction has blurred considerably, and an osteria in the center of town might now be far fancier (and pricier) than a ristorante across the street. In any sit-down establishment, however, you're generally expected to order at least a two-course meal, such as a *primo* (first course) and a *secondo* (main course) or a *contorno* (vegetable side dish); an *antipasto* (starter) followed by either a primo or secondo; or a secondo and a *dolce* (dessert).

If you'd prefer to eat less, best head to an enoteca or pizzeria, where it's more common to order a single dish. An enoteca menu is often limited to a selection of cheese, cured meats, salads, and desserts, but if there's a kitchen you can also find soups, pastas, and main courses. The typical pizzeria serves *affettati misti* (a selection of cured pork), simple salads, various kinds of bruschetta, and crostini (similar to bruschetta, with a variety of toppings).

The most convenient and least expensive places for a quick snack between sights are probably bars, cafés, and pizza *al taglio* (by the slice) spots. Pizza al taglio shops are easy to negotiate, but few have seats. They sell pizza by the slice: just point out which kind you want and how much. Since good pizza requires a wood-burning oven, which are not permitted in Venice because of the fire hazard, and since Venetians consider

Essentials

pizza to be a "foreign" food imported from Naples, pizza in Venice is in general not very good. In many cafés and in all of the al taglio places, it is heated up in a microwave.

Much better options for fast food are the kebab shops, which have flourished throughout the city. The kebabs are generally fresh and served with Middle Eastern bread made with pizza dough—a rather delicious product of gastronomic fusion.

Bars in Italy resemble what we think of as cafés and are primarily places to get a coffee and a bite to eat, rather than drinking establishments. Expect a selection of panini warmed up on the griddle (*piastra*) and tramezzini (sandwiches made of untoasted white bread triangles). Some bars also serve vegetable and fruit salads, cold pasta dishes, and gelato. Most offer beer and a variety of alcohol, as well as wines by the glass. A café is like a bar but typically has more tables.

Most places charge for table use, even if you bring the food from the counter to the table yourself. In self-service bars and cafés, it's good manners to clean your table before you leave. Menus are posted outside most restaurants (in English in tourist areas). If not, you might step inside and ask to take a look at the menu, but don't ask for a table unless you intend to stay.

If you have special dietary needs, make them known; they can usually be accommodated. Although mineral water makes its way to almost every table, you can order a carafe of tap water (acqua di rubinetto or *acqua semplice*) instead—which in Venice is quite good—but be prepared for an unenthusiastic reaction from your waiter.

A Venetian would seldom ask for olive oil and salt to dip bread in, but the culturally tolerant Venetians won't scoff if you do. They may even express mild curiosity.

But don't be surprised if there's no butter to spread on bread, unless you're eating it with anchovies, a favorite north Italian snack. Wiping your bowl clean with a (small) piece of bread is usually considered a sign of appreciation, not bad manners. Spaghetti should be eaten with a fork only, although a little help from a spoon—a southern Italian custom—won't horrify locals the way cutting spaghetti into little pieces will. Order your caffè (Italians drink cappuccino only in the morning) after dessert, not with it. Since an Italian meal generally consists of several courses, portions tend to be small.

Breakfast (*la colazione*) is usually served from 7 to 10:30, lunch (*il pranzo*) from 12:30 to 2:30, and dinner (*la cena*) from 7:30 to 10; outside those hours best head for a bar. Peak times are usually 1:30 for lunch and 9 for dinner. Enoteche and Venetian bacari (wine bars) are also open in the morning and late afternoon for cicheti (finger foods) at the counter. Most pizzerias open at 8 pm and close around midnight—later in summer and on weekends. Bars and cafés are open from 7 am until 8 or 9 pm; a few stay open until midnight.

Unless otherwise noted, the restaurants listed here are open for lunch and dinner, closing one or two days a week.

PASTICCERIE (PASTRY SHOPS)
Venetians have always loved pastry, not so much as dessert at the end of a meal, but rather as a nibble that could go well with a glass of sweet wine or a cup of hot milk. Traditional cookies are sold in *pasticcerie* (pastry shops) throughout town, either by weight or by the piece, and often come in attractive gift packages. Search for *zaeti* (cookies made with yellow corn flour and raisins), *buranelli* (S-shape cookies from Burano, which also come in heavy, fat rings), and *baicoli* (crunchy cookies made with yeast). Many

bakeries also sell pastry by the portion: from apple strudel to *crostate* (jam tarts) and *torta di mandorle* (almond cake)— just point out what you want.

After Christmas and through Carnevale, a great deal of frying takes place behind the counter to prepare the tons of pastries annually devoured by Venetians and tourists alike in the weeks preceding Lent: specialties are *frittole* (doughnuts with pine nuts, raisins, and candied orange peel, rolled in sugar), best eaten warm; the ribbonlike *galani* (crunchy, fried pastries sprinkled with confectioners' sugar); and walnut-shape *castagnole* (fried pastry dumplings rolled in sugar).

PAYING

Most restaurants have a cover charge per person, usually listed at the top of the check as *coperto* or *pane e coperto*. It should be modest (€1–€3 per person) except at the most expensive restaurants. Whenever in doubt, ask before you order to avoid unpleasant discussions later. In Venice, as in many cities in northern Italy, no tip is expected, even if the service is excellent.

The price of fish dishes is often given by weight (before cooking), so the price quoted on the menu is for 100 grams of fish, not for the whole dish. (An average fish portion is about 350 grams). So be extra careful when ordering fish as you could be presented with a huge check at the end of your meal.

Major credit cards are widely accepted in Venice; more restaurants take Visa and MasterCard than American Express or Diners Club. If you become a regular customer, you may find that the restaurant owner will give you a discount, without your asking for one. If that is the case, cash payment is preferred.

RESERVATIONS AND DRESS

Although we only mention reservations specifically when they're essential (there's no other way you'll ever get a table) or when they're not accepted, it's always safest to make one for dinner. Large parties should always call ahead to check the reservations policy. If you change your mind, be sure to cancel, even at the last minute.

We mention dress only when men are required to wear a jacket or a jacket and tie. In Venice, even the most elegant restaurants tend to be very casual about dress. Only very few restaurants will turn away patrons because they are wearing shorts.

WINES, BEER, AND SPIRITS

The grape has been cultivated in Italy since the time of the Etruscans, and Italians justifiably take pride in their local varieties, which are numerous. The Veneto and the neighboring regions of Friuli and Alto Adige are some of the prime wine-growing regions of Italy. Wine in Italy is less expensive than almost anywhere else, so it's often affordable to order a bottle of wine at a restaurant rather than sticking with the house wine (which is usually good but quite simple). Many bars have their own *aperitivo della casa* (house aperitif); Italians are imaginative with their mixed drinks, so you may want to try one.

You can purchase beer, wine, and spirits in any bar, grocery store, or enoteca, any day of the week, any time of the day. Italian and German beer is readily available, but it can be more expensive than wine.

There's no minimum drinking age in Italy. Italian children begin drinking wine mixed with water at mealtimes when they're teens (or thereabouts). Italians are rarely seen drunk in public, and public drinking, except in a bar or eating establishment, isn't considered acceptable behavior. Bars usually close

Essentials

by 11 pm; hotel and restaurant bars stay open until midnight. Brewpubs and discos serve until about 2 am.

⊙ Emergencies

No matter where you are in Italy, you can dial 113 in case of emergency: the call will be directed to the local police. Not all 113 operators speak English, so you may want to ask a local person to place the call. Asking the operator for *"pronto soccorso"* (first aid and also the emergency room of a hospital) should get you an *ambulanza* (ambulance). If you just need a doctor, ask for *"un medico."*

Italy has the *carabinieri* (national police force, their emergency number is 112 from anywhere in Italy) as well as the *polizia* (local police force). Both are armed and have the power to arrest and investigate crimes. Always report the loss of your passport to the caribinieri as well as to your embassy. When reporting a crime, you'll be asked to fill out *una denuncia* (an official report); keep a copy for your insurance company.

Pharmacies are generally open weekdays 8:30–1 and 4–8, and Saturday 9–1. Local pharmacies rotate covering the off-hours in shifts: on the door of every pharmacy is a list of which pharmacies in the vicinity will be open late.

⊕ Health & Safety

COVID–19 has disrupted travel since March 2020, and travelers should expect sporadic ongoing issues. Always travel with an FFP2-grade mask in case it's required, and keep up to date on the most recent testing and vaccination guidelines for Italy.

⊙ Hours of Operation

Religious and civic holidays are frequent in Italy. Depending on the holiday's local importance, businesses may close for the day. Businesses don't close Friday or Monday when the holiday falls on the weekend, though the Monday following Easter is a holiday.

Banks are open weekdays 8:30–1:30 and for one or two hours in the afternoon, depending on the bank. Most post offices are open Monday–Saturday 9–1:30, some until 2; central post offices are open 9–6:30 weekdays, 9–12:30 or 9–6:30 on Saturday.

Most churches are open from early morning until noon or 12:30, when they close for three hours or more; they open again in the afternoon, closing at about 6. San Marco remains open all day. Many museums are closed one day a week, often Monday or Tuesday. During low season museums often close early; during high season many stay open until late at night.

Most shops are open Monday–Saturday 9–1 and 3:30 or 4–7:30. Barbers and hairdressers, with certain exceptions, are closed Sunday and Monday. Some bookstores and fashion- or tourist-oriented shops in Venice are open all day, as well as Sunday. Many branches of large chain supermarkets, such as Billa and COOP, don't close for lunch and are usually open Sunday; smaller *alimentari* (delicatessens) and other food shops are usually closed one evening during the week and are almost always closed Sunday.

HOLIDAYS

The national holidays include January 1 (New Year's Day); January 6 (Epiphany); Easter Sunday and Monday; April 25 (Liberation Day); May 1 (Labor Day or May Day); June 2 (Festival of the Republic); August 15

(Ferragosto); November 1 (All Saints' Day); December 8 (Immaculate Conception); and December 25 and 26 (Christmas Day and the Feast of Saint Stephen).

Venice's feast of Saint Mark is April 25, the same as Liberation Day, so the Madonna della Salute on November 21 makes up for the lost holiday.

🖊 Immunizations

All visitors to Italy must have valid proof of COVID-19 vaccination and a booster; while the need and frequency of boosters is still being discussed in the medical community, it's important to verify the most recent requirements with your physician before you travel.

🛏 Lodging

Venetian magic can still linger when you retire for the night, whether you're staying in a grand hotel or budget *locanda* (inn). Some of the finest Venetian hotel rooms are lighted with Murano chandeliers and swathed in famed fabrics of Rubelli and Bevilacqua, with gilded mirrors and furnishing styles from Baroque to Biedermeier and Art Deco.

Though more contemporary decor is working its way into renovation schemes, you still may find the prized Venetian terrazzo flooring and canal views in more modest *pensioni* (small hotels). Your window will open, sometimes onto a balcony, so you may enjoy gondoliers' serenades, watch the ebb and flow of city life in the *campo* (square) below, or simply contemplate what the lack of motor traffic permits you to hear, or *not* hear.

Even if well renovated, most hotels occupy very old buildings. Preservation laws prohibit elevators in some, so if climbing stairs is an issue, check before you book. In the lower price categories, hotels may not have lounge areas, and rooms may be cramped, and the same is true of standard rooms in more expensive hotels. Space is at a premium in Venice, and even exclusive hotels have carved out small, dowdy, Cinderella-type rooms in the "standard" category. It's not at all unusual for each room to be different even on the same floor: windows overlooking charming canals and bleak alleyways are both common. En suite bathrooms have become the norm; they're usually well equipped, but sizes range from compact to more than ample; tubs are considered a luxury but are not unheard of, even in less expensive lodging. Carpeted floors are rare, as they're traditionally considered to be unhygienic. Air-conditioning is rarely a necessity until mid-June. A few of the budget hotels make do with fans. Mosquitoes can begin to pester in midsummer; turn lights off in the evening if you leave windows open, and ask the hotel staff for a Vape, an anti-mosquito device. The staff members at most Venetian hotels will be able to converse with you in English, and don't be afraid to ask for anything you need, or even to change rooms if you consider it necessary to do so.

The lodgings we list are the cream of the crop in each price category. Properties are assigned price categories based on the rate for two people sharing a standard double room in high season, including tax and service.

APARTMENT AND HOUSE RENTALS

Renting a vacation property can be economical depending on your budget and the number of people in your group. Most are owned by individuals and managed by rental agents who advertise online. In some cases rental agents

Essentials

handle only the online reservation and financial arrangements; in others, the agent and/or owner may meet you at the property for the initial check-in.

Issues to keep in mind when renting an apartment in Venice are the location (street noise, ambience, and accessibility to public transport), the availability of an elevator or number of stairs, air-conditioning and ventilation, hot water, the furnishings (including pots and linens), what's supplied on arrival (dishwashing liquid, coffee, or tea), and the cost of utilities (are all covered by the rental rate?).

HOME EXCHANGES

With a direct home exchange you stay in someone else's home while they stay in yours. Some outfits also deal with vacation homes, so you're not really occupying someone's full-time residence, just their vacant weekend place.

Venetians have historically not been as enthusiastic about home exchanges as others; however, there are some apartments in Venice owned by foreigners (Americans, English, etc.) who use the home-exchange services.

Hotel reviews have been shortened. For full information, visit Fodors.com. Prices in the reviews are the lowest cost of a standard double room in high season.

WHAT IT COSTS in Euros			
$	$$	$$$	$$$$
LODGING FOR TWO			
under €125	€125– €200	€201– €300	over €300

$ Money

Prices in Venice are high, but no higher than in Milan or in other European cities and resorts. Within Venice, there is a substantial difference between prices in the Piazza San Marco area and those in residential districts, such as Cannaregio and Santa Croce, or in the working-class neighborhood of Castello. Bars and cafés must, by law, post their prices, both for standing at the bar and for sitting at a table (whether there is table service or not). If you are in a bar or café patronized largely by tourists, you may want to consult the price list before you order or sit down. The cafés in the Piazza San Marco tack on a hefty supplementary charge for music.

ATMS AND BANKS

An ATM (*bancomat* in Italian) is the easiest way to get euros in Italy. There are numerous ATMs around Venice, and since there are ATMs at Marco Polo Airport, there is no need to buy euros before you depart the United States. Be sure to **memorize your PIN in numbers,** as ATM keypads in Italy won't always display letters. Check with your bank to confirm that you have an international PIN (*codice segreto*) that will be recognized in the countries you're visiting; to raise your maximum daily withdrawal allowance; and to learn what your bank's fee is for withdrawing money (Italian banks don't charge withdrawal fees).

■TIP→ **Be aware that PINs beginning with a 0 (zero) tend to be rejected in Italy.**

Your own bank may charge a fee for using ATMs abroad and/or for the cost of conversion from euros to dollars. Nevertheless, you can usually get a better rate of exchange at an ATM than you will at a currency-exchange office or even when changing money inside a bank with a teller, the next-best option. Whatever the

Where Should I Stay?

	NEIGHBORHOOD VIBE	PROS	CONS
San Marco	Touristy but also with some upmarket restaurants and cafés.	Closest to top attractions; pretty quiet at night.	Most touristy and most expensive.
Dorsoduro	Surrounding areas are filled with good restaurants and most of Venice's major attractions.	Everything you need is within walking distance: good eats, shopping, and many of Venice's museums and monuments.	This is the height of hustle and bustle in Venice—convenient, but often pricey; street noise may be an issue.
San Polo and Santa Croce	Home to Venice's crème de la crème for lodging and shopping.	Where all the high rollers and A-listers like to reside.	Everything is expensive; not very close to central hot spots.
Cannaregio	Plenty of options in this convenient but less trafficked neighborhood.	Hotels are much cheaper than elsewhere in Venice; central; great restaurants.	Hotels near the train station can be a bit crowded.
Castello	Somewhat removed from the hubbub, this area is a bit more refined, with fancy boutiques and hotels.	Least touristy neighborhood; lots of dining options nearby.	A bit remote from the top attractions.
The Giudecca	This calm, residential island is home to the lavish Belmond Hotel Cipriani and the iconic Hilton Molino Stucky.	Quiet area with a few great restaurants and cafés.	Area is removed from Venice's lively center and can be expensive.
The Lido	Serenity and beaches.	Tranquility, amazing views, and prime beach access.	Half-hour boat ride to Venice's historic center.
Torcello	This island has some of the more chic and funky neighborhoods in Venice.	Hotels are cheaper here than elsewhere in Venice.	Far from main tourist attractions.

2

Travel Smart ESSENTIALS

Essentials

method, extracting funds as you need them is safer than carrying around a large amount of cash. Finally, it's advisable to carry more than one card that can be used for cash withdrawal, in case something happens to your primary one.

CREDIT CARDS

It's a good idea to **inform your credit-card company before you travel,** especially if you're going abroad and don't travel internationally often. Otherwise, the credit-card company might put a hold on your card owing to unusual activity—not a welcome occurrence halfway through your trip. Record all your credit-card numbers—as well as the phone numbers to call if your cards are lost or stolen. Keep these in a safe place, so you're prepared should something go wrong. American Express, MasterCard, and Visa have general numbers you can call (collect if you're abroad) if your card is lost.

■TIP➡ **North American toll-free numbers aren't available from abroad, so be sure to obtain a local number with area code for any business you may need to contact.**

Although it's usually cheaper (and safer) to use a credit card abroad for large purchases (so you can cancel payments or be reimbursed if there's a problem), note that some credit-card companies *and* the banks that issue them add substantial percentages to all foreign transactions, whether they're in a foreign currency or not. Check on these fees before leaving home, so there won't be any surprises when you get the bill. Because of these fees, avoid using your credit card for ATM withdrawals or cash advances (use a debit or cash card instead).

Venetian merchants prefer MasterCard and Visa, but American Express is usually accepted in popular tourist destinations. Credit cards aren't accepted everywhere, though; if you want to pay with a credit card in a small shop, hotel, or restaurant, it's a good idea to make your intentions known early on.

CURRENCY AND EXCHANGE

The euro is the main unit of currency in Italy. There are 100 *centesimi* (cents) in one euro. Coins are valued at 1, 2, 5, 10, 20, and 50 centesimi, as well as 1 and 2 euros. There are seven notes: 5, 10, 20, 50, 100, 200, and 500 euros. At this writing, 1 euro was worth about 1.13 U.S. dollars.

Post offices exchange currency at good rates, but employees speak limited English, so be prepared. (Writing your request can help in these cases.)

■TIP➡ **Even if a currency-exchange booth has a sign promising no commission, rest assured that there's some kind of huge, hidden fee. You're almost always better off getting foreign currency at an ATM or exchanging money at a bank or post office.**

ⓨ Nightlife

Your first impression may well be that Venice doesn't have a nightlife. As the last rays of daylight slip away, so, too, do most signs of a bustling town. Boat traffic drops to the occasional vaporetto, shutters roll down, and signs go dark. Even though bacari (wine bars) would seem to be natural after-hours gathering spots, most close before 9 pm.

But boulevardiers, flaneurs, and those who simply enjoy a little after-dinner entertainment can take heart. Sprinkled judiciously around the city's residential-looking *calli* and *campi* (streets and squares), you'll stumble upon *locali* (nightspots) that stay open until 1 or 2 am. Some even offer live music, though rarely past midnight—a city noise ordinance prohibits too much wildness except during Carnevale.

Though there are no suitable venues for rock shows, Piazza San Marco has hosted some less-rambunctious concerts on summer evenings. Except for a few lounge bars with dancing, nightlife tends to be student oriented.

Both private and city museums regularly host major traveling art exhibits, from ancient to contemporary. Classical music buffs can rely on a rich season of concerts, opera, chamber music, and some ballet. Smaller venues and churches offer lower-priced, occasionally free performances that often highlight Venetian and Italian composers. Though the city has no English-language theater, during Carnevale you'll find foreign companies that perform in their mother tongue. All films screened at the Venice Film Festival (some in an ad-hoc amphitheater constructed in Campo San Polo) in late summer are shown in the original language, with subtitles in English, Italian, or both.

There is a variety of resources for finding what's on in Venice. Both the city and the province have tourism offices and associated websites with English versions. The calendar publication available at the APT tourist offices on the Piazza San Marco and in the Pavilion near the Vallaresso vaporetto stop provides extensive, current information on museums, churches, exhibitions, events day-by-day, useful phone numbers, gondola and taxi fares, opening hours, and more. *A Guest of Venice,* a monthly bilingual booklet free at hotels and available to download at ⊕ *www.unospitedivenezia.it,* also includes information about pharmacies, vaporetto and bus lines, and main trains and flights, as well as listings for music and art and sporting events. The *Agenda Venezia* website (⊕ *www.agendavenezia. org/en*) is another good resource. *Venezia News,* available at newsstands, has similar information but also includes in-depth

articles about noteworthy events; listings are bilingual, but most articles are in Italian. *Venezia da Vivere* (⊕ *www.veneziadavivere.com/en*) is a bilingual seasonal guide that lists nightspots and live music. It's a handy resource for up-to-date information on lots of insider restaurant and entertainment goings-on, and it features a comprehensive calendar of musical events. Last but not least, don't ignore the posters you see everywhere in the streets or the flyers hung at many locali and bacari; they're often as current as it gets.

ⓘ Passes and Discounts

Avoid lines and hassle with the online **Venezia Unica City Pass** (⊕ *www.veneziaunica.it*). This all-in-one pass can be used for public transportation and entry to museums, churches, and other attractions; you only pay for the services you wish to add. You'll receive an email with the pass, which you can show for entry at sights, though you'll still need to physically collect your transportation pass at an ACTV automatic ticket machine or ticket point located around the city.

Fifteen of Venice's most significant churches covered by the Venezia Unica City Pass are part of the **Chorus Foundation** umbrella group (☎ *041/2750462* ⊕ *www.chorusvenezia.org*), which coordinates their administration, hours, and admission fees. Churches in this group are open to visitors all day except Sunday morning. Single church entry costs €3; you have a year to visit all 15 with the €12 Chorus Pass, which you can get at any participating church or online.

The Museum Pass (€35) from **Musei Civici** (☎ *041/2405211* ⊕ *www.visitmuve. it/en/tickets*) includes single entry to 12 Venice city museums for six months.

Essentials

🌐 Passport and Visas

U.S. citizens need a valid passport to enter Italy for stays of up to 90 days.

PASSPORTS

Although somewhat costly, a U.S. passport is relatively simple to obtain and is valid for 10 years. You must apply in person if you're getting a passport for the first time; if your previous passport was lost, stolen, or damaged; or if it has expired and was issued more than 15 years ago or when you were under 16. All children under 18 must appear in person to apply for or renew a passport. Both parents must accompany any child under 14 (or send a notarized statement with their permission) and provide proof of their relationship to the child.

There are 25 regional passport offices as well as 7,000 passport acceptance facilities in post offices, public libraries, and other governmental offices. If you're renewing a passport, you may do so by mail; forms are available at passport acceptance facilities and online, where you trace the application's progress.

The cost of a new passport is $165 for adults, $135 for children under 16; renewals are $130. Allow four to six weeks for processing, both for first-time passports and renewals. For an expediting fee of $60 you can reduce this time to two to three weeks. If your trip is less than two weeks away, you can get a passport even more rapidly by going to a passport office with the necessary documentation. Private expediters can get things done in as little as 48 hours, but charge hefty fees for their services.

■ TIP→ **Before your trip, make two copies of your passport's data page (one for someone at home and another for you to carry separately). Or scan/photograph the page and email it to someone at home and/or yourself.**

General Requirements for Italy	
Passport	Must be valid for 6 months after date of arrival.
Visa	Tourist visas aren't needed for stays of 90 days or less by U.S. citizens.
Vaccinations	COVID-19
Driving	International driver's license required. CDW insurance is compulsory on car rentals and will be included in the quoted price.

VISAS

When staying for 90 days or less, U.S. citizens aren't required to obtain a visa prior to traveling to Italy. A recent law requires that you fill in a declaration of presence within eight days of your arrival—the stamp on your passport at airport arrivals is an adequate substitute.

🎭 Performing Arts

Art has been a way of life in Venice for so many centuries that it seems you need only inhale to enjoy it. From mid-June to early November in odd-number years, the Biennale Arte attracts a whirlwind of contemporary arts, showcasing several hundred contemporary artists from around the world. During Carnevale, masks and costumes let revelers dance with history. Costumed musicians will entice you to performances in the finest churches, palaces, and *scuole grandi* (large fraternal social clubs), but don't ignore the *bel canto* (meaning "beautiful singing") wafting through the canals or the opera issuing from open windows of conservatory practice halls.

MUSIC

The band Pink Floyd made rock history with a 1989 concert staged aboard a pontoon floating near Piazza San Marco. Fans made such a mess of the piazza and loud music stirred up such antipathy that the show was destined to become the city's first and last rock happening. Nearby Parco San Giuliano, Mestre, Padua, Verona, Trieste, and Treviso sometimes host artists on their European tours. Though the Biennale Musica and some clubs in Venice do spotlight contemporary music, the vast majority of the city's concerts are classical.

Numerous orchestras perform pricey "greatest hits" classical music programs marketed toward tourists—you'll easily spot ticket vendors in period costume. Groups may have a semipermanent venue, such as an ex-church or *scuola,* although they can change frequently. You'll find these promoted at your hotel, in tourist offices, at travel agencies, and in many of the previously mentioned websites and local publications. It's not usually necessary to book in advance, however, as these performances rarely sell out.

In addition to these commercial groups, there are professional orchestras that perform less regularly, usually in museums or palazzi. Churches, scuole, palazzi, and museums sometimes sponsor concerts of their own, especially around the holidays, often featuring touring musicians. Keep an eye out for notices plastered on walls along walkways for last-minute, often free concerts offered by local musicians, choirs, and city-sponsored groups.

Contemporary music options are at their richest during Biennale Musica, when concerts are held throughout Venice. These events are advertised on the Biennale website and on billboards in all principal campi, and materials are available in tourist offices.

OPERA AND BALLET

The city's main venues are Teatro La Fenice and Teatro Malibran; you can review the calendar and buy tickets for performances at both at HelloVenezia (☎ *041/2424,* 8 am–8 pm), or visit one of their sales offices (Piazzale Roma or Ferrovia). It's worth a try to head for the theater box office an hour before showtime to see if any last-minute tickets are available.

Shipping

Sending a letter or small package to the United States via Federal Express takes at least two days and costs about €50. Other package services to check are Quick Pack Europe (for delivery within Europe) and Express Mail Service (a global three- to five-day service for letters and packages). Compare prices with those of Postacelere to determine the cheapest option.

If you've purchased antiques, ceramics, or other fragile objects, ask if the vendor will do the shipping for you. In most cases this is possible, and preferable, because many merchants have experience with these kinds of shipments. If so, ask whether the article will be insured against breakage.

Shopping

It's no secret that Venice offers some excellent shopping opportunities, but the best of them are often not the most conspicuous. Look beyond the ubiquitous street vendors and the hundreds of virtually indistinguishable purse, glass, and lace shops that line the calli, and you'll discover a bounty of unique and delightful treasures—some might be kitschy, but many will show off the high level of craftsmanship for which Venice has long been known.

Essentials

Alluring shops abound. You'll find countless vendors of trademark Venetian wares such as Murano glass and Burano lace; the authenticity of some goods can be suspect, but they're often pleasing to the eye regardless of their heritage. For more sophisticated tastes (and deeper pockets), there are jewelers, antiques dealers, and high-fashion boutiques on a par with those in Italy's larger cities but often maintaining a uniquely Venetian flair. Don't ignore the contemporary, either: Venice's artisan heritage lives on in the hands and eyes of today's designers—no matter their origin.

While the labyrinthine city center can seem filled with imposing high-fashion emporiums and fancy glass shops, individual craftspeople often working off the main thoroughfares produce much of what is worth taking home from Venice. In their workshops, artful stationery is printed with antique plates; individual pairs of shoes are adroitly constructed; jewelry is handcrafted; fine fabrics are skillfully woven; bronze is poured to make gondola decor, and iron is worked into fanali lanterns; paper is glued, pressed, and shaped into masks; and oars and *fórcole* oarlocks are hewn and sculpted in the workshops of *remér* wood craftsmen.

STORE HOURS

Regular store hours are usually 9–1 and 3:30 or 4–7:30 pm; some stores are closed Saturday afternoon or Monday morning. Food shops are open 8–1 and 5–7:30 and are closed all day Sunday and Wednesday afternoon. However, many tourist-oriented shops are open all day, every day, especially those in the San Marco area. Some privately owned shops close for both a summer and a winter vacation.

It's always a good idea to mark the location of a shop that interests you on your map; even better, ask for their business card as you pass (they often have maps printed on the back). Otherwise, you may not be able to find it again in the maze of tiny streets.

TAX REFUNDS

If you make a major purchase, take advantage of tax-free shopping with the value-added tax (V.A.T., or I.V.A. in Italian) refund. On clothing and luxury-goods purchases totaling more than €154.95 made at a single store, non-EU residents are entitled to get back the up to 22% tax included in the purchase price.
⇨ *For details, see Taxes.*

WHERE TO SHOP

The rule here is simple: the closer you are to Piazza San Marco, the higher the prices. The serious jewelry and glasswork in the windows of the shops of the Procuratie Vecchie and Nuove make for a pleasant browse; in summer your stroll will be accompanied by the music from the bands that set up in front of Caffè Quadri and Caffè Florian. In the shade of the arcades of the Piazza San Marco you'll also find Murano glass vendors like Pauly and Venini, the Ravagnan Gallery, old-fashioned shops selling kitschy souvenirs, and an assortment of lace, linen blouses, silk ties, and scarves.

The area of San Marco west of the piazza (in the Frezzeria and beyond the Fenice) has a concentration of boutiques, jewelry shops, antiques dealers, and the most important art galleries in the city, including Bugno.

The Rialto district, surrounding the famous bridge on both sides of the Grand Canal in San Marco and San Polo, is the mecca for buyers of traditional, inexpensive souvenirs: *pantofole del gondoliere,* velvety slippers with rubber soles that resemble the traditional gondoliers' shoes; 18th-century-style wooden trays and coasters that look better after a little wear; and glass "candies," which make a nice, inexpensive (if inedible) gift.

Clothing and shoe shops are concentrated between the Rialto Bridge and Campo San Polo, along Ruga Vecchia San Giovanni and Ruga Ravano, and around Campo Sant'Aponal. From the Rialto heading toward Campo Santi Apostoli in Cannaregio, you'll find the elegant Murano glass and jewelry purveyor Rose Douce.

👁 Sights

It's called La Serenissima, "the most serene," a reference to the majesty, wisdom, and impressive power of this city that was for centuries the leader in trade between Europe and the East, and a major source of European culture. Built on and around a cluster of tiny islands in a lagoon by a people who saw the sea as a defense and ally, Venice is unlike any other city.

No matter how often you've seen Venice in photos and films, the city is more dreamlike than you could ever imagine. The key landmarks, the Basilica di San Marco and the Palazzo Ducale, are hardly what we normally think of as Italian: fascinatingly idiosyncratic, they are exotic mixes of Byzantine, Romanesque, Gothic, and Renaissance styles. Shimmering sunlight and silvery mist soften every perspective here; it's easy to understand how the city became renowned in the Renaissance for its artists' use of color. The city is full of secrets, inexpressibly romantic, and, in both art and everyday life, given over to an unabashed celebration of the material world.

You'll see Venetians going about their daily affairs in vaporetti (water buses),

aboard the traghetti (gondola ferries) that carry them across the Grand Canal, in the campi (squares), and along the calli (narrow streets). They are skilled—and remarkably tolerant—at dealing with the hordes of tourists from all over the world, attracted by the city's fame and splendor.

Venice proper is divided into six sestieri, or districts (the word *sestiere* means, appropriately, "sixth"): Cannaregio, Castello, Dorsoduro, San Marco, San Polo, and Santa Croce. More-sedate outer islands float around them—San Giorgio Maggiore and the Giudecca just to the south; beyond them the Lido, the barrier island; to the north, Murano, Burano, and Torcello.

💲 Taxes

A 10% V.A.T. (value-added tax) is included in the rate at all hotels. No tax is added to the bill in restaurants. A service charge of approximately 10%–15% is usually added to your check.

The V.A.T. is 22% on clothing, wine, and luxury goods. On consumer goods it's already included in the amount shown on the price tag (look for the phrase "I.V.A. *inclusa*"), whereas on services it may not be. If you're not a European citizen and your purchases in a single day total more than €154.95, you may be entitled to a refund of the V.A.T.

When making a purchase, ask whether the merchant gives refunds—not all do, nor are they required to. If they do, they'll help you fill out the V.A.T. refund form, which you then submit to a company that will issue you the refund in the form of cash, check, or credit-card adjustment.

Alternatively, as you leave the country (or, if you're visiting several European Union countries, on leaving the EU),

Essentials

present your merchandise and the form to customs officials, who will stamp it. Once through passport control, take the stamped form to a refund-service counter for an on-the-spot refund (the quickest and easiest option).

Tipping

In Venice, as in most of northern Italy, tipping is not expected in restaurants, bars, or taxis, or for other services, even for excellent service. The only exception is to tip a bellhop €2–€2.50 per bag for carrying your bags to your room.

U.S. Embassy/Consulate

For U.S. Embassy and consulate information and assistance visit ⊕ *it. usembassy.gov*. The U.S. Embassy is in Rome (☎ *06/46741*), while there are consulates in Milan (☎ *02/290351*), Florence (☎ *055/266951*), and Naples (☎ *081/5838111*).

Visitor Information

The multilingual staff of the **Venice tourism office** (☎ *041/5298711* ⊕ *www. turismovenezia.it*) can provide directions and up-to-the-minute information. Tourist office branches are in Marco Polo Airport; the Venezia Santa Lucia train station; Piazza San Marco near Museo Correr at the southwest corner; the Venice Pavilion (including a Venice-centric bookstore), on the riva (canal-front street) between the San Marco vaporetto stop and the Royal Gardens; and on the Lido at the main vaporetto stop. Daily hours are 10–6.

When to Go

Spring: Late April through early June is a good time to visit Venice: the weather is mild, but the volume of tourists is larger than it is in summer.

Summer: Summers are very warm and humid. The advantages are fewer tourists (but their numbers are still substantial), it almost never rains, and the beaches of the Lido are just a boat ride away.

Fall: Autumn, like spring, is a good time for visiting Venice. It's usually pleasant and sunny well into October, and it doesn't really begin to get cold until mid-November. Acqua alta flooding is most frequent, and severe, in late November, although the new MOSE flood defense system has lessened instances of severe floods.

Winter: Venetian winters are relatively mild, with frequent rainy spells and fog, but also many more sunny days than there are in Northern Europe or much of North America. There are substantial crowds during Carnevale, and prices for hotels and even in some restaurants skyrocket.

Contacts

Air

AIRPORT
Aeroporto Marco Polo
☎ 041/2609260 ⊕ www.veniceairport.it.
AIR TRANSFERS
Alilaguna ☎ 041/2401701
⊕ www.alilaguna.it. **ATVO**
☎ 0421/5944 ⊕ www.atvo.it.

Car

PARKING IN VENICE
Garage San Marco ⊠ Piazzale Roma 467/F, San Marco ☎ 041/5232213
⊕ www.garagesanmarco.it.

◉ Emergencies

Emergencies ☎ 113.
National and State Police ☎ 112 for Polizia (National Police), 113 for Carabinieri (State Police)
⊕ www.poliziadistato.it, www.carabinieri.it.
U.S. Department of State

☎ 877/487–2778 ⊕ travel.state.gov/passport.

Public Transportation

ACTV ⊠ Venice ☎ 041/041 Call Center ⊕ actv.avmspa.it.

⊕ Train

FS-Trenitalia
☎ 06/68475475 from outside Italy (English), 892021 in Italy ⊕ www.trenitalia.com. **Italia Rail**
☎ 877/375–7245 in U.S., 06/97632451 in Italy
⊕ www.italiarail.com.
Rail Europe ⊕ www.raileurope.com.

▤ U.S. Embassy

U.S. Embassy Rome ⊠ Via Vittorio Veneto 121
☎ 06/46741 ⊕ www.usembassy.gov/italy.
U.S. Consulate Milan
⊠ Via Principe Amedeo 2/10, Milan ☎ 02/290351
⊕ www.usembassy.

gov/italy. **U.S. Consulate Florence** ⊠ Lungarno Vespucci 38, Florence
☎ 055/266951 ⊕ www.usembassy.gov/italy.
U.S. Consulate Naples
⊠ Piazza della Repubblica, Naples ☎ 081/5838111
⊕ www.usembassy.gov/italy.

◉ Visitor Information

Venice Tourism Office
⊠ Piazzo San Marco, Piazza San Marco
☎ 041/5298711 ⊕ www.turismovenezia.it.

Great Itineraries

3 Days in La Serenissima

Three days are hardly enough to see one of the world's most beautiful cities and one of the cradles of modern Western civilization. But running from museum to museum, church to church would be a mistake, since Venice is a wonderful place to stroll or "hang out," taking in some of the atmosphere that inspired such great art.

DAY 1

The first things you will probably want to do in Venice are to take a vaporetto ride down the Grand Canal and see Piazza San Marco. These are best done in the morning; before 8:30, you'll avoid rush hour on the vaporetto, and although there's likely to be a line at the Basilica di San Marco when it opens, you'll be better off then than later in the day. Move on to the adjacent Palazzo Ducale and Sansovino's Biblioteca Marciana.

For lunch, take Vaporetto 1 to the Ca' Rezzonico stop and have a sandwich and a spritz in Campo Santa Margherita, where you can mingle with university students in one of Venice's most lively squares. From there, make your way to the Galleria dell'Accademia and spend a few hours absorbing its wonderful collection of Venetian painting. In the evening, take a walk up the Zattere and have a drink at one of the cafés overlooking the Giudecca Canal.

DAY 2

If the Accademia has whet your appetite for Venetian painting, visit some churches and institutions where you can see more of it. For Titian, go to Santa Maria Gloriosa dei Frari and Santa Maria della Salute; for Tintoretto, the Scuola Grande di San Rocco; for Bellini, San Giovanni e Paolo and San Zaccheria; for Tiepolo, Ca' Rezzonico, the Scuola Grande dei Carmini, and the Gesuati; for Carpaccio, the Scuola di San Giorgio; and for Veronese, San Sebastiano.

If your taste runs to more modern art, there is the Guggenheim Collection and, down the street from it, the Pinault Collection in the impressively refashioned Palazzo Grassi and Punta della Dogana.

In the afternoon, head for the Fondamenta Nove station to catch a vaporetto to one or more of the outer islands: Murano, where you can shop for Venetian glass and visit the glass museum and workshops; Burano, known for lace-making and colorful houses; and Torcèllo, Venice's first inhabited island, home to a beautiful cathedral.

DAY 3

Venice is more than a museum—it's a lively city, and the best way to experience that is to pay a visit to the Rialto markets. Venetians buy their fruits and vegetables here and, most important, their fish—this is one of Europe's largest and most varied fish markets. Have lunch in one of the excellent restaurants in the market area.

There's certainly a good deal more art and architecture to see in the city, and if you can't resist squeezing in another few churches, you may want to see Palladio's masterpiece of ecclesiastical architecture, the Redentore church on the Giudecca, or Tullio Lombardo's lyrical Miracoli, a short walk from the San Marco end of the Rialto Bridge.

Best Tours in Venice

If you want some expert guidance around Venice, you may opt for a private tour or large group tour. Any may include a boat tour as a portion of a longer walking tour.

A GUIDE IN VENICE

Authorized guide French-Venetian Hélène Salvadori heads a team offering a wide variety of innovative, entertaining, and informative themed tours—including master artisan, art, and architecture tours—for groups of up to eight people. Individual tours are also available and generally last two to three hours. The fee is €75 per hour for up to eight people, which does not include admissions or transportation fees. Small group tours running May–October are also available. ☎ *348/5927974* ⊕ *www.aguidein-venice.com.*

COOPERATIVA GUIDE TURISTICHE AUTORIZZATE

The Cooperativa Guide Turistiche Autorizzate has a list of more than 100 licensed guides. Two-hour tours with an English-speaking guide start at €148 for up to 30 people. Prices can double or triple for tours longer than two hours. Agree on a total price before you begin, as there can be additional administrative and pickup fees. ⊕ *www.guidevenezia.it.*

SECRET GARDENS OF VENICE

A vine creeping over a wall is often the only hint a visitor gets that this city of stone and water conceals some magnificent gardens. Secret Garden tours led by companies like Venice Guide and Boat reveal the gardens hidden behind palazzos and within the confines of convents; they are not only luxurious oases but also full of rich ornamentation and, as your guide explains, have long and colorful histories. Prices start at €330 with Venice Guide and Boat. ⊕ *www.veniceguideandboat.it.*

VENICE ART TOURS

Native English speaker and San Franciscan Eric Bagan takes small group tours around not only major artistic monuments of the city, but also residential areas that the casual visitor would probably miss on their own. The tour guide is knowledgeable and willing to adjust his itinerary to suit clients' specific artistic interests. Prices start at €280 for up to five people. ⊕ *venice-art-tours.com.*

WALKS INSIDE VENICE

For a host of particularly creative group and private tours—from history to art to gastronomy—check out Walks Inside Venice. The maximum group size is six, and tour guides include people with advanced university degrees and published authors. Rates start at €280 for the three-hour Venice for Beginners tour. ⊕ *www.walksinsidevenice.com.*

VENICE TOURISM OFFICE

Visit any Venice tourism office to book walking tours of the San Marco area (note there's no Sunday tour in winter). They can also arrange other tours including a walking tour that ends with a gondola ride, and a *pescaturismo* (fishing boat trip) around Burano.

WALKS OF ITALY

The Walks of Italy company offers a selection of Venice tours, covering the city by foot and by boat, and the guides are almost unfailingly knowledgeable and friendly. Tours start at €49. ⊕ *www. walksofitaly.com.*

SEE VENICE

Luisella Romeo is a delightful guide capable of bringing to life even the most convoluted aspects of Venice's art and history. She can customize tours depending on guests' areas of interest, including Murano and glass art, music and shopping in Venice, and photography tours. ☎ *0349/0848303* ⊕ *www. seevenice.it.*

Helpful Italian Phrases

BASICS

Yes/no	Sí/No	see/no
Please	Per favore	pear fa-**vo**-ray
Thank you	Grazie	grah-tsee-ay
You're welcome	Prego	**pray**-go
I'm sorry (apology)	Mi dispiace	mee dis-pee-**atch**-ay
Excuse me, sorry	Scusi	**skoo**-zee
Good morning/ afternoon	Buongiorno	bwohn-**jor**-no
Good evening	Buona sera	**bwoh**-na **say**-ra
Good-bye	Arrivederci	a-ree-vah-**dare**-chee
Mr. (Sir)	Signore	see-**nyo**-ray
Mrs. (Ma'am)	Signora	see-**nyo**-ra
Miss	Signorina	see-nyo-**ree**-na
Pleased to meet you	Piacere	pee-ah-**chair**-ray
How are you?	Come sta?	**ko**-may-**stah**
Hello (phone)	Pronto?	**proan**-to

NUMBERS

one-half	mezzo	**mets**-zoh
one	uno	**oo**-no
two	due	**doo**-ay
three	tre	Tray
four	quattro	**kwah**-tro
five	cinque	**cheen**-kway
six	sei	Say
seven	sette	**set**-ay
eight	otto	**oh**-to
nine	nove	**no**-vay
ten	dieci	dee-**eh**-chee
eleven	undici	**oon**-dee-chee
twelve	dodici	**doh**-dee-chee
thirteen	tredici	**trey**-dee-chee
fourteen	quattordici	kwah-**tor**-dee-chee
fifteen	quindici	**kwin**-dee-chee
sixteen	sedici	**say**-dee-chee
seventeen	dicissette	dee-chah-**set**-ay
eighteen	diciotto	dee-chee-**oh**-to
nineteen	diciannove	dee-chee-ahn-**no**-vay
twenty	venti	**vain**-tee
twenty-one	ventuno	**vent**-oo-no
thirty	trenta	**train**-ta
forty	quaranta	kwa-**rahn**-ta
fifty	cinquanta	cheen-**kwahn**-ta
sixty	sessanta	seh-**sahn**-ta
seventy	settanta	seh-**tahn**-ta
eighty	ottanta	o-**tahn**-ta
ninety	novanta	no-**vahn**-ta
one hundred	cento	**chen**-to
one thousand	mille	**mee**-lay
one million	un milione	oon **mill**-oo-nay

COLORS

black	Nero	**nair**-ro
blue	Blu	bloo
brown	Marrone	ma-**rohn**-nay
green	Verde	**ver**-day
orange	Arancione	ah-rahn-**cho**-nay
red	Rosso	**rose**-so
white	Bianco	bee-**ahn**-koh
yellow	Giallo	**jaw**-low

DAYS OF THE WEEK

Sunday	Domenica	do-**meh**-nee-ka
Monday	Lunedi	loo-ne-**dee**
Tuesday	Martedi	mar-te-**dee**
Wednesday	Mercoledi	**mer**-ko-le-**dee**
Thursday	Giovedi	jo-ve-**dee**
Friday	Venerdì	ve-ner-**dee**
Saturday	Sabato	**sa**-ba-toh

MONTHS

January	Gennaio	jen-**ay**-o
February	Febbraio	feb-**rah**-yo
March	Marzo	**mart**-so
April	Aprile	a-**pril**-ay
May	Maggio	**mahd**-joe
June	Giugno	**joon**-yo
July	Luglio	**lool**-yo
August	Agosto	a-**gus**-to
September	Settembre	se-**tem**-bre
October	Ottobre	o-**toh**-bre
November	Novembre	no-**vem**-bre
December	Dicembre	di-**chem**-bre

USEFUL WORDS AND PHRASES

Do you speak English?	Parla Inglese?	**par**-la een-**glay**-zay
I don't speak Italian	Non parlo italiano	non **par**-lo ee-tal-**yah**-no
I don't understand	Non capisco	non ka-**peess**-ko
I don't know	Non lo so	non lo **so**
I understand	Capisco	ka-**peess**-ko
I'm American	Sono Americano(a)	**so**-no a-may-ree-**kah**-no(a)
I'm British	Sono inglese	so-no een-**glay**-zay
What's your name?	Come si chiama?	**ko**-may see kee-**ah**-ma
My name is …	Mi Chiamo…	mee kee-**ah**-mo
What time is it?	Che ore sono?	kay **o**-ray **so**-no
How?	Come?	**ko**-may
When?	Quando?	**kwan**-doe
Yesterday/today/ tomorrow	Ieri/oggi/domani	**yer**-ee/ o-jee/ do-**mah**-nee

This morning	Stamattina/Oggi	sta-ma-**tee**-na/ **o**-jee
Afternoon	Pomeriggio	po-mer-**ee**-jo
Tonight	Stasera	sta-**ser**-a
What?	Che cosa?	kay **ko**-za
What is it?	Che cos'è?	kay ko-**zey**
Why?	Perchè?	pear-**kay**
Who?	Chi?	**Kee**
Where is ...	Dov'è...	doe-**veh**
the train station?	la stazione?	la sta-tsee-**oh**-nay
the subway?	la metropolitana?	la may-tro-po-lee-**tah**-na
the bus stop?	la fermata dell'autobus?	la fer-**mah**-ta del-ow-tor-**booss**
the airport	l'aeroporto	la-er-roh-**por**-toh
the post office?	l'ufficio postale	loo-**fee**-cho po-**stah**-lay
the bank?	la banca?	la **bahn**-ka
the hotel?	l'hotel...?	lo-**tel**
the museum?	Il museo	eel moo-**zay**-o
the hospital?	l'ospedale?	lo-spay-**dah**-lay
the elevator?	l'ascensore	la-shen-**so**-ray
the restrooms?	il bango?	eel **bahn**-yo
Here/there	Qui/là	kwee/la
Left/right	A sinistra/a destra	a see-**neess**-tra/a **des**-tra
Is it near/far?	È vicino/lontano?	ay vee-**chee**-no/ lon-**tah**-no
I'd like ...	Vorrei...	vo-**ray**
a room	una camera	**oo**-na **kah**-may-ra
the key	la chiave	la kee-**ah**-vay
a newspaper	un giornale	oon jore-**nah**-vay
a stamp	un francobollo	oon frahn-ko-**bo**-lo
I'd like to buy ...	Vorrei comprare...	vo-**ray** kom-**prah**-ray
a city map	una mappa della città	**oo**-na **mah**-pa **day**-la chee-**tah**
a road map	una carta stradale	**oo**-na **car**-tah stra-**dahl**-lay
a magazine	una revista	**oo**-na ray-**vees**-tah
envelopes	buste	**boos**-tay
writing paper	carta de lettera	**car**-tah dah **leyt**-ter-rah
a postcard	una cartolina	**oo**-na car-tog-**leen**-ah
a ticket	un biglietto	oon bee-**yet**-toh
How much is it?	Quanto costa?	**kwahn**-toe **coast**-a
It's expensive/ cheap	È caro/ economico	ay **car**-o/ ay-ko-**no**-mee-ko
A little/a lot	Poco/tanto	**po**-ko/**tahn**-to
More/less	Più/meno	pee-**oo**/**may**-no

Enough/too (much)	Abbastanza/ troppo	a-bas-**tahn**-sa/tro-po
I am sick	Sto male	sto **mah**-lay
Call a doctor	Chiama un dottore	kee-**ah**-mah-oondoe-**toe**-ray
Help!	Aituo!	a-**yoo**-to
Stop!	Alt!	ahlt

DINING OUT

A bottle of ...	Una bottiglia di...	**oo**-na bo-**tee**-lee-ah dee
A cup of ...	Una tazza di...	**oo**-na **tah**-tsa dee
A glass of ...	Un bicchiere di...	oon bee-key-**air**-ay dee
Beer	La birra	la **beer**-rah
Bill/check	Il conto	eel **cone**-toe
Bread	Il pane	eel **pah**-nay
Breakfast	La prima colazione	la **pree**-ma ko-la-**tsee**-oh-nay
Butter		eel **boor**-roh
Cocktail/aperitif	L'aperitivo	la-pay-ree-**tee**-vo
Dinner	La cena	la **chen**-a
Fixed-price menu	Menù a prezzo fisso	may-**noo** a **pret**-so **fee**-so
Fork	La forchetta	la for-**ket**-a
I am vegetarian	Sono vegetariano(a)	**so**-no vay-jay-ta-ree-**ah**-no/a
I cannot eat ...	Non posso mangiare	non **pose**-so mahn-gee-**are**-ay
I'd like to order	Vorrei ordinare	vo-**ray** or-dee-**nah**-ray
Is service included?	Il servizio è incluso?	eel ser-**vee**-tzee-o ay een-**kloo**-zo
I'm hungry/ thirsty	Ho fame/sede	oh **fah**-meh/**sehd**-ed
It's good/bad	E buono/cattivo	ay **bwo**-no/ka-**tee**-vo
It's hot/cold	E caldo/freddo	ay **kahl**-doe/**fred**-o
Knife	Il coltello	eel kol-**tel**-o
Lunch	Il pranzo	eel **prahnt**-so
Menu	Il menu	eel may-**noo**
Napkin	Il tovagliolo	eel toe-va-lee-**oh**-lo
Pepper	Il pepe	eel **pep**-peh
Plate	Il piatto	eel pee-**aht**-toe
Please give me ...	Mi dia...	mee **dee**-a
Salt	Il sale	eel **sah**-lay
Spoon	Il cucchiaio	eel koo-kee-ah-yo
Tea	tè	tay
Water	acqua	**awk**-wah
Wine	vino	**vee**-noh

On the Calendar

January

Festa dell'Epifania. Italians celebrate the coming of *la befana*, a folkloric old woman riding a broomstick who rewards good children with gifts, on the night of January 5.

Saldi invernali. Meanwhile, around Rialto's shops and the cluster of outlet stores in Treviso, Verona, and Padua, consumers flock to the winter sales.

February

Carnevale. Venice goes big with pre-Lent celebrations for almost two weeks up to Shrove Tuesday, with lavish masked parades, parties, and sweet treats like *frittole* and *galani*. In the 18th century, Venice was renowned for debauched Carnevale shenanigans, but they faded by the 1860s; it wasn't until the 1970s that the festivities were rebooted to attract visitors. Now, Carnevale means full-fledged concerts, street performances, masquerade balls, and contests to encourage people to don elaborate outfits and the all important *maschera* (mask). If you're not up for the revelry, crowded streets, and hike in prices, choose a quieter time to visit.

April

Festa di San Marco. The festival honoring the evangelist who for 1,000 years protected his city is somewhat eclipsed by the fact that April 25 is also Italian Liberation Day, a national holiday. On St. Mark's Day men traditionally buy *bòcoli* (red roses) for ladies in their lives (wives, mothers, sisters, cousins, friends)—the longer the stem the deeper the token of love. Legend tells of a soldier enamored of the doge's daughter who was mortally wounded in a far-off battle. As it spilled, his blood was transformed into red roses, which he entrusted his companion to bring to the girl. The story doesn't say if the flowers arrived on the saint's day, but by tradition Venetians celebrate the miracle on this date.

May

Festa della Sensa. The oldest Venetian festival, the Festival of the Ascension, was initiated by Doge Pietro II Orseolo in the year 1000, after he led the Venetian fleet to victory over the Slavic pirates (who had invaded the Istrian–Dalmatian coast) on Ascension Day. Originally the Ascension was a very simple ceremony in which the doge led a procession of boats to the entrance of the port of San Nicolò di Lido to meet the religious leader of the period, the bishop of San Pietro di Castello, who blessed the waters as a sign of peace and gratitude. In the days of the Republic, the Ascension began with a series of performances and celebrations that went on for 15 days and culminated with a large fair in Piazza San Marco. Today the Ascension is held on the Sunday following Ascension Day, the Thursday that falls 40 days after Easter, and begins at about 9 am with a procession of Venetian-oared boats led by the mayor in the Serenissima, who tosses a ring into the water and pronounces the ritual phrase *"In segno di eterno dominio, noi, Doge di Venezia, ti sposiamo o mare!"* (As a symbol of our eternal dominion, we, the Doge of

Venice, wed you, oh sea!). Masses in the Chiesa di San Nicolò and boat races follow later in the afternoon. In the Sala del Maggior Consiglio in the Palazzo Ducale, you can see several objects that are part of the ceremony, such as the thick candle, the umbrella, the gilded throne, and the eight white, red, blue, and yellow banners. The Museo Storico Navale has an 18-foot-long scale model of the gilded boat once used by the doge.

June

Venice Biennale. Every two years Venice hosts the biggest and most prestigious contemporary art show around. Traditionally, it has kicked off in June with a week-long vernissage of the international art world's entourages stroking chins and egos around the Giardini's national pavilions, Arsenale *corderie* (vast former ropework buildings), and various venues across the city. It's a buzzy time to experience the spectacle, but remember that the show runs until November if you'd like to ponder the art at quieter times. While the Biennale Arte is staged in even years, the Dance, Music, Theater, and Cinema versions roll up annually, with the Architecture biennial getting a platform in odd years. ⊕ *www.labiennale.org*.

Vogalonga. Established in 1974 by enthusiasts of *voga alla veneta* (rowing Venetian flat-bottomed vessels), this joyful and noncompetitive 20-mile race around the lagoon and Grand Canal is held on a Sunday in May or June. It attracts groups of friends in colorful costumes and some elaborate crafts, including Chinese dragon boats. It's fun to watch from the starting point at Bacino di San Marco, or at less busy vantage points around the city and lagoon, such as Burano. ⊕ *www.vogalonga.com*.

July

Festa del Redentore. On the third Sunday in July, crowds cross the Canale della Giudecca by means of a pontoon bridge, built every year to commemorate the doge's annual visit to Palladio's Chiesa del Santissimo Redentore to offer thanks for the end of a 16th-century plague. The evening before, Venetians—accompanied each year by an increasing number of tourists—set up tables and chairs along the canals. As evening falls, practically the whole city takes to the streets and tables, and thousands more take to the water. Boats decorated with colored lanterns (and well provisioned with traditional Redentore meals) jockey for position to watch the grand event. Half an hour before midnight, Venice kicks off a fireworks display over the Bacino.

August

Ferragosto. During the sweltering heat of August some businesses shut down and many head to the coast, echoing the days when Venetian nobility escaped to their cooler Veneto villas. A national holiday on August 15, originating from the Roman Feriae Augusti, sees Italians gather with family for a traditional lunch and day out with picnics.

September

Venice Film Festival. Movie stars, their entourages, critics, and film buffs mingle on the red carpet on the island of Lido and at various cinemas around the city. Open-air screenings on balmy late summer evenings bring extra magic and atmosphere to Santo Stefano and various campi, such as Campo San Polo. ⊕ *www.labiennale.org*.

On the Calendar

October

Festa del Mosto. Every first Sunday of October this fun, family-friendly event on Sant'Erasmo celebrates the island's freshly pressed grape juice.

November

Festa della Madonna della Salute. This thanksgiving festival celebrates not a harvest, but survival. Every November 21, Venetians make a pilgrimage across a temporary bridge to the church of Madonna della Salute, where they light candles to thank the Virgin Mary for liberating the city from the plague of 1630–31 and to pray for health in the year to come. A spectacular fireworks show focuses thousands of eyes on the cupola of La Salute and the Venetian skies beyond.

December

Venice Cocktail Week. This weeklong event celebrates the city's bar and cocktail scene. Participating bars create bespoke cocktails and throw parties. ⊕ *venicecocktailweek.it.*

Chapter 3

SAN MARCO

Updated by
Liz Humphreys

⊙ Sights	🍴 Restaurants	🛏 Hotels	💼 Shopping	🍸 Nightlife
★★★★★	★★★☆☆	★★★★★	★★★★★	★★☆☆☆

NEIGHBORHOOD SNAPSHOT

TOP EXPERIENCES

■ **Sip an *aperitivo* (aperitif) at sunset:** There's nothing more romantic than a spritz at dusk in Piazza San Marco.

■ **Book a room with a view:** Consider splurging on a room overlooking the Grand Canal at a fine hotel.

■ **See the Basilica di San Marco:** The 12th- and 13th-century mosaics alone are worth a trip to Venice.

■ **Cross the Ponte di Rialto:** Don't miss the spectacular Grand Canal views from Venice's famous bridge.

■ **Tour the Doge's Palace:** Be wowed by Tintoretto's paintings and the 15th-century Stairway of the Giants.

■ **Stroll and shop:** Art, fabrics, paper, jewelry, shoes—San Marco's streets are a treasure trove.

GETTING HERE

The quickest, cheapest, and most pleasant way to reach San Marco is by vaporetto (single ticket valid for 75 minutes, €7.50). There are several vaporetto stops close to Piazza San Marco: San Marco, San Zaccaria, and Vallaresso. The Rialto, San Samuele, and Sant'Angelo stops will deposit you closer to the Rialto Bridge. If your hotel is on a canal, taking a private water taxi (*motoscafi*) to and from the airport is an unforgettable Venetian experience that's worth every penny. Private taxis average about €120 one-way from Venice Marco Polo Airport to a hotel.

PLANNING YOUR TIME

You can easily spend several days seeing the historical and artistic monuments in and around Piazza San Marco alone, but at a bare minimum plan on at least an hour for the basilica, with its wonderful mosaics. Add on another half hour if you want to see its sanctuary, Pala d'Oro, and Museo di San Marco. You'll want at least an hour to appreciate the Palazzo Ducale. Leave another hour for the Museo Correr, through which you also enter the archaeological museum and the Libreria Sansoviniana. Or, take in the piazza itself from a café table with an orchestra (note there's an additional charge for the music).

VIEWFINDER

■ **Campanile di San Marco.** At 99 meters (325 feet) high, the Basilica di San Marco bell tower is the tallest building in Venice. Originally from the 9th century, it was rebuilt a few times, most recently when the tower collapsed in 1902. Today you can take an elevator to the top to see unsurpassed views of the city and the lagoon. If you can, come after dark for a romantic look at the sparkling city lights. ✉ *Piazza San Marco* ⊕ *www.basilicasanmarco.it* Ⓜ *Vaporetto: San Zaccaria, Vallaresso.*

■ **Scala Contarini del Bovolo.** Built in the 16th century, the Renaissance Gothic palace Palazzo Contarini del Bovolo no longer has much to see on the inside. But on the outside, the tallest spiral staircase in Venice—going up six floors—offers amazing views of the city spread out beneath you. Climb the 80 steps up to the domed belvedere for a 360-degree outlook unlike anywhere else in Venice. ✉ *Corte del Bovolo* ⊕ *www.gioiellinascostidivenezia.it* Ⓜ *Vaporetto: Rialto.*

Extending from Piazza San Marco (St. Mark's Square) to the Ponte di Rialto (Rialto Bridge), this *sestiere* (district) is the historical and commercial heart of Venice. From storied churches to artwork painted by Italian masters to charming shops selling unique handmade goods, you'll find the best of Venice in this bustling neighborhood. Cafés in San Marco's eponymous square—the only one in Venice given full stature as a "piazza" and, hence, often referred to simply as "the Piazza"—heave with tourists, but enjoying an aperitivo here is an unforgettable experience.

You'll find some of Venice's most unmissable sights alongside the Piazza, including the Museo Correr, a premiere collection of Venetian art and history; the Palazzo Ducale, the wondrous 10th-century doge's residence, which includes works from many of Venice's most renowned artists; and, of course, in the Piazza's pride of place, the Basilica di San Marco, with its amazing medieval mosaics.

This sestiere is also graced with some of Venice's loveliest churches, finest hotels—often with Grand Canal views—including the Gritti Palace, the St. Regis, and Bauer Palazzo, and a large concentration of fabulous art, including temporary exhibitions at the revamped Palazzo Grassi as well as galleries and studios galore. In addition, it's the city's main shopping district. Many big-name Italian designers have boutiques in San Marco, and its mazes of streets are also lined with shops from artisan producers who sell finely wrought jewelry, sumptuous fabrics, elegant leather goods, and intricate artworks.

Though it may seem like you're in a crowd of people anywhere you turn, it's worth joining the throngs to walk through the neighborhood to the Ponte di Rialto. Moving inward from the Grand Canal, you'll still find pockets of calm in hidden alleyways, where you can get a glass of wine and some *cicheti* (appetizers) to keep you fortified. And once night falls and the day-trippers have departed, San Marco feels like a dream, with the moon illuminating the water, and the narrow streets and bridges frozen in time. It's a scene you'll want to return to again and again.

Sights

★ Basilica di San Marco
(*St. Mark's Basilica*)

CHURCH | The Basilica di San Marco is not only the religious center of a great city, but also an expression of the political, intellectual, and economic aspiration and accomplishments of a place that, for centuries, was at the forefront of European culture. It is a monument not just to the glory of God, but also to the glory of Venice. The basilica was the doges' personal chapel, linking its religious function to the political life of the city, and was endowed with all the riches the Republic's admirals and merchants could carry off from the Orient (as the Byzantine Empire was then known), earning it the nickname "Chiesa d'Oro" (Golden Church). When the present church was begun in the 11th century, rare colored marbles and gold-leaf mosaics were used in its decoration. The 12th and 13th centuries were a period of intense military expansion, and by the early 13th century, the facades began to bear testimony to Venice's conquests, including gilt-bronze ancient Roman horses taken from Constantinople in 1204.

The low lighting, the single massive Byzantine chandelier, the giant iconostasis (altar screen), the matroneum (women's gallery) high above the naves—even the Greek-cross ground plan—give San Marco an exotic aspect quite unlike that of most Western Christian churches. The effect is remarkable. Here the pomp and mystery of Oriental magnificence are wedded to Christian belief, creating an intensely awesome impression.

The glory of the basilica is, of course, its medieval mosaic work; about 30% of the mosaics survive in something close to their original form. The earliest date from the late 12th century, but the great majority date from the 13th century. The taking of Constantinople in 1204 was a deciding moment for the mosaic decoration of the basilica. Large amounts of mosaic material were brought in, and a Venetian school of mosaic decoration began to develop. Moreover, a 4th- or 5th-century treasure—the Cotton Genesis, the earliest illustrated Bible—was brought from Constantinople and supplied the designs for the exquisite mosaics of the Creation and the stories of Abraham, Joseph, and Moses that adorn the narthex (entrance hall). They are among the most beautiful and best preserved in all the basilica.

In the sanctuary, the main altar is built over the tomb of St. Mark, its green marble canopy lifted high on 6th-century carved alabaster columns—again, pillaged art. The Pala d'Oro, a dazzling gilt-silver, gem-encrusted screen containing 255 enameled panels, was commissioned in 976 in Constantinople by the Venetian doge Pietro I Orseolo and enlarged over the subsequent four centuries.

Remember that this is a sacred place: guards may deny admission to people in shorts, sleeveless dresses, and tank tops. ✉ *Piazza San Marco, San Marco 328, San Marco* ☎ *041/2708311* ⊕ *www. basilicasanmarco.it* 🖾 *Basilica €3, sanctuary and Pala d'Oro €5, museum €7* Ⓜ *San Zaccaria, Vallaresso.*

Biblioteca Nazionale Marciana
(*Marciana Library*)

LIBRARY | There's a wondrous collection of centuries-old books and illuminated manuscripts at this library, located across the piazzetta from Palazzo Ducale in two buildings designed by Renaissance architect Sansovino, **Libreria Sansoviniana** (Sansovinian Library) and the adjacent **Zecca** (Mint). The complex was begun in

1537, and the Zecca was finished in 1545. Facing the Bacino (San Marco basin), the Zecca along with the Palazzo Ducale form Venice's front door. The Palazzo Ducale, built during a period of Venetian ascendance and self-confident power, is light and decidedly unmenacing. The Zecca, built in a time when the Republic had received some serious defeats and was economically strapped, is purposefully heavy and stresses a fictitious connection with the classical world. The library is, again, much more graceful and was finished according to Sansovino's design only after his death. Palladio was so impressed by the Biblioteca that he called it "beyond envy."

The books can only be viewed by written request and are primarily the domain of scholars. But the **Monumental Rooms** in the Sansoviniana are worth visiting for the works of Veronese, Tintoretto, and Titian that decorate its walls. You reach the Monumental Rooms, which often host special exhibits, through the Museo Correr. ✉ *Piazza San Marco 7, Piazza San Marco* ✛ *Enter through Museo Correr* ☎ *041/2407211* ⊕ *bibliotecanazionalemarciana.cultura.gov.it* 🎫 *Museums of San Marco Pass €25, includes Museo Correr, Museo Archeologico, Biblioteca Nazionale Marciana, and Palazzo Ducale. Museum Pass €36, includes all four museums plus eight civic museums* Ⓜ *Vaporetto: San Zaccaria, Vallaresso.*

Campanile di San Marco
(*St. Mark's Bell Tower*)
VIEWPOINT | Construction of Venice's famous brick bell tower (325 feet tall, plus the angel) began in the 9th century; it took on its present form in 1514. During the 15th century, the tower was used as a place of punishment: immoral clerics were suspended in wooden cages from the tower, some forced to subsist on bread and water for as long as a year; others were left to starve. In 1902, the tower unexpectedly collapsed, taking with it Jacopo Sansovino's marble loggia

(1537–49) at its base. The largest original bell, called the Marangona, survived. The crushed loggia was promptly reconstructed, and the new tower, rebuilt to the old plan, reopened in 1912. Today, on a clear day the stunning view includes the Lido, the lagoon, and the mainland as far as the Alps, but strangely enough, none of the myriad canals that snake through the city. ✉ *Piazza San Marco, San Marco* ☎ *041/2708311* ⊕ *www.basilicasanmarco.it* 🎫 *€10* Ⓜ *Vaporetto: San Zaccaria, Vallaresso.*

Campo Santo Stefano
PLAZA/SQUARE | In Venice's most prestigious residential neighborhood, you'll find one of the city's busiest crossroads just over the Accademia Bridge; it's hard to believe this square once hosted bullfights, with bulls or oxen tied to a stake and baited by dogs. For centuries the *campo* (square) was all grass except for a stone avenue called the *liston*. It was so popular for strolling that in Venetian dialect "*andare al liston*" still means "to go for a walk." A sunny meeting spot popular with Venetians and visitors alike, the campo also hosts outdoor fairs during Christmas and Carnevale seasons. Check out the 14th-century **Chiesa di Santo Stefano**. The pride of the church is its very fine Gothic portal, created in 1442 by Bartolomeo Bon. Inside, you'll see works by Tintoretto. ✉ *Campo Santo Stefano, San Marco* ☎ *041/2750462 Chorus Foundation* ⊕ *www.chorusvenezia.org* 🎫 *Church of Santo Stefano €3, included with Chorus Pass (€12)* Ⓜ *Vaporetto: Accademia.*

Museo Archeologico Nazionale di Venezia
(*National Archeological Museum of Venice*)
HISTORY MUSEUM | Venice is the only major Italian city without an ancient past, yet it hosts a collection of ancient art that rivals those in Rome and Naples. The small museum housing this collection was first established in 1596, when the heirs of Cardinal Domenico Grimani—a noted humanist who had left his collection of

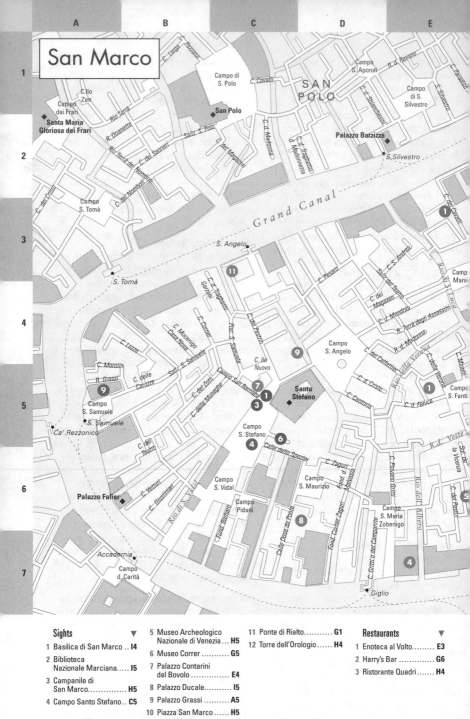

San Marco

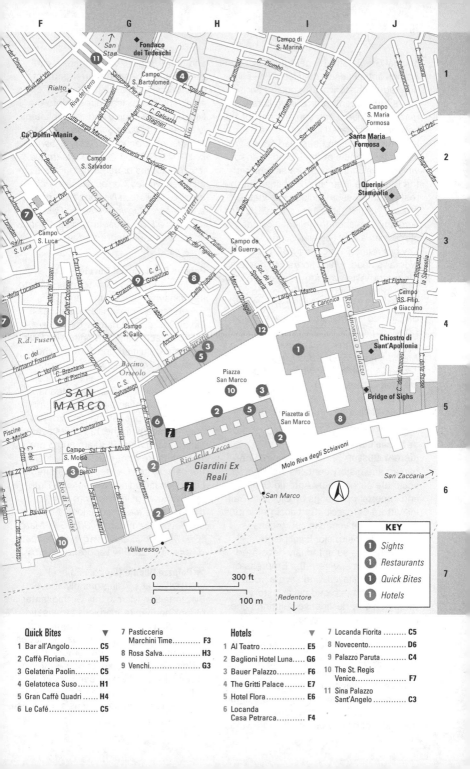

original Greek (5th–1st centuries BC) and Roman antiquities to the Republic—inaugurated the historical artworks in Sansovino's then recently completed library in Piazza San Marco. You can see part of the collection, displayed just as Grimani (or at least his immediate heirs) had conceived it, in the vestibule of the Libreria Sansoviniana, which the museum shares with the Biblioteca Marciana. Highlights in the rest of the museum include the statue of Kore (420 BC); the 1st-century BC *Ara Grimani*, an elaborate Hellenistic altar stone with a bacchanalian scene; and a tiny but refined 1st-century BC crystal woman's head, which some say depicts Cleopatra. When you arrive, scan the QR code to get a handy museum guide on your phone. ⊠ *Piazza San Marco 17/52, San Marco ⊹ Enter through Museo Correr* ☏ *041/2967663* ⊕ *polomusealeveneto.beniculturali.it* 🎫 *Museums of San Marco Pass €25, includes Museo Correr, Museo Archeologico, Biblioteca Nazionale Marciana, and Palazzo Ducale. Museum Pass €36, includes all four museums plus eight civic museums* Ⓜ *Vaporetto: San Zaccaria, Vallaresso.*

★ Museo Correr

HISTORY MUSEUM | This museum of Venetian art and history contains an important sculpture collection by Antonio Canova and important paintings by Giovanni Bellini, Vittore Carpaccio (Carpaccio's famous painting of the Venetian courtesans is here), and other major local painters. There are nine sumptuously decorated Imperial Rooms, where the Empress of Austria once stayed, and several rooms convey the city's proud naval history through highly descriptive paintings and numerous maritime objects, including ships' cannons and some surprisingly large iron mast-top navigation lights. The museum also houses curiosities like the absurdly high-soled shoes worn by 16th-century Venetian ladies (who walked with the aid of a servant) and has a significant collection of antique gems. It's also the main repository of Venetian drawings

and prints, which, unfortunately, can be seen only by special arrangement, or during special exhibitions. The Correr exhibition rooms lead directly into the Museo Archeologico and the Biblioteca Marciana. ⊠ *Piazza San Marco 52, Ala Napoleonica, opposite Basilica, San Marco* ☏ *041/2405211* ⊕ *correr.visitmuve.it* 🎫 *Museums of San Marco Pass €25, includes Museo Correr, Museo Archeologico, Biblioteca Nazionale Marciana, and Palazzo Ducale. Museum Pass €36, includes all four museums plus eight civic museums* Ⓜ *Vaporetto: San Zaccaria, Vallaresso.*

Palazzo Contarini del Bovolo

NOTABLE BUILDING | Easy to miss despite its vicinity to Piazza San Marco, this Renaissance-Gothic palace is accessible only through a narrow backstreet that connects Campo Manin with Calle dei Fuseri. Built around 1500 for the renowned Contarini family, its striking six-floor spiral staircase, the Scala Contarini del Bovolo (*bovolo* means "snail" in Venetian dialect), is the most interesting aspect of the palazzo. You can start the climb up the 133 stairs every half hour between 9:30 am and 5 pm. Though there's not much to see inside the palazzo itself, except for a limited art collection including one work by Tintoretto, the views of Venice from the top of the staircase are worth a look. ⊠ *Corte del Bovolo, San Marco 4303, San Marco* ☏ *041/3096605* ⊕ *www.gioiellinascostidivenezia.it* 🎫 *€8* Ⓜ *Vaporetto: Rialto.*

★ Palazzo Ducale (*Doge's Palace*)

CASTLE/PALACE | Rising grandly above Piazzetta San Marco, this Gothic fantasia of pink-and-white marble is a majestic expression of Venetian prosperity and power. Although the site was the doges' residence from the 10th century, the building began to take its present form around 1340; what you see now is essentially a product of the first half of the 15th century. It served not only as a residence,

A gondola floats past the Palazzo Ducale (Doge's Palace), one of Venice's top attractions.

but also as the central administrative center of the Venetian Republic.

Unlike other medieval seats of authority, the Palazzo Ducale is free of any military defenses—a sign of the Republic's self-confidence. The position of the loggias below instead of above the retaining wall, and the use of pink marble to emphasize the decorative function of that wall, gave the palazzo a light and airy aspect, one that could impress visitors— and even intimidate them, through opulence and grace rather than fortresslike bulk. You'll find yourself in an immense courtyard that holds some of the first evidence of Renaissance architecture in Venice, such as Antonio Rizzo's Scala dei Giganti (Stairway of the Giants), erected between 1483 and 1491, directly ahead, guarded by Sansovino's huge statues of Mars and Neptune, added in 1567. Though ordinary mortals must use the central interior staircase, its upper flight is the lavishly gilded Scala d'Oro (Golden Staircase), also designed by Sansovino, in 1555.

The palace's sumptuous chambers have walls and ceilings covered with works by Venice's greatest artists. Visit the Anticollegio, a waiting room outside the Collegio's chamber, where you can see *The Rape of Europa* by Veronese and Tintoretto's *Bacchus and Ariadne Crowned by Venus.* The ceiling of the Sala del Senato (Senate Chamber), featuring *The Triumph of Venice* by Tintoretto, is magnificent, but it's dwarfed by his masterpiece, *Paradise,* in the Sala del Maggiore Consiglio (Great Council Hall). A vast work commissioned for a vast hall, this dark, dynamic piece is the world's largest oil painting (23 feet by 75 feet). The room's carved gilt ceiling is breathtaking, especially with Veronese's majestic *Apotheosis of Venice* filling one of the center panels.

A narrow canal separates the palace's east side from the cramped cell blocks of the Prigioni Nuove (New Prisons). High above the water arches the enclosed marble Ponte dei Sospiri (Bridge of Sighs), which earned its name in the

Wading through the Acqua Alta

There are two ways to get anywhere in Venice: walking and by water. Occasionally you walk *through* water, when falling barometers, southeasterly winds, and even a full moon may exacerbate normally higher fall and spring tides. The result is *acqua alta*—flooding in the lowest parts of town, especially Piazza San Marco. It generally occurs in late fall and, to a lesser extent, in spring, and lasts a few hours until the tide recedes.

Venetians handle the high waters with aplomb, donning waders and erecting temporary walkways, but they're well aware of the corrosive damage caused by the salt water. Because of ongoing problems, the city launched the MOSE Project, underwater barriers that rise to block the tide's entrance into the lagoon. The barriers began to function in late 2020, though they are raised only when the tide is predicted to exceed 120 cm above sea level—little

comfort to Piazza San Marco, the lowest point in the city at a mere 85 cm. The extensive works, along with the deep channel dug years ago to accommodate cargo, have created a noticeable threat to the complex lagoon environment, and opinions conflict about this now permanent installation.

Venice has another water-related problem, arguably even more serious than acqua alta: *Motondoso*, or the waves created by the many thousands of motorboats. Venetians call it "the cancer of Venice," and it is the cause of the daily and visible deterioration of the city's foundations, not to mention the lagoon's fragile wetlands. Solutions exist, but they would require changes in the watercraft and continuous policing of speed limits, neither of which inspires any enthusiasm.

19th century, from Lord Byron's *Childe Harold's Pilgrimage*. Reserve your spot for the palazzo's popular Secret Itineraries tour well in advance. You'll visit the doge's private apartments and wind through hidden passageways to the "interrogation" (read: torture) chambers and the rooftop *piombi* (lead) prison, named for its lead roofing. Venetian-born writer and libertine Giacomo Casanova (1725–98), along with an accomplice, managed to escape from the piombi in 1756; they were the only men ever to do so. ✉ *Piazza San Marco 1, San Marco* ☏ *041/42730892 tickets* ⊕ *palazzoducale. visitmuve.it* 🎟 *Museums of San Marco Pass €25, includes Palazzo Ducale, Museo Correr, Museo Archeologico, and Biblioteca Nazionale Marciana. Museum Pass €36, includes all four museums plus eight civic museums. Secret Itineraries*

tour €28 Ⓜ *Vaporetto: San Zaccaria, Vallaresso.*

★ Palazzo Grassi

ART MUSEUM | Built between 1748 and 1772 by Giorgio Massari for a Bolognese family, this palace is one of the last of the great noble residences on the Grand Canal. Once owned by auto magnate Gianni Agnelli, it was bought by French businessman François Pinault in 2005 to showcase his highly esteemed collection of modern and contemporary art (which has now grown so large that Pinault rented the Punta della Dogana, at the entryway to the Grand Canal, for his newest acquisitions). Pinault brought in Japanese architect Tadao Ando to remodel the Grassi's interior. Check online for a schedule of temporary art exhibitions. ✉ *Campo San Samuele 3231, San Marco*

☎ *041/5231680* ⊕ *www.palazzograssi.
it* ✉ *€18, includes Punta della Dogana*
🕙 *Closed Tues.* Ⓜ *Vaporetto: San Samuele, Sant'Angelo.*

★ **Piazza San Marco** (*St. Mark's Square*)
PLAZA/SQUARE | **FAMILY** | One of the world's
most beautiful squares, Piazza San
Marco (St. Mark's Square) is the spiritual
and artistic heart of Venice, a vast open
space bordered by an orderly procession
of arcades marching toward the fairy-tale
cupolas and marble lacework of the Basilica di San Marco. From midmorning on, it
is generally packed with tourists. (If Venetians have business in the piazza, they try
to conduct it in the early morning, before
the crowds swell.) At night the piazza can
be magical, especially in winter, when
mists swirl around the lampposts and the
campanile.

Facing the basilica, on your left, the
long, arcaded building is the Procuratie
Vecchie, renovated to its present form
in 1514 as offices and residences for the
powerful procurators, or magistrates.

On your right is the Procuratie Nuove,
built half a century later in a more
imposing, classical style. It was originally
planned by Venice's great Renaissance
architect Jacopo Sansovino (1486–1570),
to carry on the look of his Libreria Sansoviniana (Sansovinian Library), but he
died before construction on the Nuove
had begun. Vincenzo Scamozzi (circa
1552–1616), a pupil of Andrea Palladio
(1508–80), completed the design and
construction. Still later, the Procuratie
Nuove was modified by architect Baldassare Longhena (1598–1682), one of
Venice's Baroque masters.

When Napoléon (1769–1821) entered
Venice with his troops in 1797, he
expressed his admiration for the piazza
and promptly gave orders to alter it. His
architects demolished a church with a
Sansovino facade in order to build the
Ala Napoleonica (Napoleonic Wing), or
Fabbrica Nuova (New Building), which

linked the two 16th-century procuratie
and effectively enclosed the piazza.

Piazzetta San Marco is the "little square"
leading from Piazza San Marco to the
waters of Bacino San Marco (St. Mark's
Basin); its *molo* (landing) once served
as the grand entrance to the Republic.
Two imposing columns tower above the
waterfront. One is topped by the winged
lion, a traditional emblem of St. Mark that
became the symbol of Venice itself; the
other supports St. Theodore, the city's
first patron, along with his dragon. (A
third column fell off its barge and ended
up in the bacino before it could be placed
alongside the others.) Although the
columns are a glorious sight today, the
Republic traditionally executed convicts
here—and some superstitious Venetians still avoid walking between them.
✉ *San Marco* Ⓜ *Vaporetto: San Zaccaria,
Vallaresso.*

★ **Ponte di Rialto** (*Rialto Bridge*)
BRIDGE | **FAMILY** | The competition to
design a stone bridge across the Grand
Canal attracted the best architects of the
late 16th century, including Michelange-
lo, Palladio, and Sansovino, but the job
went to the less famous (if appropriately
named) Antonio da Ponte (1512–95).
His pragmatic design, completed in
1591, featured shop space and was high
enough for galleys to pass beneath.
Putting practicality and economy over
aesthetic considerations—unlike the
classical plans proposed by his more
famous contemporaries—da Ponte's
bridge essentially followed the design
of its wooden predecessor. But it kept
decoration and cost to a minimum at a
time when the Republic's coffers were
low, due to continual wars against the
Turks and competition brought about by
the Spanish and Portuguese opening of
oceanic trade routes. Along the railing
you'll enjoy one of the city's most famous
views: the Grand Canal vibrant with boat
traffic. ✉ *San Marco* Ⓜ *Vaporetto: Rialto.*

Continued on page 88

THE BASILICA DI SAN MARCO

Venice's Cultural Mosaic

Standing at the heart of Venice, the spectacular Basilica di San Marco has been, for about a millennium, the city's religious center. Like other great churches—and even more so—it's also an expression of worldly accomplishments and aspirations. As you take in the shimmering mosaics and elaborate ornamentation, you begin to grasp the pivotal role Venice has played for centuries in European culture.

ORIGINS. The basilica began as a political statement. The original church, consecrated in 832, was built to house the body of St. Mark. According to legend, the saint's body had been stolen from Alexandria by two Venetians in 828. The whole enterprise was intended to establish Venice's prominence over neighboring Aquileia, a city with a glorious Roman past that claimed to have been founded by St. Mark.

Above, 17th century stamp of the winged lion, symbol of Venice

Below, façade of Basilica di San Marco

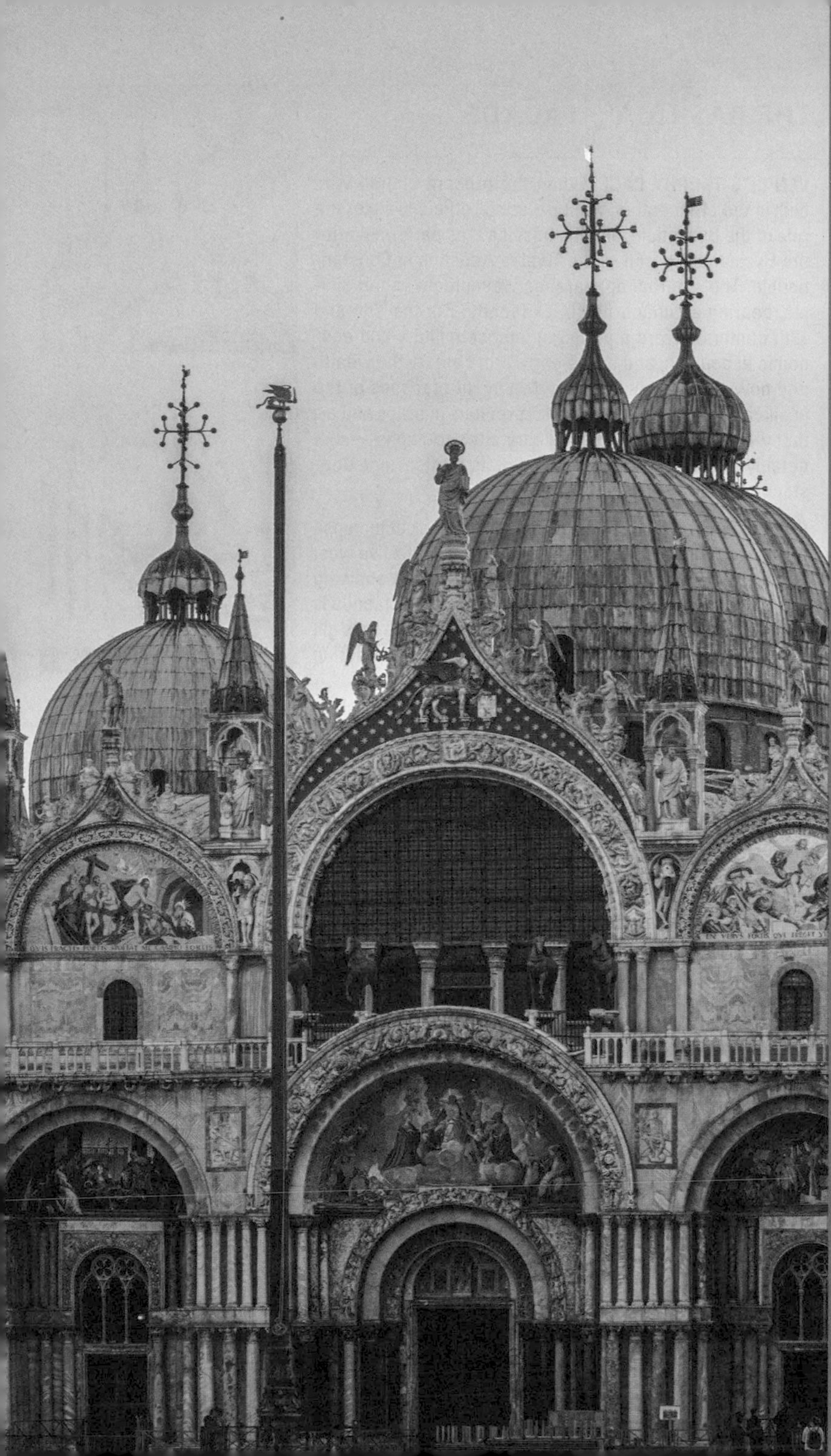

THE BASILICA'S FACADES

St. Mark and lion, main portal

VENICE'S TROPHY CASE. When the present church was built in the 11th century, Venice was still officially under the rule of the Byzantium, and the basilica was patterned after the Byzantine Church of the Twelve Apostles in Constantinople. The external appearance was initially rather simple, bearing an unadorned brick facade. But the 12th and 13th centuries were a period of intense military and economic expansion, and by the early 13th century the wealth and power of Venice were on display: the facades of the basilica were being adorned with precious marbles and art that were trophies from the military city's triumphs—most notably the conquest and sacking ot its former ruler, Constantinople, in 1204.

PORTAL OF SANT ALIPIO. Be sure to take a look at the apse of the portal of Sant Alipio, the farthest north of the five west facade portals. It bears a 13th-century mosaic showing how the church looked at that time. Note how the facade is already decorated with marble columns and the famous gilt bronze ancient Roman horses, taken by the Venetians during the sack of Constantinople.

Main portal entrance

The portal of Sant Alipio is typical of many parts of the basilica in that it contains elements that far predate the construction of the church. The base of the pointed arch beneath the mosaic, for example, dates from the 5th century, and the Byzantine capitals of the precious marble columns, as well as the window screens, are mostly from the 7th century. The use of these elements, most of them pillaged from raids and conquests, testifies to Venetian daring and power, and they create the illusion of an ancient heritage that Venice itself lacked and looked upon with envy.

Detail of bas-relief

Portal of Sant Alipio with 13th-century mosaic of the basilica

Bronze horses, facade

The details of lunette

THE MAIN PORTAL. By the time these ancient trophies were put into place, Venice had both the wealth and the talent to create its own, new decoration. On the inner arches of the main portal, look for the beautiful and fascinating Romanesque and early Gothic allegorical, biblical, and zodiac bas-reliefs.

THE TETRARCHS. The Christian relevance of some of the trophies on the basilica is scant. For a fine example of pride over piety, take a look at the fourth-century group of four soldiers in red porphyry on the corner of the south facade. It's certain that this was taken from Constantinople, because a missing fragment of one of the figures' feet can still be found attached to a building in Istanbul. The current interpretation is that they are the Tetrarchs, colleagues of the Emperor Diocletian, having little if any religious significance.

The incorporation of art from many different cultures into Venice's most important building is a sign of imperial triumph, but it also indicates an embrace of other cultures that's a fundamental part of Venetian character. (Think of Marco Polo, who was on his way to China only a few years after the first phase of decoration of the facade of the basilica began.) Venice remains, even today, arguably the most tolerant and cosmopolitan city in Italy.

Statues of tetrarchs

TREASURES INSIDE THE BASILICA

THE MOSAICS. The glory of the basilica is its brilliant, floor-to-ceiling mosaics, especially those dating from the medieval period.

The mosaics of the atrium, or porch, represent the Old Testament, while those of the interior show the stories of the Gospel and saints, ending with the image of Christ in Glory (a Renaissance copy) in the apse. Many of the mosaics of the New Testament scenes are actually somewhat earlier (mid-12th century), or contemporaneous with the 13th-century mosaics of the atrium. You wouldn't know it from the style: the figures of the atrium still bear the late classical character of the early Christian manuscript, brought to Venice after the sack of Constantinople, that inspired them. In the mosaics of the church proper, notice the flowing lines, elongated figures, and stern expressions, all characteristics of high Byzantine art. Look especially for the beautiful 12th-century mosaics in the dome of the Pentecost, the first dome in the nave of the basilica as you enter the main part of the church, and for the 12th-century mosaics in the dome of the Ascension, considered the masterpiece of the Venetian school.

The choir

Above, detail of the nave
Below, detail of mosaic

The centerpiece of the basilica is, naturally, ❶ **THE SANTUARIO (SANCTUARY)**, the main altar built over the tomb of St. Mark. Its green marble canopy, lifted high on carved alabaster columns, is another trophy dating from the fourth century. Perhaps even more impressive is the ❷ **PALA D'ORO**, a dazzling gilt silver screen encrusted with 1,927 precious gems and 255 enameled panels. Originally commissioned (976–978) in Constantinople, it was enlarged and embellished over four centuries by master craftsmen and wealthy merchants.

❸ **THE TESORO (TREASURY)**, part of the Museo di San Marco and entered from the right transept, contains treasures carried home from conquests abroad. Climb the stairway to the Galleria and the Museo di San Marco for the best overview of the basilica's interior. From here you can step out for a sweeping panorama of Piazza San Marco and across the lagoon to San Giorgio. The highlight is a close-up view of the original gilt bronze horses that were once on the outer gallery.

Right, detail of ceiling mosaics of the atrium

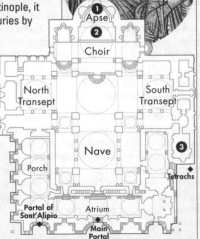

Apse

Choir

North Transept

South Transept

Nave

Porch

Tetrachs

Portal of Sant'Alipio

Atrium

Main Portal

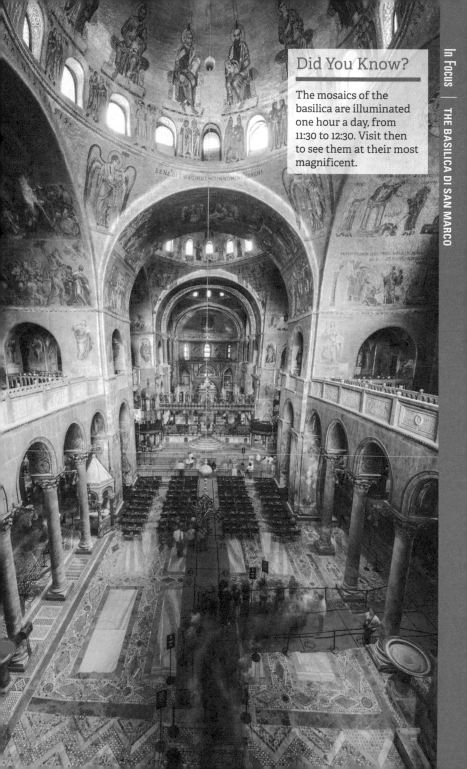

Did You Know?

The mosaics of the basilica are illuminated one hour a day, from 11:30 to 12:30. Visit then to see them at their most magnificent.

PLANNING YOUR VISIT

Be aware that guards at the basilica door turn away anyone with bare shoulders, midriff, or knees: no shorts, short skirts, or tank tops are allowed. Free guided tours in English were suspended during the COVID pandemic; call to get more information about whether they've started again.

■ **TIP→** To skip the line at the basilica entrance, reserve your arrival—at no extra cost—on the basilica Web site (choose "Booking" on the homepage). If you have luggage, you'll need to store it at the nearby bag facility at Piazza San Marco 315 (from €1.99 per locker).

✉ Piazza San Marco

☎ 041/2708318 (9:30 am -3:30 pm weekdays)

🌐 www.basilicasan-marco.it

💶 Basilica €3, Sanctuary and Pala d'Oro €5, Museum €7, Bell Tower €10

🕐 Mon.-Sat. 9:30 am-5:15 pm, Sun. 2 pm-5:15 pm (museum and bell tower open from 9:30 am); last admission 4:45 pm

Above, Piazza San Marco
Left, Crowds gather around the basilica

Did You Know?

The nobility in Venice used to be extremely competitive about their gondolas, decorating them in flamboyant colors and over-the-top ornaments. A law in the 16th century put an end to that. Today, all gondolas must be painted boring black, though they are allowed three flourishes: a curly tail, a pair of seahorses, and a multi-pronged prow.

In Venice you can try a Bellini where it was invented: Harry's Bar.

Torre dell'Orologio (*Clock Tower*)

CLOCK | FAMILY | This enameled clock, completed in 1499, was most likely designed by Venetian Renaissance architect Mauro Codussi. Twin giant figures with tarnished bronze bodies strike the hour each day, while three wise men with an angel walk out and bow to the Virgin Mary on Epiphany (January 6) and during Ascension Week (40 days after Easter). An inscription on the tower reads "*Horas non numero nisi serenas*" ("I only count happy hours"). Originally, the clock tower had a much lighter, more graceful appearance, and was freestanding. The four lateral bays were added in the early 16th century, while the upper stories and balustrades were completed in 1755. The clock itself was neglected until the 19th century, but after years of painstaking labor, it was reassembled and is fully operational. Guided tours, which start at the Museo Correr's ticket office, are held in English on Thursday at 3 pm; book in advance online or by phone. ⊠ *Piazza San Marco, north side of the Piazza, San Marco* ☎ *041/42730892 tickets (outside Italy), 84/8082000 tickets (within Italy)* ⊕ *torreorologio.visitmuve.it* ✆ *€12 for one-hour tour, includes admission to Museo Correr, Museo Archeologico, and Biblioteca Nazionale Marciana. €7 with Museums of San Marco Pass or Museum Pass* Ⓜ *Vaporetto: San Zaccaria, Vallaresso.*

 Restaurants

Enoteca al Volto

$$ | VENETIAN | A short walk from the Ponte di Rialto, this bar has been around since 1936, and the satisfying cicheti and primi have a lot to do with its staying power. Grab a table out front, or take refuge in one of the two small, dark rooms with a ceiling plastered with wine labels that provide a classic backdrop for simple fare, including a delicious risotto that is served daily from noon, plus a solid wine list of both Italian and foreign vintages. **Known for:** fantastic main courses, including risotto and pasta with seafood; great local and international wine selection; tasty and inexpensive cicheti. $ *Average* main: €17 ✉ Calle Cavalli, San Marco 4081, San Marco ☎ 041/5228945 ⊕ enotecaalvolto.com Ⓜ Vaporetto: Rialto.

★ Harry's Bar

$$$$ | VENETIAN | For those who can afford it, lunch or dinner at Harry's Bar is as much a part of a visit to Venice as a walk across Piazza San Marco or a vaporetto ride down the Grand Canal. Inside, the suave, subdued beige-on-white decor is unchanged from the 1930s, and the classic Venetian fare is carefully and excellently prepared. **Known for:** signature crepes flambées and famous Cipriani chocolate cake; being the birthplace of the Bellini cocktail; see-and-be-seen atmosphere. Ⓢ Average main: €58 ✉ Calle Vallaresso, San Marco 1323, San Marco ☎ 041/5285777 ⊕ www.cipriani.com Ⓜ Vaporetto: Vallaresso.

★ Ristorante Quadri

$$$$ | VENETIAN | Although the lavish interior has been updated by designer Philippe Starck, this restaurant above the famed café of the same name is still steeped in Venetian ambience and history (it was where Turkish coffee was introduced to the city in the 1700s). When the Alajmo family (of the celebrated Le Calandre near Padua) took over, they put their accomplished sous-chef from Padua in charge of the kitchen, resulting in the addition of dishes—best sampled with a tasting menu—that are complex and sophisticated, with a wonderful wine list to match. **Known for:** revitalized designer decor; sophisticated and modern Italian cuisine; seasonal tasting menus. Ⓢ Average main: €60 ✉ Piazza San Marco 121, San Marco ☎ 049/630303 ⊕ alajmo.it ◷ Closed Mon. and Tues., and late Jan.– mid-Feb. No lunch Wed.–Fri. Ⓜ Vaporetto: Giardinetti, Vallaresso.

☕ Coffee and Quick Bites

Bar all'Angolo

$ | CAFÉ | This corner of Campo Santo Stefano is a pleasant place to sit and watch the Venetian world go by. The café staff are in constant motion, so you'll receive your coffee, spritz, *panino* (a sandwich warmed on a griddle), or *tramezzino* (sandwich on untoasted white bread, usually with a mayonnaise-based filling) in short order; consume it at your leisure at one of the outdoor tables, at the bar, or at the tables in the back. **Known for:** good people-watching; simple yet satisfying fare, like tramezzini and panini; tasty homemade desserts, including tiramisu and cakes. Ⓢ Average main: €10 ✉ Campo Santo Stefano, San Marco 3464, just in front of Santo Stefano church, San Marco ☎ 041/5220710 ◷ Closed Sun. and Jan. Ⓜ Vaporetto: Sant'Angelo.

★ Caffè Florian

$$ | CAFÉ | Florian is not only Italy's first café (1720), but also one of its most beautiful, with glittering, neo-Baroque decor and 19th-century wall panels depicting Venetian heroes. The coffee, drinks, and snacks are good, but most people—including Venetians from time to time—come for the atmosphere and history: this was the only café to serve women during the 18th century (hence Casanova's patronage); it was frequented by artistic notables like Wagner, Goethe, Goldoni, Lord Byron, Marcel Proust, and Charles Dickens; and it was the birthplace of the international art exhibition that became the Venice Biennale. **Known for:** hot chocolate, coffee, and quick nibbles; prime location on St. Mark's Square; beautiful, historic interior. Ⓢ Average main: €16 ✉ Piazza San Marco 57, San Marco ☎ 041/5205641 ⊕ www.caffeflorian.com ◷ Closed early Jan. Ⓜ Vaporetto: Giardinetti, Vallaresso.

Italy's first café, Caffè Florian, dates back to 1720. It's still a great place to enjoy an aperitivo on Piazza San Marco.

★ Gran Caffè Quadri

$$ | CAFÉ | Come for breakfast, a pre-dinner aperitivo, or anything in between at this always lively historic coffeehouse—opened in 1775 and taken over by the famous culinary Alajmo family in 2011—in the center of the action on Piazza San Marco. Choose from a wide selection of pastries at breakfast (though the cappuccino and brioche combo is always a classic), pizzas at lunch, and tramezzini all day long, including one with lobster. **Known for:** prime people-watching; extensive (though pricey) aperitivo; celebrity owners. $ *Average main: €17* ✉ *Piazza San Marco 121, San Marco* ☎ *049/630303* ⊕ *alajmo.it* Ⓜ *Vaporetto: Giardinetti, Vallaresso.*

Le Café

$ | CAFÉ | On Campo Santo Stefano across from Paolin, Le Café has see-and-be-seen tables outside year-round. It also has bar service, light lunches, and a variety of hot chocolate drinks and desserts. **Known for:** tasty hot chocolate; appealing breakfast options; sandwiches and pizza.

$ *Average main: €13* ✉ *Campo Santo Stefano, San Marco 2797, San Marco* ☎ *041/5230002* ⊕ *www.lecafevenezia.com* Ⓜ *Vaporetto: San Samuele, Sant'Angelo.*

PASTICCERIE (PASTRY SHOPS)

Rosa Salva

$ | BAKERY | FAMILY | There are several branches to this venerable *pasticceria* in town; the headquarters is a small shop on Calle Fiubera in San Marco. Rosa Salva features a wide selection of pastry and savory snacks as well as bar service at the counter. **Known for:** Venetian Carnival fritters (*frittelle*); Venetian cookies; traditional cakes. $ *Average main: €3* ✉ *Calle Fiubera, San Marco 950, San Marco* ☎ *041/5210544* ⊕ *www.rosasalva.it* ⊗ *Closed Sun.* Ⓜ *Vaporetto: Rialto.*

★ Pasticceria Marchini Time

$ | BAKERY | FAMILY | This popular breakfast spot close to the Rialto attracts a mix of locals and tourists. Enjoy your pastry and coffee inside the old-time pastry shop or, if you're lucky, snag a seat outside.

Known for: Tasty espresso; traditional Venetian pastries; friendly, helpful staff. ⑤ *Average main: €5* ✉ *Campo San Luca, San Marco 4589, San Marco* ☎ *041/2413087* Ⓜ *Vaporetto: Rialto.*

GELATERIE (ICE CREAM SHOPS)

Gelateria Paolin

$ | **ICE CREAM** | The morning sun draws crowds of all ages and nationalities to take a seat on busy Campo Santo Stefano and enjoy a little cup at this favorite café-gelateria. A scoop of *limone* (lemon) gelato is particularly refreshing on a hot summer day. **Known for:** good aperitivo; *gianduia* (hazelnut and chocolate) gelato; lively terrace. ⑤ *Average main: €5* ✉ *Campo Santo Stefano 2962, San Marco* ☎ *041/5225576* Ⓜ *Vaporetto: San Samuele, Sant'Angelo.*

Gelatoteca Suso

$ | **ICE CREAM** | **FAMILY** | Try this fun shop for gelato that's out of the ordinary: think walnut cream with carmelized fig, or vanilla with rum-raisins and Malaga wine. Sorbets and milkshakes are also on offer. **Known for:** unusual flavors; vegan ice cream options; convenient location on way to Rialto Bridge. ⑤ *Average main: €5* ✉ *Sotoportego de la Bissa, San Marco 5453, San Marco* ☎ *0348/5646545* ⊕ *tastesu.so* Ⓜ *Vaporetto: Rialto.*

★ Venchi

$ | **ICE CREAM** | **FAMILY** | This 19th-century chocolate shop serves up delicious (what else?) chocolate ice creams, along with refreshing sorbets. For the ultimate experience, add seasonal sprinkles, such as Piedmont hazelnuts, to your sweet treat. **Known for:** cones topped with chocolate; rich dark-chocolate gelato; green pistachio from Sicily. ⑤ *Average main: €6* ✉ *Calle dei Fabbri, San Marco 989, San Marco* ☎ *041/2412314* ⊕ *eu.venchi.com* Ⓜ *Vaporetto: Rialto, San Marco.*

 # Hotels

Al Teatro

$$$ | **B&B/INN** | **FAMILY** | The renovated home of owner Eleonora behind the Fenice Opera House offers three spacious, comfortable, and conscientiously appointed rooms; each has its own private bath and overlooks a gondola-filled canal. **Pros:** good for families; airy rooms; convenient San Marco location. **Cons:** canal noise, especially from singing gondoliers; early checkout time; the intimacy of a family B&B is not for everyone. ⑤ *Rooms from: €210* ✉ *Fondamenta della Fenice, San Marco 2554, San Marco* ☎ *0333/9182494* ⊕ *www.bedandbreakfastalteatro.com* ⥱ *3 rooms* ❍❙ *Free Breakfast* Ⓜ *Vaporetto: Giglio.*

★ Baglioni Hotel Luna

$$$$ | **HOTEL** | **FAMILY** | Just a short stroll from Piazza San Marco—though on a quiet side street that seems a world away—this charming hotel will please those seeking traditional Venetian decor in an ultra-convenient location. **Pros:** extremely helpful concierge; beautifully appointed rooms and public spaces; wonderful breakfast selection. **Cons:** no spa; some rooms feel a bit cramped; not all rooms have canal views. ⑤ *Rooms from: €502* ✉ *San Marco 1243, San Marco* ☎ *041/5289840* ⊕ *www.baglionihotels.com* ⥱ *91 rooms* ❍❙ *Free Breakfast* Ⓜ *Vaporetto: San Marco, Vallaresso.*

Bauer Palazzo

$$$$ | **HOTEL** | This palazzo with an ornate 1930s neo-Gothic facade facing the Grand Canal has large (by Venetian standards), lavishly decorated guest rooms with high ceilings, tufted walls of Bevilacqua and Rubelli fabrics, Murano glass, marble bathrooms, damask drapes, and reproduction antique furniture. **Pros:** pampering service; Venice's highest rooftop terrace; high-end luxury. **Cons:** no spa on-site; furnishings are, as is the facade, an imitation; decor could be a bit dark and old-fashioned for some. ⑤ *Rooms*

from: €301 ✉ *Campo San Moisè, San Marco 1459, San Marco* ☎ *041/5207022* ⊕ *www.bauervenezia.com* 🛏 *191 rooms* ⦿ *No Meals* Ⓜ *Vaporetto: Vallaresso.*

★ The Gritti Palace

$$$$ | HOTEL | With handblown chandeliers, sumptuous textiles, and sweeping canal views, this grande dame (whose history dates from 1525, when it was built as the residence of the prominent Gritti family) represents aristocratic Venetian living at its best. **Pros:** classic Venetian experience; truly historical property; Grand Canal location. **Cons:** food served at the hotel gets mixed reviews; major splurge; few spa amenities. ⑤ *Rooms from:* €1470 ✉ *Campo Santa Maria del Giglio 2467, San Marco* ☎ *041/794611* ⊕ *www.thegrittipalace.com* 🛏 *82 rooms* ⦿ *No Meals* Ⓜ *Vaporetto: Giglio.*

Hotel Flora

$$ | HOTEL | The elegant and refined facade announces a charming, and reasonably priced, place to stay; the hospitable staff, the tastefully decorated rooms, and the lovely garden, where guests can breakfast or drink, do not disappoint. **Pros:** excellent breakfast; peaceful hidden garden; central location. **Cons:** no water views; some rooms can be on the small side; old-fashioned lobby doesn't invite hanging out. ⑤ *Rooms from:* €160 ✉ *Calle Bergamaschi, San Marco 2283/A, just off Calle Larga XXII Marzo, San Marco* ☎ *041/5205844* ⊕ *www.hotelflora.it* 🛏 *40 rooms* ⦿ *Free Breakfast* Ⓜ *Vaporetto: Vallaresso.*

Locanda Casa Petrarca

$ | B&B/INN | Neatly decorated and light-filled rooms between St. Marks Square and the Rialto Bridge offer guests something rare in Venice—a central yet quiet base from which to explore the city. **Pros:** extensive breakfast; gentle prices; quiet for a central location. **Cons:** difficult to find; small rooms; basic amenities. ⑤ *Rooms from:* €109 ✉ *Calle de le Schiavine, San Marco 4386, San Marco* ☎ *041/5200430* ⊕ *www.casapetrarca.*

com 🛏 *7 rooms* ⦿ *Free Breakfast* Ⓜ *Vaporetto: Rialto.*

Locanda Fiorita

$ | B&B/INN | Tucked behind Campo San Stefano in a charming little courtyard, this oasis offers small but peaceful rooms decorated in 18th-century Venetian style. **Pros:** air-conditioning in all rooms; central location; romantic setting. **Cons:** hallways can be noisy; basic bathrooms; rooms and bathrooms are indeed small. ⑤ *Rooms from:* €90 ✉ *Campiello Novo, San Marco 3457, San Marco* ☎ *041/5234754* ⊕ *www.locandafiorita.com* 🛏 *10 rooms* ⦿ *Free Breakfast* Ⓜ *Vaporetto: Sant'Angelo.*

★ Novecento

$$ | HOTEL | A stylish yet intimate retreat tucked away on a quiet *calle* (street) midway between Piazza San Marco and the Accademia Bridge offers exquisite rooms tastefully decorated with original furnishings and tapestries from the Mediterranean and Far East. **Pros:** complimentary afternoon tea; unique design sensibility; intimate, romantic atmosphere. **Cons:** no elevator; most rooms only have showers, not tubs; some rooms can be noisy. ⑤ *Rooms from:* €184 ✉ *Calle del Dose, San Marco 2683/84, off Campo San Maurizio, San Marco* ☎ *041/2413765* ⊕ *www.novecento.biz* 🛏 *9 rooms* ⦿ *Free Breakfast* Ⓜ *Vaporetto: Santa Maria del Giglio.*

★ Palazzo Paruta

$$$ | HOTEL | Steeped in lavish Venetian ambience, junior suites are palatial, superior rooms comfortably sized, bright, and well appointed, and ornate frescoes, pastel bas-reliefs, and splendid coffered and carved beamed ceilings abound. **Pros:** good location with restaurants and bars nearby; few small lodgings compare in terms of comfort and opulence; some rooms have canal views. **Cons:** noise from other rooms can be an issue; breakfast could be better; standard rooms are quite small. ⑤ *Rooms from:* €255 ✉ *Campo Sant'Angelo, San Marco 3824, San Marco* ☎ *041/2410835* ⊕ *palazzoparuta.com*

Did You Know?

Housed in a 17th-century palace, the Palazzo Paruta hotel is not only opulent and atmospheric, it's also centrally located in San Marco and opens up to an idyllic canal.

The view of the Grand Canal from the St. Regis Venice is legendary.

🛥 *19 rooms* ⊙❙ *Free Breakfast* Ⓜ *Vaporetto: Sant'Angelo.*

Sina Palazzo Sant'Angelo

$$$ | **HOTEL** | This elegant palazzo is large enough to deliver expected facilities and services but small enough to pamper its guests; rooms have red-and-gold tapestry-adorned walls and carpeting and Carrara and Alpine marble in the bath, and those facing the Grand Canal have balconies. **Pros:** convenient to vaporetto stop; distinguished yet comfortable; classic Venetian style. **Cons:** bathrooms can be on the small side; no restaurant; modest breakfast. Ⓢ *Rooms from: €257* ✉ *Campo Sant'Angelo, San Marco 3878/b, San Marco* ☎ *041/2411452* ⊕ *www.sinahotels.com* 🛥 *26 rooms* ⊙❙ *Free Breakfast* Ⓜ *Vaporetto: Sant'Angelo.*

★ The St. Regis Venice

$$$$ | **HOTEL** | Whimsical design details evoking the Venetian landscape abound in this elegant, contemporary hotel constructed from five historic palazzi with phenomenal views onto the Grand Canal. **Pros:** wonderful central location; St. Regis butler service for all guests; terraces with unbeatable views. **Cons:** few spa amenities (no pool or saunas); standard rooms on the small side; sleek modern style not for fans of Venetian opulence. Ⓢ *Rooms from: €931* ✉ *San Marco 2159, San Marco* ☎ *041/2400001* ⊕ *www.marriott.com* 🛥 *169 rooms* ⊙❙ *Free Breakfast* Ⓜ *Vaporetto: Vallaresso.*

Nightlife

Bacarando in Corte dell'Orso

WINE BARS | It is easy to see why this place is popular with the locals, offering fairly priced cocktails, a reasonable assortment of cicheti, and a good selection of Italian wine, but the warm ambience, friendly staff, and occasional live jazz are the main draws. The kitchen stays open until late. ✉ *Corte Dell'Orso, San Marco 5495, San Marco* ⊕ *Tucked away in alley across from Church of San Giovanni Grisostomo* ☎ *041/5238280* ⊕ *www.bacarando.com* Ⓜ *Vaporetto: Rialto.*

Bacaro Jazz

BARS | This Venetian-style dive bar has strong cocktails, a jazz soundtrack, and hundreds of bras hanging from the ceiling. The lively daily happy hour is a great time to visit. ✉ *San Marco 5546, San Marco* ☎ *041/5285249* ⊕ *bacarojazz. it* Ⓜ *Vaporetto: Rialto.*

★ Bar Longhi

BARS | The Gritti Palace is home to one of the most exclusive watering holes in town (though thankfully open to the public), lined with 18th-century paintings and Murano chandeliers. You can also enjoy your cocktail on the patio with prime views onto the Grand Canal. ✉ *The Gritti Palace, Campo Santa Maria del Giglio, San Marco 2467, San Marco* ☎ *041/794611* ⊕ *www.thegrittipalace. com* Ⓜ *Vaporetto: Giglio.*

★ Caffè Baglioni

BARS | Just outside Piazza San Marco (near the Museo Correr), Hotel Luna Baglioni's pleasant bar—complete with 16th-century art pieces and an 18th-century fireplace—is perfect for an intimate chat in the cold winter months. ✉ *Calle Larga de l'Ascension, San Marco 1243, San Marco* ☎ *041/5289840* ⊕ *www.baglionihotels.com* Ⓜ *Vaporetto: Vallaresso.*

Performing Arts

Teatro La Fenice

OPERA | One of Italy's oldest opera houses has witnessed many memorable operatic premieres, including, in 1853, the dismal first-night flop of Verdi's *La Traviata*. It has also witnessed its share of disasters: the most recent being a horrific fire that burned most of the interior; it was deliberately set in January 1996, and was followed by endless delays in a complicated reconstruction. In keeping with its name (which translates as "The Phoenix," coined when it was built over the ashes of its predecessor in 1792), La Fenice rose again. It was restored and once again hosts seasons of symphony, opera, and dance.

The acoustics of the reconstructed theatre have received mainly positive reviews, but attitudes expressed toward the decoration (replicated based on the style of the early-19th century, but using cheaper, less exacting techniques) have been mixed. According to music critics, in recent years less well-known and accomplished artists have been booked, the production quality has deteriorated somewhat, and some operas (because of budget cuts) are presented in *concertante* (just sung, without staging). Visits to the theater are available daily from 9:30–6; download the La Fenice app, available in several languages, for a free 35-minute self-guided audio tour for adults and a 30-minute tour for children. ✉ *Campo San Fantin, San Marco 1965, San Marco* ☎ *041/786654, 041/2722699 tickets* ⊕ *www.teatrolafenice.it* Ⓜ *Vaporetto: Sant'Angelo, Giglio.*

🛍 Shopping

ART AND ANTIQUES DEALERS

Kleine Galerie

ANTIQUES & COLLECTIBLES | This is a good address for antique books and prints, majolica pottery, and other ceramics. ✉ *Calle delle Botteghe, San Marco 2972, San Marco* ☎ *338/7389194* Ⓜ *Vaporetto: Sant'Angelo or San Samuele.*

Linea d'Acqua

ANTIQUES & COLLECTIBLES | Fine antique print and book aficionados will fall in love with this gem of a store run by the extremely knowledgeable Luca Zentilini. His focus is on Venetian culture and limited editions, with special interest in illustrated books from the 18th century. A large selection of Venetian maps are on offer, as well as etchings by masters including Piranesi, Visentini, Tiepolo, and Carlevarijs. ✉ *Calle della Mandola, San Marco 3717/D, San Marco* ☎ *041/5224030* ⊕ *lineadacqua.it* Ⓜ *Vaporetto: Sant'Angelo.*

ART GALLERIES

★ Bugno Art Gallery

ART GALLERIES | This retailer of modern and contemporary art, along with photography, puts together windows representative of the whole gallery. ✉ Campo San Fantin, San Marco 1996/D, San Marco ☎ 041/5231305 ⊕ www.bugnoartgallery. com Ⓜ Vaporetto: Sant'Angelo, San Giglio.

★ Caterina Tognon Arte Contemporanea

ART GALLERIES | Contemporary visual artists who employ glass as their medium are featured by Caterina in her marvelous art gallery. ✉ Ca' Nova di Palazzo Treves in Corte Barozzi, San Marco 2158, San Marco ☎ 041/5201566 ⊕ www.caterinatognon.com Ⓜ Vaporetto: Vallaresso.

Contini Art Gallery

ART GALLERIES | Contini shows only 20th-century artists and is Italy's only dealer for Botero, Zoran Music, and the marble and bronze sculptures by Mitoraj. ✉ Calle Larga XXII Marzo, San Marco 2288, San Marco ☎ 041/5230357 ⊕ www.continiarte.com Ⓜ Vaporetto: Giglio, Vallaresso.

Holly Snapp Gallery

ART GALLERIES | The focus is on the works by the eclectic English-born artist Geoffrey Humphries, including paintings, drawings, and etchings ranging from landscapes to portraits; he also produces watercolors of Venetian vistas. ✉ Calle delle Botteghe, San Marco 3133, San Marco ☎ 041/2960824 ⊕ www.hollysnappgallery.com Ⓜ Vaporetto: San Samuele, Sant'Angelo.

Livio De Marchi Galleria

ART GALLERIES | Signor De Marchi's swift hands turn wood into outstanding full-scale sculptures that perfectly reproduce everyday objects such as hats, laundry hung out to dry, telephones, jackets, books, fruit, lace—even underwear. ✉ Campo San Maurizio, San Marco 2742/A, San Marco ☎ 041/5285694 ⊕ www.liviodemarchi.com Ⓜ Vaporetto: Giglio.

Ravagnan Gallery

ART GALLERIES | The exclusive dealer since 1967 of some of the most famous living artists on the Italian scene shows work by Venetian surrealist Ludovico De Luigi, metaphysical painter Andrea Vizzini, and glass sculptor Primo Formenti. ✉ Procuratie Nuove, Piazza San Marco 50/A, San Marco ☎ 041/5203021 ⊕ www.ravagnangallery.com Ⓜ Vaporetto: San Marco.

BOOKSTORES

Libreria Studium

BOOKS | Studium is a good stop for books in English, especially guidebooks and books on Venetian culture and food. It's also particularly strong on English-language fiction with Italian, mostly Venetian, settings and themes; in addition, it has a small but worthy collection of recent hardcover fiction. ✉ Calle della Canonica, San Marco 337, San Marco ☎ 041/5222382 ⊕ www.libreriastudium. eu Ⓜ Vaporetto: San Zaccaria.

CLOTHING

★ Al Duca d'Aosta

MIXED CLOTHING | The most stylish of Venetians and visitors alike come here for women's and men's designer labels for every taste. Brands include Burberry, Givenchy, Jil Sander, Lanvin, Moncler, and many others; be prepared to be wowed. ✉ San Marco 284, San Marco ☎ 041/5220733 ⊕ www.alducadaosta. com Ⓜ Vaporetto: San Marco, Zaccaria.

★ Godi Fiorenza

WOMEN'S CLOTHING | At Godi Fiorenza, Patrizia Fiorenza's designs in silk chiffon appear more sculpted than sewn—they're highly tailored pieces that both conceal and expose. Her sister Samanta is a jewelry designer and silversmith whose unique pieces compliment any outfit. ✉ Rio Terà San Paternian, San Marco 4261, San Marco ☎ 041/2410866 ⊕ www.fiorenzadesign.com Ⓜ Vaporetto: Rialto.

COSTUMES AND ACCESSORIES
Atelier Antonia Sautter

OTHER SPECIALTY STORE | Antonia Sautter's opulent, fanciful display of 18th-century Venetian gowns often causes passersby to pause and ponder. Hers is the atelier of the prestigious Ballo del Doge Carnival ball, along with many other extraordinarily fantastically coutured Venetian events. You'll also find medieval-style garments, masks, and accessories behind the curtains inside. ⊠ *Frezzeria, San Marco 1286, San Marco* ☎ *041/5224426* ⊕ *www.antoniasautter.it* Ⓜ *Vaporetto: San Marco.*

★ Giuliana Longo

HATS & GLOVES | A hat shop that's been around since 1901 offers an assortment of Venetian and gondolier straw hats, Panama hats from Ecuador, caps and berets, and some select scarves of silk and fine wool; there's even a special corner dedicated to accessories for antique cars. ⊠ *Calle del Lovo, San Marco 4813, San Marco* ☎ *041/5226454* ⊕ *www.giulianalongo.com* Ⓜ *Vaporetto: San Marco.*

DEPARTMENT STORES
T Fondaco dei Tedeschi

DEPARTMENT STORE | This 15th-century Renaissance commercial center served as Venice's main post office for many years, but was remodeled and returned to its historical roots as a luxury department store. Here you can find a large assortment of high-end jewelry, clothing, and other luxury items, plus fabulous views from the rooftop terrace; book online for a free 15-minute visit. ⊠ *Calle Fondaco dei Tedeschi, near San Marco end of Ponte di Rialto, San Marco* ☎ *041/3142000* ⊕ *www.dfs.com* Ⓜ *Vaporetto: Rialto.*

GIFTS
Atmosfera Veneziana

JEWELRY & WATCHES | One stop might fit the bill when you've got last-minute gifts to buy: American Theresa works only with Murano artisans and offers an abundant, tasteful selection of reasonably priced beads, vases, goblets, and jewelry, even mirrors and chandeliers. ⊠ *Calle dei Fuseri, San Marco 4340, San Marco* ☎ *041/2413256* ⊕ *www.atmosferaveneziana.com* Ⓜ *Vaporetto: Rialto, Vallaresso.*

★ Fonderia Artistica Valese

CRAFTS | This studio has been casting brass, bronze, copper, and pewter into artistic handles, menorahs, Carnevale masks, and real gondola decorations (which make great paperweights, bookends, or shelf pieces) since 1913. The coups de grâce are the brass chandeliers, exactly like those that hang in the Oval Office in the White House. Call to arrange a visit to the studio in Cannaregio when they pour. ⊠ *Calle Fiubera, San Marco 793, San Marco* ☎ *041/5227282* ⊕ *www.valese.it* Ⓜ *Vaporetto: San Marco.*

Materialmente

OTHER SPECIALTY STORE | Artists Maddalena Venier and Alessandro Salvadori of Materialmente envision "balancing the precious with the everyday." They succeed with a fascinating collection of fanciful, light-as-air sculpture, lamps, jewelry, and housewares. ⊠ *Ramo Marzaria San Salvador, San Marco 4850, San Marco* ☎ *041/5286881* ⊕ *www.materialmentevenezia.com* Ⓜ *Vaporetto: Rialto.*

GLASS
L'Isola

GLASSWARE | This lovely store features chic, contemporary glassware designed in the style of Murano master Carlo Moretti. ⊠ *Calle de la Botteghe, San Marco 2970, San Marco* ☎ *041/5231973* ⊕ *www.lisola.com* Ⓜ *Vaporetto: San Samuele, Sant'Angelo.*

★ MuranoVitrum

GLASSWARE | You'll find Murano-made glassworks, including glasses, vases, chandeliers, mirrors, and sculptures, in this friendly family-owned shop. ⊠ *San Marco 1229, San Marco* ☎ *041/5206358* ⊕ *www.muranovitrum.com* Ⓜ *Vaporetto: Vallaresso.*

The stores leading to the Rialto Bridge are handy for picking up Venetian souvenirs, such as Murano glass.

JEWELRY

Gianluca Bastianello

JEWELRY & WATCHES | Classic handmade jewelry here includes pieces made with semiprecious stones. ✉ *San Marco 5192, San Marco* ☎ *041/5231851* ⊕ *www. gianlucabastianello.it* Ⓜ *Vaporetto: Rialto.*

★ Nardi

JEWELRY & WATCHES | Exquisite earrings, rings, necklaces, and brooches are studded with diamonds, rubies, or emeralds in this shop owned by the Nardi family since the 1920s. ✉ *Under Procuratie Nuove, Piazza San Marco, San Marco 69, San Marco* ☎ *041/5225733* ⊕ *www.nardi-venezia.com* Ⓜ *Vaporetto: Vallaresso.*

★ Paropàmiso

JEWELRY & WATCHES | This fascinating shop stocks antique jewelry from Europe and Asia, along with stunning Venetian glass beads. ✉ *Frezzeria, San Marco 1701, San Marco* ☎ *041/5227120* ⊕ *www.paropamisovenezia.com* Ⓜ *Vaporetto: Vallaresso.*

Salvadori Diamond Atelier

JEWELRY & WATCHES | Established in 1857, Salvadori features sparkling diamonds and other precious stones set in the shop's own designs. They have two other shops in Piazza San Marco that specialize in watches: Boutique Rolex (Piazza San Marco 44) and Panerai Venezia (Piazza San Marco 47). ✉ *Piazza San Marco 67, San Marco* ☎ *041/5230609* ⊕ *www. salvadori-venezia.com* Ⓜ *Vaporetto: San Marco.*

LACE, LINEN, AND FABRIC

★ Bevilacqua

FABRICS | This renowned studio has kept the weaving tradition alive in Venice since 1875, using 18th-century hand looms for its most precious creations. Its repertoire of 3,500 different patterns and designs yields a ready-to-sell selection of hundreds of brocades, Gobelins, damasks, velvets, taffetas, and satins. You'll also find tapestry, cushions, and braiding. Fabrics made by this prestigious firm have been used to decorate the Vatican, the Royal Palace of Stockholm, and the

White House. There is another location behind the San Marco Basilica. If you're interested in seeing the actual 18th-century looms in action making the most precious fabrics, request an appointment at the Luigi Bevilacqua production center in Santa Croce. ✉ *Campo di Santa Maria del Giglio, San Marco 2520, San Marco* ☎ *041/2410662 main retail outlet, 041/5287581 retail outlet behind Basilica, 041/721566 Santa Croce production center* ⊕ *bevilacquatessuti.com* Ⓜ *Vaporetto: Giglio.*

★ Jesurum Venezia 1870

FABRICS | A great deal of so-called Burano Venetian lace is now machine-made in China—and there really is a difference. Unless you have some experience, you're best off going to a trusted place. Jesurum has been the major producer of handmade Venetian lace since 1870. Its lace is, of course, all modern production, but if you want an antique piece, the people at Jesurum can point you in the right direction. ✉ *Calle Veste, San Marco 2024, San Marco* ☎ *041/5238969* ⊕ *www.jesurum.it* Ⓜ *Vaporetto: Vallaresso.*

★ Rubelli — Showroom & Historic Archives

FABRICS | Founded in1858, Rubelli offers the same sumptuous brocades, damasks, and cut velvets used by the world's most prestigious decorators. ✉ *Ca' Pisani Rubelli, San Marco 3393, San Marco* ☎ *041/5236110* ⊕ *www.rubelli.com* Ⓜ *Vaporetto: San Samuele, Sant' Angelo.*

LEATHER GOODS

★ Atelier Segalin di Daniela Ghezzo

SHOES | This artist turned master shoemaker produces one-of-a-kind creations from exotic leathers. Though the shoes start at €650 and usually take at least six weeks to finish, you'll truly feel like you're wearing a masterpiece. ✉ *Calle dei Fuseri, San Marco 4365, San Marco* ☎ *041/5222115* ⊕ *www.danielaghezzo.it* Ⓜ *Vaporetto: Rialto.*

★ Dittura Massimo

SHOES | Run by a second-generation shoemaker, this shop is one of the only places left in the city still producing Venice's iconic friulane slippers, invented in the 19th century and handstitched from velvet and rubber. The shoes are still worn by gondoliers today. ✉ *Calle Fiubera, San Marco 943, San Marco* ☎ *041/5231163* ⊕ *ditturamassimo.it* Ⓜ *Vaporetto: San Marco.*

La Parigina

SHOES | A Venetian institution shows off its shoes in five large windows in two neighboring shops. You'll find the house collection plus a dozen lesser-known designers, as well as luxury sportswear. ✉ *Merceria San Zulian, San Marco 727, San Marco* ☎ *041/5226743* ⊕ *laparigina.it* Ⓜ *Vaporetto: Rialto, San Marco.*

★ René Caovilla

SHOES | René Caovilla's shoes are meant for showing off, not walking around town (especially in Venice). The evening shoes here are so glamorous and over-the-top that you might feel compelled to buy a pair and then create an occasion to wear them. ✉ *Calle Seconda a l'Ascensione, San Marco 1296, San Marco* ☎ *041/5238038* ⊕ *www.renecaovilla.com* Ⓜ *Vaporetto: San Marco.*

PAPER GOODS

Alberto Valese Ebrû

STATIONERY | The name is a Turkish word meaning "cloudy" and refers to the technique that Alberto Valese uses to decorate paper, as well as silk ties and paperweights. ✉ *Campo Santo Stefano, San Marco 3471, San Marco* ☎ *041/5238830* ⊕ *www.albertovalese-ebru.it* Ⓜ *Vaporetto: Sant'Angelo.*

Antica Legatoria Piazzesi

STATIONERY | One of the oldest bookbinderies in Venice is known for its historic *stampi,* hand-printed paper using carved wood plates, which artisans carefully filled with colored inks. Don't let the sporadic opening times discourage you from trying to visit or purchase their exquisite papers. ⊠ *Campo della Feltrina near Campo Santa Maria del Giglio, San Marco 2511, San Marco* ☎ *0333/8950095* ⊕ *www.facebook.com/AnticaLegatoriaPiazzesiVeneziArchivioStorico* Ⓜ *Vaporetto: Santa Maria del Giglio.*

Fabriano Boutique

STATIONERY | The name has been synonymous with high-quality paper since 1264 and is esteemed by publishers, writers, and artists. The boutique offers a glimpse into their full range of products from luxurious stationery to journals and specialized notebooks. They also offer a line of writing instruments and leather items. ⊠ *Calle del Lovo, San Marco 4816, San Marco* ☎ *041/5286988* ⊕ *www.fabrianoboutique.com* Ⓜ *Vaporetto: Rialto.*

La Ricerca

STATIONERY | A broad assortment of writing materials, bound journals and albums, book covers, medieval sketchbooks, and handmade marble paper are made in a nearby laboratory. New products are introduced often so that no two visits to the store are ever the same. ⊠ *Ponte delle Ostreghe near Campo Santa Maria del Giglio, San Marco 2431, San Marco* ☎ *041/5212606* ⊕ *www.laricerca.it* Ⓜ *Vaporetto: Giglio.*

WINE

★ Millevini

WINE/SPIRITS | Lorenzo will be more than happy to assist you in exploring the broad selection of wines from across the region, the entire Italian landscape, and beyond. You'll also find liquors and brandies, lovely bubbles, and even a few microbrews. ⊠ *Ramo del Fontego dei Tedeschi, just off the Rialto Bridge, San Marco 5362, San Marco* ☎ *041/5206090* ⊕ *www.enotecamillevini.it* Ⓜ *Vaporetto: Rialto.*

Chapter 4

DORSODURO

Updated by
Erla Zwingle

👁 Sights	🍴 Restaurants	🛏 Hotels	👜 Shopping	🍸 Nightlife
★★★★☆	★★★★☆	★★★★☆	★★★★☆	★★★★★

NEIGHBORHOOD SNAPSHOT

TOP EXPERIENCES

- **Explore Venice's best art museums:** Ca' Rezzonico and the Gallerie dell'Accademia are must-sees.

- **Observe student life:** Campo Santa Margherita is a lively hangout spot for many university-goers.

- **Stroll the Zattere:** Take a cue from locals and head out for a passeggiata (stroll) along the promenade.

- **Barhop:** Whether at a café, *bacaro* (bar), or jazz club, this is perhaps Venice's best neighborhood for nightlife.

- **Take in the views:** Canals wind their way toward the Santa Maria della Salute and the Punta della Dogana.

PLANNING YOUR TIME

You can easily spend a full day in the neighborhood, exploring the streets and squares, stepping into churches, having a coffee or "spritz" with the students in Campo Santa Margherita, or strolling the Fondamenta delle Zattere with gelato in hand. Devote at least a half an hour to admiring the Titians in the imposing and monumental Santa Maria della Salute, and another half hour for the wonderful Veroneses in the peaceful church of San Sebastiano. The Gallerie dell'Accademia demands a few hours, but if time is short an audio guide can help you cover the highlights in about an hour. Ca' Rezzonico deserves at least an hour, as does the Peggy Guggenheim Collection. Those interested in contemporary art should spend an hour at the François Pinault Foundation museum at the Punta della Dogana.

GETTING HERE

Dorsoduro stretches from the western edge of Venice at Piazzale Roma to the east, ending at the Punta della Dogana, overlooking the basin of San Marco. If you want to begin your exploration from Piazzale Roma, the closest vaporetto stops are Piazzale Roma or San Basilio. If you want to begin at the Punta della Dogana, your stop is "Salute."

VIEWFINDER

- **Top of the Accademia Bridge:** Sweeping views of the Grand Canal, the dome of the Salute church, and the basin of San Marco are best at dawn or sunset. Ⓜ *Vaporetto: Accademia, Zattere.*

- **The Squero di San Trovaso:** This traditional gondola workshop is easily visible from the Fondamenta Nani looking across the rio de San Trovaso. Ⓜ *Vaporetto: Accademia, Zattere.*

- **Church of San Trovaso:** Entering from the *campo*, just inside the main entrance is the small altar once dedicated to the guild of boatbuilders, with the rough outline of a gondola cut into the marble to the left of the altar and the outline of a seagoing ship cut into the marble to the right. Ⓜ *Vaporetto: Accademia, Zattere.*

The *sestiere* (district) Dorsoduro (nicknamed "hard back" for its solid, compact soil foundation) is across the Grand Canal to the south of San Marco. It is a place of meandering canals, the city's finest art museums, monumental churches, *scuole* (Renaissance civic institutions) filled with works by Titian, Veronese, and Tiepolo, and a promenade called the Zattere, where on sunny days you'll swear half the city is out for a passeggiata. The eastern tip of the peninsula, the Punta della Dogana, is capped by the dome of Santa Maria della Salute and was once the city's maritime customs point; the old customs house is now a museum of contemporary art.

Dorsoduro is home to the Gallerie dell'Accademia, with an unparalleled collection of Venetian painting, and the gloriously restored Ca' Rezzonico, which houses the Museo del Settecento Veneziano. Another of its landmark sites, the Peggy Guggenheim Collection, has a fine selection of 20th-century art.

Both of the city's universities are in Dorsoduro: The Università Ca' Foscari headquartered in the former grand palace of the Foscari family on the Grand Canal at the Rio Novo (its departments are scattered around the city) and the University of Architecture, near San Basilio. Students often fill the streets and nearby cafés, providing a refreshing vibrancy to the neighborhood. Add to this some wonderful restaurants, charming places to stay, and inviting bars for an early-evening spritz, and you've got a sestiere well worth exploring.

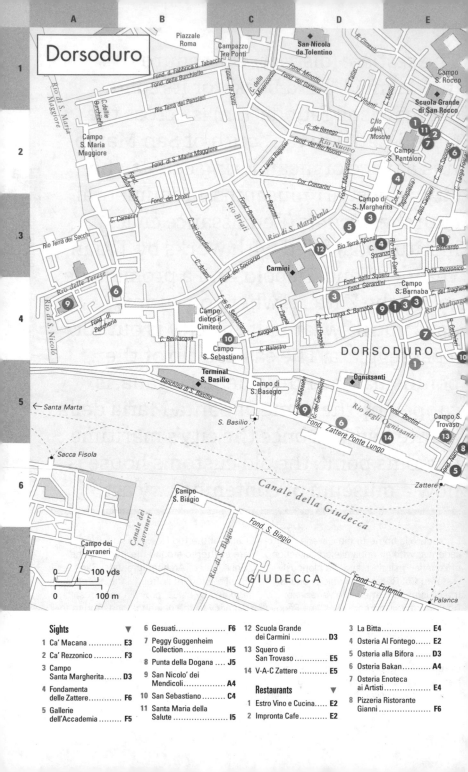

Dorsoduro

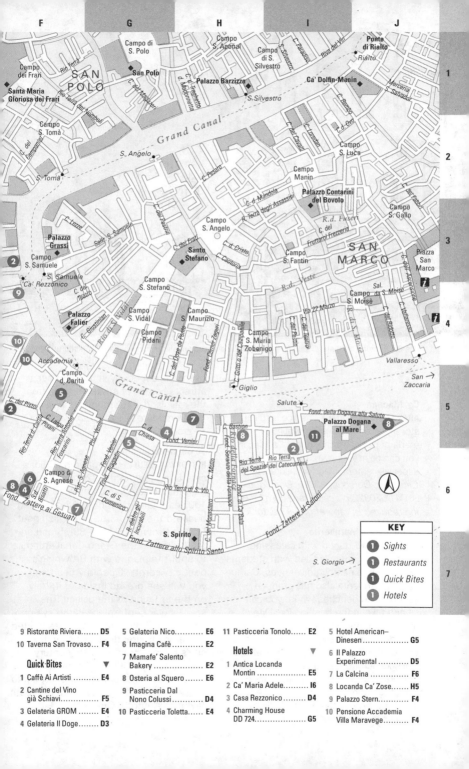

KEY

- ① Sights
- ① Restaurants
- ① Quick Bites
- ① Hotels

9 Ristorante Riviera........ **D5**
10 Taverna San Trovaso... **F4**

Quick Bites ▼
1 Caffè Ai Artisti **E4**
2 Cantine del Vino
già Schiavi.............. **F5**
3 Gelateria GROM **E4**
4 Gelateria Il Doge........ **D3**
5 Gelateria Nico........... **E6**
6 Imagina Cafè **E2**
7 Mamafe' Salento
Bakery **E2**
8 Osteria al Squero **E6**
9 Pasticceria Dal
Nono Colussi **D4**
10 Pasticceria Toletta...... **E4**
11 Pasticceria Tonolo...... **E2**

Hotels ▼
1 Antica Locanda
Montin **E5**
2 Ca' Maria Adele.......... **I6**
3 Casa Rezzonico **D4**
4 Charming House
DD 724................... **G5**
5 Hotel American–
Dinesen **G5**
6 Il Palazzo
Experimental **D5**
7 La Calcina **F6**
8 Locanda Ca' Zose....... **H5**
9 Palazzo Stern............ **F4**
10 Pensione Accademia
Villa Maravege........... **F4**

The Ca' Rezzonico vaporetto stop on the Grand Canal is convenient to many sights in Dorsoduro.

Sights

Ca' Macana

ARTS CENTERS | FAMILY | Venice is full of stores selling fanciful Carnival masks made of papier-mâché, but at Ca'Macana you can paint your own. This activity is especially entertaining for children. ⊠ *Calle Cappeller, Dorsoduro 3215, Dorsoduro* ☎ *041/5203229* ⊕ *camacana.com* ☞ *Booking required* Ⓜ *Vaporetto: Ca' Rezzonico.*

Campo Santa Margherita

PLAZA/SQUARE | Lined with cafés and restaurants generally filled with students from the two nearby universities, Campo Santa Margherita also has produce vendors and benches where you can sit and take in the bustling local life of the campo. Also close to Ca' Rezzonico and the Scuola Grande dei Carmini, and only a 10-minute walk from the Gallerie dell'Accademia, the square is the center of Dorsoduro social life. It takes its name from the church to one side, closed since the early 19th century and now used as an auditorium. On weekend evenings, especially in the summer, it attracts hordes of students, even from the mainland. ⊠ *Campo Santa Margherita, Dorsoduro* Ⓜ *Vaporetto: Zattere, Ca' Rezzonico.*

★ Ca' Rezzonico

HISTORY MUSEUM | Designed by Baldassare Longhena in the 17th century, this gigantic palace was completed nearly 100 years later by Giorgio Massari and became the last home of English poet Robert Browning (1812–89). Stand on the bridge by the Grand Canal entrance to spot the plaque with Browning's poetic excerpt, "Open my heart and you will see graved inside of it, Italy...," on the left side of the palace. The spectacular centerpiece is the eye-popping Grand Ballroom, which has hosted some of the grandest parties in the city's history, from its 18th-century heyday to the 1969 Bal Fantastica (a Save Venice charity event that attracted every notable of the day, from Elizabeth Taylor to Aristotle Onassis).

Today the upper floors of the Ca' Rezzonico are home to the especially delightful Museo del Settecento (Museum of Venice in the 1700s). Its main floor successfully retains the appearance of a magnificent Venetian palazzo, decorated with period furniture and tapestries in gilded salons, as well as Gianbattista Tiepolo ceiling frescoes and oil paintings. Upper floors contain a fine collection of paintings by 18th-century Venetian artists, including the famous Pulcinella frescoes by Tiepolo's son, Giandomenico, moved here from the Villa di Zianigo. There's even a restored apothecary, complete with powders and potions. ⊠ *Fondamenta Rezzonico, Dorsoduro 3136, Dorsoduro* ☎ *041/2410100* ⊕ *carezzonico. visitmuve.it* ⊠ *€10 (free with Museum Pass)* ⊘ *Closed Mon.–Wed.* Ⓜ *Vaporetto: Ca' Rezzonico.*

Fondamenta delle Zattere

PROMENADE | This broad, bustling waterfront promenade is one of Venice's prime stretches for strolling; thanks to its southern orientation along the Giudecca Canal, it is full of families, students, children, and dogs whenever there is the slightest ray of sunshine. Come in spring or winter to warm up a little, or in the summer to cool off under café umbrellas with drinks or gelato. Restaurant terraces over the water lure diners until late. The name Zattere means "rafts," and this was the area designated by the Venetian government for storing the vast platforms of tree trunks that were floated down rivers from the nearby Alps destined to become pilings, beams, ships, or any other item made of wood. ⊠ *Dorsoduro* Ⓜ *Vaporetto: Zattere, San Basilio, Spirito Santo.*

★ Gallerie dell'Accademia

ART MUSEUM | The greatest collection of Venetian paintings in the world hangs in these galleries founded by Napoléon back in 1807 on the site of a religious complex he had suppressed. The galleries were carefully and subtly restructured between 1945 and 1959 by the renowned Venetian architect Carlo Scarpa.

Jacopo Bellini is considered the father of the Venetian Renaissance, and in Room 2 you can compare his *Madonna and Child with Saints* with such later works as *Madonna of the Orange Tree* by Cima da Conegliano (circa 1459–1517) and *Ten Thousand Martyrs of Mt. Ararat* by Vittore Carpaccio (circa 1455–1525). Jacopo's more accomplished son Giovanni (circa 1430–1516) attracts your eye not only with his subject matter but also with his rich color. Rooms 4 and 5 have a good selection of his madonnas. Room 5 contains *The Tempest* by Giorgione (1477–1510), a revolutionary work that has intrigued viewers and critics for centuries. It is unified not only by physical design elements, as was usual, but more importantly by a mysterious, somewhat threatening atmosphere. In Room 10, *Feast in the House of Levi,* commissioned as a Last Supper, got Veronese summoned to the Inquisition over its depiction of dogs, jesters, and other extraneous and unsacred figures. The artist responded with the famous retort, *"Noi pittori ci prendiamo le stesse libertà dei poeti e dei pazzi"* ("We painters permit ourselves the same liberties as poets and madmen"). He resolved the problem by simply changing the title, so that the painting represented a different, less solemn biblical feast. Don't miss the views of 15th- and 16th-century Venice by Carpaccio and Gentile Bellini, Giovanni's brother—you'll easily recognize places you have passed in your walks around the city.

Booking tickets in advance isn't essential but helps during busy seasons and costs only an additional €1.50. A free map notes art and artists, and the bookshop sells a more informative English-language booklet. In the main galleries a €4 audio guide saves reading but adds little to each room's excellent annotation. As of late 2021, a valid certificate of vaccination against COVID-19 is required for visitors to all Italian museums; check with the

Gentile Bellini's work in the Gallerie dell'Accademia presents a view of Venice at the end of the 15th century.

gallery to verify this is still required on the day you wish to visit. ✉ *Campo de la Carità, Dorsoduro 1050, Campo della Carità just off Accademia Bridge, Dorsoduro* ☏ *041/5222247, 041/5243354 reservations when calling from outside Italy* ⊕ *www.gallerieaccademia.it/en* ✆ *€12; subject to increases for special exhibitions* Ⓜ *Vaporetto: Accademia, Zattere.*

Gesuati

(*Church of Santa Maria del Rosario*)
CHURCH | When the Dominicans took over the church of Santa Maria della Visitazione from the suppressed order of Gesuati laymen in 1668, Giorgio Massari, the last of the great Venetian Baroque architects, was commissioned to build this structure between 1726 and 1735. It has an important Gianbattista Tiepolo (1696–1770) illusionistic ceiling and several other of his works, plus those of his contemporaries Giambattista Piazzetta (1683–1754) and Sebastiano Ricci (1659–1734). Outside on the right-hand wall above a small staircase is a bronze door decorated with a series of panels

showing scenes from the life of Jesus by noted Venetian sculptor Francesco Scarpabolla. ✉ *Fondamenta Zattere ai Gesuati, Dorsoduro* ☏ *041/2750462 Chorus Foundation, 041/5205921 church office* ⊕ *www.chorusvenezia.org* ✆ *€3 (free with Chorus Pass)* ⊘ *Closed Sun.* Ⓜ *Vaporetto: Zattere.*

Peggy Guggenheim Collection

ART MUSEUM | **FAMILY** | Housed in the incomplete but nevertheless charming Palazzo Venier dei Leoni, this choice selection of 20th-century painting and sculpture represents the taste and extraordinary style of the late heiress Peggy Guggenheim. Through wealth, social connections, and a sharp eye for artistic trends, Guggenheim (1898–1979) became an important art dealer and collector from the 1930s through the 1950s, and her personal collection here includes works by Picasso, Kandinsky, Pollock, Motherwell, and Ernst (her onetime husband). The museum serves beverages, snacks, and light meals in its refreshingly shady and artistically sophisticated garden. ⌧ *Fondamenta Venier dei Leoni, Dorsoduro 701-704, Dorsoduro* ☎ *041/2405411* ⊕ *www.guggenheim-venice.it* 🎫 *€15* ⊙ *Closed Tues.* ⚲ *Timed tickets must be purchased online in advance. Weekend tickets must be booked at least one day ahead* Ⓜ *Vaporetto: Accademia, Salute.*

★ Punta della Dogana

ART MUSEUM | Funded by the billionaire who owns a major share in Christie's Auction House, the François Pinault Foundation commissioned Japanese architect Tadao Ando to redesign this fabled customs house—sitting at the *punta,* or point of land, at the San Marco end of the Grand Canal—now home to a changing roster of works from Pinault's renowned collection of contemporary art. The streaming light, polished surfaces, and clean lines of Ando's design contrast beautifully with the massive columns, sturdy beams, and brick of the original Dogana. Even if you aren't into contemporary art, a visit is worthwhile just to see Ando's amazing architectural transformation. Be sure to walk down to the punta for a magnificent view of the Venetian basin. Check online for a schedule of temporary exhibitions. ⌧ *Punta della Dogana, Dorsoduro* ☎ *041/2401308* ⊕ *www.palazzograssi.it* 🎫 *€15 with Palazzo Grassi* ⊙ *Closed Tues. and Dec. 25* Ⓜ *Vaporetto: Salute.*

★ San Sebastiano

CHURCH | Paolo Veronese (1528–88), though still in his twenties, was already the official painter of the Republic when he began the ceiling oil panels and wall frescoes at San Sebastiano in 1555. For decades he continued to embellish the church with very beautiful illusionistic scenes. The cycles of scenes in San Sebastiano are considered to be his supreme accomplishment. His three oil paintings in the center of the ceiling depict scenes from the life of Esther, a rare theme in Venice. Veronese is buried beneath his bust near the organ. The

Museum Mile

Four popular museums—Punta Della Dogana, Peggy Guggenheim Collection, Accademia, and Palazzo Cini Gallery—live close together in the easternmost part of Dorsoduro, and are collectively termed "Museum Mile" (note: it's not actually a mile!). If you plan to visit more than one of the participating museums, buy your ticket to the first of the four, and when you show it at the next museum you'll receive a discount on the ticket price there. If you think you'll want to see more than one of these exceptional museums, the plan saves you money and is valid for 7 days.

church itself, remodeled by Scarpagnino and finished in 1548, offers a rare opportunity to see a monument in Venice where both the architecture and the pictorial decoration all date from the same period. Be sure to check out the portal of the ex-convent, now part of the University of Venice, to the left of the church; it was designed in 1976–78 by Carlo Scarpa, a Venetian and one of the most important Italian architects of the 20th century. ⌧ *Campazzo San Sebastiano, Dorsoduro* ☎ *041/2750462* ⊕ *www.chorusvenezia.org* 🎫 *€3 (free with Chorus Pass)* ⊙ *Closed Sun.* Ⓜ *Vaporetto: San Basilio.*

San Nicolò dei Mendicoli

CHURCH | San Nicolò is one of the oldest churches in Venice (7th century), though the present building dates from 1300, and the covered porch was added in the 15th century. It was dedicated to the patron saint of sailors and fishermen. "Mendicoli" might refer to its earliest neighbors ("mendici," or beggars), or to "mendigola," the original name of the little island on which it stands. Under the Venetian Republic, the inhabitants of this

Located at the tip of Dorsoduro, Santa Maria della Salute is one of the most iconic landmarks of Venice.

area were categorically called "Nicolotti" (those from the easternmost part of Venice were "Castellani") and granted many special privileges by the doge. They elected their own "doge" in this church, and he was allowed, among other things, to follow directly behind the doge's barge on the Feast of the Ascension.

The church interior always seems a little dark, despite an unusual amount of gold leaf, not only on the picture frames but under the arches of the stone columns. You'll notice the classic three-nave Roman basilica design, and that the walls are covered with paintings, many by artists of the school of Veronese. The round painting by Francesco Montemezzano, *St. Nicholas in Glory,* in the center of the ceiling may well be one of the most chaotic scenes of its type ever created. The imposing gilt wooden statue of Saint Nicholas in the niche above the high altar is from the mid-15th century. Parts of the classic horror film *Don't Look Now* (1973) were filmed here. ⊠ *Campo San Nicolò, Dorsoduro 1907, Dorsoduro*

☎ *041/2750382* ⊕ *www.anzolomendicoli. it* ⊙ *Closed Sun. afternoon* Ⓜ *Vaporetto: San Basilio, Piazzale Roma.*

★ Santa Maria della Salute

CHURCH | The most iconic landmark of the Grand Canal, "La Salute" (as this church is commonly called) is most unforgettably viewed from the Riva degli Schiavoni at sunset, or from the Accademia Bridge by moonlight. En route to becoming Venice's most important Baroque architect, 32-year-old Baldassare Longhena won a competition in 1631 to design a shrine honoring the Virgin Mary for saving Venice from a plague that in the space of two years (1629–31) killed 47,000 residents, or one-third of the city's population, including the doge. It was not completed, however, until 1687—five years after Longhena's death.

Outside, this ornate white Istrian stone octagon is topped by a colossal cupola with snail-like ornamental buttresses—in truth, piers encircled by finely carved "ropes," an allusion to the sail-making industry of the city (or so say today's art historians). Inside, a white-and-gray color scheme is complemented by a polychrome marble floor and the six chapels. The Byzantine icon above the main altar has been venerated as the Madonna della Salute (Madonna of Health) since 1670, when Francesco Morosini brought it here from Crete. Above it is a dramatic marble sculpture by Giusto Le Court showing Venice on her knees before the Madonna as she implores aid and a cherub drives the plague from the city.

Do not leave the church without visiting the Sacrestia Maggiore, which contains a dozen works by Titian, including his *San Marco Enthroned with Saints* altarpiece. You'll also see Tintoretto's *Wedding at Cana*. For the Festa della Salute, held November 21, a votive bridge is constructed across the Grand Canal from Campo Santa Maria del Giglio to San Gregorio, and Venetians make a pilgrimage here to light candles in prayer for another year's health. ⊠ *Punta della Dogana, Dorsoduro* ☎ *041/2743928* ⊕ *basilicasalutevenezia.it* ⊠ *Church free, sacristy €4* Ⓜ *Vaporetto: Salute.*

Scuola Grande dei Carmini

HISTORIC SIGHT | When the order of Santa Maria del Carmelo commissioned Baldassare Longhena to finish the work on the Scuola Grande dei Carmini in the 1670s, their confraternity was one of the largest and wealthiest in Venice. Little expense was spared in the stuccoed ceilings and carved wooden paneling, and the artwork is remarkable. The paintings by Gianbattista Tiepolo that adorn the Baroque ceiling of the **Sala Capitolare** (Chapter House) are particularly alluring. In what many consider his best work, the artist's nine canvases vividly transform some rather conventional religious themes into dynamic displays of color and movement. ⊠ *Campo dei Carmini, Dorsoduro 2617, Dorsoduro* ☎ *041/5289420* ⊕ *www. scuolagrandecarmini.it* ⊠ *€7* Ⓜ *Vaporetto: Ca' Rezzonico.*

Squero di San Trovaso

HISTORIC SIGHT | **FAMILY** | San Trovaso is one of only four *squeri*, or boatbuilding yards specifically dedicated to gondolas and other Venetian wooden boats, still operating in Venice. (There once were at least 45). Dating from the 17th century, it is a registered monument where you can really observe and appreciate a unique mode of transportation that still thrives today. If the small wooden buildings seem to resemble an Alpine chalet, it's because Venice's boatbuilders historically came from the nearby mountains. Notice the wooden planks stacked outside to season (a gondola is made of eight different types of wood). Half-hour visits can be booked. ⊠ *Campo San Trovaso, Dorsoduro 1097, Dorsoduro* ☎ *041/5229146* ⊕ *squerosantrovaso.com* ⊗ *Closed Sun.* Ⓜ *Vaporetto: Zattere, Accademia.*

V-A-C Zattere

ARTS CENTER | When it comes to contemporary art, Venice's Biennale may get all the ink, but this new art center on the Zattere gives it a run for its money. Set up within the Palazzo Clary, it features both permanent and temporary exhibitions of thought-provoking contemporary art. Be aware that some of its shows are dense, technical creations. When you work up an appetite, café/restaurant Sudest 1401 features classic and innovative dishes from the Piemonte and Valle d'Aosta regions, uncommon elsewhere in Venice. A bonus: it's one of the few museums open on Monday. ⊠ *Fondamenta delle Zattere, Dorsoduro 1401, Dorsoduro* ☎ *041/0996840* ⊕ *v-a-c. org/en/zattere* ⊠ *Free* ⊗ *Closed Wed.* Ⓜ *Vaporetto: San Basilio, Zattere.*

🍴 Restaurants

★ Estro Vino e Cucina

$$$$ | **MODERN ITALIAN** | Wine lovers shouldn't miss this cozy and compact eatery run by the Spezzamonte brothers, which offers a fantastic selection of organic wines along with modern

4

Dorsoduro

Venice through the Ages

Beginnings

Venice was founded in the 5th century when the Veneti, inhabitants of the mainland region roughly corresponding to today's lower Veneto, fled their homes to escape invading Germanic tribes. The unlikely city, built on islands in the lagoon and atop wooden posts driven into the marshes, would evolve into a maritime republic lasting over a thousand years.

Venice's early fortunes grew as a result of its active role in the Crusades, beginning in 1095 and culminating in the Venetian-led sacking of Constantinople in 1204. The defeat of rival Genoa in the Battle of Chioggia (1380) established Venice as the dominant sea power in Europe.

Early Government

As early as the 7th century, Venice was governed by a ruler, the doge, elected by the nobility of the city to a lifetime term. Venice was, therefore, from its beginnings a republic; the common people, however, had little political power, and the city was never a democracy in the modern sense. Beginning in the 12th century, the doge's power was increasingly subsumed by a growing number of councils, commissions, and magistrates. By the late 13th century, power rested foremost with the Great Council, which at times numbered as many as 2,000 members.

A Long Decline

Venice reached the height of its wealth and territorial expansion in the early 15th century, during which time its domain included all of the Veneto region and part of Lombardy, but the seeds of its decline were soon to be sown. By the beginning of the 16th century, Pope Julius II, threatened by Venice's mainland expansion, organized the League of Cambrai, allying most of the major powers in Western Europe against Venice, and defeated her in 1505, putting a stop to the Republic's mainland territorial designs. The Ottoman Empire blocked Venice's Mediterranean trade routes, and newly emerging sea powers, such as Britain and the Netherlands, ended Venice's monopoly by opening oceanic trading routes.

When Napoléon arrived in 1797, he starved the city into submission, gave it briefly to the Austrians, and then got it back in 1805. With his defeat Venice was ceded again to the Austrians at the Council of Vienna in 1815, and they occupied the city until 1848. In that tumultuous year throughout Europe, the Venetians rebelled, but the rebellion was defeated the following year. Venice remained in Austrian hands until 1866, when it joined the recently formed (1861) Italian Republic.

Venetians regard the period of Austrian rule as a misfortune, but admit that the Austrians modernized Venice in important ways. They built the causeway that connects Venice to the mainland, now named Ponte della Libertà, though it was then limited to trains. (The carriageway for cars was built in 1933.) They paved all the streets with stone and installed street lighting to replace the pale flames from candles or lamps at religious shrines and street corners. They also filled in enough of the canals to make it possible to traverse Venice on foot; previously, parts of the city were accessible only by boat.

takes on classic Venetian dishes, such as *scampi in saor* (marinated langoustines) and grilled local amberjack. If you can't choose, let the helpful servers suggest the perfect vino from their list of more than 700 bottles to pair with your à la carte dishes or tasting menu. **Known for:** vibrant atmosphere; ambitious local cuisine; extensive natural wine list. $ *Average main: €38* ⊠ *Crosera San Pantalon, Dorsoduro 3778, Dorsoduro* ☎ *041/4764914* ⊕ *www.estrovenezia.com* ⊗ *Closed Tues.* Ⓜ *Vaporetto: San Tomà.*

Impronta
$$$ | **VENETIAN** | This sleek café is a favorite lunchtime haunt for professors from the nearby university and local businesspeople, when you can easily have a beautifully prepared *primo* (first course) or *secondo* (second course), plus a glass of wine, for a reasonable price; there's also a good selection of sandwiches and salads. Unlike most local eateries, this spot is open from breakfast through late dinner, and you can dine well in the evening on imaginative pasta, seafood, and meat dishes. **Known for:** all-day dining; imaginative dishes; contemporary decor. $ *Average main: €25* ⊠ *intersection of Calle Crosera and Calle San Pantalon, Dorsoduro 3815, Dorsoduro* ☎ *041/2750386* ⊕ *www.improntacafe-venice.com* ⊗ *Closed Sun. and 2 wks in Aug.* Ⓜ *Vaporetto: San Tomà.*

★ La Bitta
$$$ | **NORTHERN ITALIAN** | For a break from all the fish and seafood options in Venice, this is your place; the meat-and veggie-focused menu (inspired by the cuisine of the Venetian mainland) presents a new temptation at every course, and market availability keeps the dishes changing almost every day. The homemade desserts are all luscious (it's been said that La Bitta serves the best panna cotta in town), and you can trust the owner's selections from her excellent wine and grappa lists, which tend to

favor small local producers. **Known for:** friendly and efficient service; meat dishes (no seafood); seasonally inspired menus. $ *Average main: €25* ⊠ *Calle Lunga San Barnaba, Dorsoduro 2753/A, Dorsoduro* ☎ *041/5230531* ⊕ *facebook. com/LaBittaVenezia* ⊟ *No credit cards* ⊗ *Closed Sun. No lunch* Ⓜ *Vaporetto: Ca' Rezzonico, Zattere.*

Osteria Al Fontego
$$ | **ITALIAN** | This small eatery hides a historic secret: indoors are the visible underground remains of three medieval brick vats that were used for dying cloth, discovered during renovation work years ago. A menu for the whole family varies from *cicheti* (appetizers) to pasta to dessert. **Known for:** umbrella-covered outdoor seating; fine setting for a coffee or spritz; historic past. $ *Average main: €15* ⊠ *Campo Santa Margherita, Dorsoduro 3426, Dorsoduro* ☎ *041/5710877* Ⓜ *Vaporetto: Ca' Rezzonico.*

★ Osteria alla Bifora
$$ | **VENETIAN** | A beautiful and atmospheric bacaro, Alla Bifora has such ample, satisfying fare that most Venetians consider it a full-fledged restaurant. Offerings include overflowing trays of cold, sliced meats and cheeses; various preparations of *baccalà* (cod); and Venetian classics, such as *polpette* (croquettes), sarde in saor, and marinated anchovies. **Known for:** warm and friendly owners; good selection of regional wines by the glass; *seppie in nero con polenta* (cuttlefish in ink with polenta). $ *Average main: €18* ⊠ *Campo Santa Margherita, Dorsoduro 2930, Dorsoduro* ☎ *041/5236119* ⊗ *Closed Jan. and Aug.* Ⓜ *Vaporetto: Ca' Rezzonico.*

Osteria Bakan
$$$$ | **VENETIAN** | Outstanding fish, from the simplest steamed sea bass to decadent swordfish ravioli, is served at Bakan, its name a reference to the part of the lagoon near Sant'Erasmo that's popular for swimming and clamming. You'll see more students and locals than tourists

here, and there are tables outside.
Known for: outdoor seating; local patrons; seafood classics like *baccalà mantecato* (whipped salt cod). $ *Average main:* €50 ⊠ *Corte Mazor, Dorsoduro 2314/A, Dorsoduro* ☎ *041/5647658* ⊙ *Closed Mon. and Tues.* Ⓜ *Vaporetto: San Basilio, Piazzale Roma.*

★ Osteria Enoteca ai Artisti

$$$ | VENETIAN | Pop into this canalside restaurant at lunch for a satisfying primo or come for dinner to sample fine and fresh offerings; the candlelit tables that line the *fondamenta* (quay) suggest romance, and the service is friendly and welcoming. The posted menu—with choices like tagliatelle with porcini mushrooms and tiger prawns, or a filleted John Dory with tomatoes and pine nuts—changes daily (spot the date at the top) and seasonally. **Known for:** truly helpful service; delicious pasta and seafood offerings; superlative tiramisu. $ *Average main: €25* ⊠ *Fondamenta della Toletta, Dorsoduro 1169a, Dorsoduro* ☎ *041/5238944* ⊕ *www.enotecaartisti. com* ⊙ *Closed Sun. and Mon.* Ⓜ *Vaporetto: Ca' Rezzonico, Zattere.*

Pizzeria Ristorante Gianni

$ | VENETIAN | One of several restaurants on the Zattere with an over-water terrace, Gianni offers much more than pizza. They also serve unusually good preparations of favorites such as spaghetti with clams, tiramisu, and coffee. **Known for:** sunset views; pasta, fish, and pizza; relaxed service. $ *Average main: €12* ⊠ *Fondamenta Zattere ai Gesuati, Dorsoduro 918, Dorsoduro* ☎ *041/5237210* ⊙ *Closed Sun.* Ⓜ *Vaporetto: Zattere, Accademia.*

Ristorante Riviera

$$$$ | NORTHERN ITALIAN | The impressive panorama from their Zattere terrace attracts travelers yearning for a view, and the Riviera certainly offers that. Choose from contemporary takes on a variety of traditional Venetian dishes, including calf's liver with figs; "guitar string" pasta with shrimp, tiny green beans, and mint;

and venison with blueberry sauce. **Known for:** stunning views; regional wine list; Venetian classics. $ *Average main: €50* ⊠ *Zattere, Dorsoduro 1473, Dorsoduro* ☎ *041/5227621* ⊕ *www.ristoranteriviera. it* ⊙ *Closed Mon., Tues. and 4 wks in Jan. and Feb.* Ⓜ *Vaporetto: San Basilio.*

Taverna San Trovaso

$ | ITALIAN | FAMILY | A wide choice of Venetian dishes served in robust portions, economical fixed-price menus, pizzas, and house wine by the glass or pitcher keep this two-floor, no-nonsense, reliable tavern abuzz with young locals and budget-conscious visitors. It's always packed, and table turnover is fast, so it's not for lingering. **Known for:** quick service; solid northern Italian food; proximity to Gallerie dell'Accademia. $ *Average main: €12* ⊠ *Calle Contarini Corfù, Dorsoduro 1016, Dorsoduro* ☎ *041/5203703* ⊕ *www. tavernasantrovaso.it* Ⓜ *Vaporetto: Accademia, Zattere.*

☕ Coffee and Quick Bites

Caffè Ai Artisti

$ | CAFÉ | Caffè Ai Artisti gives locals, students, and travelers alike good reason to pause and refuel. The location is central, pleasant, and sunny—perfect for people-watching and taking a break before the next destination—and the hours are long. **Known for:** chilling with the locals; relaxing with a coffee; evening Aperol spritz or wine. $ *Average main: €8* ⊠ *Campo San Barnaba, Dorsoduro 2771, Dorsoduro* ☎ *3939680135, 041/5238994* Ⓜ *Vaporetto: Ca' Rezzonico.*

★ Cantine del Vino già Schiavi

$ | WINE BAR | A mainstay for anyone living or working in the area, this beautiful, family-run, 19th-century bacaro across from the squero (gondola boatyard) of San Trovaso has original furnishings and one of the city's best wine cellars, and the walls are covered floor-to-ceiling with bottles for purchase. The cicheti here are some of the most inventive—and

CANTINE del VINO · già SCHIAVI

freshest—in Venice (feel free to compliment the signora, who makes them up to twice a day); everything's eaten standing up, as there's no seating. **Known for:** boisterous local atmosphere; excellent quality cicheti; plenty of wine choices. [$] *Average main: €8* ⊠ *Fondamenta Nani, Dorsoduro 992, Dorsoduro* ☎ *041/5230034* ⊕ *www.cantinaschiavi. com* ⊘ *Closed Sun. and 3 wks in Aug.* Ⓜ *Vaporetto: Accademia, Zattere.*

Gelateria GROM

$ | ICE CREAM | FAMILY | Founded in 2003 by two men from Torino (one of them named Federico Grom), this modest *gelateria* (ice cream shop) has expanded across the globe, including to 23 Italian cities and eight international cities. Natural ingredients such as Ecuadorian or Venezuelan chocolate, Sicilian lemon, and Mawardi pistachios add intense flavors, and the selection changes with the seasons. **Known for:** seasonal menu; flavor-packed gelato and sorbet; international following. [$] *Average main: €3* ⊠ *Campo San Barnaba, Dorsoduro* ☎ *041/9340140* ⊕ *www.grom.it* Ⓜ *Vaporetto: Ca' Rezzonico.*

Gelateria il Doge

$ | ICE CREAM | This popular takeout gelateria, just off Campo Santa Margherita, offers a wide selection of flavors, from a few low-calorie options, including yogurt and soy, to the extra-rich *strabon* (Venetian for "more than good," which in this case means made with cocoa, espresso, and chocolate-covered almonds), as well as granitas in summer. It's worth a detour, and it's open late most of the year. **Known for:** late hours; gelato; granitas. [$] *Average main: €2* ⊠ *Campo Santa Margherita, Dorsoduro 3058/A, Dorsoduro* ☎ *041/5234607* ⊘ *Closed Nov.–Feb.* Ⓜ *Vaporetto: Ca' Rezzonico, Zattere.*

Gelateria Nico

$ | ICE CREAM | FAMILY | Enjoy the Zattere's most scrumptious treat—Nico's famous *gianduiotto*, a slab of chocolate-hazelnut ice cream floating on a cloud of whipped cream—and relax on the big, welcoming deck. Nico's is one of the few places still serving authentic homemade (*artigianale*) ice cream and has been seducing Venetians since 1935. **Known for:** abundant seating; divine hazelnut ice cream; waterfront location. [$] *Average main: €5* ⊠ *Zattere al Ponte Lungo, Dorsoduro 922, Dorsoduro* ☎ *041/5225293* ⊕ *www. gelaterianico.com* ▭ *No credit cards* Ⓜ *Vaporetto: Zattere.*

Imagina Cafè

$ | ITALIAN | This friendly café and art gallery, located between Campo Santa Margherita and Campo San Barnaba, is a great place to stop for a spritz, or even for a light lunch or dinner. The highlights are the freshly made salads, but their *panini* and *tramezzini* (sandwiches) are also among the best in the area. **Known for:** pleasant outdoor seating; good wines and cocktails; tasty sandwiches and salads. [$] *Average main: €10* ⊠ *Rio Terà Canal, Dorsoduro 3126, Dorsoduro* ☎ *041/2410625* ⊕ *www.imaginacafe.it/ english.html* Ⓜ *Vaporetto: Ca' Rezzonico.*

Mamafè Salento Bakery

$$ | SOUTHERN ITALIAN | FAMILY | If you're hungry but don't know what you want, head to this bar, café, restaurant, and pizzeria for a bite. Here you can sample all types of southern Italian specialties from the Salento area of Puglia, the "heel" of the Italian "boot." Divided into two locations across the street from each other on Calle San Pantalon, the café has some tables inside, while the bakery focuses on takeout. **Known for:** takeout snacks and pastries; *puccia* (cross between a sandwich and pizza); cappuccino. [$] *Average main: €20* ⊠ *Dorsoduro 3743 and 3755, Calle San Pantalon, Dorsoduro* ☎ *366/2188789* Ⓜ *Vaporetto: Ca' Rezzonico, San Tomà.*

Osteria al Squero

$$ | ITALIAN | It wasn't long after this lovely little wine bar (not, as its name implies, a restaurant) appeared across from Squero San Trovaso that it became

a neighborhood—and citywide—favorite. The Venetian owner has created a personal vision of what a good bar should offer: a variety of sumptuous cicheti, panini, and cheeses to be accompanied by just the right regional wines (ask for his recommendation). **Known for:** pretty canal views; tasty cicheti; good veggie options. ⑤ *Average main: €20* ✉ *Fondamenta Nani, Dorsoduro 943/944, Dorsoduro* ☎ *335/6007513* ⊕ *osteriaalsquero. wordpress.com* ⊗ *Closed Sun.* Ⓜ *Vaporetto: Zattere, Accademia.*

Pasticceria Dal Nono Colussi

$ | BAKERY | Nono ("grandfather" in Venetian) Colussi starts every day at 4 am in the pastry shop he began in 1956. Working with granddaughter Marina in the kitchen and daughter Linda at the counter, he turns out classic Venetian delicacies such as *fugassa*, a soft and sweet raised cake, and *krapfen*, a sweet roll filled with pastry cream. **Known for:** fresh pastries, made with love; family business; zaletti cookies. ⑤ *Average main: €2* ✉ *Calle Lunga San Barnaba, Dorsoduro 2864/A, Dorsoduro* ☎ *041/5231871* ⊕ *dalnonocolussi.com* ⊗ *Closed Sun. and Mon.* Ⓜ *Vaporetto: Ca' Rezzonico, San Basilio.*

Pasticceria Toletta

$ | BAKERY | Monica Gozzi runs this tiny pastry shop on one of Venice's busiest streets, between Campo San Barnaba and the Accademia. Delectable croissants and other breakfast pastries are fresh every morning, and her cakes and assorted sweets are among the best in Venice. **Known for:** memorable pastries; *sfogliatelle* (lobster tail pastry); bustling location. ⑤ *Average main: €2* ✉ *Calle de la Toletta, Dorsoduro 1192, Dorsoduro* ☎ *041/5227451* ⊕ *facebook.com/Pasticceriatoletta* Ⓜ *Vaporetto: Accademia, Ca' Rezzonico.*

Pasticceria Tonolo

$ | BAKERY | One of Venice's premier confectioneries has been in operation since 1886. During Carnevale it's still one of the best places in town for *frittelle*, or fried doughnuts (traditional raisin or cream-filled), and at Christmas and Easter, this is where Venetians order their *focaccia veneziana*, the traditional raised cake—well in advance. **Known for:** can't-miss doughnuts; arguably the best pastries in Venice; excellent coffee. ⑤ *Average main: €5* ✉ *Calle San Pantalon, Dorsoduro 3764, Dorsoduro* ☎ *041/5237209* ⊕ *pasticceria-tonolo-venezia.business.site* ⊗ *Closed Mon.* Ⓜ *Vaporetto: San Tomà.*

🛏 Hotels

Antica Locanda Montin

$ | HOTEL | A true Venetian institution, this small, historic hotel with a beautiful garden restaurant has hosted such famous guests as Gabriele D'Annunzio, Ezra Pound, Robert De Niro, and David Bowie. **Pros:** historic charm; spacious rooms; close to the Gallerie dell'Accademia. **Cons:** can feel hidden away; restaurant is hit or miss; old-fashioned. ⑤ *Rooms from: €100* ✉ *Fondamenta de Borgo, Dorsoduro 1147, Dorsoduro* ☎ *041/5227151* ⊕ *locandamontin.com* ↩ *12 rooms* �ⓄⅠ *No Meals* Ⓜ *Vaporetto: Zattere, Ca' Rezzonico.*

★ Ca' Maria Adele

$$$$ | HOTEL | One of the city's most intimate and elegant getaways blends terrazzo floors, dramatic Murano chandeliers, and antique-style furnishings with contemporary touches, particularly in the African-wood reception area and breakfast room. **Pros:** tranquil yet convenient spot near Santa Maria della Salute; quiet and romantic; imaginative decor. **Cons:** bathrooms on the small side; no elevator and lots of stairs; no restaurant (just breakfast room). ⑤ *Rooms from: €462*

4

Dorsoduro

Ca' Maria Adele hotel's Sala del Doge room is draped in red velvet, a chandelier, and antique furnishings.

✉ *Campo Santa Maria della Salute, Dorsoduro 111, Dorsoduro* ☎ *041/5203078* ⊕ *www.camariaadele.it* ⊗ *Closed 3 wks in Jan.* ⇆ *14 rooms* ⦿ *Free Breakfast* Ⓜ *Vaporetto: Salute.*

Casa Rezzonico

$$ | B&B/INN | Some pleasant if generic guest rooms overlook a sunny fondamenta and canal, and others a spacious private garden, where breakfast is served in good weather. **Pros:** canal views at a reasonable rate; two lively squares nearby; great for families. **Cons:** some rooms are quite small; ground-floor rooms are dark; must reserve well in advance. ⑤ *Rooms from: €150* ✉ *Fondamenta Gherardini, Dorsoduro 2813, Dorsoduro* ☎ *041/2770653* ⇆ *6 rooms* ⦿ *Free Breakfast* Ⓜ *Vaporetto: Ca' Rezzonico.*

Charming House DD724

$$$$ | HOTEL | These ultramodern surroundings abandon all things traditionally Venetian, opting instead to create the air of a stylish residence with impeccable, minimalist decor and a contemporary, warmly romantic, and occasionally even dramatic atmosphere. **Pros:** variety of lodging options; unique decor; convenient location to the Guggenheim. **Cons:** some rooms on the smaller side; can be expensive; not traditional Venetian style. ⑤ *Rooms from: €350* ✉ *Ramo da Mula off Campo San Vio, Dorsoduro 724, Dorsoduro* ☎ *041/2770262* ⊕ *www.thecharminghouse.com* ⇆ *9 rooms* ⦿ *Free Breakfast* Ⓜ *Vaporetto: Accademia.*

Hotel American Dinesen

$$ | HOTEL | If you're in Venice to see art, you can't beat the location of this hotel, where all the spacious rooms have brocade fabrics and Venetian-style lacquered furniture. **Pros:** some rooms have canal-view terraces; wonderfully located near Gallerie dell'Accademia, Peggy Guggenheim Collection, and Punta della Dogana; on a bright, quiet, exceptionally picturesque canal. **Cons:** style could be too understated for those expecting Venetian opulence; canal-view rooms are more expensive; bathrooms can feel cramped. ⑤ *Rooms from: €171* ✉ *Fondamenta*

Bragadin, Dorsoduro 628, Dorsoduro ☎ 041/5204733 ⊕ www.hotelamerican. it ⌁ 34 rooms ⎟◯⎟ No Meals Ⓜ Vaporetto: Accademia, Salute, Zattere.

Il Palazzo Experimental

$$$ | HOTEL | Of-the-moment Parisian designer Dorothée Meilichzon composed the striped pastel color palette at this hip boutique hotel— the first Experimental Group property in Italy—hidden inside a Renaissance palazzo facing the Giudecca Canal. **Pros:** trendy cocktail bar on-site; fun, whimsical decor; quiet location away from the Venice crowds. **Cons:** little storage space in bathrooms; not all rooms have water views; no gym. *⑤ Rooms from: €270 ⊠ Fondamenta Zattere Al Ponte Lungo, Dorsoduro 1411, Dorsoduro ☎ 041/0980200 ⊕ www.palazzoexperimental.com ⌁ 32 rooms ⎟◯⎟ No Meals Ⓜ Vaporetto: Zattere, San Basilio.*

La Calcina

$$ | HOTEL | Many notables (including Victorian-era art critic John Ruskin) have stayed at this hotel, though they might not recognize it after its series of upscale renovations; it has an enviable location along the sunny Zattere, as well as comfy rooms and apartments with parquet floors, original 19th-century furniture, and firm beds. **Pros:** well-regarded restaurant with terrace over the Giudecca Canal; panoramic views from some rooms; quiet, peaceful atmosphere. **Cons:** no elevator; not for travelers who prefer ultramodern surroundings; most rooms on the small side. *⑤ Rooms from: €130 ⊠ Zattere, Dorsoduro 780, Dorsoduro ☎ 041/5206466 ⊕ www.lacalcina.com ⌁ 25 rooms ⎟◯⎟ Free Breakfast Ⓜ Vaporetto: Zattere.*

Locanda Ca' Zose

$$ | HOTEL | The idea that the Campanati sisters named the 15 rooms in their renovated 17th-century locanda after the stars and constellations of the highest magnitude in the Northern Hemisphere says something about how personally this place is run. **Pros:** quiet but convenient

location; canal views; efficient, personal service. **Cons:** no outdoor garden or terrace; no Wi-Fi in rooms (but free in lounge, as is computer use); unimpressive breakfast. *⑤ Rooms from: €165 ⊠ Calle del Bastion, Dorsoduro 193/B, Dorsoduro ☎ 041/5226635 ⊕ www. hotelcazose.com ⌁ 15 rooms ⎟◯⎟ Free Breakfast Ⓜ Vaporetto: Salute.*

★ Palazzo Stern

$$ | HOTEL | This opulently refurbished neo-Gothic palazzo features marble-column arches, terrazzo floors, frescoed ceilings, mosaics, and a charming carved staircase, and some rooms have tufted walls and parquet flooring. **Pros:** modern renovation retains historic ambience; excellent hotel service; lovely views from many rooms. **Cons:** Grand Canal–facing rooms can be a bit noisy; standard rooms don't have views; no restaurant, gym, or spa. *⑤ Rooms from: €192 ⊠ Calle del Traghetto, Dorsoduro 2792, Dorsoduro ☎ 041/2770869 ⊕ www. palazzostern.com ⌁ 24 rooms ⎟◯⎟ Free Breakfast Ⓜ Vaporetto: Ca' Rezzonico.*

Pensione Accademia Villa Maravege

$$ | HOTEL | Behind iron gates in one of the most densely packed parts of the city is this renowned Gothic-style villa with gardens and charmingly decorated accommodations with Venetian-style antique reproductions and fine tapestry. **Pros:** a unique villa in the heart of Venice; complimentary drinks and snacks at the bar; two gardens where guests can breakfast, drink, and relax. **Cons:** no restaurant; bathrooms can be on the small side; no guest rooms have Grand Canal views. *⑤ Rooms from: €128 ⊠ Fondamenta Bollani, Dorsoduro 1058, Dorsoduro ☎ 041/5210188 ⊕ www.pensioneaccademia.it ⌁ 27 rooms ⎟◯⎟ Free Breakfast Ⓜ Vaporetto: Accademia.*

Nightlife

BARS

Al Chioschetto

BARS | Although this popular place consists only of a kiosk set up to serve some outdoor tables, it is located on the Zattere and thus provides a wonderful view of the Giudecca Canal. It's a handy meet-up spot for locals, especially students from the nearby university, and a useful stop-off for tourists in nice weather for a spritz or a panino. Keep in mind, though, that "the kiosk" exists for quick refreshments and not for lingering. The view and the sunshine (and especially the sunset) are the main draw; the food and drink, while acceptable, are not exceptional. ⊠ *Fondamenta delle Zattere, Dorsoduro 1406/A, Dorsoduro* ☎ *348/3968466* ⊗ *Closed Sun; Jan.* Ⓜ *Vaporetto: San Basilio, Zattere.*

★ Il Caffè Rosso (*Bar Rosso*)

BARS | The sign above the door simply says "CAFFÈ," but it has long since been called "Bar Rosso" for its bright-red exterior. The ideal people-watching spot on one of the busiest campos, it has far more tables outside than inside. A favorite with students and faculty from the nearby university, it's a good place to start the day with coffee and croissant, or to enjoy a spritz—the preferred Venetian aperitif of white wine, Campari or Aperol, sparkling water, an olive, and a slice of orange. It has excellent tramezzini (among the best in town) and panini, and a hip, helpful staff. High-school students from the mainland tend to crowd in on weekend nights, so it can be more enjoyable around lunchtime or in the early evening. ⊠ *Campo Santa Margherita, Dorsoduro 2963, Dorsoduro* ☎ *041/5287998* ⊕ *facebook.com/cafferosso.venezia* ⊗ *Closed Sun.* Ⓜ *Vaporetto: Ca' Rezzonico.*

Impronta

CAFÉS | Just a few steps from Campo Santa Margherita, this is one of the rare locales that has a kitchen serving until midnight also offers a bar menu until 2. It's also a good spot for nightcap—you can expect a fairly lively atmosphere right up until closing time. ⊠ *Calle Crosera, Dorsoduro 3815, Dorsoduro* ☎ *041/2750386* ⊕ *www.improntacafevenice.com* ⊗ *Closed Sun.* Ⓜ *Vaporetto: San Tomà.*

Margaret Duchamp

CAFÉS | The French-sounding name befits this artfully minimalist café-brasserie in Campo Santa Margherita. Classic Venetian cocktails are served alongside warm sandwiches and light salads all day until 2 am. The tables face westward, so there's lots of sun in the afternoon. ⊠ *Campo Santa Margherita, Dorsoduro 3019, Dorsoduro* ☎ *041/5286255* ⊕ *facebook.com/MargaretDuchampVenezia* Ⓜ *Vaporetto: Ca' Rezzonico.*

Orange

BARS | Modern, hip, and complemented by an internal garden, this welcoming bar anchors the south end of Campo Santa Margherita, the liveliest campo in Venice. You can have *piadine* (thin flatbread) sandwiches, salads, and drinks while watching soccer games on a massive screen inside, or sit at the tables facing the campo. Despite being close to the university, Orange is frequented primarily by young working people from the mainland and tourists. ⊠ *Campo Santa Margherita, Dorsoduro 3054/A, Dorsoduro* ☎ *041/5234740* ⊕ *facebook.com/OrangeVenezia/* Ⓜ *Vaporetto: Ca' Rezzonico.*

Piccolo Mondo

DANCE CLUBS | Piccolo Mondo is the city's only disco, still going strong since 1963 (it was renovated in 2018). ⊠ *Calle Contarini Corfù, Dorsoduro 1056/A, Dorsoduro* ☎ *041/8878154, 041/5200371 Number active from 11 pm–4 am* ⊕ *elsouk.it* ⊗ *Closed Sun.–Tues.* Ⓜ *Vaporetto: Accademia, Zattere.*

Senso Unico

BARS | This popular neighborhood hangout is decorated in wood and brick and has a couple of tables that have a great view of the canal. There are beers on tap and plenty of wine and sandwich choices from 10 am to 1 am. ✉ *Near Campo San Vio before the Guggenheim, Dorsoduro 684, Dorsoduro* ☎ *348/3720847* ☾ *Closed Tues.* Ⓜ *Vaporetto: Accademia.*

Venice Jazz Club

LIVE MUSIC | Owner Federico is on the piano while his band plays live jazz, in styles including classic, modern, Latin jazz, and bossa nova, at this intimate venue. Concerts usually start at 9 pm every night except Thursday and Sunday, and dinner is available beforehand for an extra charge. ✉ *Ponte dei Pugni, Dorsoduro 3102, Dorsoduro* ☎ *041/5232056, 3401504985* ⊕ *venicejazzclub.weebly. com* ☾ *Closed Sun. and Thurs.* ☞ *€20 entrance fee includes one drink* Ⓜ *Vaporetto: Ca' Rezzonico.*

🛍 Shopping

ANTIQUES AND ART DEALERS

Antichità Pietro Scarpa

ANTIQUES & COLLECTIBLES | This distinguished shop next to the Gallerie dell'Accademia sells old master paintings—originals, not copies—with accordingly rarified prices. ✉ *Campo della Carità, Dorsoduro 1023/A, Dorsoduro* ☎ *041/5239700* ⊕ *antichitapietroscarpa.business.site* ☾ *Closed Sun.* Ⓜ *Vaporetto: Accademia.*

Augusto Mazzon

ANTIQUES & COLLECTIBLES | Mazzon is a master woodworker specializing in intaglio, framing, gilding, and restoration of anything wooden. His sublimely cluttered workshop contains figurines of various sizes, from just-carved cherubs to an elegantly simple madonna shining in gold leaf, with picture and mirror frames all carved by hand. He is the fourth generation of his family to do this work. ✉ *Calle del Traghetto, Dorsoduro 2783, Calle del Traghetto at San Barnaba, Dorsoduro* ☎ *379/1493408 call cell if closed; owner will come up from his home downstairs* Ⓜ *Vaporetto: Ca' Rezzonico.*

Claudia Canestrelli

ANTIQUES & COLLECTIBLES | In her tasteful shop, Claudia has amassed a limited choice of antiques, small paintings, original etchings from the 16th to 19th centuries, and plenty of interesting-looking bric-a-brac, including silver ex-votos and period souvenirs, such as brass ashtrays in the shape of lions' heads and various doorknockers. Baroque-looking earrings are made of cultured pearls and bits of old brass or bronze. ✉ *Campiello Barbaro, near the Peggy Guggenheim Collection, Dorsoduro 364/A, Dorsoduro* ☎ *340/5776089* ⊕ *evenice.it/claudia-canestrelli-antiquariato* ☾ *Closed Sun. but will open by appointment* Ⓜ *Vaporetto: Salute, Accademia.*

BOOKSTORES

Ca' Foscarina

BOOKS | The bookstore of Università di Venezia Ca' Foscari has a reasonable selection of titles in English. Shelves teem with literature and history, but there's also a handful of travel books, as well as the latest best sellers. ✉ *Campiello Squelini, Dorsoduro 3259, Dorsoduro* ☎ *041/2404802* ⊕ *www.cafoscarina.it* ☾ *Closed Sun.* Ⓜ *Vaporetto: Ca' Rezzonico.*

Libreria Toletta

BOOKS | A linchpin in the city's literary history, Libreria Toletta offers a varied selection of English books and numerous volumes about the city of Venice in addition to their vast literary, art, and architecture offerings in Italian. Their staff is friendly and knowledgeable. (Note: "Libreria" means bookstore; "biblioteca" means library.) ✉ *Sacca de la Toletta, Dorsoduro 1213, Dorsoduro* ☎ *041/5232034* ⊕ *www.latoletta.com* Ⓜ *Vaporetto: Ca' Rezzonico, Accademia, Zattere.*

CLOTHING

Arras

MIXED CLOTHING | This shop sells scarves as well as blouses and jackets, all handwoven using looms built to ancient specifications. Not only are their products made to a very high standard in wool or silk, but the weavers are part of a social cooperative called Laguna Fiorita that employs the mentally disabled; their families formed the association in 1993. The store also occasionally organizes weaving workshops. ☒ *Campiello dei Squelini, Dorsoduro 3235, Dorsoduro* ☎ *041/5226460* ⊕ *arrastessuti.wordpress.com* ☉ *Closed Sun.* Ⓜ *Vaporetto: Ca' Rezzonico, San Tomà.*

Solo Se

MIXED CLOTHING | Mere steps from the Accademia, stocked with elegant yet understated fashion, this small shop will dress you for virtually any occasion. A coat, some slippers, a dress, a silk blouse, even a simple piece of jewelry or scarf from here will make your ordinary outfits sing. It's like having your own personal stylist. ☒ *Dorsoduro 1057/E, Calle Contarini Corfu, Dorsoduro* ☎ *041/5227727* ⊕ *www.soloseabbigliamento.it* Ⓜ *Vaporetto: Accademia, Zattere.*

GIFTS

Aqua Altra

CRAFTS | **FAMILY** | A play on the term for Venice's flooding, *acqua alta*, this tiny but bountiful shop operated by a social cooperative sells natural, fair-trade products, some from Third World artisans (therefore "altra," or "other"). The quality is notably higher than some similar stores, and there is a wide range of items, including shampoo, jam, hand-knitted scarves, reusable cotton cloth to wrap food, herbal teas, coffee, water bottles, and more. If nothing else, buy a bar of the delectable Modica chocolate, made in Sicily following the Mesoamerican cold-processing techniques introduced by the Spanish. ☒ *Campo Santa Margherita, Dorsoduro 2999, Dorsoduro* ☎ *041/3030605* ⊕ *bottegaaquaaltra. tumblr.com* ☉ *Closed Sun.* Ⓜ *Vaporetto: Ca' Rezzonico, Zattere.*

Madera

CRAFTS | Craftswoman and architect Francesca Meratti and a team of local and international artisans combine traditional and contemporary design to create a mix of most-appealing objects, including dishware, carved wooden bowls, jewelry, and ceramic pieces. ☒ *Campo San Barnaba, Dorsoduro 2762, Dorsoduro* ☎ *041/5224181* ⊕ *www.maderavenezia.it* ☉ *Closed Sun.* Ⓜ *Vaporetto: Ca' Rezzonico, Zattere.*

Signor Blum

SOUVENIRS | Solid, large-piece jigsaw puzzles (painted or in natural wood colors) depict animals, views of Venice, and trompe l'oeil scenes. Ideal for toddlers, the puzzles also look nice hanging on a wall. ☒ *Fondamenta Gherardini off Campo San Barnaba, Dorsoduro 2840, Dorsoduro* ☎ *041/5226367* ⊕ *www.signorblum. com* Ⓜ *Vaporetto: Ca' Rezzonico.*

GLASS

Designs.188

JEWELRY & WATCHES | American-born but Venetian by choice, glass-bead artist Trina Tygrett opened her studio after completing her studies at the city's Academy of Fine Arts. She married into one of the oldest surviving families of traditional Venetian glassblowing and was able to study some of the older techniques founded on Murano. Her signature jewelry is a breath of fresh air as she mixes her beads with materials such as metal fabric, silver, and precious stones to create unique and eclectic pieces. A second shop is only a few steps away at Dorsoduro 167. ☒ *Calle del Bastion, Dorsoduro 188, Dorsoduro* ☎ *041/5239426* ⊕ *www. designs188.com* Ⓜ *Vaporetto: Accademia, Salute.*

Le Forcole de Saverio Pastor preserves the Venetian craft of handmade gondola oars and oarlocks.

Genninger Studio

JEWELRY & WATCHES | This is the retail outlet for Leslie Ann Genninger, an American from Ohio who was the first woman to enter the male-dominated world of Murano master bead-makers. She established her own line of jewelry, called Murano Class Act, in 1994 using period-glass beads, and when she could no longer find antique beads she started designing her own. ⊠ *Campiello Barbaro, Dorsoduro 364, Dorsoduro* ☎ *041/5225565* ⊕ *www.genningerstudio.com* Ⓜ *Vaporetto: Accademia, Salute.*

Marina and Susanna Sent

JEWELRY & WATCHES | The beautiful and elegant glass jewelry of Marina and Susanna Sent has been featured in *Vogue.* Look also for vases and other exceptional design pieces. Other locations are on the Fondamenta Serenella on Murano and in San Polo under the Sotoportego dei Oresi at Rialto. ⊠ *Campo San Vio, Dorsoduro 669, Dorsoduro* ☎ *041/5208136 for Dorsoduro, 041/5210016 for San Polo, 041/5274665*

for Murano ⊕ *www.marinaesusannasent. com* Ⓜ *Vaporetto: Salute, Accademia, Zattere.*

GOLD, WOOD, AND METALWORK

Cornici Trevisanello

CRAFTS | This second-generation family of artisans make Byzantine and rich Renaissance handcrafted frames of gold-leafed wood and inset with antique glass beads, mosaic tesserae, and small ceramic tiles. The more-elaborate pieces look their best when used to frame an old mirror. ⊠ *Fondamenta Bragadin off Campo San Vio, Dorsoduro 662, Dorsoduro* ☎ *041/5207779* ⊘ *Closed Sun.* Ⓜ *Vaporetto: Accademia, Salute, Zattere.*

★ Le Forcole di Saverio Pastor

CRAFTS | The sculpted walnut-wood oarlocks *(forcole)* used exclusively by Venetian rowers may be utilitarian, but they are beautiful, custom-made objects that make for uniquely Venetian gifts or souvenirs. Saverio Pastor (along with Paolo Brandolisio) is one of the few remaining oar and forcola makers left in Venice. ⊠ *Fondamenta Soranzo, Dorsoduro 341,*

Venetian carnival masks became popular when Carnevale was revived in the 1970s.

Dorsoduro ☎ *041/5225699* ⊕ *www.forcole.com* ⊙ *Closed Sun.* Ⓜ *Vaporetto: Salute, Accademia, Zattere.*

3D Concept

CRAFTS | Among the attractive assortment of rather generic gifts, there is a selection of complicated models to be assembled by your favorite puzzle enthusiast. Pieces of precisely laser-cut birch fit together to make 3-D objects such as a *Triceratops* or a functional zodiac clock. They are not unreasonably priced for such spectacular creations. ✉ *Crosera San Pantalon at Calle San Rocco, Dorsoduro 3812A, Dorsoduro* ☎ *347/0534982* Ⓜ *Vaporetto: San Tomà.*

JEWELRY
Gualti

JEWELRY & WATCHES | Creative earrings, brooches, and necklaces are done in colored resin that looks as fragile as glass but is as strong and soft as rubber. Silk shoes can be custom "garnished" with jewelry. ✉ *Rio Terà Canal near Campo Santa Margherita, Dorsoduro 3111, Piazza San Marco* ☎ *041/5201731*

⊕ *www.gualti.it* ⊙ *Closed Sun.* Ⓜ *Vaporetto: Ca' Rezzonico.*

LACE, LINEN, AND FABRIC
Annelie Pizzi e Ricami

OTHER SPECIALTY STORE | This lace and embroidery shop offers a highly appealing selection—from Venice and beyond—that includes fine cotton and linen tablecloths, baby clothing, shirts, nightgowns, sheets, and curtains as delightful and unique as the proprietor herself. Ask to see antique lace. ✉ *Calle Lunga San Barnaba, Dorsoduro 2748, Dorsoduro* ☎ *041/5203277* ⊙ *Closed Sun.* Ⓜ *Vaporetto: Ca' Rezzonico, Zattere.*

LEATHER GOODS
Il Grifone

HANDBAGS | Of Venice's few remaining artisan leather shops, Il Grifone is the standout with respect to quality, tradition, and the guarantee of an exquisite product. For more than 30 years, Antonio Peressin has been making bags, purses, belts, and smaller leather items that have a wide following because of his precision and attention to detail. His goods remain

Venice's Signature Crafts: Masks

When Carnevale was revived in the late 1970s, mask making returned as well, with travelers inspiring its evolution to its current ornate form. Although many workshops stick to centuries-old techniques, none has been in business for more than 55 years.

A key date in the history of Venetian masks is 1436, when the *mascareri* (mask makers) founded their guild. By then the techniques were well established: a mask is first modeled in clay, then a chalk cast is made from it and lined with papier-mâché, glue, gauze, and wax.

Masks were popular well before the mascareri's guild was established. Local laws regulating their use appeared as early as 1268, often intended to prevent people from carrying weapons when masked or in an attempt to prohibit the then-common practice of masked men disguised as women entering convents to seduce nuns. Even on religious holidays—when masks were theoretically prohibited—they were used by Venetians going to the theater or attempting to avoid identification at the city's brothels and gaming tables.

In the 18th century actors started using masks for the traditional roles of the commedia dell'arte. Arlecchino, Pantalone, Pulcinella, and company would wear leather masks designed to amplify or change their voices. It's easy to spot these masks in stores today: Arlecchino (Harlequin) has the round face and surprised expression, Pantalone has the curved nose and long mustache, and Pulcinella has the protruding nose.

The least expensive mask is the white larva, smooth and plain with a long upper lip and no chin, allowing the wearer to eat and drink without having to remove it. In the 18th century it was an integral part of the Bauta costume, composed of the larva, a black tricornered hat, and a black mantled cloak. The Moretta is the Bauta's female counterpart; she kept her oval mask on by biting down on a button inside it, thus rendering her mute.

The pretty Gnaga, which resembles a cat's face, was used by gay men to "meow" compliments and proposals to good-looking boys. The most interesting of the masks is perhaps the Medico della Peste (the Plague Doctor), with glasses and an enormous nose shaped like a bird's beak. During the plague of 1630 and 1631, doctors took protective measures against infection: as well as wearing this mask, they examined patients with a rod to avoid touching them and wore waxed coats that didn't "absorb" the disease. Inside the nose of the mask they put medical herbs and fragrances thought to filter the infected air, while the glasses protected the eyes. This mask was created by a French doctor as a serious part of the physician's equipment; it's only today that it has become a feature of fun.

Following the boom of mask shops, numerous costume rental stores opened in the 1990s. Here you'll find masks and simplified versions of 18th-century costumes. If you plan to rent a costume during Carnevale, it's a good idea to reserve several months in advance.

reasonably and accessibly priced. ✉ *Fondamenta del Gafaro, Dorsoduro 3516, Dorsoduro* ☎ *041/5229452* ⊕ *www.ilgrifonevenezia.it* ⊗ *Closed Sun. and Mon.* Ⓜ *Vaporetto: Piazzale Roma.*

MARKETS
Campo Santa Margherita
MARKET | Dorsoduro's liveliest square is the setting for a colorful morning food market. ✉ *Campo Santa Margherita, Dorsoduro* ⊗ *Closed Sun.* Ⓜ *Vaporetto: Ca' Rezzonico.*

MASKS
Ca' Macana
CRAFTS | A large showroom offering lots of gilded creations, both traditional and new, is a must-see. Ask about mask-making workshops. ✉ *Calle Cappeller, Dorsoduro 3215, Dorsoduro* ☎ *041/5203229* ⊕ *camacana.com* Ⓜ *Vaporetto: Ca' Rezzonico.*

PAPER GOODS
Il Pavone
OTHER SPECIALTY STORE | The name aptly translates as "The Peacock," and the shop offers a great selection of *coda di pavone,* a kind of paper with colors and patterns resembling peacock feathers. Artisans here are particularly proud of their hand-painted paper. ✉ *Fondamenta Venier dei Leoni, Dorsoduro 721, Dorsoduro* ☎ *041/5234517* ⊕ *www.ilpavonevenezia.com* Ⓜ *Vaporetto: Salute, Accademia.*

WINE
Cantine del Vino Già Schiavi
WINE/SPIRITS | One of Venice's finest wine bars is just as popular for the ample choice of excellent bottled wines and spirits sold to go. ✉ *Fondamenta Nani at Ponte San Trovaso, Dorsoduro 992, Dorsoduro* ☎ *041/5230034* ⊕ *www.cantinaschiavi.com* ⊗ *Closed Sun.* Ⓜ *Vaporetto: Accademia, Zattere.*

 # Activities

Cajgo Sport Shop
RUNNING | **FAMILY** | Love to run on vacation? Venice might seem the least likely place for your morning or evening mile, but shop owner Gianni Autorino offers guided tours in short and long itineraries for runners, Nordic walkers, and fitness walkers. (Pronounced kah-*ee*-go, Cajgo is Venetian for "fog.") ✉ *Calle del Vento, Dorsoduro 1517/A, Dorsoduro* ☎ *041/2413019, 393/2117310* ⊕ *www.cajgo.com* 💷 *From €59, including running shirt* ⊗ *Closed Sun.* Ⓜ *Vaporetto: San Basilio, Zattere.*

5

SAN POLO AND SANTA CROCE

Updated by
Erla Zwingle

👁 Sights
★★★★☆

🍴 Restaurants
★★★★★

🛏 Hotels
★★★★☆

👜 Shopping
★★★★☆

🍸 Nightlife
★★☆☆☆

NEIGHBORHOOD SNAPSHOT

TOP EXPERIENCES

- **Shop the Rialto markets:** Fresh fruit, vegetables, and fish abound at markets by the Rialto Bridge.

- **Admire churches:** 15th-century stunners like Santa Maria Gloriosa dei Frari grace the neighborhoods.

- **Sample *cicheti* (finger foods) at a *bacaro* (bar):** Try wine and shareable plates at the many bars and restaurants near Rialto.

- **Peruse stellar museums:** Ca' Pesaro will entertain you for an afternoon with Kandinsky and Matisse; the Scuole will take you back through Venetian history.

- **Relax on the *campo* (square):** Watch the world go by from the many open squares in these neighborhoods.

PLANNING YOUR TIME

To do San Polo justice requires at least the better part of a morning. Come early to beat the crowds for food shopping at the Rialto markets; they close at 1 pm. Next, spend an hour at Santa Maria Gloriosa dei Frari, which contains some of the most important art in Venice. Another hour should be devoted to the two floors of floor-to-ceiling Tintorettos in the Scuola Grande di San Rocco. Leave a few minutes to see the Scuola Grande San Giovanni Evangelista.

In Santa Croce, the church of San Stae is well worth a 15- to 20-minute detour, and fans of modern art will want to spend an hour in the collections in Ca' Pesaro. Any visitor who wants to see the real Venice should idle in Campo San Giacomo dall'Orio.

GETTING HERE

If you arrive by bus or car to Piazzale Roma, you will be in Santa Croce. On foot, you can walk farther into Santa Croce and, still farther along, San Polo, by following the signs pointing toward Rialto, Frari, or San Marco. To reach San Polo from the train station or Piazzale Roma, take the #1 vaporetto to Rialto Market or San Tomà (get off at Riva de Biasio or San Stae for Santa Croce). From San Marco, just walk over the Rialto Bridge. If you arrive by tour bus at Tronchetto, take the #2 to Piazzale Roma.

PAUSE HERE

- **Giardini Papadopoli.** On the Grand Canal between Piazzale Roma and the train station is this lush garden, complete with a small playground for children. Ⓜ *Vaporetto: Piazzale Roma, Ferrovia.*

- **Campo San Polo.** Sit on the benches in the shade under the trees in the square with their low, broad branches, a welcome refuge on a hot day. Ⓜ *Vaporetto: San Silvestro, San Tomà.*

VIEWFINDER

- **Campo San Stae.** Stand on the square looking across the Grand Canal to Palazzo Barbarigo, the palace facing you at the corner of a side canal. You can see several large patches of frescoes on the facade, painted by Camillo Bellini in the second half of the 1500s, a rare example of what was once common exterior decoration. Ⓜ *Vaporetto: San Stae.*

- **Sotoportego dei Oresi.** Walk along the covered passageway stretching between the Rialto Bridge and Ruga Vecchia S. Giovanni. Admire the restored frescoes in the vaults of the ceiling and what were once storerooms for the gold used by the *oresi*, or goldsmiths, whose workshops are now bars and stores. Ⓜ *Vaporetto: Rialto Mercato.*

The two smallest of Venice's six *sestieri* (districts), San Polo and Santa Croce, were named after their main churches, although the church of Santa Croce was demolished in 1810. The city's most famous bridge, the Ponte di Rialto, unites San Marco (east) with San Polo (west). The Rialto takes its name from Rivoaltus, the high ground on which it was built. You'll find some of Venice's most lauded restaurants here, and shops abound in the area closest to the bridge. On the San Marco side you'll find fashion, on the San Polo side, food.

Visitors generally explore San Polo and Santa Croce together, as there is little natural division between them; even Venetians are sometimes unaware of where one ends and the other begins. However, San Polo is most known for its concentration of bacaro and cafés near the Rialto markets, and Santa Croce is most known for its beautiful artwork at the Ca' Pesaro museum galleries.

area surrounding the western end of the Rialto Bridge, which connects San Polo with San Marco. You can shop for fruits and vegetables and buy fish along with the Venetians at the Rialto markets at the San Polo end of the bridge. If you want to go shopping but avoid the crowds around San Marco, the main route from the markets toward the train station (clearly marked) is lined with a variety of shops, particularly glass and masks.

San Polo

San Polo has three major sights, Santa Maria Gloriosa dei Frari, the Scuola Grande di San Rocco, and the Scuola Grande San Giovanni Evangelista, as well as some worthwhile but lesser-known churches. Food shops abound in the

 Sights

Campo San Polo

PLAZA/SQUARE | Only Piazza San Marco is larger than this square, and the echo of children's voices bouncing off the surrounding palaces makes the space seem even bigger. Campo San Polo once

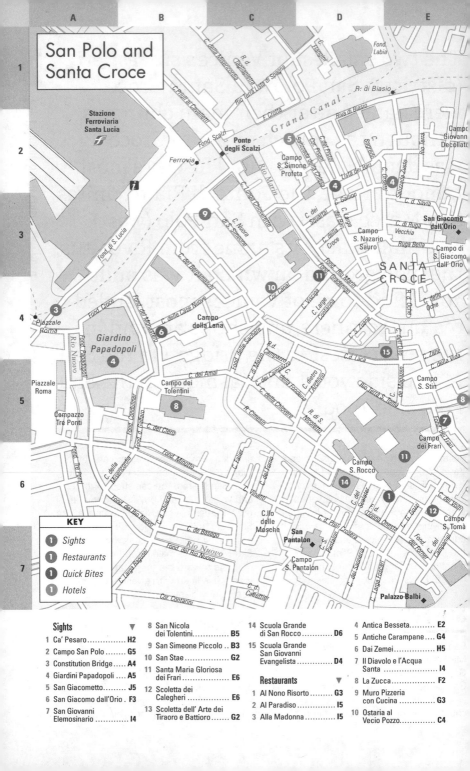

San Polo and Santa Croce

KEY

- ⬤ Sights
- ⬤ Restaurants
- ⬤ Quick Bites
- ⬤ Hotels

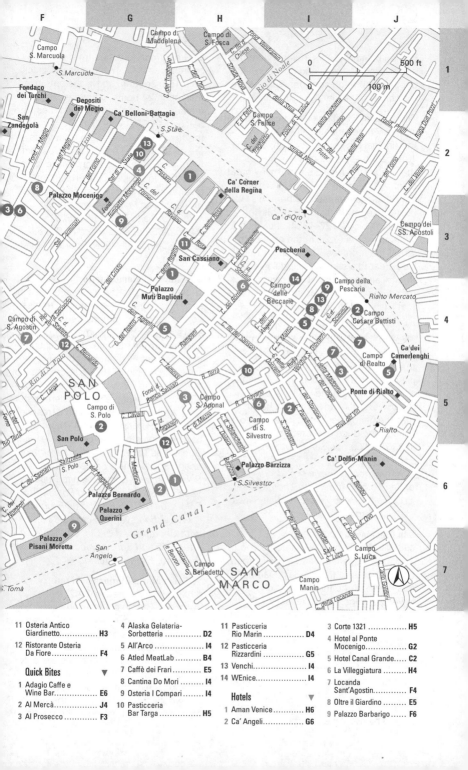

11 Osteria Antico
Giardinetto............... **H3**

12 Ristorante Osteria
Da Fiore................. **F4**

Quick Bites ▼

1 Adagio Caffe e
Wine Bar............... **E6**

2 Al Mercà................. **J4**

3 Al Prosecco **F3**

4 Alaska Gelateria-
Sorbetteria **D2**

5 All'Arco **I4**

6 Atled MeatLab **B4**

7 Caffè dei Frari **E5**

8 Cantina Do Mori **I4**

9 Osteria I Compari **I4**

10 Pasticceria
Bar Targa **H5**

11 Pasticceria
Rio Marin **D4**

12 Pasticceria
Rizzardini **G5**

13 Venchi.................... **I4**

14 WEnice................... **I4**

Hotels ▼

1 Aman Venice............ **H6**

2 Ca' Angeli................ **G6**

3 Corte 1321 .... **H5**

4 Hotel al Ponte
Mocenigo................ **G2**

5 Hotel Canal Grande..... **C2**

6 La Villeggiatura **H4**

7 Locanda
Sant'Agostin............ **F4**

8 Oltre il Giardino **E5**

9 Palazzo Barbarigo **F6**

hosted bullfights, fairs, military parades, and packed markets, and now comes especially alive on summer nights, when it's home to the city's outdoor cinema.

The Chiesa di San Polo has been restored so many times that little remains of the original 9th-century church, and the 19th-century alterations were so costly that, sadly, the friars sold off many great paintings to pay bills. Although Gianbattista Tiepolo is represented here, his work is outdone by 16 paintings by his son Giandomenico (1727–1804), including the *Stations of the Cross* in the oratory to the left of the entrance. The younger Tiepolo also created a series of expressive and theatrical renderings of the saints. Look for altarpieces by Tintoretto and Veronese that managed to escape auction.

San Polo's bell tower (begun 1362) across the street from the entrance to the church, remained unchanged over the centuries—don't miss the two lions, playing with a disembodied human head and a serpent, on the wall just above the tower's doorway. Tradition has it that the head refers to that of Marino Faliero, the doge executed for treason in 1355. ⊠ *Campo San Polo, San Polo* ☎ *041/2750462 Chorus Foundation* ⊕ *www.chorusvenezia.org* ✉ *Chiesa di San Polo €3 (free with Chorus Pass)* ⊘ *Closed Sun.* Ⓜ *Vaporetto: San Silvestro, San Tomà.*

San Giacometto

CHURCH | Officially titled San Giacomo Apostolo, but affectionately nicknamed San Giacometto ("Little Saint James"), this is one of the three oldest churches in Venice. Legend says its establishment coincides with the mythic date of Venice's founding on March 25, 421, but in fact it was built when the market was established in 1097. It's a tiny Romanesque jewel in Greek-cross form that miraculously survived the conflagration that leveled much of the Rialto area in 1514. The porch (15th century) is supported by five Veneto-Byzantine columns

of Greek marble dating from when the church was built. The impressive clock (mid-15th century) above the entrance, marked in 24 hours, governed the market's opening and closing times. The bell gable (1792) was installed to replace the tower damaged in the disastrous fire of 1514; its economical but perfectly functional style is seen on several other churches in Venice. Concerts are often given here. ⊠ *Campo San Giacomo di Rialto, San Polo* ✛ *A few steps from the Rialto bridge* ☎ *3482815492, 041/5238090 Parish office of San Silvestro, 041/5224745* Ⓜ *Vaporetto: Rialto Mercato.*

San Giovanni Elemosinario

CHURCH | Storefronts make up the facade, and market guilds—poulterers, messengers, and fodder merchants—built the altars at this church intimately bound to the Rialto markets. The original church was completely destroyed by a fire in 1514 and rebuilt in 1531 by Scarpagnino, who had also worked on the Scuola di San Rocco. During a more recent restoration, workers stumbled upon a frescoed cupola by Pordenone (1484–1539) that had been painted over centuries earlier. Don't miss Titian's *St. John the Almsgiver* and Pordenone's *Sts. Catherine, Sebastian, and Roch.* ⊠ *Rialto Ruga Vecchia San Giovanni, San Polo 480, San Polo* ☎ *041/2750462 Chorus Foundation* ⊕ *www.chorusvenezia.org* ✉ *€3 (free with Chorus Pass)* ⊘ *Closed Mon.–Sat. after 1:15 and Sun.* Ⓜ *Vaporetto: San Silvestro, Rialto Mercato.*

★ Santa Maria Gloriosa dei Frari

CHURCH | Completed in 1442, this immense Gothic church of russet-color brick, known locally as "I Frari," is famous worldwide for its array of spectacular Venetian paintings and historic tombs. It is also noteworthy for being the only important church in Italy that has preserved its elaborately carved, freestanding wooden choir in front of the high altar, a common feature in the medieval

Behind its redbrick facade, Santa Maria Gloriosa dei Frari holds some of the most brilliant artwork of any church in Venice.

period (for the use of the monks in the attached monastery, still active today).

Visit the sacristy first, to see Giovanni Bellini's 1488 triptych *Madonna and Child with Saints* in all its mellow luminosity, painted for precisely this spot. The Corner Chapel on the other side of the chancel is graced by Bartolomeo Vivarini's (1415–84) 1474 altarpiece *St. Mark Enthroned and Saints John the Baptist, Jerome, Peter, and Nicholas,* which is much more conservative, displaying an attention to detail generally associated with late medieval painting. In the first south chapel of the choir, there is a fine sculpture of St. John the Baptist by Donatello, dated 1438 (perhaps created before the artist came to Venice), which conveys a psychological intensity rare for early Renaissance sculpture. You can see the rapid development of Venetian Renaissance painting by contrasting Bellini with the heroic energy of Titian's *Assumption,* over the main altar, painted only 30 years later. Unveiled in 1518, it was the artist's first public commission

and, after causing a bit of controversy, did much to establish his reputation. Upon viewing this painting at the far end of the nave, you'll first think it has been specially spotlit: up close, however, you'll discover this impression is due to the painter's unrivaled use of light and color.

Titian's masterpiece, the *Madonna di Ca' Pesaro,* is in the left aisle. The painting took seven years to complete (finished in 1526), and in it Titian disregarded the conventions of his time by moving the Virgin out of center and making the saints active participants. The composition, built on diagonals, anticipates structural principals of Baroque painting in the following century. The work is brought to life by the unconventional gaze of young Leonardo Pesaro, who seems to look directly at the viewer.

The Frari also holds a Sansovino sculpture of St. John the Baptist and Longhena's impressive Baroque tomb designed for Doge Giovanni Pesaro. Titian, who died during the plague of 1576, is buried near his luminous *Madonna di Ca' Pesaro;* the massive marble monument

Venice's Scuola Days

An institution you'll inevitably encounter from Venice's glory days is the *scuola*. These weren't schools, as the word today translates, but important fraternal institutions. The smaller ones (*scuole piccole*) were established by different social groups—enclaves of foreigners, tradesmen, followers of a particular saint, and parishioners. The *scuole grandi*, however, were open to all citizens and included people of different occupations and ethnicities. They formed a more democratic power base than the Venetian governmental Grand Council, which was limited to nobles.

For the most part secular, despite their devotional activities, the scuole concentrated on charitable work, either helping their own membership or assisting the city's neediest citizens. The tradesmen's and servants' scuole formed social-security nets for elderly and disabled members. Wealthier scuole assisted orphans or provided dowries so poor girls could marry.

By 1500 there were more than 200 minor scuole in Venice but only six scuole grandi, some of which contributed substantially to the arts. The Republic encouraged their existence—the scuole kept strict records of the names and professions of contributors to the brotherhood, which helped when it came time to collect taxes.

to him near the main entrance was commissioned by the emperor of Austria in 1838 in recognition of the artist who had worked at the court of his forefathers. The black marble tomb of musician Claudio Monteverdi, one of the greatest composers of the 17th century, is in the chapel of the Milanese to the left of the high altar. There are always roses lying on it, left by anonymous admirers. ⊠ *Campo dei Frari, San Polo* ☎ *041/2728618, 041/2750462 Chorus Foundation* ⊕ *www. basilicadeifrari.it* ✉ *€3 (free with Chorus Pass), €1.50 for students under 30 with ID card* Ⓜ *Vaporetto: San Tomà.*

Scoletta dei Cale.gheri
ARTS CENTER | The "little scuola" of the shoemakers conducted its affairs in its headquarters in this charming building on Campo San Tomà. It is now used for community meetings and lectures open to the public, as well as small exhibitions. Most notable is the relief carving (Pietro Lombardo, 1478) above the main door that vividly portrays San Marco miraculously healing Aniano, a poor shoemaker and the scuola's patron saint. The story

goes that San Marco had arrived in Alexandria, Egypt, and was directed by the archangel Michael to go to Aniano to fix his broken sandal. He found the shoemaker in terrible pain from having injured himself with one of his tools. Marco preached the gospel to him, and then created a substance by mixing his saliva with dust from the road that healed the injury immediately. Aniano converted to Christianity and was baptized by Marco himself. ⊠ *Campo San Tomà, Calle del Traghetto 2857, San Polo* Ⓜ *Vaporetto: San Tomà.*

★ Scuola Grande di San Rocco
ART MUSEUM | This elegant example of Venetian Renaissance architecture was built between 1516 and 1549 for the essentially secular charitable confraternity bearing the saint's name. The Venetian scuole were organizations that sometimes had loose religious affiliations, through which the artisan class could exercise some influence upon civic life. San Rocco was venerated as a protector against the plague, and his scuola was one of the city's most magnificent. While

the building is bold and dramatic outside, its contents are even more stunning—a series of more than 60 paintings by Tintoretto. In 1564, Tintoretto edged out competition for a commission to decorate a ceiling by submitting not a sketch, but a finished work, which he moreover offered free of charge, calculating correctly that a gift could not be rejected. *Moses Striking Water from the Rock, The Brazen Serpent,* and *The Fall of Manna* represent three afflictions—thirst, disease, and hunger—that San Rocco, and later his brotherhood, sought to relieve.

There are also paintings by Giorgione, Titian, and Gianbattista Tiepolo. The grand staircase is flanked by two dramatic monumental paintings by Antonio Zanchi and Pietro Negri representing the Virgin saving Venice from the plague. Equally famous are the 24 wooden doors of cupboards that once contained documents in the main room. These masterpieces of low-relief carving by Giovanni Marchiori, made between 1741 and 1743, show scenes from the life of San Rocco. This was the only scuola that escaped suppression by Napoléon in 1806, and it is still active today. ⊠ *Campo San Rocco, San Polo 3052, San Polo* ☎ *041/5234864* ⊕ *www.scuolagrandesanrocco.it* ⊠ *€10* ⊘ *Closed Dec. 25 and Jan. 1* Ⓜ *Vaporetto: San Tomà.*

Scuola Grande San Giovanni Evangelista
HISTORIC SIGHT | Another of the six "great" scuole, San Giovanni Evangelista, founded in 1261, is only a few steps from the Frari and San Rocco, but undeservedly lacks the popularity of San Rocco, despite its impressive Renaissance architecture by two of the greatest architects of the 15th century (Pietro Lombardo and Mauro Codussi). The wealth of paintings by Titian, Palma il Giovane, and Giandomenico Tiepolo favor depictions of St. John's visions of the Apocalypse. The famous paintings of the "Miracles of the Reliquary of the Holy Cross," created by Giovanni Bellini in 1490 for the scuola,

are in the Accademia Gallery. The grand staircase was redesigned in 1498 by Mauro Codussi, who employed several visual tricks to make it seem larger than its small space would allow, and the mosaic marble pavement of the Salone (Giorgio Massari, 1752) is a masterpiece of the stoneworker's art. If you don't have time to visit the scuola itself, be sure to stop in its unique semi-enclosed medieval courtyard. The marble wall (Pietro Lombardo, 1481) is surmounted by a cross, eagle, and books, all symbols of St. John. The pavement (1759) echoes the designs seen on Piazza San Marco. ⊠ *Campo San Giovanni Evangelista, San Polo 2454, San Polo* ☎ *041/718234* ⊕ *www.scuolasangiovanni.it/en* ⊠ *€10* Ⓜ *Vaporetto: San Tomà, Piazzale Roma.*

🍴 Restaurants

★ Al Paradiso
$$$$ | MODERN ITALIAN | In a small dining room made warm and cozy by its pleasing and unpretentious decor, proprietor Giordano makes all diners feel like honored guests. Unlike many elegant restaurants, Al Paradiso serves generous portions, and many of the delicious *antipasti* and *primi* are quite satisfying; you may want to follow the traditional Italian way of ordering and wait until you've finished your antipasto or your *primo* before you order your *secondo*. **Known for:** central location near the Ponte di Rialto; large appetizer and pasta portions; tasty meat and fish mains. ⑤ *Average main: €40* ⊠ *Calle del Paradiso, San Polo 767, San Polo* ☎ *041/5234910* ⊕ *www. ristorantealparadiso.com* ⊘ *Closed 3 wks Jan.–Feb.* Ⓜ *Vaporetto: San Silvestro.*

Alla Madonna
$$$ | VENETIAN | "The Madonna" used to be world-famous as *the* classic Venetian trattoria, but in recent decades has settled into middle age. Owned and operated by the Rado family since 1954, this Venetian institution looks like one, with wood beams, stained-glass windows,

and a panoply of paintings on white walls. **Known for:** old-time atmosphere; freshly prepared seafood; traditional Venetian cuisine. $ *Average main: €30* ✉ *Calle della Madonna, San Polo 594, San Polo* ☎ *041/5223824* ⊕ *www.ristoranteallamadonna.com* ⊗ *Closed Wed. and Jan.* Ⓜ *Vaporetto: San Silvestro, Rialto Mercato.*

★ Antiche Carampane

$$$$ | SEAFOOD | Judging by its rather modest and unremarkable appearance, you wouldn't guess that Piera Bortoluzzi Librai's trattoria is among the finest fish restaurants in the city both because of the quality of the ingredients and because of the chef's creative magic. You can choose from a selection of classic dishes with a modern and creative touch. **Known for:** popular with visitors and locals (so book ahead); superlative fish and seafood; modernized Venetian dishes. $ *Average main: €40* ✉ *Rio Terà delle Carampane, San Polo 1911, San Polo* ☎ *041/5240165* ⊕ *www.antichecarampane.com* ⊗ *Closed Sun. and Mon., 10 days in Jan., and 3 wks July– Aug.* Ⓜ *Vaporetto: Rialto Mercato, San Silvestro.*

Il Diavolo e l'Acqua Santa

$$ | VENETIAN | Despite its name "the devil and holy water" (a common way of describing a person whose personality swings between these two extremes), this small bar and restaurant has a reliable kitchen and a homey, neighborhood atmosphere. Go on Saturday morning, when old friends tend to stop for an ombra and cicheto. **Known for:** small bites; Venetian classics like cuttlefish ink pasta; local favorite. $ *Average main: €20* ✉ *Calle della Madonna, San Polo 561, San Polo* ☎ *041/2770307* ⊗ *Closed Tues.* Ⓜ *Vaporetto: San Silvestro, Rialto Mercato.*

★ Ristorante Osteria Da Fiore

$$$$ | VENETIAN | The understated atmosphere, simple decor, and quiet elegance featured alongside Da Fiore's modern take on traditional Venetian cuisine certainly merit its international reputation. With such beautifully prepared cuisine, you would expect the kitchen to be run by a chef with a household name; however, the kitchen is headed by owner Maurizio Martin's wife, Mara, who learned to cook from her grandmother. **Known for:** reservations required; sophisticated traditional Venetian dishes; delicious tasting menus. $ *Average main: €50* ✉ *Calle del Scaleter, San Polo 2202, San Polo* ☎ *041/721308* ⊕ *www.ristorantedafiore.com* ⊗ *Closed 3 wks in Jan. and Sun. No dinner Fri. and Sat.* Ⓜ *Vaporetto: San Tomà, San Silvestro.*

☕ Coffee and Quick Bites

Adagio Caffè e Wine Bar

$ | ITALIAN | Even if this café/wine bar wasn't at one of the city's busiest intersections, on the corner between the Frari and the Scuola of San Rocco, it would be worth the trip. It's small but with an amazing variety of drinks, cicheti, and pastries, plus an energetic and welcoming atmosphere. **Known for:** central location; outdoor dining; bustling energy. $ *Average main: €10* ✉ *Salizada San Rocco, San Polo 3028, San Polo* ☎ *320/3881122* ⊕ *www.adagiocaffe.it* Ⓜ *Vaporetto: San Tomà.*

All'Arco

$ | WINE BAR | Just because it's noon and you only have enough time between sights for a sandwich doesn't mean that it can't be a satisfying, even awe-inspiring, one. There's no menu at All'Arco, but a scan of what's behind the glass counter is all you need; order what entices you, or have Roberto or Matteo (father and son) suggest a cicheto or panino. **Known for:** friendly and helpful service; top-notch cicheti; platters of meats and cheeses. $ *Average main: €8* ✉ *Calle Arco, San Polo 436, San Polo* ☎ *041/5205666* ⊗ *Closed Wed.* Ⓜ *Vaporetto: Rialto Mercato, San Silvestro.*

Al Mercà

$ | **WINE BAR** | It's easy to spot this tiny bacaro shoved into a corner of the campo adjoining Campo San Giacometto just beyond the Rialto markets: it's the one mobbed with chatty patrons—dressed in suits, jeans, or travel wear, shouldering messenger bags or backpacks, with strollers or carts loaded with market acquisitions—each with a glowing spritz or glass of wine in hand. Step up to the bar, scan the chalkboards for the lists of wines (whites on the left, reds on the right), then choose from the myriad cicheti (meat, tuna, or eggplant croquettes; crostini and panini with imaginative combos of radicchio, artichokes, fish, *sopressa* [pork salami], *ossocollo* [cured pork neck], and more) in the glass case. **Known for:** popular location; wide selection; lively atmosphere. $ *Average main: €5* ⊠ *Campo Bella Vienna già Cesare Battisti, San Polo 213, San Polo* ☎ *346/8340660* ☉ *Closed Sun.* Ⓜ *Vaporetto: Rialto Mercato.*

Caffè dei Frari

$ | **CAFÉ** | Just over the bridge in front of the Frari church is this old-fashioned place where you'll find an assortment of sandwiches and snacks, but it is the atmosphere, and not the food, that is the main attraction. Established in 1870, it's one of the last Venetian tearooms with its original decor, and while prices are a bit higher than in cafés in nearby Campo Santa Margherita, the vibe and the friendly "retro" atmosphere make the added cost worthwhile. **Known for:** quality cicheti; lovely historic setting; well-made cocktails. $ *Average main: €8* ⊠ *Fondamenta dei Frari, San Polo 2564, San Polo* ☎ *347/8293158* ⊕ *www.ilmercantevenezia.com/il-locale* ☉ *Closed Sun and Mon. No dinner* Ⓜ *Vaporetto: San Tomà.*

Cantina Do Mori

$ | **WINE BAR** | This is the original bacaro, in business continually since 1462; cramped but warm and cozy under hanging antique copper pots, it has served generations of workers from the Rialto markets. In addition to young local whites and reds, the well-stocked cellar offers reserve labels, many available by the glass; between sips you can choose to munch the wide range of cicheti on offer, or a few tiny well-stuffed tramezzini, appropriately called *francobolli* (postage stamps). **Known for:** delicious *baccalà mantecato* (creamy whipped salt cod), with or without garlic and parsley; good choice of wines by the glass; fine selection of cicheti and sandwiches. $ *Average main: €8* ⊠ *Calle dei Do Mori, San Polo 429, San Polo* ☎ *041/5225401* ☉ *Closed Sun.* Ⓜ *Vaporetto: Rialto Mercato.*

Dai Zemei

$ | **WINE BAR** | Loads of travelers happily "discover" this relatively new arrival on the bacaro scene traversing west from the Rialto markets, and a fortunate find it is. It's easy to make a light meal of the inspired bites offered here; the difficult part is choosing among crostini and panini of *lardo e rucola*, radicchio and *alici* (fresh anchovy), spicy Neapolitan sausage, and duck breast with truffle oil. **Known for:** wine list; outdoor dining; quick bites. $ *Average main: €2* ⊠ *Ruga Ravana, San Polo 1045/B, San Polo* ☎ *041/5208596* ▭ *No credit cards* ☉ *Closed Tues.* Ⓜ *Vaporetto: San Silvestro, Rialto Mercato.*

Osteria I Compari

$$ | **VENETIAN** | This small corner bar/café is a vibrant spot full of personality with a remarkable menu, thanks to the highly enterprising Simone Lazzari and his nephew, Devis. Along with a selection of tempting, original cicheti, it serves more classic Venetian bites, such as *sarde in saor* (marinated sardines), baccalà mantecato, *seppie* (cuttlefish), and *nervetti* (boiled beef cartilage with raw onions). **Known for:** neighborhood staple; cicheti; boiled octopus. $ *Average main: €20* ⊠ *Campo de la Pescaria, San Polo 255/A, San Polo* ✛ *Corner of Calle Donzella* ☎ *329/2183540* ⊕ *facebook.com/simonelazzari6* ☉ *Closed Sun.* Ⓜ *Vaporetto: Rialto Mercato.*

Pasticceria Bar Targa

$ | **ITALIAN** | **FAMILY** | You can see straight into the kitchen that churns out delectable pastries at Targa every morning. Beside the ever-present croissants are Venice's best *kipferl* (here pronounced *kee*-fer); their version of the Austrian cookie is reimagined as a flaky croissant filled with marzipan and dusted with powdered sugar. **Known for:** cookies and pastries; *frittelle* (fritters or fried doughnuts) during Carnevale; pizzas. ⑤ *Average main: €5* ✉ *Ruga Vecchia S. Giovanni, San Polo 1050, San Polo* ☎ *041/5236048* ⊘ *Closed Mon.* Ⓜ *Vaporetto: San Silvestro.*

Pasticceria Rizzardini

$ | **BAKERY** | This is not only the tiniest and prettiest pastry shop in Venice, it's also the oldest, being in almost continuous operation since 1742. It's most famous for its Venetian classics such as frittelle during Carnival, or *baicoli* and other cookies. **Known for:** a Venice institution; Zurigo (light, flaky apple pastry); *salatine* (pastry with ham or cheese and vegetables). ⑤ *Average main: €2* ✉ *Calle dei Meloni, San Polo 1415, San Polo* ☎ *041/5223835* ▭ *No credit cards* ⊘ *Closed Tues.* Ⓜ *Vaporetto: San Silvestro.*

Venchi

$ | **ICE CREAM** | One of several shops in Venice belonging to this internationally famous luxury chocolatier, Venchi was founded in Turin in 1878. Once purveyor to the royal Italian household, Venchi has now created 90 flavors of gelato and countless types of chocolates, boxed or loose, from truffles and spreads to chocolate cigars and baking products. **Known for:** gelato; chocolates; dipped ice cream cones. ⑤ *Average main: €10* ✉ *Ruga dei Spezieri, San Polo 269, San Polo* ☎ *041/2438443* ⊕ *it.venchi.com* Ⓜ *Vaporetto: Rialto Mercato.*

WEnice

$$ | **ITALIAN** | Ideal for those whose perfect meal is "lots of appetizers," this little place in the fish market is a one-stop shop for tasting many Venetian recipes. It's set up primarily for takeout, but there are a few tables with high stools. **Known for:** *fritto misto* (fried mixed seafood and vegetables); bite-size classics; closes at 3 pm. ⑤ *Average main: €15* ✉ *Calle de le Beccarie, San Polo 319, San Polo* ☎ *348/3465373, 041/8220298* ⊕ *www.wenice.it* Ⓜ *Vaporetto: Rialto Mercato.*

 ## Hotels

Aman Venice

$$$$ | **RESORT** | The restored Palazzo Papadopoli (sometimes referred to as "the place where George Clooney got married") provides its guests with sumptuous period details alongside elegant contemporary design, an expansive private garden facing the Grand Canal, a rooftop terrace, and light-filled and spacious rooms with garden or canal views. **Pros:** excellent facilities; frescoed ceilings in some rooms; stunning views from common areas. **Cons:** basic rooms don't offer much historical detail; a bit distant from San Marco; breakfast not included. ⑤ *Rooms from: €1000* ✉ *Palazzo Papadopoli, Calle Tiepolo, San Polo 1364, San Polo* ☎ *041/2707333* ⊕ *www.aman.com* ⤴ *24 rooms* ⑪ *No Meals* Ⓜ *Vaporetto: San Silvestro.*

Ca' Angeli

$$ | **B&B/INN** | **FAMILY** | The heirs of an important Venetian architect have transformed his former residence, on the third and top floors of a palace along the Grand Canal, into an elegant lodging with views of either the Grand Canal or a side canal—or in the case of the smallish Room 6, rooftops, from a terrace twice the size of the room. **Pros:** helpful staff; historic residence with Grand Canal

views; traditional yet innovative style. **Cons:** credit cards accepted only for stays of two or more nights; not central; a bit of a walk from the vaporetto stop. ⑤ *Rooms from: €200* ✉ *Calle del Traghetto de la Madoneta, San Polo 1434, San Polo* ☎ *041/5232480* ⊕ *www.caangeli.it* ➥ *8 rooms* ⑧ *Free Breakfast* Ⓜ *Vaporetto: San Silvestro.*

Corte 1321

$$ | **B&B/INN** | If you're looking to escape the 18th-century-style decor that predominates in Venetian lodging, check out these spacious, carefully renovated rooms where ceramic lamps, tapestries, and carved platform beds are combined with standard Venetian features such as beamed ceilings and parquet flooring. **Pros:** convivial, eclectic atmosphere; contemporary decor; interior courtyard. **Cons:** not super close to San Marco; can occasionally hear lively conversations in shared spaces; all rooms but one open onto the courtyard. ⑤ *Rooms from: €200* ✉ *Campiello Ca' Bernardi, San Polo 1321, San Polo* ⊹ *Just off Calle Perdon between Campo Sant'Aponal and Campo San Polo* ☎ *041/5224923* ⊕ *www.facebook.com/corte1321* ☾ *Closed Jan.* ➥ *5 rooms* ⑧ *Free Breakfast* Ⓜ *Vaporetto: San Silvestro.*

La Villeggiatura

$ | **HOTEL** | If eclectic Venetian charm is what you seek, this luminous residence near the Rialto has it: each of the individually decorated guest rooms has its own theater-theme wall painting by a local artist. **Pros:** meticulously maintained; relaxed atmosphere and friendly, personalized service; well located near markets, artistic monuments, and restaurants. **Cons:** no restaurant (though breakfast is served); no elevator and lots of stairs; no view to speak of, despite the climb. ⑤ *Rooms from: €104* ✉ *Calle dei Botteri, San Polo 1569, San Polo* ☎ *041/5244673* ⊕ *www.lavilleggiatura.it* ➥ *6 rooms*

⑧ *Free Breakfast* Ⓜ *Vaporetto: Rialto Mercato.*

Locanda Sant'Agostin

$$ | **B&B/INN** | You'll find enough classic Venetian characteristics to remind you of where you are, but not so many as to be stuffy or ostentatious. **Pros:** good location near the Frari; tranquil atmosphere; attentive service; authentic period renovation. **Cons:** no Wi-Fi in rooms; no elevator (but all rooms are only one flight up); a bit of a walk from the vaporetto stop. ⑤ *Rooms from: €195* ✉ *Campo Sant'Agostin, San Polo 2344, San Polo* ☎ *041/8223645* ⊕ *locandasantagostin.italia-it.info/en* ➥ *10 rooms* ⑧ *Free Breakfast* Ⓜ *Vaporetto: San Tomà, San Silvestro, San Stae.*

★ Oltre il Giardino

$$$ | **HOTEL** | Behind a brick wall, just over the bridge from the Frari church, this palazzo is hard to find but well worth the effort: a sheltered location, large garden, and individually decorated guest rooms make it feel like a country house. **Pros:** friendly owners happy to share their Venice tips; glorious walled garden; peaceful, gracious, and convenient setting. **Cons:** rooms book up quickly; a beautiful, but not particularly Venetian, ambience; no in-house restaurant (though breakfast served). ⑤ *Rooms from: €218* ✉ *Fondamenta Contarini, San Polo 2542, San Polo* ☎ *041/2750015* ⊕ *www.oltreilgiardino-venezia.com* ☾ *Closed Jan.* ➥ *6 rooms* ⑧ *Free Breakfast* Ⓜ *Vaporetto: San Tomà.*

Palazzo Barbarigo

$$$ | **HOTEL** | This former palace was formally named Palazzo Barbarigo della Terrazza because of its unique open-air terrace. **Pros:** an uncommon ambience; intimate; lavish. **Cons:** at times, unpleasant odors waft from the side canal; standard rooms have pleasant side canal, but not Grand Canal, views. ⑤ *Rooms from: €300* ✉ *Calle Corner, San Polo 2765, San Polo* ☎ *041/740172*

palazzobarbarigo.com 🛏 *14 rooms*
🍴 *Free Breakfast* Ⓜ *Vaporetto: San Tomà.*

 Nightlife

BARS
★ Il Mercante
COCKTAIL LOUNGES | When the clock strikes 6 pm, historic Caffè dei Frari transforms into this lively craft cocktail bar that will dazzle your inner adventurer. Relax on a velvet sofa while savoring remarkably inventive drinks paired with flavorful small bites. Each pairing has a distinctive name; "Amatriciana" is composed of vodka, dry vermouth, and black tea, served with Parmesan foam, pineapple gel, and balsamic vinegar (billed as "strong, smoky, tasty"). ✉ *Fondamenta dei Frari, San Polo 2564, San Polo* ☎ *347/8293158* ⊕ *www.ilmercantevenezia.com* ⊙ *Closed Sun.* Ⓜ *Vaporetto: San Tomà.*

Naranzaria
BARS | At the friendliest of the several bar-restaurants that line the Erbaria, near the Rialto markets, enjoy a cocktail outside, along the Canal Grande, or at a cozy table inside the renovated 16th-century warehouse. Although the food is acceptable, the ambience is really the main attraction. After the kitchen closes at 10:30, light snacks are served until midnight, and there is live music (usually jazz, Latin, or rock) occasionally on Sunday evening. On summer evenings, especially the weekend, the market area draws crowds of young people from Venice, the lagoon islands, and the mainland. ✉ *L'Erbaria, San Polo 130, San Polo* ☎ *041/7241035* ⊕ *www.naranzaria.it* Ⓜ *Vaporetto: Rialto Mercato.*

🛍 Shopping

CLOTHING
Emilio Ceccato
OTHER SPECIALTY STORE | This shop selling gondolier's garb has been at the foot of the Rialto Bridge since 1902. There are no cheap knockoffs here; the wool sweaters, straw hats, and down vests are all worn by working gondoliers and made of quality materials intended to withstand a long day out in all weather. A charming selection of gifts, such as tote bags, stuffed toys, refrigerator magnets, and so forth, all bear the crest of the gondoliers' association. ✉ *Sotoportego degli Oresi, San Polo 16/17, at the foot of the Rialto bridge, San Polo* ☎ *041/3198826* ⊕ *emilioceccato.com/en* Ⓜ *Vaporetto: Rialto Mercato.*

Zazù
MIXED CLOTHING | Clothing and accessories here have a definite Eastern feel. Owner Federica Zamboni is also a jewelry expert; ask to see her collection of antique Indian necklaces and earrings. ✉ *Calle dei Saoneri, San Polo 2750, San Polo* ☎ *041/715426* ⊙ *Closed Sun.* Ⓜ *Vaporetto: San Tomà.*

COSTUMES AND ACCESSORIES
Atelier Pietro Longhi
MIXED CLOTHING | Costumes for sale or rent are inspired by 18th- and 19th-century models, with masks (for sale only) to match. Large sizes are available for both sexes. By appointment only, but well worth the effort. ✉ *Campo San Polo 2454, San Polo* ☎ *3289706572* ⊕ *www.pietrolonghi.com* Ⓜ *Vaporetto: San Tomà.*

★ Il Tabarro San Marco di Monica Daniele
OTHER SPECIALTY STORE | This petite shop is the best place in town to find traditional Venetian wool capes, known as *tabarro*, and classic hats, such as the Ezra Pound (curved hat with a brim), the *tricorno* (three-cornered hat), and the *cilindro* (top hat). ✉ *Calle del Scaleter, San Polo 2235, San Polo* ☎ *041/5246242, 375/5355420* ⊕ *www.monicadaniele.com* Ⓜ *Vaporetto: San Stae, San Silvestro.*

GIFTS
Il Baule Blu
SOUVENIRS | The "Blue Trunk" specializes in antique toys of all sorts, but their *orsi artistici*, mohair teddy bears, are their trademark treasures. Painstakingly

handmade in many sizes and colors with articulated paws and glass eyes, they can either grumble or play a carillon tune when squeezed. Some are unclothed; others are dressed in old baby garments trimmed with lace and ribbons. ⊠ *Calle del Traghetto, San Polo 2916/A, San Polo* ☎ *041/719448* ⊘ *Closed Sun.* Ⓜ *Vaporetto: San Tomà.*

Sabbie e Nebbie

SOUVENIRS | The Japanese aesthetic is quite apparent in the ceramic and porcelain bowls, plates, vases, and teapots, with inviting clean, natural lines and muted colors, of artist-owner Maria Teresa Laghi and her collaborators. Her silk scarves are just as appealing. ⊠ *Calle dei Nomboli, San Polo 2768/A, San Polo* ☎ *041/719073* ⊘ *Closed Sun.* Ⓜ *Vaporetto: San Tomà.*

GOLD, WOOD, AND METALWORK
Gilberto Penzo

CRAFTS | The gondola and lagoon boat expert in Venice creates scale models of a wide variety of Venetian boats in his nearby *laboratorio* (workshop). (If the retail shop is closed, a sign posted on the door will explain how to find Signor Penzo.) When he's not busy sawing and sanding, Mr. Penzo writes historical and technical books about traditional Venetian boats, including the gondola. Here you'll also find gondola model kits, as well as some *forcole* (Venetian rowing oarlocks). ⊠ *Calle Seconda dei Saoneri, San Polo 2681, San Polo* ☎ *041/5246139* ⊕ *www. veniceboats.com* ⊘ *Closed Sun.* Ⓜ *Vaporetto: San Tomà.*

JEWELRY
Attombri

JEWELRY & WATCHES | Celebrated brothers Daniele and Stefano blend and weave copper and silver wire with Murano glass beads to render stylish, contemporary pieces with a timeless feel. ⊠ *Sotoportego dei Oresi, San Polo 65, San Polo* ☎ *041/5212524* ⊕ *www.attombri. com* ⊘ *Closed Sun.* Ⓜ *Vaporetto: Rialto Mercato.*

Gems of Venice

JEWELRY & WATCHES | Name a gemstone—aquamarine, garnet, jade, amber, opal—and you will almost certainly find it here, in both classic and unique settings from traditional to gorgeous. This is the ideal place to find a special piece featuring your birthstone. ⊠ *Rugheta Ravano, San Polo 1044, San Polo* ☎ *041/5225148* ⊕ *www.gemsofvenice.it* Ⓜ *Vaporetto: San Silvestro, Rialto Mercato.*

Il Mercante di Sabbia

JEWELRY & WATCHES | French-born owner-designer Claudia Puschi travels across Europe to fill her store with eclectic and intriguing home accessories and jewelry. Her unique items can't be found anywhere else in the city; in fact, she herself designed many of the purses you'll see in the store—which she deftly and stylishly transformed from a former butcher shop. ⊠ *Calle Seconda dei Saoneri, San Polo 2724, San Polo* ☎ *041/5243865* ⊕ *ilmercantedisabbia.com/en* Ⓜ *Vaporetto: San Tomà.*

★ Laberintho

JEWELRY & WATCHES | A tiny bottega near Campo San Polo is run by a team of young goldsmiths and jewelry designers specializing in inlaid stones and mosaic tesserae. The work on display in their shop is exceptional, and they also create customized pieces. ⊠ *Calle del Scaleter, San Polo 2236, San Polo* ☎ *041/710017* ⊕ *www.laberintho.com* ⊘ *Closed Sun.* Ⓜ *Vaporetto: San Tomà.*

LACE, LINEN, AND FABRIC
Cenerentola

CRAFTS | "Cinderella" creates unique handmade lampshades out of silk, old lace, and real parchment, embroidered and decorated with gold braids and cotton or silk trim. It also sells restored lace and embroidered vintage clothing. The pieces on display are a perfect match for country- and antique-style furniture. The owner will be happy to discuss special orders. ⊠ *Calle dei Saoneri, San Polo 2718/A, San Polo* ☎ *348/2263559,*

041/4256386 ⊕ *cenerentoladisimona-*
tomartina.it ⊘ *Closed Sun.* Ⓜ *Vaporetto: San Tomà.*

LEATHER GOODS
Fanny Gloves
LEATHER GOODS | Run by a family of market stall sellers, Fanny combines good value, friendly service, and cheerful design. Come here for an exceptional selection of soft leather gloves as well as leather and suede bags. ✉ *Calle Seconda dei Saoneri, San Polo 2723, San Polo* ☎ *041/5228266* ⊕ *www.fannygloves.it* Ⓜ *Vaporetto: San Tomà.*

Francis Model
LEATHER GOODS | A tiny workshop specializes in superb handmade leather bags in all shapes and sizes. The craftsmanship is exceptional; get Bottega Veneta look-alikes at half the price. ✉ *Rughetta Ravaño, San Polo 773/A, San Polo* ☎ *041/5212889* ⊕ *www.francismodel.it* Ⓜ *Vaporetto: San Silvestro.*

MARKETS
Drogheria Mascari
OTHER SPECIALTY STORE | Since 1948 the Mascari family has been selling a wide range of treats, such as bits of dried sugared fruit, balsamic vinegar, chestnut flour, fennel seeds, Swiss chocolate, honey, olive oil, and an exceptional collection of Italian wines and liquors. Try some traditional cookies from many different Italian regions, including *baicoli*, the crunchy Venetian dipping cookie. If nothing else, you will almost certainly stop to admire the window full of pyramids of loose spices, a vibrant reminder that much of Venice's wealth derived from the spice trade. ✉ *Ruga dei Spezieri, San Polo 381, San Polo* ☎ *041/5229762* ⊕ *www.imascari.com* ⊘ *Closed Sun.* Ⓜ *Vaporetto: Rialto Mercato.*

Rialto markets
MARKET | **FAMILY** | The Rialto fish, fruit, and vegetable markets have been operational in this same location for more than a thousand years. It's a food potpourri;

scan the stalls to see what you might be dining on during your stay (or better yet, rent an apartment and experiment yourself). Look for the word "nostrano" when shopping to identify the most local fish and produce. For enthusiasts of seppie (cuttlefish), be aware that the older the fish is, the more black ink will be covering it. ✉ *Campiello della Pescheria, San Polo* ⊘ *Fish stalls closed Mon.* Ⓜ *Vaporetto: Rialto Mercato.*

MASKS
L'Arlecchino
CRAFTS | This tiny shop contains an abundance of masks made of papier-mâché, but Marilisa Dal Cason's skill and imagination shine best in her original creations made of cut-up resin masks (the plain white ones on sale everywhere for €1), which she ingeniously reshapes and paints into fantastic forms. From an octopus to flames covered with gold leaf, every shape is unique. Considering that each is one of a kind, her masks, though somewhat expensive, are possibly the most economical purchase of Venetian art you'll make. ✉ *Ruga Vecchia S. Giovanni, San Polo 789, San Polo* ☎ *041/5208220* ⊕ *www.arlecchino-masks.com* Ⓜ *Vaporetto: San Silvestro.*

★ La Bottega dei Mascareri
CRAFTS | Despite the great popularity of the Venetian Carnevale, mask-making is a dying art in the city. The large majority of masks for sale in the shops and kiosks of Venice are kitsch made in Asia and have little (if any) relationship to the popular local tradition. A shining exception is Sergio and Massimo Boldrin's Bottega dei Mascareri. Staunch traditionalists, the Boldrin brothers recreate beautiful and historically accurate versions of the masks of the Venetian commedia dell'arte. They have also carefully extended their repertoire to include masks inspired by characters in Tiepolo's paintings, thereby inventing new masks while remaining true to the spirit of 18th-century Carnevale. A mask from Bottega is

about as close to the "real thing" as you can get. ⊠ *Ruga dei Oresi at the foot of the Rialto Bridge, San Polo 80, San Polo* ☎ *041/5223857* ⊕ *www.mascarer.com* Ⓜ *Vaporetto: Rialto Mercato.*

Tragicomica

CRAFTS | This store has arguably the best selection, in both quality and quantity, of handmade masks in Venice. Gualtiero Dall'Osto studied art at the Accademia and is a trove of historical information as well as an excellent source of information about Carnevale parties. The shop also turns out a limited number of costumes made from hand-printed cotton fabric. ⊠ *Rio terà dei Nomboli, San Polo 2800, San Polo* ☎ *041/721102* ⊕ *www.tragicomica.it* ⊗ *Closed Sun.* Ⓜ *Vaporetto: San Tomà.*

PAPER GOODS

Carterìa ai Frari

OTHER SPECIALTY STORE | Elisabetta and Stefano, with their daughter, Giulia, founded this shop in 2008 and have made it one of the city's most remarkable sources for handmade paper and an astonishing variety of objects made from it. Their handiwork always combines charm, style, and imagination. ⊠ *Calle Larga Prima, San Polo 2954, San Polo* ☎ *041/5242619* ⊕ *carteriaaifrari.it* ⊗ *Closed Sun.* Ⓜ *Vaporetto: San Tomà.*

Legatoria Polliero

BOOKS | One of Venice's oldest, and certainly most renowned, bookbinders is in the expert hands of Anselmo Polliero, the third generation of his family to create beautiful leather-bound blank books, desk accessories, picture frames, and more. He also prints serigraphs of Venetian views, and prints designs on paper using antique woodcut blocks. ⊠ *Campo dei Frari, San Polo 2995, San Polo* ☎ *041/5285130* ⊕ *facebook.com/LegatoriaPolliero* ⊗ *Closed Sun.* Ⓜ *Vaporetto: San Tomà.*

Santa Croce

Santa Croce's two important churches are San Stae on the Grand Canal and San Nicola dei Tolentini, near Piazzale Roma. The quarter's most pleasing architectural assemblage is the Campo San Giacomo dall'Orio, one of Venice's liveliest squares. Having a spritz or a coffee in the pretty campo is an excellent alternative to doing the same in one of the packed squares in San Marco or Dorsoduro. The rooms in Ca' Pesaro museum on the Grand Canal fill out Venice's offering of modern art and present the only public collection of Asian art in the city.

Sights

Ca' Pesaro

ART MUSEUM | Baldassare Longhena's grand Baroque palace, begun in 1676, is the beautifully restored home of two impressive collections. The Galleria Internazionale d'Arte Moderna has works by 19th- and 20th-century artists, such as Klimt, Kandinsky, Matisse, and Miró. It also has a collection of representative works from the Venice Biennale that amounts to a panorama of 20th-century art. The pride of the Museo Orientale is its collection of Japanese art—and especially armor and weapons—of the Edo period (1603–1868). It also has a small but striking collection of Chinese and Indonesian porcelains and musical instruments. ⊠ *Fondamenta Pesaro, Santa Croce 2076, Santa Croce* ☎ *041/721127 Galleria, 041/5241173 Museo Orientale* ⊕ *capesaro.visitmuve.it* ⊠ *€10, includes both museums* ⊗ *Closed Mon.–Wed.* Ⓜ *Vaporetto: San Stae.*

Constitution Bridge

BRIDGE | Commonly referred to as the "Calatrava Bridge" after its designer, Santiago Calatrava, this swooping modern arch crossing the Grand Canal connects Piazzale Roma to the train station. Opinions have differed wildly on its aesthetic

Giardini Papadopoli is a leafy garden oasis in Santa Croce.

ever since its inauguration in 2008, but no one can deny its long-overdue usefulness—as many as 5,000 people a day cross it when arriving, departing, or daily commuting. It has become notorious for its structural flaws, most notably slippery steps made of Murano glass that are now in the process of being replaced by concrete. Whatever your thoughts on its beauty, the views from its graceful summit are always engaging. ⊠ *Ponte della Costituzione, Santa Croce* Ⓜ *Vaporetto: Piazzale Roma, Ferrovia.*

Giardini Papadopoli
GARDEN | **FAMILY** | Located between Piazzale Roma and the train station, this lush oasis was created in the 1830s by demolishing the former monastery of Santa Croce. A tranquil place to sit in the shade, the gardens feature flowers, large, leafy trees, and a small playground for children. Pause to admire the marble statue of civil engineer Pietro Paleòcapa; not a Venetian, but one of the great 19th-century hydraulic engineers modifying rivers and swamps in Italy and Europe. He served in Venice as Director of Public Works and crowned his career by collaborating with Luigi Negrelli in the planning of the Suez Canal. ⊠ *Santa Croce* ☏ *041/2748111* ⊕ *www.comune. venezia.it* Ⓜ *Vaporetto: Piazzale Roma, Ferrovia.*

San Giacomo dall'Orio
PLAZA/SQUARE | This lovely square was named after a laurel tree (*orio*), and today trees lend it shade and character. Add benches and a fountain (with a drinking bowl for dogs), and the pleasant, oddly shaped campo becomes a welcoming place for friendly conversation and neighborhood kids at play. The church of San Giacomo dall'Orio was founded in the 9th century on an island still populated (the legend goes) by wolves. The current church dates from 1225; its short, unmatched Byzantine columns survived renovation during the Renaissance, and the church never lost the feel of an ancient temple sheltering beneath its 14th-century ship's-keel roof. In the sanctuary, large marble crosses are

Inside the San Stae church, you can see artwork by Tiepolo, Ricci, and Piazzetta.

surrounded by a group of small medieval Madonnas. The altarpiece is *Madonna with Child and Saints* (1546) by Lorenzo Lotto (1480–1556), and the sacristy contains 12 works by Palma il Giovane (circa 1544–1628). ⊠ *Campo San Giacomo dall'Orio, Santa Croce* ☎ *041/2750462 Chorus Foundation* ⊕ *www.chorusvenezia.org* ⌨ *Church €3 (free with Chorus Pass)* ⊙ *Church closed Sun.* Ⓜ *Vaporetto: San Stae, Riva de Biasio.*

San Nicola dei Tolentini

CHURCH | Officially named "San Nicola da Tolentino," Vincenzo Scamozzi's Baroque building (1602; facade 1714 by Andrea Tirali) is named for Saint Nicholas as venerated in the town of Tolentino in the Marche region of Italy. A black cannonball is stuck into the wall just to the right of the front door as you enter the church; this is a relic of the Austrian bombardment during the failed Venetian uprising in 1848. It didn't land here by itself, but was placed here as a memorial; an identical cannonball is on the facade of the

church of San Salvador. It has a squad of doges' tombs: Giovanni I Cornaro (d. 1629), his son Francesco Cornaro (d. 1656), Giovanni II Cornaro (d. 1722), and Paolo Renier (d. 1789). The adjoining monastery now serves as a branch of IUAV, the University of Architecture. ⊠ *Campo dei Tolentini, Santa Croce 265, Santa Croce* ☎ *041/2728611* ⊙ *Closed Thurs.* Ⓜ *Vaporetto: Piazzale Roma.*

San Simeone Piccolo

CHURCH | Built in 1738 by Giovanni Antonio Scalfarotto, this neoclassical behemoth is the first thing you see when you exit the train station. It makes a breathtaking first impression, though it's obvious that its proportions are very unbalanced. When Napoléon saw it, he famously quipped, "I've seen churches with domes before, but this is the first time I've seen a dome with a church." It is open daily but only for mass at 11 am, conducted in Latin according to the Roman ritual. It is under the care of FSSP (Fraternità Sacerdotale San

Pietro), a missionary confraternity of priests. ⊠ *Santa Croce 698, Santa Croce* ✛ *Facing the train station* ☎ *348/9353936* ⊕ *venezia.fssp.it/chiesa* Ⓜ *Vaporetto: Piazzale Roma, Ferrovia.*

San Stae

CHURCH | The church of San Stae—the Venetian name for Sant'Eustachio (St. Eustace)—was reconstructed in 1687 by Giovanni Grassi and given a new facade in 1707 by Domenico Rossi. Renowned Venetian painters and sculptors of the early 18th century decorated this church around 1717 with the legacy left by Doge Alvise II Mocenigo, who's buried in the center aisle. San Stae affords a good opportunity to see the early works of Gianbattista Tiepolo, Sebastiano Ricci, and Piazzetta, as well as those of the previous generation of Venetian painters, with whom they had studied. ⊠ *Campo San Stae, Santa Croce* ☎ *041/2750462 Chorus Foundation* ⊕ *www.chorusvenezia.org* 🎟 *€3 (free with Chorus Pass)* 🕙 *Closed Sun.* Ⓜ *Vaporetto: San Stae.*

Scoletta dell'Arte dei Tiraoro e Battioro

NOTABLE BUILDING | The charming rust-color building tucked beside the church of San Stae was the headquarters of the gold guild, including the gold "pullers" (gold wire and thread) and gold beaters (gold leaf). Although it was a very old guild, it was one of the smallest (only 48 members); their building was constructed only in 1711, and closed in 1798, a year after the fall of the Venetian Republic. After changing hands several times, in the early 20th century it became the property of a Venetian antiques dealer, whose family still owns it today. While it is not open to the public, the building is used for elegant private events. ⊠ *Campo San Stae, Santa Croce 1980, Santa Croce* ☎ *041/2750606* ⊕ *www.scolettabattioro.it/en* Ⓜ *Vaporetto: San Stae.*

 Restaurants

Al Nono Risorto

$$$ | VENETIAN | FAMILY | This friendly trattoria popular with the locals is only a short walk from the Rialto markets. The pizza—not a Venetian specialty, generally speaking—is pretty good here, but the star attractions are the generous appetizers and excellent shellfish pastas. **Known for:** pretty outdoor garden seating; traditional starters and pastas; quite tasty pizzas. ⑤ *Average main: €25* ⊠ *Sotoportego de Siora Bettina, Santa Croce 2338, Santa Croce* ☎ *041/5241169* ⊕ *alnonorisortovenezia.com* 🕙 *Closed Wed. and Jan.* Ⓜ *Vaporetto: Rialto Mercato.*

Antica Besseta

$$$ | VENETIAN | Tucked away in a quiet corner of Santa Croce, with a few tables under an ivy shelter, the Antica Besseta dates from the 19th century, and it retains some of its old feel. The menu focuses on vegetables and fish, according to what's at the market, with some pasta and meat dishes, too. **Known for:** charming old-fashioned feel; classic Italian pastas, like spaghetti *con vongole* (with clams); simple menu of fish and meat choices. ⑤ *Average main: €35* ⊠ *Salizzada de Ca' Zusto, Santa Croce 1395, Santa Croce* ☎ *041/721687* ⊕ *www.anticabesseta.it* 🕙 *Closed Tues.* Ⓜ *Vaporetto: Riva de Biasio.*

La Zucca

$$$ | NORTHERN ITALIAN | Simple place settings, wood lattice walls, and a mélange of languages make La Zucca (The Pumpkin) feel much like a typical, somewhat sophisticated vegetarian restaurant that you could find in any European city. What makes La Zucca special is simply great cooking and the use of fresh, local ingredients—many of which, like the particularly sweet zucca itself, aren't normally found outside northern

Italy. **Known for:** flan di zucca, a luscious pumpkin pudding topped with aged ricotta cheese; seasonal vegetarian-focused dishes; home-style Italian cooking. ⑤ *Average main: €25* ⊠ *Calle del Tentor, at Ponte del Megio, Santa Croce 1762, Santa Croce* ☎ *041/5241570* ⊕ *www. lazucca.it* ☉ *Closed Sun.* Ⓜ *Vaporetto: San Stae.*

Muro Pizzeria con Cucina

$$$ | **ITALIAN** | **FAMILY** | Don't let the name *pizzeria con cucina* fool you: Muro offers its mostly youthful clientele a varied menu and uses high-quality ingredients, taking its cue from its more refined sister restaurant, Muro Rialto. Select from excellent Venetian fare and pizza in classic and innovative forms—try the *arrotolata amoretesoro* (a rolled pizza) with *bresaola* (thinly sliced air-cured beef), *scamorza* (a delicately flavored melting cheese made from cow's milk), and radicchio. **Known for:** *piatti unici* (one-dish meals); rolled pizza; beer on tap. ⑤ *Average main: €30* ⊠ *Campiello dello Spezier, Santa Croce 2048, Santa Croce* ☎ *041/5241628* ⊕ *www.murovenezia. com* Ⓜ *Vaporetto: San Stae.*

Ostaria al Vecio Pozzo

$$ | **ITALIAN** | **FAMILY** | This friendly neighborhood restaurant named for the old well nearby offers a wide selection of favorite Italian dishes. The pizza is made with locally milled flour that is left to mature for two days, and the pasta is handmade every day. **Known for:** seasonal pizza toppings like truffle and pumpkin; outdoor dining; local favorite. ⑤ *Average main: €20* ⊠ *Corte Canal, Santa Croce 656, Santa Croce* ☎ *041/5242760* ⊕ *www.veciopozzo.it* ☉ *Closed Sun.* Ⓜ *Vaporetto: Piazzale Roma.*

Osteria Antico Giardinetto

$$$$ | **ITALIAN** | The name refers to the intimate garden where co-owner Larisa will welcome you warmly, once you've wound your way from the Rialto or San Stae down the narrow calle to this romantic locale. (There's an indoor dining room as well, but the garden is covered and heated in winter.) Larisa's husband, Virgilio, mans the kitchen, where he prepares such dishes as sea bass in salt crust and a grilled fish platter. Be sure to try the homemade gnocchi or pasta—perhaps the *tagliolini* (thin spaghetti) with scallops and artichokes. **Known for:** romantic garden setting; homemade gnocchi; regional wines. ⑤ *Average main: €40* ⊠ *Calle dei Morti, Santa Croce 2253, Santa Croce* ☎ *041/5240325* ⊕ *www. anticogiardinetto.it* ☉ *Closed Mon. and Jan. 4–31* Ⓜ *Vaporetto: San Stae.*

☕ Coffee and Quick Bites

Al Prosecco

$$ | **WINE BAR** | Locals drop into this friendly bacaro to explore wines from this region and elsewhere in Italy, which accompany a carefully chosen selection of meats, cheeses, and other food from small, artisanal producers, used in tasty panini like the *porchetta romane verdure* (roasted pork with greens) and in elegant cold platters. A young, friendly staff reel off the day's specials with ease. **Known for:** outdoor seating on the lively campo; lovely meat and cheese platters; great selection of biodynamic wines, including prosecco. ⑤ *Average main: €20* ⊠ *Campo San Giacomo dall'Orio, Santa Croce 1503, Santa Croce* ☎ *041/5240222* ⊕ *www.alprosecco.com* ☉ *Closed Sun.* Ⓜ *Vaporetto: San Stae.*

Alaska Gelateria-Sorbetteria

$ | ICE CREAM | This shop whips up delicious gelato completely from scratch, and is endlessly experimenting with imaginative flavors. Combine a tried-and-true favorite with, say, asparagus, fennel, or pistachio. **Known for:** inventive flavors; homemade ice cream; creative toppings. $ Average main: €2 ⊠ Calle Larga dei Bari, Santa Croce 1159, Santa Croce ☎ 041/715211 Ⓜ Vaporetto: Riva de Biasio.

Atled MeatLab

$ | AMERICAN | If you need a break from Venice's abundant fish and pasta, head to this smokehouse for barbecue ribs, smoked pulled pork, pastrami, and chicken gyro. Vegetarians and vegans will enjoy the smoked eggplant with hummus on a bun, fried jalapeños, and more. **Known for:** Texas-style barbecue; pulled pork; veggie options. $ Average main: €10 ⊠ Fondamenta dei Tolentini, Santa Croce 220, Santa Croce ☎ 041/4588914 ⊕ atled-meat-lab.business.site ⊗ Closed Tues. Ⓜ Vaporetto: Piazzale Roma, Ferrovia.

Pasticceria Rio Marin

$ | BAKERY | Besides the usual selection of small pastries and drinks, you can enjoy a piece of crostata di marroni (chestnut tart) or spicy cookies made with chili at one of the tables along a quiet canal. **Known for:** relaxed atmosphere; cookies and small bites; canal setting. $ Average main: €4 ⊠ Fondamenta Rio Marin, Santa Croce 784, Santa Croce ☎ 041/718523 ⊟ No credit cards Ⓜ Vaporetto: Riva de Biasio.

Hotels

★ Hotel al Ponte Mocenigo

$ | HOTEL | At this hotel—once home to the Santa Croce branch of the Mocenigo family, which counts a few doges in its lineage—a columned courtyard welcomes you, and guest room decor nods to the building's history, with canopied beds, striped damask fabrics, lustrous terrazzo flooring, and gilt-accented furnishings. **Pros:** enchanting courtyard (the perfect spot for an aperitivo [aperitif, or pre-meal drink]); fantastic value; friendly and helpful staff. **Cons:** standard rooms are small; beds are on the hard side; rooms in the annex can be noisy. $ Rooms from: €110 ⊠ Salizzada San Stae, Santa Croce 1985, Santa Croce ☎ 041/5244797 ⊕ www.alpontemocenigo.com ⇌ 11 rooms �(○)| Free Breakfast Ⓜ Vaporetto: San Stae.

Hotel Canal Grande

$$$$ | HOTEL | Conveniently near the train station, this small hotel couples 18th-century elegance with modern amenities; the decoration, inspired by Venetian history, includes lush damasks, gold-framed mirrors, and plenty of Murano glass and Rezzonico-style floors. **Pros:** free Wi-Fi; Grand Canal views; helpful and informative staff; excellent position for those traveling by train. **Cons:** far from Piazza San Marco; a little on the pricey side. $ Rooms from: €310 ⊠ Campo San Simeone Grande, Santa Croce 932, Santa Croce ☎ 041/2440148 ⊕ www.hotelcanalgrande.it ⇌ 22 rooms �(○)| Free Breakfast Ⓜ Vaporetto: Riva de Biasio.

Shopping

La Margherita Venezia

CERAMICS | Margherita Rossetto has been creating unique, deliciously appealing faience-style majolica since 1989. Pieces include figures of animals, flowers, and fruit as well as abstract designs on a white background. She also fashions handmade greeting cards that are one-of-a-kind works of art in themselves. ⊠ *Corte Canal near Campo de la Lana, Santa Croce 659, Santa Croce* ☎ *393/2100272* ⊕ *www.lamargheritavenezia.com* Ⓜ *Vaporetto: Riva de Biasio, Piazzale Roma.*

La Mascareta

CRAFTS | This tiny shop is overflowing with masks of all types, all handmade by the owner/artisan (you can often watch him making them). There's an excellent selection of styles at competitive prices. ⊠ *Calle del Tentor, Santa Croce 2100, Santa Croce* ☎ *041/8221229* Ⓜ *Vaporetto: San Stae, Rialto Mercato.*

Mare di Carta

BOOKS | FAMILY | Since 1997 the "Sea of Paper" has been Venice's best book and gift shop devoted to nautical themes. Books, calendars, navigation charts, and instruments, plus postcards, prints, toys, children's books and games, and even bags made of old sails are among the treasures you'll find here. There is also a wide variety of books on the Venetian lagoon and traditional Venetian boats. ⊠ *Fondamenta dei Tolentini, Santa Croce 222, Santa Croce* ☎ *041/716304* ⊕ *maredicarta.com/libreria-nautica-a-venezia* ⊗ *Closed Sun.* Ⓜ *Vaporetto: Piazzale Roma.*

Chapter 6

CANNAREGIO

Updated by
Nick Bruno

👁 Sights	🍴 Restaurants	🧳 Hotels	💼 Shopping	🍸 Nightlife
★★★★☆	★★★★☆	★★★★☆	★★★★☆	★★★★☆

NEIGHBORHOOD SNAPSHOT

TOP EXPERIENCES

■ **Visit the Jewish Ghetto.** Learn about the fascinating and moving history of the Ghetto, an emblematic place in Jewish identity and a lesson for humanity.

■ **Walk in Tintoretto's footsteps.** The *calli* (streets) and *campi* (squares) of the artist's childhood neighborhood are also home to the Madonna dell'Orto, filled with his work.

■ **Experience the nightlife.** Spend an evening eating and dancing with Venice's youthful crowd in and around the canal-side *locali* (nightspots) of Fondamenta della Misericordia and Fondamenta degli Ormesini.

■ **Get on the water.** Learn how to row a traditional *batellina* vessel exploring Cannaregio's serene canals.

■ **Sip a spritz.** When it's late afternoon along Fondamente Nove, enjoy a refreshing drink and the warm rays and sunset views of the San Michele.

■ **Shop the market stalls.** Mix with locals shopping at the fruit, vegetable, and seafood stalls on the Strada Nova at Rio Terà San Leonardo.

PLANNING YOUR TIME

Although it's more residential and less sight-rich than other Venice neighborhoods, you'll still need several hours here to explore the Ca' d'Oro palace and Madonna dell'Orto and Santa Maria dei Miracoli churches and to wander the Jewish Ghetto. Cannaregio is a great place to spend a morning before taking the vaporetto to Murano and Burano, which departs from the Fondamente Nove stop.

GETTING HERE

Venice's busy Ferrovia di Santa Lucia train station drops visitors straight into the Cannaregio *sestiere* (district). Vaporetti shuttle to and from the Ferrovia: Routes 1 and A travel the Canale Grande, stopping on the Cannaregio side at San Marcuola and Ca' d'Oro. Other routes head north along the Canale di Cannaregio, stopping at Guglie and Tre Archi, then onto the open northern lagoon.

PAUSE HERE

■ **Campo dei Gesuiti.** Cannaregio has intimate and tranquil campi where you can find a bench and sample local Venetian life. Approaching the towering Gesuiti church facade, Campo dei Gesuiti is one such relaxing spot, with a few trees providing welcome shade. Here you can sit, have a picnic with goods bought from the market stalls nearby, and watch the world go by. Ⓜ *Vaporetto: Fondamente Nove.*

■ **Campo Santa Maria Nova.** Near Rialto, you can escape the crowds and take a breather at this intimate square with views of Santa Maria dei Miracoli church. There are plenty of benches and an interesting bookshop on the square that will retain your attention for ages. Ⓜ *Vaporetto: Fondamente Nove.*

VIEWFINDER

■ **Ponte dei Mendicanti.** For stunning views of the northern lagoon and the nearby cemetery island San Michele, head along the Fondamente Nove to this gently humped stone bridge, which straddles the *sestieri* (district) of Cannaregio and Castello. On a clear day you can take in the view of greenish waters, skyscapes, boat traffic, and the snow-capped Dolomites on the horizon. Ⓜ *Vaporetto: Fondamente Nove.*

Seen from above, this part of town seems like a wide field plowed by several long, straight canals linked by perpendicular streets—not typical of Venice, where the shape of the islands usually defines the shape of the canals. The daylight reflected off the bright-green canals (cut through a vast bed of reeds; hence the name Cannaregio, which may mean "Reed Place") makes this a particularly luminous area. It's no surprise, perhaps, that Titian and Tintoretto had houses in the sestiere.

Cannarégio, first settled in the 14th century, is one of the more "modern" of Venice's neighborhoods, with *fondamente* (walkways) along the major canals, making it ideal for waterside strolls with views of spectacular Gothic and Baroque facades. The Strada Nova (literally, "New Street," as it was opened in 1871) is Cannaregio's main thoroughfare and the longest street in Venice. Lined with fruit and vegetable stalls, quiet shops, gelaterias, and bakeries, it serves as a pedestrian passage from the train station to the Campo Sant'Apostoli, just a few steps from the Rialto. The Jewish Ghetto, with five historically and artistically important synagogues, is in this quarter, and the churches of Madonna dell'Orto and Miracoli are among the most beautiful and interesting buildings in the city. Once you leave the Strada Nova, you'll find the sestiere blessedly free of tourists.

 Sights

★ Ca' d'Oro

HISTORY MUSEUM | One of the classic postcard sights of Venice, this exquisite Venetian Gothic palace was once literally a "Golden House," when its marble tracery and ornaments were embellished with gold. It was created by Giovanni and Bartolomeo Bon between 1428 and 1430 for the patrician Marino Contarini, who had read about the Roman emperor Nero's golden house in Rome, the Domus Aurea, and wished to imitate it as a present to his wife. Her family owned the land and the Byzantine *fondaco* (palace-trading house) previously standing on it; you can still see the round Byzantine arches incorporated into the Gothic building's entry porch.

The last proprietor, Baron Giorgio Franchetti, left Ca' d'Oro to the city after

Ca' d'Oro, a Venetian palace filled with important artwork, is located on the Grand Canal in Cannaregio.

having it carefully restored and furnished with antiquities, sculptures, and paintings that today make up the Galleria Franchetti. Besides Andrea Mantegna's *St. Sebastian* and other Venetian works, the Galleria Franchetti contains the type of fresco that once adorned the exteriors of Venetian buildings (commissioned by those who could not afford a marble facade). One such detached fresco displayed here was made by the young Titian for the facade of the Fondaco dei Tedeschi near the Rialto. ✉ *Calle Ca' d'Oro, Cannaregio 3933, Cannaregio* ☎ *041/5200345* ⊕ *www.cadoro.org* ✉ *€6* Ⓜ *Vaporetto: Ca' d'Oro.*

★ Gesuiti
(*Chiesa di Santa Maria Assunta*)
CHURCH | The interior walls of this early-18th-century church (1715–30) resemble brocade drapery, and only touching them will convince skeptics that rather than embroidered cloth, the green-and-white walls are inlaid marble. This trompe-l'oeil decor is typical of the late Baroque's fascination with optical

illusion. Toward the end of his life, Titian tended to paint scenes of suffering and sorrow in a nocturnal ambience. A dramatic example of this is on display above the first altar to the left: Titian's daring *Martyrdom of St. Lawrence* (1578), taken from an earlier church that stood on this site. Titian's *Assumption* (1555), originally commissioned for the destroyed Crociferi church, demands reverence. The Crociferi's surviving Oratory features some of Palma Giovane's best work, painted between 1583 and 1591. ✉ *Campo dei Gesuiti, Cannaregio* ☎ *041/5286579* ✉ *Gesuiti €1; oratory €3* ⊙ *Oratory closed Mon.–Wed., Jan.–mid-Feb., and Sept.–Oct.* Ⓜ *Vaporetto: Fondamente Nove.*

★ Jewish Ghetto
HISTORIC DISTRICT | The neighborhood that gave the world the word "ghetto" is today a quiet area surrounding a large campo. It is home to Jewish institutions, several kosher restaurants, a rabbinical school, and five synagogues. Present-day Venetian Jews live all over the city, and

the contemporary Jewish life of the ghetto, with the exception of the Jewish Museum and the synagogues, is an enterprise conducted almost exclusively by American Hasidic Jews of eastern European descent and tradition.

Although Jews may have arrived earlier, the first synagogues weren't built and a cemetery (on the Lido) wasn't founded until the Ashkenazi, or eastern European Jews, came in the late 1300s. Dwindling coffers may have prompted the Republic to sell temporary visas to Jews, who were over the centuries alternately tolerated and expelled. The Rialto commercial district, as mentioned in Shakespeare's *The Merchant of Venice*, depended on Jewish moneylenders for trade and to help cover ever-increasing war expenses.

In 1516, relentless local opposition forced the Senate to confine Jews to an island in Cannaregio, then on the outer reaches of the city, named for its *geto* (foundry). The term "ghetto" also may come from the Hebrew "ghet," meaning separation or divorce. Gates at the entrance were locked at night, and boats patrolled the surrounding canals. Jews were allowed only to lend money at low interest, operate pawnshops controlled by the government, trade in textiles, or practice medicine. Jewish doctors were highly respected and could leave the ghetto at any hour when on duty. Though ostracized, Jews were nonetheless safe in Venice, and in the 16th century, the community grew considerably—primarily with refugees from the Inquisition, which persecuted Jews in Spain, Portugal, and southern and central Italy. The ghetto was allowed to expand twice, but it still had the city's densest population and consequently ended up with the city's tallest buildings.

Although the gates were pulled down after Napoléon's 1797 arrival, the ghetto was reinstated during the Austrian occupation. The Jews realized full freedom only in 1866 with the founding of the

Italian state. Many Jews fled Italy as a result of Mussolini's 1938 racial laws, so that on the eve of World War II, there were about 1,500 Jews left in the ghetto. Jews continued to flee, and the remaining 247 were deported by the Nazis; only eight returned.

The area has Europe's highest density of Renaissance-era synagogues, and visiting them is interesting not only culturally, but also aesthetically. Though each is marked by the tastes of its individual builders, Venetian influence is evident throughout. Women's galleries resemble those of theaters from the same era, and some synagogues were decorated by artists who were simultaneously active in local churches; Longhena, the architect of Santa Maria della Salute, renovated the Spanish synagogue in 1635. ⊠ *Campo del Ghetto Nuovo, Cannaregio.*

★ **Madonna dell'Orto**

CHURCH | Though built toward the middle of the 14th century, this church takes its character from its beautiful late-Gothic facade, added between 1460 and 1464; it's one of the most beautiful Gothic churches in Venice. Tintoretto lived nearby, and this, his parish church, contains some of his most powerful work. Lining the chancel are two huge (45 feet by 20 feet) canvases, *Adoration of the Golden Calf* and *Last Judgment.* In glowing contrast to this awesome spectacle is Tintoretto's *Presentation of the Virgin at the Temple* and the simple chapel where he and his children, Marietta and Domenico, are buried. Paintings by Domenico, Cima da Conegliano, Palma Giovane, Palma Vecchio, and Titian also hang in the church. A chapel displays a photographic reproduction of a precious *Madonna with Child* by Giovanni Bellini. The original was stolen one night in 1993. Don't miss the beautifully austere, late-Gothic cloister (1460), which you enter through the small door to the right of the church; it is frequently used for exhibitions but may be open at other times as well. ⊠ *Campo*

The Jewish Ghetto is anchored by a quiet campo surrounded by restaurants, museums, and synagogues.

della Madonna dell'Orto, Cannaregio ☎ *041/795993* ✉ *€3, free with Chorus Pass* Ⓜ *Vaporetto: Orto.*

Museo Ebraico (*Jewish Museum*)
SYNAGOGUE | The small but well-arranged museum highlights centuries of Venetian Jewish culture with splendid silver Hanukkah lamps and Torahs and beautifully decorated wedding contracts handwritten in Hebrew. Tours of the ghetto and its five synagogues in Italian and English leave from the museum hourly (on the half hour). ✉ *Campo del Ghetto Nuovo, Cannaregio 2902/B, Cannaregio* ☎ *041/715359* ⊕ *www.museoebraico. it* ✉ *€8* ⊘ *Closed Sat.* Ⓜ *Vaporetto: San Marcuola, Guglie.*

Palazzo Vendramin-Calergi
CASINO | Hallowed as the site of Richard Wagner's death and today Venice's most glamorous casino, this magnficent edifice found its fame centuries earlier: Venetian star architect Mauro Codussi (1440–1504) essentially invented Venetian Renaissance architecture with this design. Built for the Loredan family around 1500,

Codussi's palace married the fortresslike design of the Florentine Alberti's Palazzo Rucellai with the lightness and delicacy of Venetian Gothic. Note how Codussi beautifully exploits the flickering light of Venetian waterways to play across the building's facade and to pour in through the generous windows. Consult the website for upcoming free guided tours of the small Museo Wagner upstairs, where an archive, events, and concerts may interest Wagnerians.

Venice has always prized the beauty of this palace. In 1652 its owners were convicted of a rather gruesome murder, and the punishment would have involved, as was customary, the demolition of their palace. The murderers were banned from the Republic, but the palace, in view of its beauty and historical importance, was spared. Only a newly added wing was torn down. ✉ *Cannaregio 2040, Cannaregio* ☎ *041/5297111* ⊕ *www.casinovenezia.it* ✉ *Casino €5–€10; free for visitors staying at a Venice hotel* Ⓜ *Vaporetto: San Marcuola.*

Let's Get Lost

Getting around Venice presents some unusual problems: the city's layout has few straight lines; house numbering seems nonsensical; and the six sestieri of San Marco, Cannaregio, Castello, Dorsoduro, Santa Croce, and San Polo all duplicate each other's street names. What's more, addresses in Venice are given by sestiere rather than street, making them of limited help in getting around. Venetians commonly give directions by pinpointing a major landmark, such as a church, and telling you where to go from there.

The numerous vaporetto lines can be bewildering, too, and often the only option for getting where you want to go is to walk. Yellow signs, posted on many busy corners, point toward the major landmarks—San Marco, Rialto, Accademia, and so forth—but don't count on finding such markers once you're deep into residential neighborhoods. Even buying a good map at a newsstand—the kind showing all street names and vaporetto routes—won't necessarily keep you from getting lost. To make matters worse, map apps on smart phones, for some reason, give frequently erroneous results for Venice.

Fortunately, as long as you maintain your patience, getting lost in Venice can be a pleasure. For one thing, being lost is a sign that you've escaped the tourist throngs. And although you might not find the Titian masterpiece you'd set out to see, you could wind up coming across an ageless *bacaro* (a traditional wine bar) or a quirky shop that turns out to be the highlight of your afternoon. Opportunities for such serendipity abound. Keep in mind that the city is self-contained: sooner or later, perhaps with the help of a patient native, you can rest assured you'll regain your bearings.

Sant'Alvise

CHURCH | For Tiepolo fans, trekking to the outer reaches of a pleasant residential section of Cannaregio to visit the unassuming Gothic church of Sant'Alvise is well worth the trouble. The little church holds Gianbattista Tiepolo's three panels of the Passion of Christ. He painted these panels, which display a new interest in dramatic intensity, and perhaps the influence of Tintoretto and Titian, for the church during his middle period, between 1737 and 1740. ⊠ *Campo Sant'Alvise, Campo Sant' Alvise, Cannaregio* ☎ *041/2750462 Chorus Foundation* ⛱ *€3, free with Chorus Pass* Ⓜ *Vaporetto: Sant'Alvise.*

★ Santa Maria dei Miracoli

CHURCH | Tiny yet harmoniously proportioned, this Renaissance gem, built between 1481 and 1489, is sheathed in marble and decorated inside with exquisite marble reliefs. Architect Pietro Lombardo (circa 1435–1515) miraculously compressed the building to fit its lot, then created the illusion of greater size by varying the color of the exterior, adding extra pilasters on the building's canal side and offsetting the arcade windows to make the arches appear deeper. The church was built to house *I Miracoli*, an image of the Virgin Mary by Niccolò di Pietro (1394–1440) that is said to have performed miracles—look for it on the high altar. ⊠ *Campo Santa Maria Nova, Cannaregio* ☎ *041/2750462 Chorus*

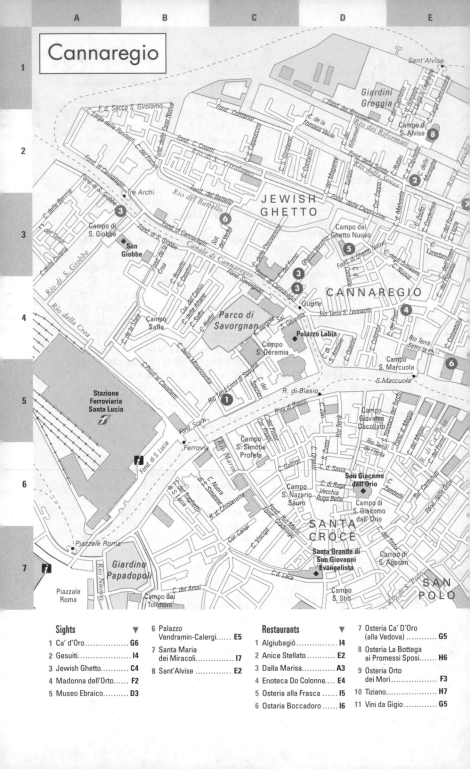

Cannaregio

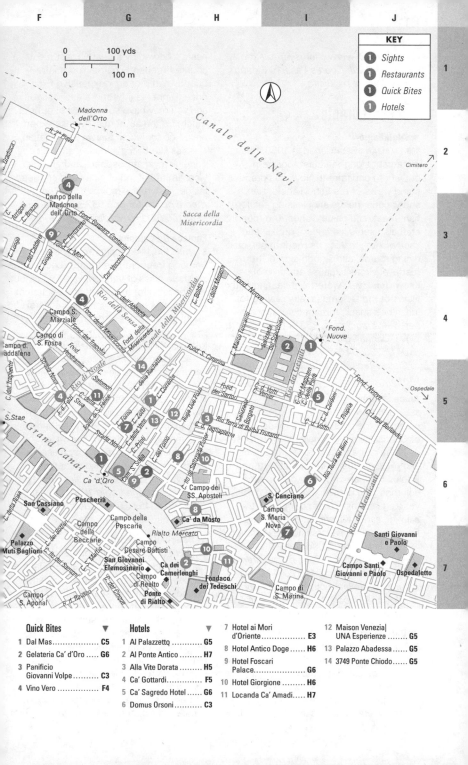

Foundation ⊕ www.chorusvenezia.org ✉ €3 (free with Chorus Pass) ⊘ Closed Sun. Ⓜ Vaporetto: Rialto.

🍴 Restaurants

★ Algiubagiò

$$$ | ITALIAN | Established in 1950, this restaurant along the quiet, northern outlier of Fondamente Nove has grandstand views of the San Michele island and various menus showcasing seasonal fish, meat, and pasta dishes. The friendly staff also serve ice cream, drinks, and sandwiches, making its modern bar, chic dining rooms, and lagoon-side platform restful environs to pause any time of day. **Known for:** lovely waterfront seating with views of the Dolomites; airy respite for lunch or a snack; romantic spot for dinner. ⑤ Average main: €33 ✉ Fondamente Nove, Cannaregio 5039, Cannaregio ☎ 041/5236084 ⊕ www.algiubagio.net ⊘ Closed Tues. Ⓜ Vaporetto: Fondamente Nove.

Anice Stellato

$$$ | VENETIAN | Off the main concourse on one of the most tranquil fondamente of Cannaregio, this small, family-run osteria is the place to stop for artful seafood and meat dishes in a romantic setting. Book a table among the wooden tables, columns, and mosaic floor of the rustic yet elegant dining room or right by the calming canal. **Known for:** seasonal seafood; exuberant flavors and presentation; relaxed fine dining. ⑤ Average main: €25 ✉ Fondamenta de la Sensa, Cannaregio 3272, Cannaregio ☎ 041/720744 ⊕ www. osterianicestellato.com ⊘ Closed Sun. and Mon. Ⓜ Vaporetto: San Alvise or San Marcuola.

★ Dalla Marisa

$$ | ITALIAN | This is the most famous restaurant in Venice for the city's working class; if you can get a table for lunch, you'll eat, without any choice, what Marisa prepares for her local clientele— generally, enormous portions of excellent pasta followed by a hearty roast meat course (frequently game, more infrequently fish), for an inexpensive fixed price. Dinner is a bit more expensive, and you may have some choice, but not much; for the authentic "Marisa experience," go for lunch. **Known for:** Venetian classics like baccalà mantecato (salt cod); genuine local atmosphere and gruff service; limited menu choices and cramped inside. ⑤ Average main: €15 ✉ Fondamenta di San Giobbe 652B, Cannaregio ☎ 041/720211 ⊘ No dinner Sun.–Tues.

Enoteca Do Colonne

$ | WINE BAR | Venetians from the neighborhood frequent this friendly bacaro, not just for a glass of very drinkable wine, but also because of its excellent selection of traditional Venetian cicheti (appetizers) for lunch. There's a large assortment of sandwiches and panini, as well as luscious tidbits like grilled vegetables, breaded and fried sardines and shrimp, and a superb version of baccalà mantecato, along with Venetian working-class specialties, such as musetto (a sausage made from pigs' snouts served warm with polenta) and nervetti (veal tendons with lemon and parsley). **Known for:** the best musetto in town; a cozy place for locals to hang out; classic cicheti and sandwiches. ⑤ Average main: €10 ✉ Rio Terà Cristo, Cannaregio 1814, Cannaregio ☎ 041/5240453 ⊕ www.docolonne.it Ⓜ Vaporetto: San Marcuola.

★ Ostaria Boccadoro

$$ | VENETIAN | Anchored on peaceful Campo Widman since the '90s is Ostaria Boccadoro, where purist chef Luciano Orlandi brings fresh seafood from the Chioggia market to the plate raw or lightly cooked with the subtlest of seasoning. Ask Luciano to suggest a wine from his carefully edited Veneto-dominated selection, then peruse the menu of Boccadoro classics like succulent canestrelli (tiny Venetian scallops), daily homemade pasta, tuna tartare, a crispy frittura (fritter), and perfectly grilled fish of

the day like *orata* (gilt-head bream) with zucchini sauce; there are meat options as well. **Known for:** professional, friendly service; simply prepared seafood; romantic setting. $ *Average main: €20* ⊠ *Campo Widman, Cannaregio 5405/a, Cannaregio* ☎ *041/5211021* ⊕ *www.boccadorovenezia.it.*

Osteria alla Frasca

$$ | SEAFOOD | Far from the maddening San Marco crowds, this tiny eatery nestled under a grapevine on a remote campiello charms before you even taste the seafood (think: grilled *seppie* [cuttlefish], *canoce* [mantis shrimp], excellent baccalà mantecato, or *sarde in saor* [sweet-and-sour sardines]). Wines are an important part of the meal here; ask for a recommendation from the ample list of predominantly regional selections. **Known for:** small, pricey plates; outdoor terrace; seafood staples. $ *Average main: €18* ⊠ *Corte de la Carità, Cannaregio 5176, Cannaregio* ☎ *041/2412585* Ⓜ *Vaporetto: Fondamente Nove.*

Osteria Ca' d'Oro (alla Vedova)

$ | VENETIAN | "The best polpette in town," you'll hear fans of the venerable Vedova say, and that explains why it's an obligatory stop on any *giro d'ombra* (bacaro tour); the *polpette* (meatballs) are always hot and crunchy—and also gluten-free, as they're made with polenta. Ca' d'Oro is a full-fledged trattoria as well, but make sure to reserve ahead: it's no secret to those seeking traditional Venetian fare at reasonable prices, locals and travelers alike. **Known for:** house wine served in tiny traditional glasses; classic Venetian cuisine; famous polpette. $ *Average main: €13* ⊠ *Calle del Pistor, Cannaregio 3912, off Strada Nova, Cannaregio* ☎ *041/5285324* ⊗ *Closed Thurs. and Sun. morning* Ⓜ *Vaporetto: Ca' d'Oro.*

Osteria La Bottega ai Promessi Sposi

$$ | VENETIAN | Join locals at the *banco* (counter) premeal for an *ombra* (small glass of wine) and cicheti like polpette or violet eggplant rounds, or reserve a table for a full meal in the dining room or the intimate courtyard. A varied, seasonal menu includes local standards like calf's liver or grilled canestrelli, along with creative variations on classic Venetian fare, such as homemade ravioli stuffed with radicchio di Treviso or orecchiette with a scrumptious minced-duck sauce. **Known for:** friendly, helpful service; creative cicheti and wine; regularly changing menu with both traditional and modern choices. $ *Average main: €19* ⊠ *Calle de l'Oca, just off Campo Santi Apostoli, Cannaregio 4367, Cannaregio* ☎ *041/2412747* ⊗ *No lunch Mon.* Ⓜ *Vaporetto: Ca' d'Oro.*

Osteria l'Orto dei Mori

$$$ | ITALIAN | This small, popular neighborhood osteria—located canalside, just under the nose of the campo's famous corner statue—specializes in creative versions of classic Italian (but not necessarily Venetian) dishes; don't skip dessert, as their tiramisu wins raves. Dine in the artsy and atmospheric interior or outside in the intimate, echoing square for a truly memorable experience. **Known for:** buzzing atmosphere with locals and tourists alike; traditional Italian dishes with modern accents; choice local wine selection. $ *Average main: €26* ⊠ *Campo dei Mori, Fondamenta dei Mori, Cannaregio 3386, Cannaregio* ☎ *041/5243677* ⊕ *www.osteriaortodeimori.com* ⊗ *Closed Tues. and Wed.* Ⓜ *Vaporetto: Orto, Ca' d'Oro, San Marcuola.*

Tiziano

$ | ITALIAN | A fine variety of excellent *tramezzini* (sandwiches made of untoasted white bread triangles) lines the display cases at this *tavola calda* (roughly the Italian equivalent of a cafeteria) on the main thoroughfare from the Rialto to Santi Apostoli; inexpensive salad plates and daily pasta specials are also served. This is a great place for a light meal or snack before a performance at the nearby Teatro Malibran. **Known for:** efficient (if occasionally grumpy) service; quick meals or snacks, especially tramezzini; modest prices. $ *Average main: €8* ⊠ *Salizada San Giovanni Crisostomo, Cannaregio 5747, Cannaregio* ☎ *041/5235544* Ⓜ *Vaporetto: Rialto.*

★ Vini da Gigio

$$$ | **VENETIAN** | A brother-sister team run this refined trattoria, where you're made to feel as if you've been personally invited to lunch or dinner. Indulge, perhaps, in rigatoni with duck sauce or arugula-stuffed ravioli, seafood risotto made to order, or sesame-encrusted tuna. Just note, though, that it's the meat dishes that steal the show: the steak with red-pepper sauce and the *tagliata di agnello* (sautéed lamb fillet with a light, crusty coating) are both superb, and you'll never enjoy a better *fegato alla veneziana* (Venetian-style liver with onions). **Known for:** helpful and professional service; superb meat dishes like fegato alla veneziana; one of the city's best wine cellars. $ *Average main: €25* ⊠ *Fondamenta San Felice, Cannaregio 3628/A, Cannaregio* ☎ *041/5285140* ⊕ *www.vinidagigio.com* ⊘ *Closed Mon. and Tues. and 2 wks in Aug.* Ⓜ *Vaporetto: Ca' d'Oro.*

☕ Coffee and Quick Bites

★ Dal Mas

$ | **BAKERY** | Filled brioche, exquisite chocolates and pastries, such as *kranz* (a braided pastry filled with almond paste and raisins) and strudel from the Friuli region, and bar service make Dal Mas a great choice for breakfast. It's been a local favorite since 1906. **Known for:** savory snacks and drinks; handy pit-stop near the station; delicious pastries like Pastine di Riso. $ *Average main: €4* ⊠ *Lista di Spagna, Cannaregio 150/A, Cannaregio* ☎ *041/715101* ⊕ *www. dalmaspasticceria.it* ⊘ *Closed Tues.* Ⓜ *Vaporetto: Stazione.*

Gelateria Ca' d'Oro

$ | **BAKERY** | **FAMILY** | Here you'll find the usual array of gelato flavors, which change with the seasons, plus more unusual ones like licorice. You can also enjoy a granita (regular and Sicilian), *panna in ghiaccio* (a brick of frozen cream between wafers), and some specialties (chocolate-covered and otherwise) in front of the counter. **Known for:** cakes and *semifreddi* (a dessert between ice cream and mousse); fresh fruit sorbets; generous scoops. $ *Average main: €3* ⊠ *Strada Nova near Campo Santi Apostoli, Cannaregio 4273/B, Cannaregio* ☎ *041/5228982* Ⓜ *Vaporetto: Ca' d'Oro.*

Panificio Giovanni Volpe

$ | **BAKERY** | This is the only place in town that still bakes traditional Venetian-Jewish pastry and delicious *pane azimo* (matzo bread) year round, though days of operation give away that the shop is not kosher. **Known for:** Bisse biscuits for dunking; savory pantry goods; bread and panini for packed lunches. $ *Average main: €4* ⊠ *Calle del Ghetto Vecchio, Cannaregio 1143, Cannaregio* ☎ *041/715178* ▭ *No credit cards* ⊘ *Closed Sun.* Ⓜ *Vaporetto: Guglie.*

★ Vino Vero

$ | **WINE BAR** | Swing by this pint-sized wine bar for cicheti and crostini that are just a bit different and fresher than what you'll find elsewhere, along with a fine selection of natural wines. Though there's not much space inside, try to snag one of the coveted seats by the canal. **Known for:** pretty canalside seating; large selection of both Italian and international natural wines; delectable small bites. $ *Average main: €12* ⊠ *Fondamenta de la Misericordia, Cannaregio 2497, Cannaregio* ☎ *041/2750044* ⊕ *vinovero.wine* ⊘ *No lunch Mon.* Ⓜ *Vaporetto: Madonna dell'Orto, Ca' d'Oro.*

Al Ponte Antico hotel is housed in a 16th-century palace overlooking the Grand Canal.

Hotels

Al Palazzetto

$$ | **B&B/INN** | **FAMILY** | Understated Venetian decor, original exposed-beam ceilings and terrazzo flooring, and large rooms suitable for families or small groups are hallmarks of this intimate, family-owned guesthouse. **Pros:** good value; authentic 18th-century palace; clean and quiet. **Cons:** not many amenities; old-fashioned decor; a bit rough around the edges. $ *Rooms from: €149* ✉ *Calle delle Vele, Cannaregio 4057, Cannaregio* ☎ *041/2750897* ⊕ *www.guesthouse.it* ⇆ *5 rooms* ¶ *Free Breakfast* Ⓜ *Vaporetto: Ca' d'Oro.*

★ Al Ponte Antico

$$$$ | **HOTEL** | This hospitable 16th-century palace inn has lined its Gothic windows with tiny white lights, creating an inviting glow that's emblematic of the luxurious, distinctively Venetian warmth inside. **Pros:** excellent service; upper-level terrace overlooks Grand Canal; family-run warmth. **Cons:** beds a little hard for some; in one of the busiest areas of the city (although not particularly noisy); books up quickly. $ *Rooms from: €330* ✉ *Calle dell'Aseo, Cannaregio 5768, Cannaregio* ☎ *041/2411944* ⊕ *www.alponteantico.com* ⇆ *9 rooms* ¶ *Free Breakfast* Ⓜ *Vaporetto: Rialto.*

Alla Vite Dorata

$$ | **B&B/INN** | Newly restored and thoughtfully appointed lodgings at the end of a narrow calle have beamed ceilings, large windows that invite in light and provide canal views, and space-liberating iron and glass furniture. **Pros:** Canal views; handy for sightseeing; lots of restaurant and bacari options nearby. **Cons:** can sometimes hear noise outside; some small rooms; ground-level lodgings might not appeal to everyone. $ *Rooms from: €150* ✉ *Rio Terà Barba Frutariol, Cannaregio 4690 B, Cannaregio* ☎ *041/2413018* ⊕ *www.allavitedorata.com* ⇆ *6 rooms* ¶ *Free Breakfast* Ⓜ *Vaporetto: Ca' d'Oro, Fondamente Nove.*

Ca' Gottardi

$$$ | HOTEL | Traditional Venetian style mixes with contemporary design: the clean white-marble entrance leading up to the luminous *piano nobile* (main floor) of the 15th-century palace gracefully contrasts with the opulent Murano chandeliers and rich wall brocades. **Pros:** canal views; great location; alluring mix of old and new. **Cons:** standard rooms are quite small; sometimes there's noise outside; no outdoor garden or terrace. ⑤ *Rooms from: €250* ✉ *Strada Nova, Cannaregio 2283, Cannaregio* ☎ *041/2759333* ⊕ *www.cagottardi.com* ✈ *7 rooms, 2 suites* ⦿| *Free Breakfast* Ⓜ *Vaporetto: Ca' d'Oro.*

Ca' Sagredo Hotel

$$$ | HOTEL | This expansive palace has been the Sagredo family residence since the mid-1600s and has the decor to prove it: a massive staircase has Longhi wall panels soaring above it; large common areas are adorned with original art by Tiepolo, Longhi, and Ricci; and a traditional Venetian style dominates guest rooms, many of which have canal views and some of which have original art and architectural elements. **Pros:** rooftop terrace and indoor bar; excellent location; some of the city's best preserved interiors. **Cons:** heat in rooms controlled by front desk; more opulent than intimate; no coffee- or tea-making facilities in rooms. ⑤ *Rooms from: €280* ✉ *Campo Santa Sofia, Cannaregio 4198/99, Cannaregio* ☎ *041/2413111* ⊕ *www.casagredohotel.com* ✈ *42 rooms* ⦿| *No Meals* Ⓜ *Vaporetto: Ca' d'Oro.*

Domus Orsoni

$ | B&B/INN | The grounds of the famous Orsoni Mosaics factory is the setting for these five spacious rooms with quirky golden mosaic flourishes. **Pros:** no bridges and few steps to deal with; a fine option for anyone looking for a unique experience in lodging; pretty garden. **Cons:** no sweeping views; some rooms need a refresh; near vaporetto stops but

a bit removed from the action (which can be a plus). ⑤ *Rooms from: €120* ✉ *Sottoportego dei Vedei, Cannaregio 1045, Cannaregio* ☎ *041/2759538* ⊕ *www.domusorsoni.it* ✈ *5 rooms* ⦿| *Free Breakfast* Ⓜ *Vaporetto: Guglie, Tre Archi, or Crea.*

Hotel ai Mori d'Oriente

$$ | HOTEL | Though the atmosphere harkens back to Venice's connection with the Silk Road, the surroundings and amenities are everything you'd expect from a 21st-century establishment, and the staff is highly accommodating. **Pros:** quiet area; canal-side bar for breakfast or cocktails; Tintoretto's district. **Cons:** pricey bar; patchy AC; perhaps too quiet for some. ⑤ *Rooms from: €180* ✉ *Fondamenta della Sensa, Cannaregio 3319, Cannaregio* ☎ *041/711001* ⊕ *www.morihotel.com* ✈ *21 rooms* ⦿| *Free Breakfast* Ⓜ *Vaporetto: San Marcuola or Madonna dell'Orto.*

Hotel Antico Doge

$$$ | HOTEL | Once the home of Marino Faliero, a 14th-century doge who was executed for treason, this palazzo has been attentively "modernized" in elegant 18th-century Venetian style: all rooms are adorned with brocades, damask-tufted walls, gilt mirrors, and parquet floors—even the breakfast room has a stuccoed ceiling and Murano chandelier. **Pros:** romantic, atmospheric decor; some rooms have whirlpool tubs; convenient to the Rialto and beyond. **Cons:** area outside hotel can get very busy; no elevator; no outdoor garden or terrace. ⑤ *Rooms from: €230* ✉ *Campo Santi Apostoli, Cannaregio 5643, Cannaregio* ☎ *041/2411570* ⊕ *www.anticodoge.com* ✈ *20 rooms* ⦿| *Free Breakfast* Ⓜ *Vaporetto: Ca' d'Oro, Rialto.*

Hotel Foscari Palace

$$$ | HOTEL | Venetian grandeur meets a modern, relaxed ambience in this extensively renovated 16th-century palazzo overlooking the Grand Canal and bustling Campo Santo Sofia. **Pros:** handy for

Did You Know?

In the late 1400s, Venice was the printing capital of the world, and nowadays you'll find dozens of *legatori* (bookbinderies) around town.

walking, vaporetto, and gondola *traghetto* (ferry); stunning view over the rooftops and Grand Canal from the terrace; huge beds in some rooms. **Cons:** has a less distinctively Venetian feel than some other options; some bathrooms on the small side; on a busy square. $ *Rooms from: €240* ⊠ *Campo Santo Sofia, Cannaregio 4200/1/2, Cannaregio* ☎ *041/5297611* ⊕ *www.hotelfoscaripalace.com* ⌁ *26 rooms* ⦿ *Free Breakfast* Ⓜ *Vaporetto: Ca' d'Oro.*

Hotel Giorgione

$$$ | HOTEL | Set in a quiet corner of Cannaregio, with an attractive pool, courtyard, and guest rooms accented with rich Venetian furnishings and gold leaf flourishes, this is a decent option, especially if the Superior Deluxe rooms are on offer. **Pros:** elegant garden; relaxing ambience; heated saltwater whirlpool. **Cons:** area prone to *acqua alta* (flooding); some rooms are small and business-like; no canal views. $ *Rooms from: €230* ⊠ *Off Campo Santi Apostoli, Cannaregio 4587, Cannaregio* ☎ *041/5225810* ⊕ *www.hotelgiorgione.com* ⌁ *76 rooms* ⦿ *Free Breakfast* Ⓜ *Vaporetto: Ca' d'Oro or Fondamente Nove.*

Locanda Ca' Amadi

$$ | HOTEL | A historic 13th-century palazzo near the Rialto markets is a welcome retreat on a tranquil *corte,* (court) and individually decorated rooms have tufted walls and views of a lively canal or a quiet courtyard. **Pros:** handy for sightseeing; classic Venetian style; some canal-view rooms. **Cons:** no restaurant (simple continental breakfast served, though); rooms vary a lot in size and quality; reception staff not always helpful or available. $ *Rooms from: €130* ⊠ *Corte Amadi, Cannaregio 5815, Cannaregio* ☎ *041/5285210* ⊕ *www.caamadi.it* ⌁ *6 rooms* ⦿ *Free Breakfast* Ⓜ *Vaporetto: Rialto.*

Maison Venezia | UNA Esperienze

$$$ | HOTEL | Up a narrow calle and across the bridge from the bustling Strada Nova, this 15th-century palazzo sits by a tranquil canal and an evocative little campo; inside you'll find traditional Venetian decor and guest rooms featuring silk damasks tufted onto multiwindowed walls. **Pros:** excellent customer service; an intimate, boutique hideaway that's handy for exploring the city; complimentary afternoon drinks and snacks. **Cons:** some bathrooms look tired; some may find the decor gaudy; classic rooms are quite small. $ *Rooms from: €230* ⊠ *Ruga Do Pozzi, Cannaregio 4173, Cannaregio* ☎ *041/2442711* ⊕ *www.gruppouna.it/en* ⌁ *34 rooms* ⦿ *Free Breakfast* Ⓜ *Vaporetto: Ca' d'Oro.*

★ Palazzo Abadessa

$$ | HOTEL | At this late-16th-century palazzo, you can experience warm hospitality, a luxurious atmosphere, a lush private garden, and unusually spacious guest rooms well appointed with antique-style furniture, frescoed or stuccoed ceilings, and silk fabrics. **Pros:** enormous walled garden, a rare and delightful treat in crowded Venice; superb guest service; unique and richly decorated guest rooms. **Cons:** Wi-Fi can be iffy; no restaurant (buffet breakfast served); some bathrooms are small and plain. $ *Rooms from: €160* ⊠ *Calle Priuli, Cannaregio 4011, off Strada Nova, Cannaregio* ☎ *041/2413784* ⊕ *www.abadessa.com* ⦵ *Closed last 2 wks in Jan.* ⌁ *15 rooms* ⦿ *Free Breakfast* Ⓜ *Vaporetto: Ca' d'Oro.*

3749 Ponte Chiodo

$ | B&B/INN | Spending time at this charming guesthouse near the Ca' d'Oro vaporetto stop is like staying with a friend: service is warm and helpful, with lots of suggestions for dining and sightseeing. **Pros:** pretty private garden; highly attentive service; relaxed atmosphere. **Cons:** not for those looking for large-hotel amenities (no spa or gym); no restaurant, though breakfast is served in the garden; some bathrooms are smallish. $ Rooms from: €105 ⊠ Calle Racheta, Cannaregio 3749, Cannaregio ☎ 041/2413935 ⊕ www.pontechiodo.it ↩ 6 rooms ⦾ Free Breakfast Ⓜ Vaporetto: Ca' d'Oro.

Nightlife

BARS

El Sbarlefo

WINE BARS | The odd name is Venetian for "smirk," although you'll be hard-pressed to find one at this cheery, familiar bacaro with a wine selection as ample as the cicheti on offer. The spread of delectables ranges from classic polpette of meat and tuna to tomino cheese rounds to speck and robiola rolls, and the selection of wines is equally intriguing. There's often live jazz and blues on Friday and Saturday nights. El Sbarlefo has a second location in Dorsoduro, in the calle just behind the church of San Pantalon. ⊠ Salizada del Pistor, off Campo Santi Apostoli, Cannaregio 4556/C, Cannaregio ☎ 041/5246650 ⊕ www.elsbarlefo.it Ⓜ Vaporetto: Ca' d'Oro.

The Irish Pub

PUBS | Guinness and gab flow freely from 5 pm to 1 am at this pub, a favorite expat and student hangout since the 1990s. There are Irish, Italian, and Belgian brews plus cider on tap, as well as sports on TV and occasional live music, either Irish or rock. Small sandwiches are available until late (the *segalini* are divine). ⊠ Corte dei Pali, off Strada Nova, Cannaregio 3847, Cannaregio ☎ 041/0990196 ⊕ theirishpubvenice.wordpress.com Ⓜ Vaporetto: Ca' d'Oro.

Paradiso Perduto

BARS | Paradiso Perduto has been catering to night owls since the '80s with drinks, wine, and slightly overpriced fish dishes (a better option is the cicheti). The old piano has witnessed Chet Baker and Archie Shepp jams, and the place still

serves up live music—mainly local and international jazz groups. It attracts young people and students alongside tourists, creating a very lively atmosphere. In temperate weather, patrons fill the fondamenta until they're shooed away. ⊠ Fondamenta della Misericordia, Cannaregio 2540, Cannaregio ☎ 041/720581 ⊗ Closed Tues. and Wed.

TiME Social Bar

COCKTAIL LOUNGES | The seasonal cocktails at this charming mixology bar, many of which use fruit and homemade bitters, win rave reviews from visitors and locals alike. There are also small nibbles on offer if hunger strikes. ⊠ Rio Terà Farsetti, Cannaregio 1414, Cannaregio ☎ 0338/3636951 ⊕ timesocialbar.it Ⓜ Vaporetto: San Marcuola Casino.

Un Mondo di Vino

WINE BARS | Recharge with some wine or a cicheto or two—meat, fish, and vegetarian choices are on offer—at this cozy, friendly spot near the Miracoli church. Numerous wines are available by the glass, and the helpful servers are often happy to crack open a bottle for sampling if there's something you fancy. ⊠ Salizzada San Cancian, Cannaregio ☎ 041/5211093 ⊕ www.bacarounmondodivino.it Ⓜ Vaporetto: Rialto, Ca' d'Oro.

CASINOS

Palazzo Vendramin-Calergi

THEMED ENTERTAINMENT | The city-run casino in splendid Palazzo Vendramin-Calergi is a classic scene of well-dressed high rollers playing French roulette, Caribbean poker, chemin de fer, 30–40, and slots. You must be at least 18 to enter, and men must wear jackets after 8:30 pm to access the "VIP" area. ⊠ Campiello Vendramin, Cannaregio 2040, Cannaregio ☎ 041/5297111 ⊕ casinovenezia.it Ⓜ Vaporetto: San Marcuola.

🎭 Performing Arts

Teatro Malibran

OPERA | La Fenice's more intimate sister venue was built by the powerful Grimani family in 1677, opening as the Teatro Grimani a San Gristostomo and soon becoming one of Europe's most famous theaters. The theater at first hosted theatrical productions, including many works by Metastasio and, later, Goldoni. It became an opera house in the early 19th century and was renamed Malibran in 1835, after Maria García Malibran, the great soprano of her day. It was converted into a movie theater in 1927 and then reopened for live performances in 2001 after lengthy restoration. Be careful when booking as some seats have restricted views. ✉ *Campiello del Teatro Malibran, Cannaregio 5870, Cannaregio* ☎ *041/272 2699 La Fenice* ⊕ *www.teatrolafenice.it* Ⓜ *Vaporetto: Rialto.*

🛍 Shopping

ART GALLERIES

Vittorio Constantini

ANTIQUES & COLLECTIBLES | **FAMILY** | This glass artist's workshop features unusual, intricate pieces inspired by nature—birds, butterflies, beetles, and other insects—appreciated by adults and children alike. ✉ *Calle del Fumo, Cannaregio 5311, Cannaregio* ☎ *041/5222265* ⊕ *www.vittoriocostantini.com* Ⓜ *Vaporetto: Fondamente Nove.*

BOOKSTORES

★ **Libreria Miracoli**

BOOKS | A long-established treasure trove of unusual books, historic prints, and quirky postcards spills out of this crammed bookshop onto the pretty campo by the Miracoli church. ✉ *Campo Santa Maria Nova 6062, Cannaregio* ☎ *041/523 4060* Ⓜ *Vaporetto: Ca' d'Oro.*

COSTUMES AND ACCESSORIES

Nicolao Atelier

MIXED CLOTHING | The largest costume-rental showroom in town has outfitted many a period film (including *Casanova*). They have nearly 7,000 choices ranging from the historical to the fantastic, including thematic costumes ideal for group masquerades. ✉ *Fondamenta Misericordia, Cannaregio 2590, Cannaregio* ☎ *041/5207051* ⊕ *www.nicolao.com* Ⓜ *Vaporetto: Ca d'Oro.*

Vladì Shoes

SHOES | These sassy shoes have just enough fantasy to be stylish, but not too much to be over the top. ✉ *Rio tera' de la Maddalena, Cannaregio 2340, San Polo* ☎ *041/2440084* ⊕ *www.vladishoes.it* Ⓜ *Vaporetto: San Marcuola.*

GIFTS

★ **Gianni Basso Stampatore**

STATIONERY | Beloved of artists and celebrities, this traditional printer creates handmade business cards, stationery, and invitations using vintage letterpress machinery. You can choose from the selection on offer, or have your own custom-designed and shipped to you at home. ✉ *Calle del Fumo, Cannaregio 5306, Cannaregio* ☎ *041/5234681* Ⓜ *Vaporetto: Fondamente Nove.*

Il Forcolaio Matto

OTHER SPECIALTY STORE | Swing by the carpentry workshop of Piero Dri to see how he crafts the *remi* (oars) and *fórcole* (rowlocks) that adorn the city's gondola and Voga alla Veneta flat-bottomed boats. With his walnut-wood off-cuts, Piero creates gorgeous sculptural pieces to purchase. ✉ *Calle dell'Oca, Cannaregio* ☎ *041/8778823* ⊕ *www.ilforcolaiomatto.it* Ⓜ *Vaporetto: Ca' d'Oro.*

Massimiliano Caldarone

GLASSWARE | Hailing from Turin, Massimiliano shows his love of his adopted city and Murano glassmaking in his eclectic lampwork creations. Pop in to see him at work, commission a piece, or browse the glassware, which varies from elegant wine glasses and sculptures to nautical-theme pieces and saucily themed jewelry. ⊠ *Campiello Widmann già Biri, 5419B, Cannaregio* ☎ *345/8179190 Cell* ⊕ *www.facebook.com/Caldarone.creazioni* Ⓜ *Vaporetto: Fondamente Nove.*

Vestopazzo

OTHER SPECIALTY STORE | One of three outlets in Venice, this Roman business inspired by travel and ethical goods is filled with unusual gifts and fashion accessories, from recycled aluminum jewelry and scarves to men's wallets and hats. ⊠ *Calle del Magazen 5585, Cannaregio* ☎ *041/5645773* ⊕ *shop.vestopazzo.it* Ⓜ *Vaporetto: Ca' d'Oro.*

JEWELRY

Rose Douce

JEWELRY & WATCHES | The enticing selection of tasteful Murano glass accessories, figures, and chalices at Rose Douce includes jewelry made with antique Murano beads and braided gold. ⊠ *Salizzada S Giovanni Cristostomo, Rialto area, Cannaregio 5782, Cannaregio* ☎ *041/5227232* Ⓜ *Vaporetto: Rialto.*

MARKETS

Mercati di Rio Terà e Canale Cannaregio

MARKET | These weekday markets stretch along the busy canal and nearby Strada Nova, where locals come to pick up fruit, vegetables, and fish. ⊠ *Rio Terà San Leonardo, Cannaregio* Ⓜ *Vaporetto: Guglie.*

WINE

Enoteca Vintido

WINE/SPIRITS | This small wine shop by the Canale Cannaegio is lined with flasks, and the friendly owners give tastings to help you decide which of the Veneto vintages you wish to buy. ⊠ *Fondamenta Cannaregio 1116, Cannaregio* ☎ *041/5206090.*

 Activities

Holistic Massage Apsara

SPAS | Professional holistic massages of the reflexology, sports, Californian, and hot stone varieties are on offer at this relaxing private studio. Massages are by appointment only. ⊠ *Cannaregio 914, Cannaregio* ⊕ *apsaravenezia.wixsite.com/website* ⊠ *From €50 for a massage.*

Row Venice

BOATING | Learn the traditional Voga alla Veneta rowing style with these fun lessons along Cannaregio's quiet canals. The beginner's session starts aboard a traditional and stable *batellina* craft, where you learn to row *a prua* (at the prow) while still moored. As you set off, there's time to practice the stroke and learn how to steer before reaching the open lagoon. The meeting point is Sacca Misericordia/Ponte de la Sacca. ⊠ *Ponte de la Sacca, Cannaregio* ☎ *347/7250637 contact by text first* ⊕ *rowvenice.org* ⊠ *From €85 for 1-2 people.*

Chapter 7

CASTELLO

Updated by
Nick Bruno

⊙ Sights	🍴 Restaurants	🛏 Hotels	🛍 Shopping	🍸 Nightlife
★★★★☆	★★★★★	★★★★☆	★★★★☆	★★★☆☆

NEIGHBORHOOD SNAPSHOT

TOP EXPERIENCES

■ **Marvel at Renaissance masterpieces:** The artistic riches of Bellini, Veronese, and others await at Santi Giovanni e Paolo and the Querini Stampalia.

■ **See Biennale exhibits:** If you're here during the international art exhibition, explore the galleries.

■ **Check out the foodie scene:** Linger with a drink and innovative bites in the neighborhood *campi* (squares).

■ **Get off the beaten path:** A visit to San Francesco della Vigna makes you feel as far away from the tourists of San Marco as possible.

■ **Explore Venice's naval history:** The Arsenale and the Museo Storico Navale are windows into the city's nautical past and present.

PLANNING YOUR TIME

It will take at least half a day to do justice to the many worthwhile sights in Castello since they are scattered throughout the largest *sestiere* (neighborhood) in Venice. Schedule at least a half hour to see the Carpaccios at the Scuola di San Giorgio, and an hour for the interior of Santi Giovanni e Paolo and the adjacent campo. The Querini Stampalia museum will take an hour, and the churches of San Zaccaria and San Francesco della Vigna at least a half hour each. You will not want to miss the beautiful Renaissance entry to the Arsenale. If the Biennale dell'Arte is running, you'll want to visit its main exhibition areas, which are in Castello; this should take a full day.

GETTING HERE

To reach Castello directly from San Marco airport the most direct (and expensive) options are water taxi or the Alilaguna Linea Blu ferry to one of the stops nearest your accommodation: Ospedale or Bacini for the northern part, Arsenale or Zattere for the southern part. It's a long journey and pricey, so if you're mobile and not burdened with too much luggage, take the airport bus to Piazzale Roma, then a vaporetto, such as Line 1, 2, or N (at night), to your destination.

VIEWFINDER

■ **The Arsenale.** The naval shipyards occupy a large swathe of Castello's northern reaches. In and around the imposing redbrick architecture are wonderful views and photo opportunities. Approaching from the Arsenale vaporetto stop, the Renaissance gateway Porta Magna (1460) comes into view. Its four lions, including a curious looking 2,000-year-old, 10-foot feline pillaged from Athens, make alluring backdrops to any photo. Head to the wooden bridge Ponte de L'Arsenal o del Paradiso for different perspectives; and take the opportunity to wander the Arsenale's *corderie* (ropeworks) and proto-industrial landscapes during Biennale shows or other events. Ⓜ *Vaporetto: Arsenale.*

Castello, Venice's largest sestiere, includes all the land from east of Piazza San Marco to the city's easternmost tip. Its name probably comes from a fortress that once stood on one of the eastern islands. During the days of the Republic, eastern Castello was the primary neighborhood for workers in the shipbuilding Arsenale located in its midst and now home to the Venice Biennale. Foodies flock here for some of the city's most creative modern Italian cuisine.

Castello isn't lacking in colorful history. In the early 15th century, large Greek and Dalmatian communities moved into the area along the Riva degli Schiavoni, where many of them sold dried fish and meat; the Confraternity of San Marco, based in what is now the hospital on Campo Santi Giovanni e Paolo, was patronized by Venetian high society in the 16th to 18th centuries; and nearby Campo Santa Maria Formosa served as a popular open-air theater for shows of various kinds (some including livestock among the cast members).

Not every well-off Venetian family could manage to build a palazzo on the Grand Canal. Many that couldn't instead settled in western Castello, taking advantage of its proximity to the Rialto and San Marco, and built the noble palazzi that today distinguish this area from the fisher's enclave in the more easterly streets of the sestiere.

There is a lot to see here. Carpaccio's paintings at the Scuola di San Giorgio degli Schiavoni are worth a long look. San Francesco della Vigna, with a Palladio facade and Sansovino interior, certainly deserves a stop, especially as the local area is a wonderful tranquil corner of Castello to wander around. The churches of Santi Giovanni e Paolo and San Zaccaria are major attractions, as is the Querini Stampalia museum. You can learn about Venice's naval history at the small and quirky Museo Storico Navale.

Castello, like parts of Cannaregio and Giudecca, is the place to soak up genuine Venetian life. In Castello's *calli* (streets) and campi. Venetian families meet and chat and do their shopping, and kids play freely. Away from the tourist hordes of San Marco and Rialto, it's here that you get a feel for the local rhythm, particularly along the wide Via Garibaldi, where people have their morning cappuccino and brioche in the bars or a late night, spritz-fueled chat at an outside table.

During the Biennales d'Arte e Architettura, the neighborhood takes on a curious atmosphere with the influx of international creative types and tourists. The Giardini and the Arsenale's corderie, repurposed rope works and industrial spaces, give up their haunted, abandoned atmosphere of the winter months in exchange for a buzz of activity and a cornucopia of curious (and often eye-opening) art-related sideshows.

Distant, clanging echoes of the former shipyards of the Arsenale and the thousands of men and women who toiled here to build the formidable Venetian fleet can be felt behind the high redbrick walls. If you can, enter the fascinating, rusty industrial landscape: the military base authorities occasionally allow visitors to see beyond the magnificent lions of the complex's Porta Magna Renaissance gateway.

 Sights

Arsenale

MILITARY SIGHT | Visible from the street, the Porta Magna (1460), an impressive Renaissance gateway designed by Antonio Gambello, was the first classical structure to be built in Venice. It is guarded by four lions—war booty of Francesco Morosini, who took the Peloponnese from the Turks in 1687. The 10-foot-tall lion on the left stood sentinel more than 2,000 years ago near Athens, and experts say its mysterious inscription is runic "graffiti" left by Viking mercenaries hired to suppress 11th-century revolts in Piraeus. If you look at the winged lion above the doorway, you'll notice that the Gospel at his paws is open but lacks the customary *Pax* inscription; praying for peace perhaps seemed inappropriate above a factory that manufactured weapons. The interior is not regularly open to the public, since it belongs to the Italian Navy,

but it opens for special events like the art and architecture Biennales. If you're here at those times, don't miss the chance to look inside; you can enter from the back via a northern-side walkway leading from the Ospedale vaporetto stop.

The Arsenale is said to have been founded in 1104 on twin islands. The immense facility that evolved—it was the largest industrial complex in Europe built prior to the Industrial Revolution—was given the old Venetian dialect name *arzanà*, borrowed from the Arabic *darsina'a*, meaning "workshop." At the height of its activity, in the early 16th century, it employed as many as 16,000 *arsenalotti*, workers who were among the most respected shipbuilders in the world. The Arsenale developed a type of pre–Industrial Revolution assembly line, which allowed it to build ships with astounding speed and efficiency. The Arsenale's efficiency was confirmed time and again—whether building 100 ships in 60 days to battle the Turks in Cyprus (1597) or completing one perfectly armed warship, start to finish, while King Henry III of France attended a banquet. ⊠ *Campo de la Tana 2169, Castello* Ⓜ *Vaporetto: Arsenale.*

Campo Santi Giovanni e Paolo

PLAZA/SQUARE | This large, attractive square is the site of two city landmarks: the imposing namesake Gothic church and the Scuola Grande di San Marco, with one of the loveliest Renaissance facades in Italy. The *scuola's* (men's fraternal institution) exterior is the combined work of Venice's most prominent Renaissance architects. The facade was begun by Pietro Lombardo in the 1480s, then in 1490 the work was given over to Mauro Codussi, who also added a grand stairway in the interior. In the 16th century, Sansovino designed the facade facing the Rio dei Mendicanti. The campo also contains the only equestrian monument ever erected by La Serenissima. The rider, Bartolomeo Colleoni, served Venice well as a *condottiere,* or mercenary commander—the Venetians preferred to pay others to fight for them on land. When he died in 1475, he left his fortune to the city on the condition that a statue be erected in his honor "in the piazza before San Marco." The Republic's shrewd administrators coveted Colleoni's ducats but had no intention of honoring anyone, no matter how valorous, with a statue in Piazza San Marco. So they collected the money, commissioned a statue by Florentine sculptor Andrea del Verrocchio (1435–88), and put it up before the Scuola Grande di San Marco. ⊠ *Campo Santi Giovanni e Paolo, Campo Santi Giovanni e Paolo, Castello.*

Chiesa della Pietà

RELIGIOUS BUILDING | Unwanted babies were left on the steps of this religious institute, founded by a Franciscan friar in 1346. The adjoining orphanage provided the children with a musical education. The quality of the performances here reached continental fame—the in-house conductor was none other than Antonio Vivaldi (1678–1741), who wrote some of his best compositions here for the hospice. The present church was designed in the 18th century by Giorgio Massari, but the facade was completed only in the early 20th century. The main reason for a visit is to view the magnificent ceiling fresco by Gianbattista Tiepolo. In a room to the left of the entrance is a tiny collection of Baroque instruments, including the violin played by Vivaldi. There are guided tours Tuesday through Sunday. ⊠ *Riva degli Schiavoni, Castello 3701, Castello* ☎ *041/5222171* ⊕ *www. pietavenezia.org* 🎫 *€3* ⊘ *No guided tours Mon.* Ⓜ *Vaporetto: San Zaccaria.*

Chiostro di Sant'Apollonia

RELIGIOUS BUILDING | Within this Benedictine monastery is a peacefully shady 12th-century cloister that has been modified over the centuries. It remains the only surviving example of a Romanesque cloister in Venice. The brick pavement is original, and the many inscriptions

and fragments on display (some from the 9th century) are all that remain of the first Basilica di San Marco. ⊠ *Ponte della Canonica, Castello 4312, Castello* ☎ *041/5229166* ⊕ *www.patriarcato-venezia.it* Ⓜ *Vaporetto: Vallaresso, San Zaccaria.*

Museo Storico Navale

(*Museum of Naval History*)
OTHER MUSEUM | FAMILY | The impressive boat collection here includes scale models, such as the doges' ceremonial *Bucintoro,* and full-size boats, such as Peggy Guggenheim's private gondola complete with romantic *felze* (cabin). There's a range of old galley and military pieces, a section dedicated to Admiral Morosini (who plundered the Arsenale's Porta Magna lions nearby), and a large collection of seashells. A visit to the Paglione delle Nave, a part of the museum, allows you to see a portion of the interior of the Arsenale otherwise closed to visitors. ⊠ *Campo San Biagio, Castello 2148, Castello* ☎ *041/2441399* 🎫 *€5* Ⓜ *Vaporetto: Arsenale.*

Querini Stampalia

ART MUSEUM | A connoisseur's delight, the art collection at this late-16th-century palace includes Giovanni Bellini's *Presentation in the Temple* and Sebastiano Ricci's triptych *Dawn, Afternoon, and Evening.* Portraits of newlyweds Francesco Querini and Paola Priuli were left unfinished on the death of Palma Vecchio (1480–1528); note the groom's hand and the bride's dress. Original 18th-century furniture and stuccowork are a fitting background for Pietro Longhi's portraits. Nearly 70 works by Gabriele Bella (1730–99) capture scenes of Venetian street life; downstairs is a café. The entrance hall and the small, charming rear garden were designed by famous Venetian architect Carlo Scarpa during the 1950s. ⊠ *Campo Santa Maria Formosa, Castello 5252, Castello* ☎ *041/2711411* ⊕ *www.querinistampalia. org* 🎫 *€14* ⊘ *Closed Mon.* Ⓜ *Vaporetto: San Zaccaria.*

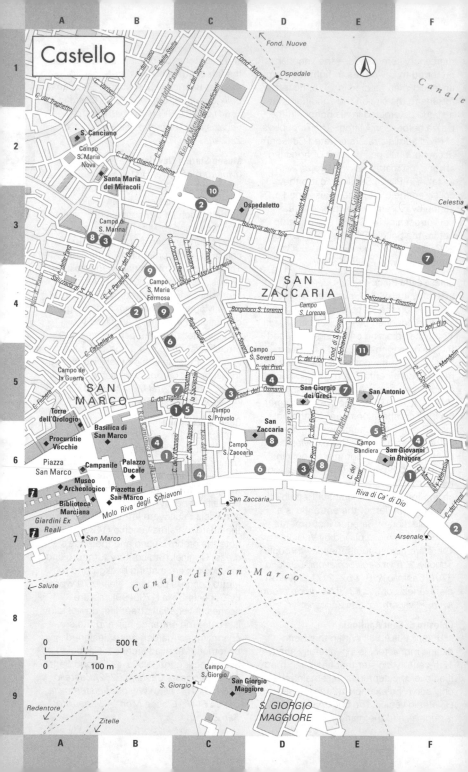

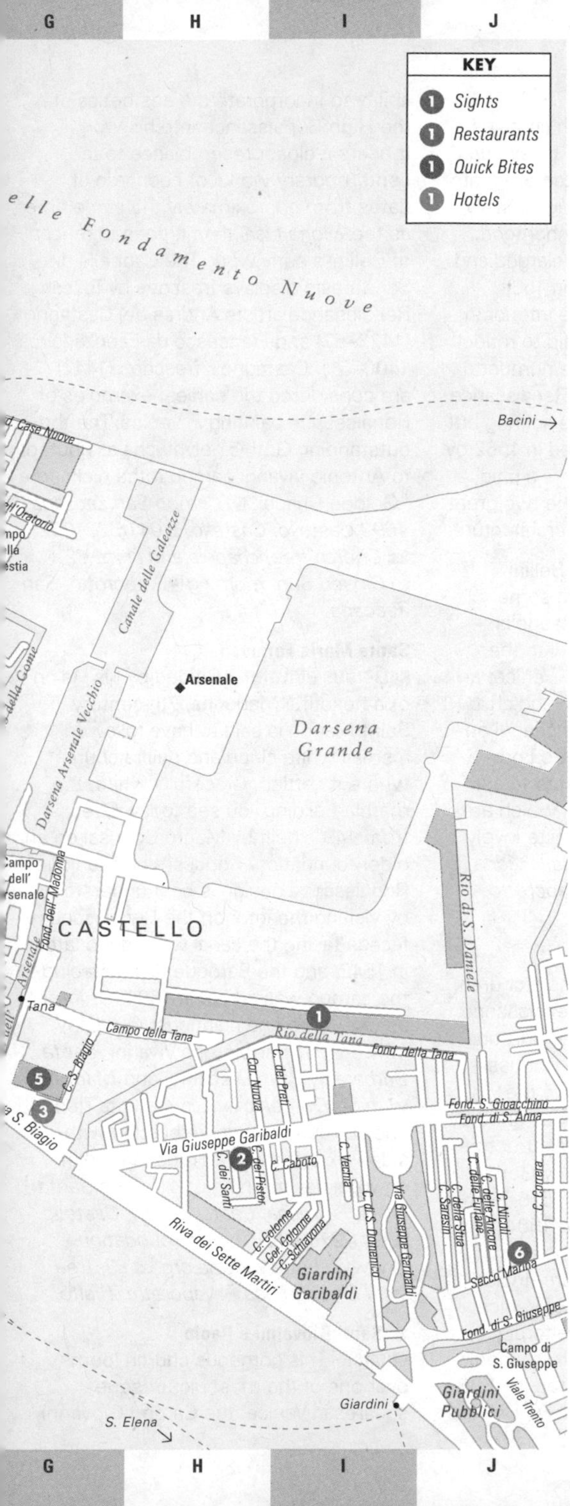

G
H
I
J
KEY
Sights
Restaurants
Quick Bites
Hotels
Fondamento Nuove
Bacini
Canale delle Galeazze
Arsenale
Darsena Grande
Darsena Arsenale Vecchio
Fond. dell' Madonna
CASTELLO
Rio di S. Daniele
Tana
Campo della Tana
Rio della Tana
Fond. della Tana
C. S. Biagio
Cor. Nuova
C. dei Preti
Fond. S. Gioacchino
Fond. di S. Anna
Via Giuseppe Garibaldi
C. dei Santi
C. del Pistor
C. Caboto
C. Vecchia
C. di S. Domenico
Via Giuseppe Garibaldi
C. delle Furlane
C. delle Ancore
C. della Stua
C. Saresin
C. Nicoli
C. Correra
C. Colonne
Cor. Colonne
C. Schiavona
Giardini Garibaldi
Riva dei Sette Martiri
Secco Marina
Fond. di S. Giuseppe
Campo di S. Giuseppe
Viale Trento
Giardini Pubblici
Giardini
S. Elena
G
H
I
J

Sights

1 Arsenale I7
2 Campo Santi Giovanni e Paolo C3
3 Chiesa della Pietà D6
4 Chiostro di Sant'Apollonia B6
5 Museo Storico Navale G7
6 Querini-Stampalia B5
7 San Francesco della Vigna F3
8 San Zaccaria D6
9 Santa Maria Formosa B4
10 Santi Giovanni e Paolo C3
11 Scuola di San Giorgio degli Schiavoni E5

Restaurants

1 Al Covo F6
2 Alle Testiere B4
3 Antica Sacrestia C5
4 CoVino F6
5 Il Ridotto C5
6 La Trattoria ai Tosi J8
7 Local E5
8 Osteria di Santa Marina A3

Quick Bites

1 Aciugheta C5
2 El Rèfolo H8
3 Pasticceria Italo Didovich B3
4 Wine Bar 5000 .... D5

Hotels

1 Ca 'dei Dogi B6
2 Ca' di Dio F7
3 Hotel Bucintoro G7
4 Hotel Danieli C6
5 Hotel La Residenza E6
6 Hotel Londra Palace D6
7 Locanda Casa Querini C5
8 Metropole E6
9 Ruzzini Palace Hotel B4

★ San Francesco della Vigna

CHURCH | Although this church contains some interesting and beautiful paintings and sculptures, it's the architecture that makes it worth the hike through a lively, middle-class residential neighborhood. The Franciscan church was enlarged and rebuilt by Jacopo Sansovino in 1534, giving it the first Renaissance interior in Venice; its proportions are said to reflect the mystic significance of the numbers three and seven dictated by Renaissance neo-Platonic numerology. The soaring but harmonious facade was added in 1562 by Palladio. The church represents a unique combination of the work of the two great stars of 16th-century Veneto architecture.

As you enter, a late Giovanni Bellini *Madonna with Saints* is down some steps to the left, inside the Cappella Santa. In the Giustinian chapel to the left is Veronese's first work in Venice, an altarpiece depicting the Virgin and child with saints. In another, larger chapel on the left are bas-reliefs by Pietro Lombardo and his son Tullio. Be sure to ask to see the attached cloisters, which are usually open to visitors and quite lovely. ⊠ *Campo di San Francesco della Vigna, Castello* ☎ *041/5206102* Ⓜ *Vaporetto: Celestia.*

★ San Zaccaria

CHURCH | More a museum than a church, San Zaccaria has a striking Renaissance facade, with central and upper portions representing some of Mauro Codussi's best work. The lower portion of the facade and the interior were designed by Antonio Gambello. The original structure of the church was 14th-century Gothic, with its facade completed in 1515, some years after Codussi's death in 1504, and it retains the proportions of the rest of the essentially Gothic structure. Inside is one of the great treasures of Venice, Giovanni Bellini's celebrated altarpiece, *La Sacra Conversazione,* easily recognizable in the left nave. Completed in 1505, when the artist was 75, it shows Bellini's ability to incorporate the aesthetics of the High Renaissance into his work. It bears a closer resemblance to the contemporary works of Leonardo (it dates from approximately the same time as the *Mona Lisa*) than it does to much of Bellini's early work. The Cappella di San Tarasio displays frescoes by Tuscan Renaissance artists Andrea del Castagno (1423–57) and Francesco da Faenza (circa 1400–51). Castagno's frescoes (1442) are considered the earliest examples of Renaissance painting in Venice. The three outstanding Gothic polyptychs attributed to Antonio Vivarini earned it the nickname "Golden Chapel." ⊠ *Campo San Zaccaria, 4693 Castello, Castello* ☎ *041/5221257* 🖃 *Church free, chapels and crypt €2* ⊙ *Closed Sun. morning* Ⓜ *Vaporetto: San Zaccaria.*

Santa Maria Formosa

RELIGIOUS BUILDING | Guided by his vision of a beautiful Madonna, 7th-century Saint Magno is said to have followed a small white cloud and built a church where it settled. Gracefully white, the marble building you see today dates from 1492, built by Mauro Codussi on an older foundation. Codussi's harmonious Renaissance design is best understood by visiting the interior; the Renaissance facade facing the canal was added later, in 1542, and the Baroque facade facing the campo was added in 1604. Of interest are three fine paintings: *Our Lady of Mercy* by Bartolomeo Vivarini, *Santa Barbara* by Palma Vecchio, and *Madonna with St. Domenic* by Gianbattista Tiepolo. The surrounding square bustles with sidewalk cafés and a produce market on weekday mornings. ⊠ *Campo Santa Maria Formosa, Castello 5267, Castello* ☎ *041/2750462 Chorus Foundation* ⊕ *www.chorusvenezia.org* 🖃 *€3, free with Chorus Pass* Ⓜ *Vaporetto: Rialto.*

★ Santi Giovanni e Paolo

CHURCH | This gorgeous church looms over one of the most picturesque squares in Venice: the Campo Giovanni

It's hard to say what's more impressive about San Zaccaria: its Renaissance facade or the interior artwork by Bellini.

e Paolo, centered on the magnificent 15th-century equestrian statue of Bartolomeo Colleoni by the Florentine Andrea del Verrocchio. Also note the beautiful facade of the Scuola Grande di San Marco (now the municipal hospital), begun by Pietro Lombardo and completed after the turn of the 16th century by Mauro Codussi. The massive Italian Gothic church itself is of the Dominican order and was consecrated in 1430. Bartolomeo Bon's portal, combining Gothic and classical elements, was added between 1458 and 1462, using columns salvaged from Torcello. The 15th-century stained-glass window near the side entrance is breathtaking for its brilliant colors and beautiful figures; it was made in Murano from drawings by Bartolomeo Vivarini and Girolamo Mocetto (circa 1458–1531). The second official church of the Republic after San Marco, San Zanipolo (as its known in Venetian) is Venice's equivalent of London's Westminster Abbey, with a great number of important people, including 25 doges, buried here.

Artistic highlights include an early (1465) polyptych by Giovanni Bellini (right aisle, second altar) where the influence of Mantegna is still very evident, Alvise Vivarini's *Christ Carrying the Cross* (sacristy), and Lorenzo Lotto's *Charity of St. Antonino* (right transept). Don't miss the Cappella del Rosario (Rosary Chapel), off the left transept, built in the 16th century to commemorate the 1571 victory of Lepanto in western Greece, when Venice led a combined European fleet to defeat the Turkish Navy. The chapel was devastated by a fire in 1867 and restored in the early years of the 20th century with works from other churches, among them the sumptuous Veronese ceiling paintings. However quick your visit, don't miss the Pietro Mocenigo tomb to the right of the main entrance, by Pietro Lombardo and his sons. Note also Tullio Lombardo's tomb of Andrea Vendramin, the original home of Tullio's *Adam*, which has recently been restored in New York City's Metropolitan Museum of Art. ✉ *Campo dei Santi Giovanni e Paolo, Castello* ☎ *041/5235913* ⊕ *www.*

The Scuola di San Giorgio degli Schiavoni houses impressive artwork by Carpaccio.

santigiovanniepaolo.it 🖃 *€3.50* ⊗ *Closed weekends* Ⓜ *Vaporetto: Fondamente Nove, Rialto.*

★ **Scuola di San Giorgio degli Schiavoni**
HISTORIC SIGHT | Founded in 1451 by the Dalmatian community, this small *scuola,* or confraternity, was, and still is, a social and cultural center for migrants from what is now Croatia. It contains one of Italy's most beautiful rooms, harmoniously decorated between 1502 and 1507 by Vittore Carpaccio. Although Carpaccio generally painted legendary and religious figures against backgrounds of contemporary Venetian architecture, here is perhaps one of the first instances of "Orientalism" in Western painting. Note the turbans and dress of those being baptized and converted, and even the imagined, arid Middle Eastern or North African landscape in the background of several of the paintings. In this scuola for immigrants, Carpaccio focuses on "foreign" saints especially venerated in Dalmatia: Sts. George, Tryphon, and Jerome. He combined keen empirical

observation with fantasy, a sense of warm color, and late medieval realism. (Look for the priests fleeing St. Jerome's lion, or the body parts in the dragon's lair.) ■**TIP→ Opening hours are quite flexible. Since this is a must-see site, book in advance so you won't be disappointed.** 🖃 *Calle dei Furlani, Castello 3259/A, Castello* ☎ *041/5228828* ⊕ *www.scuoladalmatavenezia.com* 🖃 *€5* Ⓜ *Vaporetto: Arsenale, San Zaccaria.*

 **Restaurants**

Al Covo
$$$ | **VENETIAN** | For years, Diane and Cesare Binelli's Al Covo has set the standard of excellence for traditional, refined Venetian cuisine; the Binellis are dedicated to providing their guests with the freshest, highest-quality fish from the Adriatic, and vegetables, when at all possible, from the islands of the Venetian Lagoon and the fields of the adjacent Veneto region. Although their cuisine could be correctly termed "classic Venetian," it always offers

surprises, like the juicy crispness of their legendary *fritto misto* (fried mixed seafood and vegetables)—reliant upon an unconventional secret ingredient in the batter—or the heady aroma of their fresh anchovies marinated in wild fennel, an herb somewhat foreign to Veneto. **Known for:** Diane's chocolate cake for dessert; sophisticated Venetian flavors; top-notch local ingredients. $ *Average main: €28* ✉ *Campiello Pescaria, Castello 3968, Castello* ☎ *041/5223812* ⊕ *www.ristorantealcovo.com* ⊘ *Closed Tues. and Wed., 3 wks. in Jan., and 10 days in Aug.* Ⓜ *Vaporetto: Arsenale.*

★ Alle Testiere

$$$ | VENETIAN | The name is a reference to the old headboards that adorn the walls of this tiny, informal restaurant, but the food (not the decor) is undoubtedly the focus. Local foodies consider this one of the most refined eateries in the city thanks to chef Bruno Gavagnin's gently creative take on classic Venetian fish dishes; the chef's artistry seldom draws attention to itself, but simply reveals new dimensions of familiar fare, creating dishes that stand out for their lightness and balance. **Known for:** wonderful wine selection; daily changing fish offerings, based on what's fresh at the market; excellent pasta with seafood. $ *Average main: €28* ✉ *Calle del Mondo Novo, Castello 5801, Castello* ☎ *041/5227220* ⊕ *www.osterialletestiere.it* ⊘ *Closed Sun. and Mon., 3 wks in Jan.–Feb., and 4 wks in July–Aug.*

★ Antica Sacrestia

$$$ | VENETIAN | Housed in the atmospheric, deconsecrated ecclesiastical buildings of the Chiesa di San Giovanni Novo, this special restaurant run by the attentive Giuseppe Calliandro marries classic Venetian cuisine with some inventive flavor combinations. In colder months dine amid magnificent wooden beams, religious artworks, and quirky objects; in warmer times, the pretty, plant-filled courtyard is the place to sit.

Known for: simple, fresh flavors; quality meat and seafood platters to share; pizza and pasta. $ *Average main: €26* ✉ *Calle de la Corona, Castello 4463, Castello* ☎ *041/5230749* ⊕ *www.anticasacrestia.it* ⊘ *Closed Mon.* Ⓜ *Vaporetto: San Marco.*

CoVino

$$$$ | ITALIAN | A charming new concept in Venetian eateries, diminutive CoVino offers a fixed-price, three-course menu, from which you'll choose among several traditionally inspired *antipasti* (starters), *secondi* (second course), and desserts with innovative—and satisfying—twists. At this Slow Food presidio, you can watch the cook construct your sliced tuna dressed with Bronte pistachios and eggplant; Bra sausage "imported" from the Piedmont alla Valpolicella with tiny green beans; or perhaps even fresh gazpacho. **Known for:** locally sourced ingredients; wine selection; light lunch option for €30. $ *Average main: €42* ✉ *Calle del Pestrin, Castello 3829a-3829, Castello* ☎ *041/2412705* ⊕ *www.covinovenezia.com* ▭ *No credit cards* ⊘ *Closed Tues. and Wed. No lunch Thurs.* Ⓜ *Vaporetto: Arsenale.*

★ Il Ridotto

$$$$ | MODERN ITALIAN | Longtime restaurateur Gianni Bonaccorsi (proprietor of the popular Aciugheta nearby) has established an eatery where he can pamper a limited number of lucky patrons with his imaginative cuisine and impeccable taste in wine. *Ridotto* means "small, private place," which this very much is, evoking an atmosphere of secrecy and intimacy; the innovative menus tend toward lighter but wonderfully tasty versions of classic dishes. **Known for:** extensive wine recommendations; some of the most creative cuisine in Venice; excellent five- or seven-course tasting menus. $ *Average main: €40* ✉ *Campo SS. Filippo e Giacomo, Castello 4509, Castello* ☎ *041/5208280* ⊕ *www.ilridotto.com* ⊘ *Closed Wed., no lunch Tues. and Thurs.* Ⓜ *Vaporetto: San Zaccaria.*

Known for its classic seafood dishes, Alle Testiere is one of Castello's many fantastic restaurants.

La Trattoria ai Tosi

$ | **VENETIAN** | **FAMILY** | Getting off the beaten track to find good, basic local cuisine isn't easy in Venice, but La Trattoria ai Tosi (aka Ai Tosi Piccoli) fits the bill with its somewhat remote, tranquil location, homey atmosphere, and variety of fine traditional fare at prices that make it worth the walk from anywhere in the city. The *baccalà mantecato* (whipped salted cod) "sanwicini" are excellent, as are the classic frittura mista and the traditional Venetian *bigoli in salsa* (thick, homemade spaghetti with an anchovy-onion sauce). **Known for:** fried seafood; outdoor seating for a spritz *aperitivo* (pre-meal drink); excellent pizza. Ⓢ *Average main: €12* ✉ *Seco Marina, Castello 738, Castello* ☎ *041/5237102* ☺ *Closed Mon.* Ⓜ *Vaporetto: Giardini.*

★ Local

$$$$ | **VENETIAN** | In a simple yet charming setting with beamed ceilings and terrazzo floors, a sister and brother team oversee their "New Venetian Cuisine," where local ingredients are used to prepare reinvented traditional dishes, often with Japanese influences. It's tasting-menu only, with seven or nine courses (or a less expensive three-course option at weekday lunch), and wine pairings from their extensive list are a recommended treat. **Known for:** tiramigiù dessert: coffee, marsala, and mascarpone; highly attentive staff; ingredients from Italian producers and daily catch. Ⓢ *Average main: €110* ✉ *Salizzada dei Greci, Castello 3303, Castello* ☎ *041/2411128* ⊕ *www.ristorantelocal.com* ☺ *Closed Tues. and Wed.* Ⓜ *Vaporetto: San Zaccaria.*

★ Osteria di Santa Marina

$$$ | **VENETIAN** | The candlelit tables on this romantic campo are inviting enough, but it's the intimate restaurant's imaginative kitchen that's likely to win you over; you can order consistently excellent pasta, fish, or meat dishes à la carte or opt for one of the rewarding tasting menus. The wine list is ample and well thought out, and the service is gracious, warm, and professional. **Known for:** wonderful wine pairings; innovative and artfully presented modern Venetian food; charming

setting. $ Average main: €30 ⊠ Campo Santa Marina, Castello 5911, Castello ☎ 041/5285239 ⊕ www.osteriadisantamarina.com ⊗ Closed Sun. and 2 wks in Aug. No lunch Mon. Ⓜ Vaporetto: Rialto.

Coffee and Quick Bites

Aciugheta

$$ | **WINE BAR** | Almost an institution, the "Tiny Anchovy" (as the name translates) doubles as a pizzeria-trattoria, but the real reason for coming is the bar's tasty *cicheti* (finger foods), like the eponymous anchovy minipizzas, the *arancioni* (stuffed fried rice balls), and the *polpette* (meatballs or croquettes). Wines by the glass change daily, but there is always a good selection of local wines on hand, as well as some Tuscan and Piedmontese choices thrown in for good measure. **Known for:** good selection of Italian wines by the glass; *pizzetta con l'acciuga* (minipizza with anchovy); mix of traditional and more modern cicheti. $ *Average main: €15* ⊠ Campo SS. Filippo e Giacomo, Castello 4357, Castello ☎ 041/5224292 ⊗ Closed Mon. Ⓜ Vaporetto: San Zaccaria.

El Rèfolo

$$ | **WINE BAR** | At this contemporary cantina and hip hangout in a very Venetian neighborhood, the owner pairs enthusiastically chosen wines and artisanal beers with select meat, savory cheese, and seasonal vegetable combos. With outside-only seating (not particularly comfortable), it's more appropriate for an aperitivo and a light meal. **Known for:** boisterous atmosphere outside in nice weather; good selection of wine and beer; filling meat and cheese plates. $ *Average main: €16* ⊠ Via Garibaldi, Castello 1580, Castello ☎ 344/1636759 ⊕ www.elrefolo.it ⊗ Closed Mon. Ⓜ Vaporetto: Arsenale.

Pasticceria Italo Didovich

$ | **BAKERY** | At this long-established, family-run locale, you'll find excellent pastries, including delicious filled cannoli, as well as good-value savory bites. You can enjoy a *primo* (first course) at lunchtime outside at one of the campo-side tables, although it's much cheaper to stand at the bar or take out. **Known for:** lasagna, eggs 'n' bacon, and other daily savory plates; fab (if pricey) pastries; great cappuccino and brioche breakfast stop. $ *Average main: €12* ⊠ Campo di Santa Marina, Castello 5909, Castello ☎ 041/5230017 ☐ No credit cards ⊗ Closed Sun. June–Sept.; closed Sun. afternoon Oct.–May Ⓜ Vaporetto: Rialto.

Wine Bar 5000

$ | **WINE BAR** | Nibble on a selection of cicheti or a cheese or meat plate at this cozy wine bar on Campo San Severo, near the Basilica dei Frari. You can either dine inside the brick-walled, Murano glass–chandeliered space, or watch the gondolas sail by at a table outdoors next to the quiet adjacent Severno canal. **Known for:** small but well-prepared choice of cicheti; large wine list, including biodynamic options; lovely outdoor seating area. $ *Average main: €10* ⊠ Campo San Severo, Castello 5000, Castello ☎ 041/5201557 ⊕ www.lunasentada.it/winebar5000 ⊗ Closed Tues. and Wed. Ⓜ Vaporetto: San Zaccaria.

🛏 Hotels

★ Ca' dei Dogi

$ | **HOTEL** | A quiet courtyard secluded from the San Marco melee offers an island of calm in six guest rooms and two apartments (some with private terraces overlooking the Doge's Palace, one with a Jacuzzi), which are individually decorated with contemporary furnishings and accessories. **Pros:** balconies with wonderful views; traditional Italian restaurant on-site; amazing location close to Doge's Palace and Piazza San Marco.

A marble staircase leads to rooms at the Hotel Danieli, a palazzo steeped in history.

Cons: bathrooms can feel cramped; no elevator and lots of stairs; rooms are on the small side. ⑤ *Rooms from: €116* ✉ *Corte Santa Scolastica, Castello 4242, Castello* ☎ *041/2413751* ⊕ *www. cadeidogi.it* ⊘ *Closed 3 wks. in Dec.* ⊠ *6 rooms* ⑩ *Free Breakfast* Ⓜ *Vaporetto: San Zaccaria.*

Ca' di Dio

$$$$ | HOTEL | Housed in a palace dating from 1272, with interiors updated by of-the-moment architect Patricia Urquiola, this deluxe hotel offers rooms with views of San Giorgio Maggiore island, two restaurants, and two internal courtyards, all within striking distance of the Venice Biennale grounds. **Pros:** on-site gym and spa; convenient to the Biennale; most guest rooms are suites. **Cons:** not for fans of traditional design; quite expensive; a walk from traditional Venetian sights. ⑤ *Rooms from: €565* ✉ *Riva Ca' di Dio, Castello 5866, Castello* ☎ *041/0980238* ⊕ *vretreats.com/en/ ca-di-dio* ⊠ *66 rooms* ⑩ *Free Breakfast* Ⓜ *Vaporetto: Arsenale.*

Hotel Bucintoro

$$$$ | HOTEL | "All rooms with a view" touts this *pensione* (modest lodging)-turned-four-star-hotel—and the views are indeed expansive: from the hotel's waterfront location near lively Via Garibaldi, your windows swing open to a panorama that sweeps from the Lido across the basin to San Giorgio and San Marco; upper-floor vistas are particularly inspiring. **Pros:** near the Arsenale vaporetto stop; lagoon views from all rooms; waterfront without the San Marco crowds. **Cons:** noise from boats when windows are open; some rooms on the small side; yachts sometimes dock outside, blocking lagoon views, and without those views the hotel is really overpriced. ⑤ *Rooms from: €375* ✉ *Riva degli Schiavoni, Castello 2135/A, Castello* ☎ *041/5209909* ⊕ *www. hotelbucintoro.com* ⊠ *21 rooms* ⑩ *Free Breakfast* Ⓜ *Vaporetto: Arsenale.*

Hotel Danieli

$$$$ | HOTEL | Welcoming guests with one of the most sumptuous, quintessentially Venetian loggia-lobbies (part of the late-14th-century Palazzo Dandolo, built by the family of the doge who conquered Constantinople), this fabled monument of Venetian history retains much of its luxury luster, with marble columns here, carved archways there, and plush furniture everywhere. **Pros:** fabulous terrace; a sense of history; spectacular views. **Cons:** service is patchy; some rooms are small and need attention; the restaurant isn't to the standard of the rest of the hotel. Ⓢ *Rooms from: €800* ✉ *Riva degli Schiavoni, Castello 4196, Castello* ☎ *041/5226480* ⊕ *www.danielihotel-venice.com* ⤵ *225 rooms* ⓘ⦿ *No Meals* Ⓜ *Vaporetto: San Zaccaria.*

Hotel La Residenza

$$$ | HOTEL | Set in a quiet campo, this renovated 15th-century Gothic-Byzantine palazzo has simple but spacious rooms and lovely public spaces filled with chandeliers, 18th-century paintings, and period reproduction furnishings. **Pros:** affordable rates; lavish salon and breakfast room; quiet residential area, steps from Riva degli Schiavoni and 10 minutes from Piazza San Marco. **Cons:** basic guest rooms; no elevator; sparse breakfast. Ⓢ *Rooms from: €210* ✉ *Campo Bandiera e Moro (or Bragora), Castello 3608, Castello* ☎ *041/5285315* ⊕ *www.venicela-residenza.com* ⤵ *15 rooms* ⓘ⦿ *No Meals* Ⓜ *Vaporetto: Arsenale.*

Hotel Londra Palace

$$$$ | HOTEL | A wall of windows soaks up extraordinary, sweeping views of the lagoon and the island of San Giorgio, enjoyed from many of the individually decorated guest rooms and suites, which have fine fabric, damask drapes, Biedermeier furniture, Venetian glass, and marble bathrooms. **Pros:** excellent Do Leoni restaurant; superlative views;

attentive service. **Cons:** decor may not be for those with contemporary tastes; some rooms are small for such a price; busy, touristy area. Ⓢ *Rooms from: €495* ✉ *Riva degli Schiavoni, Castello 4171, Castello* ☎ *041/5200533* ⊕ *www.londrapalace.com* ⤵ *53 rooms* ⓘ⦿ *Free Breakfast* Ⓜ *Vaporetto: San Zaccaria.*

Locanda Casa Querini

$$ | B&B/INN | Pastel lacquered furnishings and mock-flock wallpaper pay tribute to 18th-century Venetian style in the six bedrooms of this small pensione on a charming Castello campo; ask for one that overlooks the neighborhood life out front. **Pros:** good value for Venice; handy location between San Zaccaria and Campo Santa Maria Formosa; sunny outside seating area for people-watching. **Cons:** dated decor; very limited public space; no elevator. Ⓢ *Rooms from: €150* ✉ *Campo San Giovanni Novo, Castello 4388, Castello* ☎ *041/2411294* ⊕ *www.locandaquerini.com* ⤵ *6 rooms* ⓘ⦿ *Free Breakfast* Ⓜ *Vaporetto: San Zaccaria.*

★ Metropole

$$$$ | HOTEL | Atmosphere prevails in this labyrinth of opulent, intimate spaces featuring classic Venetian decor combined with Eastern influences: the owner—a lifelong collector of unusual objects—has filled the common areas and sumptuously appointed guest rooms with an assortment of antiques and curiosities. **Pros:** great food and cocktails in the gorgeous Oriental Bar & Bistrot; hotel harkens back to the gracious Venice of a bygone era; suites have private roof terraces with water views. **Cons:** rooms with views are considerably more expensive; one of the most densely touristed locations in the city; quirky, eccentric collections on display not for everyone. Ⓢ *Rooms from: €400* ✉ *Riva degli Schiavoni, Castello 4149, Castello* ☎ *041/5205044* ⊕ *www.hotelmetropole.com* ⤵ *67 rooms* ⓘ⦿ *Free Breakfast* Ⓜ *Vaporetto: San Zaccaria.*

7

Castello

Ruzzini Palace Hotel

$$$ | HOTEL | Renaissance- and Baroque-style common areas are soaring spaces with Venetian terrazzo flooring, frescoed and exposed beam ceilings, and Murano chandeliers; guest rooms tastefully mix historical style with contemporary furnishings and appointments. **Pros:** great buffet breakfast (not included in all rates); a luminous, aristocratic ambience; located on a lively Venetian campo not frequented by tourists. **Cons:** relatively far from a vaporetto stop; plain bathrooms; no restaurant on-site. $ *Rooms from: €250* ⊠ *Campo Santa Maria Formosa, Castello 5866, Castello* ☎ *041/2410447* ⊕ *www.ruzzinipalace.com* ⌐ *28 rooms* ❄ *No Meals* Ⓜ *Vaporetto: San Zaccaria, Rialto.*

Nightlife

Bar Dandolo

COCKTAIL LOUNGES | Even if you're not staying at Hotel Danieli, it's worth a stop to marvel at its bar's over-the-top decor inside a 14th-century palace. Though pricey, it's a highly atmospheric place to sample their signature Vesper martini (gin, vodka, martini dry, and Angostura bitters), or another cocktail of your choice, usually accompanied by live piano music. ⊠ *Hotel Danieli, Riva degli Schiavoni, Castello 4196, Castello* ☎ *041/5226480* ⊕ *www.marriott.com* Ⓜ *Vaporetto: San Zaccaria.*

Inishark

PUBS | The popular Italo-Irish pub Inishark, located midway between San Marco and Rialto, is known for its variety of international beers, live music, and live sports on the TV. ⊠ *Calle Mondo Novo near San Lio, Castello 5787, Castello* ☎ *041/5235300* Ⓜ *Vaporetto: Rialto.*

Zanzibar

CAFÉS | This kiosk bar is very popular on warm summer evenings with Venetians and tourists. Although there's food, it's mostly limited to conventional Venetian sandwiches and commercial ice cream. The most interesting thing about the place is its location with a view of the church of Santa Maria Formosa, which makes it a pleasant place for a drink and a good place for people-watching. ⊠ *Campo Santa Maria Formosa, Castello 5840, Castello* ☎ *345/9423998* Ⓜ *Vaporetto: San Zaccaria.*

 Performing Arts

Querini Stampalia Fondazione

MUSIC | This palazzo/museum occasionally stays open late to host curated evenings of music, from jazz to centuries-old music played on antique instruments. The Caffè Letterario on the premises has food and drink available. ⊠ *Campo Santa Maria Formosa, Castello 5252, Castello* ☎ *041/2711411.*

Shopping

CLOTHING

★ Banco Lotto No. 10

WOMEN'S CLOTHING | All the one-of-a-kind clothes and bags on sale at this vintage-inspired boutique were designed and created by residents of the women's prison on Giudecca island. ⊠ *Salizada Sant'Antonin, Castello 3478/A, Castello* ☎ *041/5221439* Ⓜ *Vaporetto: San Zaccaria.*

★ Barbieri Arabesque

OTHER ACCESSORIES | Scarves and shawls for all come in myriad colors, textures, designs, and shapes. They've been a perennial favorite of Venetians and travelers alike since they opened in 1945. ⊠ *Ponte dei Greci, Castello 3403, Castello* ☎ *041/5228177* ⊕ *www.barbieriarabesque.com* Ⓜ *Vaporetto: San Zaccaria.*

CRAFTS

Scriba

CRAFTS | A delightful husband-and-wife team sells exclusive Italian-made crafts, along with maps, fine prints, and paintings by Italian and international artists.

An artisan decorates a papier-mâché Venetian mask.

☒ *Castello Salizada S. Lio 5728, Castello* ☏ *041/4769324* ⊕ *www.scribavenice.com* Ⓜ *Vaporetto: Rialto.*

GLASS

Vetrofantasia Di Fuin Michele

GLASSWARE | Pop in and see Michele at work in his workshop and browse the wonderful glass creations, including various jewelry pieces and glass-ball bottle stoppers. The vibrant handcrafted objects here are far more affordable than in many overpriced glass outlets in Venice. ☒ *Calle del Dose, 3800, Castello* ☏ *041/4767067* ⊕ *vetrofantasia-di-fuin-michele-lavorazi-one.business.site* Ⓜ *Vaporetto: San Zaccaria.*

GOLD, WOOD, AND METALWORK

Cose Antiche di Luca Sumiti

CRAFTS | Luca Sumiti carries on the work of his father, Maurizio; traditional wrought-iron chandeliers and lamps come unadorned, gilded, or tastefully enameled in bright colors. Here you'll also find conspicuous, five-foot-tall wooden sculptures of *mori veneziani* (Venetian Moors). ☒ *Calle delle Bande, Castello*

5274, Castello ☏ *041/5205621* Ⓜ *Vaporetto: Rialto or San Zaccaria.*

Jonathan Ceolin

CRAFTS | Carrying on the traditions of his adopted city, this craftsman makes traditional wrought-iron chandeliers, wall lamps, and Venetian lanterns, either plain black or gilded (like in the old days), in his tiny workshop near Campo Santa Maria Formosa. ☒ *Ponte Marcello off Campo Santa Marina, Castello 6106, Castello* ☏ *041/5200609* ⊕ *www.ceolinjonathan.com* Ⓜ *Vaporetto: Rialto.*

★ Paolo Brandolisio

CRAFTS | Paolo Brandolisio's workshop is a lofty tribute to his craft; this is where Brandolisio apprenticed with his famous mentor, Giuseppe Carli (spot photos of him and a youthful Paolo dotting the walls). Gondoliers' oars await pickup, piled underneath the skylight; you can purchase a tiny hand-carved oarlock as a very special souvenir. ☒ *Calle Corte Rota, Castello 4725, Castello* ☏ *041/5224155* ⊕ *www.paolobrandolisio.it* Ⓜ *Vaporetto: San Zaccaria.*

LEATHER GOODS

★ Giovanna Zanella

SHOES | Cobbler-designer Giovanna Zanella Caeghera creates whimsical contemporary footwear in a variety of styles and colors. She was a student of the famous Venetian master cobbler Rolando Segalin. ✉ *Calle Carminati off Campo San Lio, Castello 5641, Castello* ☎ *041/5235500* ⊕ *giovannazanella.com* Ⓜ *Vaporetto: Rialto.*

Kalimala

LEATHER GOODS | This shop should not be missed if you are looking for soft leather bags that are a perfect match for almost any outfit, handmade leather shoes, or quality belts. ✉ *Salizzada San Lio, Castello 5387, Castello* ☎ *041/5283596* ⊕ *kalimala.net* Ⓜ *Vaporetto: Rialto.*

MARKETS

Via Garabaldi food market

MARKET | Fresh foods, including farm-fresh cheeses and other dairy products, are available at the morning market near the Giardini della Biennale. There's also a handy Coop supermarket nearby. ✉ *Via Garabaldi 1796, Castello* Ⓜ *Vaporetto: Arsenale.*

MASKS

★ Kartaruga

OTHER SPECIALTY STORE | This is a treasure trove of papier-mâché objects, panels, and masks designed for the theater stage. Their masks have starred on catwalks and in commercials and films, including *Casanova*, *Gambit*, and *Eyes Wide Shut*. Mask-making classes are offered by appointment. ✉ *Calle delle Bande, Castello 5369/70, Castello* ☎ *041/5210393* ⊕ *kartaruga.com* Ⓜ *Vaporetto: Rialto or San Marco.*

★ Papier Mache—Laboratorio di Artigianato Artistico

OTHER SPECIALTY STORE | **FAMILY** | If you're looking for an authentic Venetian mask, this is the place to come. Owner Stefano and his talented team of artists create exquisite handmade masks that can be custom-ordered if you don't see what you want, as well as shipped worldwide. ✉ *Calle Lunga Santa Maria Formosa, Castello 5174/B, Castello* ☎ *041/5229995* ⊕ *www.papiermache. it* Ⓜ *Vaporetto: Ospedale.*

Scheggi di Arlecchino

OTHER SPECIALTY STORE | What distinguishes family-owned-and-operated Scheggi di Arlecchino is that many of their masks are inspired by the works of famous painters, including Picasso, Klimt, and de Chirico, to name but a few. ✉ *Calle Lunga Santa Maria Formosa, Castello 6185, Castello* ☎ *041/5225789* Ⓜ *Vaporetto: Rialto.*

WINE

Al Canton del Vin

WINE/SPIRITS | This friendly neighborhood enoteca has an excellent array of regional wines plus a selection of craft beer and spirits, chocolate, and other gourmet treats. ✉ *Salizada Santa Giustina 2907/A, Castello* ☎ *041/2770449* Ⓜ *Vaporetto: Celestia.*

🏃 Activities

Nico Venice Tour

WALKING TOURS | Friendly licensed tour guide Nico, a native of Asolo with a master's in History of Arts and Conservation, leads various tours focusing on culture and food and wine, including boat tours around Venice and the islands of the lagoon. During the Biennales Arte and Architettura. he also guides tours of the Giardini pavilions and gallery spaces around Castello. ✉ *Castello* ☎ *340/2692866 cell* ⊕ *www.nicovenicetour.com* 🎫 *From €48 for Secrets of Venice tour.*

Treasures of Venice

BOAT TOURS | **FAMILY** | Skipper and licensed tour guide Max steers the rudder of his 20-foot-long boat *Alice*, offering forays around the lagoon, including a 3–6 hour Sunrise over Burano tour (€390). There's room for four passengers, but there's no cabin, so check the forecast before booking and bring suitable clothing. ✉ *Castello* ☎ *347/3723761 cell* ⊕ *boatinvenice.com* 🎫 *From €240 for Panoramic City Tour.*

Chapter 8

SAN GIORGIO MAGGIORE AND THE GIUDECCA

8

Updated by
Nick Bruno

👁 Sights	🍴 Restaurants	🛏 Hotels	🛍 Shopping	🍸 Nightlife
★★★☆☆	★★★★☆	★★★☆☆	★★☆☆☆	★☆☆☆☆

NEIGHBORHOOD SNAPSHOT

TOP EXPERIENCES

Explore the Cini Foundation. Discover handsome cloisters, galleries, a garden maze, and archives.

Climb the campanile. Reach the top of San Giorgio's church tower for views of the lagoon.

Stroll the *fondamenta* (quay, or walkway). Grab a seat or walk the long promenade to observe Giudecca life.

Appreciate the architecture. Visit Palladio's architectural masterpiece on the Giudecca, Il Redentore.

Splash out at Hotel Cipriani. Jet-setters flock to this lavish hotel for the epitome of Venetian luxury.

PLANNING YOUR TIME

You will probably want to see San Giorgio together with the adjacent island of the Giudecca. Allow a half hour to see the church of San Giorgio, more if you want to catch the view from the top of the bell tower. Allot an extra hour or two if you wish to see one of the frequent excellent art exhibits in the Cini Foundation adjacent to the church and to glance into the serene Palladian cloister.

The only major site on the Giudecca is Palladio's masterpiece, the church of the Santissimo Redentore, whose major attraction is its architecture itself; so, a visit should not take more than a half hour. Any additional time depends upon how long you want to spend soaking up the local atmosphere, exploring the new crop of arts spaces, and enjoying the spectacular views of Venice proper.

GETTING HERE

To reach Giudecca directly from Marco Polo airport, take Alilaguna Line Blu to Giudecca Stucky (for the eastern end) or the seasonal Linea Rosso, which also alights at Zitelle for the western side. The cheapest way to reach San Giorgio from Venice is to take Vaporetto Line 2, which runs between the hubs of nearby San Zaccaria and Piazzale Roma/Rialto. At night take Vaporetto N. Lines 2, 4.2, and N all stop at Zitelle, Redentore, and Palanca on Giudecca.

OFF THE BEATEN PATH

■ **Sacca Fisola.** East of the imposing Molino Stucky is the adjoining artificial island of Sacca Fisola. With much of Venice dominated by tourism and veneration of the past, as if it were an open-air museum, walking around this residential district is a chance to experience contemporary life for today's dwindling population of Venetians. Ⓜ *Vaporetto: Palanca.*

PAUSE HERE

■ **Il Convento dei Santi Cosma e Damiano.** Duck into and along narrow Calle del Pestor to find this secluded former convent. The cloister here is a wonderful, atmospheric place to pause with a picnic and for shade or shelter, depending on the weather. The complex houses many intriguing art galleries and studios where you can meet a number of talented artists at work. Ⓜ *Vaporetto: Palanca.*

Life is slower on San Giorgio Maggiore and Giudecca, two Venetian islands just off Dorsoduro. Here, visitors can escape the well-trodden tourist trail and meet artists and curators at work, or while away the afternoon strolling and, on Giudecca, dining, along the panoramic fondamenta promenade. The two islands' close proximity makes them easy to visit together, but each has a charm all its own.

San Giorgio Maggiore, the island across from Piazza San Marco, is graced with its magnificent namesake church, a panoramic campanile, and interesting cultural center. Its Benedictine monastery was established in 982, but it wasn't until 1580 that the gleaming church became a major symbol of La Serenissima ("the most serene," a nickname for Venice). Alongside Palladio's church there are a few unusual places that may divert you for a few hours. Instead of restaurants, shops, or secular attractions, you can take in views from San Giorgio Maggiore's neoclassical campanile over Venice, the islands, and beyond. Or, you can spend a day at the Fondazione Giorgio Cini, a vast monastery complex turned cultural institute with important archives, interesting exhibitions, and events, including fabulous concerts. It's worth a visit for its cloisters by Palladio, the 17th-century library by Baldassare Longhena, the Teatro Verde, and the verdant grounds, including the meditative Borges Labyrinth.

Just to the west of San Giorgio is Giudecca, an island that paints a picture of local Venetian family life. It has retained much of its working class roots and today attracts creative types and the odd jet-setter lured by the lavish Hotel Cipriani. Although administratively a part of Dorsoduro, Giudecca feels detached from the main action over the busy waters of Canale di Giudecca.

The island is known for Palladio's magnificent Redentore church, built to give thanks to the Redeemer for deliverance from the 1576 plague that decimated the Venetian population. Venetians continue to give thanks here every third Saturday of July with an exuberant party on boats, pontoons, and restaurants. But it doesn't have to be festival time to enjoy the island. The real charm of a visit to Giudecca is just to wander along the fondamenta that faces Venice. Grab a seat at one of the seafood restaurants and take in the contrasting architecture and serene grounds of the luxe Hotel Cipriani and former flour-mill Molino Stucky, which lie at opposing ends of the island. Lots of intriguing buildings and enterprises lie between. In recent years locals and newcomers have created an intimate and friendly arts scene here. Giudecca's new allure is in its numerous small galleries, backstreet workshops, and repurposed Santi Cosma e Damiano Convent, which form part of the Giudecca Art District.

San Giorgio Maggiore

Beckoning travelers across St. Mark's Basin is the island of San Giorgio Maggiore, separated by a small channel from the Giudecca. A tall brick campanile on that distant bank complements the Campanile of San Marco. Beneath it looms the stately dome of one of Venice's greatest churches, San Giorgio Maggiore, the creation of Andrea Palladio.

You can reach San Giorgio Maggiore via Vaporetto Line 2 from San Zaccaria. The next three stops on the line take you to the Giudecca.

■TIP→ **Food options are limited to the San Giorgio Café at the Fondazione Cini, which has a wonderful waterside terrace but can be inconsistent. Bring light refreshments and snacks, and suspend your appetite for a meal on nearby Giudecca.**

Sights

★ Fondazione Giorgio Cini
(*Cini Foundation*)
OTHER MUSEUM | Adjacent to San Giorgio Maggiore is a complex that now houses the Cini Foundation, established in 1951 as a cultural center dedicated to humanist research. It contains a beautiful cloister designed by Palladio in 1560, his refectory, a library designed by Longhena, and various archives. In a woodland area you can wander amid 10 "Vatican Chapels" created for the 2018 Architecture Biennale by renowned architects, including Norman Foster. Another stunning feature is the Borges Labyrinth, a 1-km (½-mile) path through a boxwood hedge that allows visitors to take a 45-minute contemplative walk. It was designed by Randoll Coate and inspired by the Jorge Luis Borges short story "The Garden of Forking Paths." An evocative audio guide, composed by Antonio Fresa and performed by Teatro La Fenice's orchestra, may accompany your pensive stroll. Guided tours are given daily (except Wednesday, November through mid-March), and reservations are required. ✉ *Isola di San Giorgio Maggiore, San Giorgio Maggiore* ☎ *366/4202181 WhatsApp for info and guided tours reservations* ⊕ *www.cini. it* ≦ *€14 for guided tour of either the Foundation buildings or the Vatican Chapels; €18 for guided tour of both the Foundation buildings and the Vatican Chapels* ⊙ *Closed Wed. Nov.–mid-Mar.* ⚲ *Reservations required* Ⓜ *Vaporetto: San Giorgio.*

Le Stanze del Vetro
ART GALLERY | Set in the west wing of a former boarding school within the Cini Foundation complex, these sleek gallery rooms host exhibitions exploring 20th- and 21st-century glass, from art pieces to commercial producers, including Venini. ✉ *Isola di San Giorgio Maggiore, 8, Giudecca* ☎ *041/5229138* ⊕ *lestanzedelvetro.org* ≦ *Free* ⊙ *Closed Wed.* Ⓜ *Vaporetto: San Giorgio.*

★ San Giorgio Maggiore
CHURCH | There's been a church on this island since the 8th century, with the addition of a Benedictine monastery in the 10th. Today's refreshingly airy and simply decorated church of brick and white marble was begun in 1566 by Palladio and displays his architectural

San Giorgio Maggiore, as seen from across the Bacino di San Marco.

hallmarks of mathematical harmony and classical influence. *The Last Supper* and the *Gathering of Manna*, two of Tintoretto's later works, line the chancel. To the right of the entrance hangs *The Adoration of the Shepherds* by Jacopo Bassano (1517–92); affection for his home in the foothills, Bassano del Grappa, is evident in the bucolic subjects and terra-firma colors. If they have time, monks are happy to show Carpaccio's *St. George and the Dragon,* which hangs in a private room. The campanile (bell tower) dates from 1791, the previous structures having collapsed twice. ■TIP➔ **Climb to the top of the campanile for unparalleled 360-degree views of the lagoon, islands, and Venice itself.** ⊠ *Isola di San Giorgio Maggiore, San Giorgio Maggiore* ☎ *041/5227827 San Giorgio Maggiore* ⊕ *www.abbaziasangiorgio.it* ☞ *Church free, campanile €6* Ⓜ *Vaporetto: San Giorgio.*

The Giudecca

The 2-km (1-mile)–long island of Giudecca, also known as Spinalonga (or "long spine"), has a becalming residential feel. It is most notably tied to Venetian heartstrings as the location of July's exuberant festival, Festa del Redentore.

Giudecca's name is something of a mystery. It may come from a possible 14th-century Jewish settlement, or because 9th-century nobles condemned to *giudicato* (exile) were sent here. It became a pleasure garden for wealthy Venetians during the Republic's long and luxurious decline, but today it's populated by a combination of working-class Venetians and generally expatriate gentrifiers. The Giudecca provides spectacular views of Venice. Thanks to several bridges, you can walk the entire length of its promenade, relaxing at one of several restaurants or just taking in the tranquil atmosphere.

While visiting San Giorgio Maggiore, stroll through the Borges Labyrinth, a garden maze at the Cini Foundation.

You can reach the Giudecca via vaporetto Line 2 from San Zaccaria. After San Giorgio Maggiore, the next stops on the line take you to the Giudecca, crossing over to the Zattere in Venice proper between the Giudecca stops. The island's past may be shrouded in mystery, but today it's about as down to earth as you can get, and despite substantial gentrification, it remains one of the city's few essentially working-class neighborhoods. The view of Venice from the rooftop bar at the Hilton hotel (Molino Stucky—it used to be a 19th-century flour mill) is perhaps even more spectacular than the one from San Marco's Campanile.

Sights

★ Casa dei Tre Oci

ART GALLERY | Housed in a handsome palazzo with three distinct windows (hence *oci*, or eyes in Venetian dialect), this fabulous art gallery is a must-visit for those seeking interesting art photography exhibitions and cultural events in a very special place. ⊠ *Fondamenta Zitelle 43, Giudecca* ☎ *041/2412332* ⊕ *treoci. org* 🖼 *€13* ⊘ *Closed Tues.* Ⓜ *Vaporetto: Zitelle.*

Giudecca Art District

ART GALLERY | Launched in 2019 and housed mainly in the former Dreher brewery industrial complex, GAD art village comprises a number of spaces, including those of renowned artist Fabrizio Plessi, and galleries including

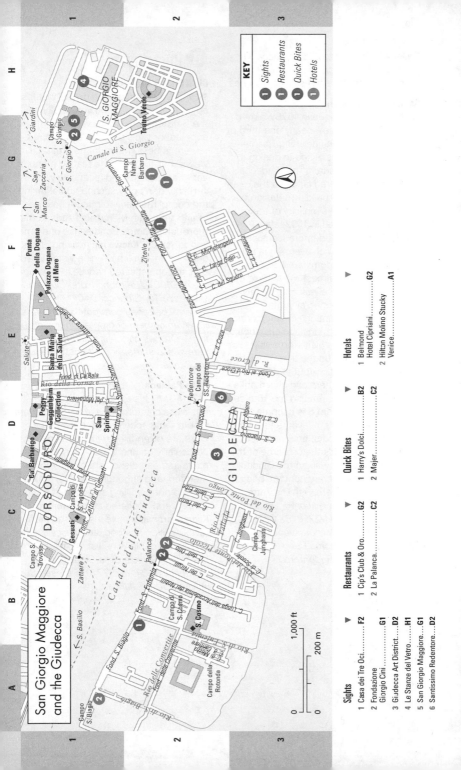

San Giorgio Maggiore and the Giudecca

KEY
- 1 Sights
- 1 Restaurants
- 1 Quick Bites
- 1 Hotels

0 — 200 m
0 — 1,000 ft

Sights ▶
1 Casa dei Tre Oci..........**F2**
2 Fondazione
   Giorgio Cini..............**G1**
3 Giudecca Art District....**D2**
4 Le Stanze del Vetro......**H1**
5 San Giorgio Maggiore....**G1**
6 Santissimo Redentore....**D2**

Restaurants ▶
1 Cip's Club & Oro..........**G2**
2 La Palanca................**C2**

Quick Bites ▶
1 Harry's Dolci.............**B2**
2 Majer....................**C2**

Hotels ▶
1 Belmond
   Hotel Cipriani..........**G2**
2 Hilton Molino Stucky
   Venice..................**A1**

Galleria Michela Rizzo. ✉ *Giudecca 211, Giudecca* ⊕ *www.giudecca-art-district. com* ⊗ *Closed Jan.* Ⓜ *Vaporetto: Palanca.*

Santissimo Redentore

CHURCH | After a plague in 1576 claimed some 50,000 people—nearly one-third of the city's population (including Titian)—Andrea Palladio was asked to design a commemorative church. The Giudecca's Capuchin friars offered land and their services, provided the building's design was in keeping with the simplicity of their hermitage. Consecrated in 1592, after Palladio's death, the Redentore (considered Palladio's supreme achievement in ecclesiastical design) is dominated by a dome and a pair of slim, almost minaretlike bell towers. Its deceptively simple, stately facade leads to a bright, airy interior. There aren't any paintings or sculptures of note, but the harmony and elegance of the interior makes a visit worthwhile. For hundreds of years, on the third weekend in July, it was tradition for the doge to make a pilgrimage here and give thanks to the Redeemer for ending the 16th-century plague. The event has become the Festa del Redentore, a favorite Venetian festival featuring boats, fireworks, and outdoor feasting. It's the one time of the year when you can walk to the Giudecca—across a temporary pontoon bridge connecting Redentore with the Zattere. ✉ *Fondamenta San Giacomo, Giudecca* ☎ *041/5231415, 041/2750462 Chorus Foundation* ⊕ *www.chorusvenezia.org* 🎫 *€3 (free with Chorus Pass)* ⊗ *Closed Sun.* Ⓜ *Vaporetto: Redentore.*

🍴 Restaurants

Cip's Club & Oro

$$$$ | **VENETIAN** | Located on the water's edge, looking out at the Venice skyline, the Belmond Cipriani's exclusive outdoor-indoor Cip's Club bar and Oro restaurant is best known for its breathtaking views, but the exquisite tasting menu of Venetian classics and extensive wine list certainly don't play second fiddle. Taking the complimentary 10-minute boat ride to and from San Marco also adds to the thoroughly James Bond sense of drama and romance. **Known for:** relaxing lunch destination; sublime Venice vistas with a Bellini; sophisticated service. ⑤ *Average main: €100* ✉ *Belmond Hotel Cipriani, Giudecca 10, Giudecca* ☎ *041/240801* ⊕ *www.belmond.com/hotels/europe/ italy/venice/belmond-hotel-cipriani/dining* 🏛 *Oro: elegant informal (no shorts, sleeveless shirts, or flip-flops)* Ⓜ *Vaporetto: Zitelle.*

★ La Palanca

$$ | **ITALIAN** | It's all about the views at this classic, informal wine bar–restaurant, where tables perched on the water's edge are often filled with chatty patrons, particularly at lunchtime. The homemade pasta and fish dishes are highly recommended, and although they don't really serve dinner, a filling selection of *cicheti* (appetizers) is offered in the evening. **Known for:** superlative views; sea bass ravioli, grilled seafood, and *baccalà* (cod); good, affordable wine list. ⑤ *Average main: €16* ✉ *Isola della Giudecca 448, Giudecca* ☎ *041/5287719* ⊗ *Closed Sun.* Ⓜ *Vaporetto: Palanca.*

☕ Coffee and Quick Bites

Harry's Dolci

$$$ | BAKERY | With tables offering a spectacular view of the Zattere outside and an elegant room inside, Harry's (of Cipriani fame) makes for a very indulgent pit stop. While you can linger for lunch or dinner, you can also order or fill your bag to go with light bites, sandwiches, and sweet goodies, such as cake and gelato. **Known for:** location and fame that come with a price tag; salads; cakes and pastries. ⑤ *Average main: €26* ⊠ *Fondamenta San Biagio, Giudecca 773, Giudecca* ☎ *041/5224844* ⊕ *www.cipriani.com/gb/harrys-dolci* ⊗ *Closed Mon. and Tues.* Ⓜ *Vaporetto: Palanca.*

★ Majer

$$ | VENETIAN | Set by the Palanca waterside with lagoon views and clean, contemporary interiors, Majer is a reliable, quality bet at any time of day. Start as early as 7 am for breakfast cappuccino and pastries or arrive later for brunch bites, leisurely pasta lunches, picnic bakes, *aperitvo* (aperitif) with vino, or dinner dates until 10 pm. **Known for:** all-day snacks; *sbrisòlona* (a traditional crumbly almond cake); biscotti, cakes, and *semifreddi* (dessert with a texture between ice cream and mousse); grilled seafood and wagyu steak for dinner. ⑤ *Average main: €22* ⊠ *Fondamenta Sant'Eufemia 461, Giudecca* ☎ *041/5211162* ⊕ *www.majer.it.*

🛏 Hotels

★ Belmond Hotel Cipriani

$$$$ | HOTEL | With amazing service, wonderful rooms, fab restaurants, and a large pool and spa—all just a five-minute boat ride from Piazza San Marco (the hotel water shuttle leaves every 15 minutes, 24 hours a day)—the Cipriani is Venetian luxe at its best. **Pros:** old-world charm meets modern luxury; Olympic-size heated saltwater pool; Michelin-starred restaurant. **Cons:** gym not open 24 hours; may be too quiet for some; very expensive. ⑤ *Rooms from: €967* ⊠ *Giudecca 10, Giudecca* ☎ *041/240801* ⊕ *belmond.com* ⊗ *Closed mid-Nov.–late Mar.* ⇌ *96 rooms* ⦿l *Free Breakfast* Ⓜ *Vaporetto: Zitelle.*

Hilton Molino Stucky Venice

$$$ | HOTEL | FAMILY | Wooden beams and iron columns are some of the original details still visible in this redbrick former flour mill-turned-hotel, which also features sublime views across the lagoon to Venice, particularly from the lively rooftop bar. **Pros:** ample breakfast buffet; extremely helpful staff; shuttle boat to San Marco. **Cons:** hotel itself a bit confusing to navigate; can hear noise from other rooms; food offerings on the pricey side. ⑤ *Rooms from: €215* ⊠ *Giudecca 810, Giudecca* ☎ *041/2723311* ⊕ *www.hilton.com* ⇌ *379 rooms* ⦿l *No Meals* Ⓜ *Vaporetto: Palanca.*

Nightlife

★ Skyline Rooftop Bar

COCKTAIL LOUNGES | For arguably the best views of Venice anywhere, visit this buzzy eighth-floor hotel cocktail bar. There are regular DJ and live music events during the summer months. ⊠ *Hilton Molino Stucky Venice, Giudecca 810, Giudecca* ☎ *041/2723316* ⊕ *www. skylinebarvenice.it* Ⓜ *Vaporetto: Palanca.*

Shopping

GLASS

Stefano Morasso Studio

GLASSWARE | For exquisite, vibrantly colored handmade glass and a meeting with the artist Stefano and his wife Nicoletta, seek out the serene convent cloister of the Santi Cosma e Damiano. Call in advance to make sure the studio is open. ⊠ *Giudecca 621/E, Giudecca* ☎ *041/5647224* ⊕ *www.stefanomorasso. it* Ⓜ *Vaporetto: Palanca.*

LACE, LINEN, AND FABRIC

Fortuny Tessuti Artistici

FABRICS | The original Fortuny textile factory, built on former convent grounds, has been converted into a showroom. Prices are over-the-top, but it's worth a trip to see the extraordinary colors and textures of their hand-printed silks and velvets. Call in advance to arrange a tour of the buildings and gorgeous gardens. ⊠ *Fondamenta San Biagio, Giudecca 805, Giudecca* ☎ *393/8257651, 041/5287697* ⊕ *fortuny.com* Ⓜ *Vaporetto: Palanca.*

Activities

Canottieri Giudecca

SAILING | For a taste of rowing in the traditional Voga Veneta style and a chance to sail in the lagoon, sign up with this venerable rowing club, which also has a gym for members. ⊠ *Giudecca 259/B, Giudecca* ☎ *041/5287409* ⊕ *www. canottierigiudecca.com* Ⓜ *Vaporetto: Redentore.*

ISLANDS OF THE LAGOON

Updated by
Liz Humphreys

◉ Sights	🍴 Restaurants	🛏 Hotels	💼 Shopping	🍸 Nightlife
★★★★☆	★★★☆☆	★★★☆☆	★★★★☆	★★☆☆☆

WELCOME TO
ISLANDS OF THE LAGOON

TOP REASONS TO GO

★ **Gaze at glass:** Murano's glass producers will wow you with their magnificent creations, whether you plan to buy or simply to window shop.

★ **Get some beach time:** On the southern border of the Venice lagoon, the Lido's beach clubs make for a perfect day in the sun for the whole family.

★ **Explore the Basilica di Santa Maria Assunta:** This 11th-century church on Torcello showcases amazingly well-preserved Byzantine mosaics, including the gorgeous *Last Judgment*.

★ **Pose with brightly colored houses:** Burano is filled with fisherman's homes painted in the colors of the rainbow to make them easier to find in the fog.

★ **Visit San Michele in Isola:** Renaissance architect Mauro Codussi designed this beautiful 15th-century church, dating from 1469.

★ **See Venice's vineyards:** Venissa, a charming restaurant/hotel across the bridge from Torcello on the island of Mazzorbo, boasts the only working vineyards in the Venetian islands.

1 The Lido. Venice's legendary beachfront still retains elements of belle epoque grandeur.

2 Torcello. This tiny island is renowned for its beauty, breathing room, and 12th-century mosaics.

3 Murano. This bustling island is famed for its outstanding glass artisans and its informative glass museum.

4 Burano. With a long history of lace production, fishing traditions, and brightly painted houses, Burano is full of charm.

5 San Michele. Venice's cemetery island is the resting place of many artists and home to the beautiful church San Michele in Isola.

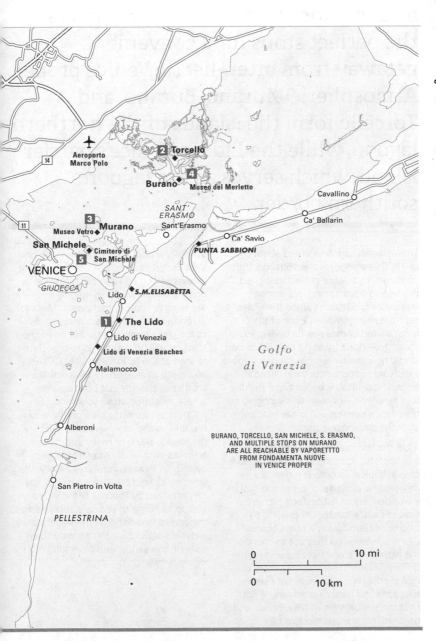

14

Aeroporto
Marco Polo

2 Torcello

4

Burano   Museo del Merletto

Cavallino

SANT'
ERASMO

Ca' Ballarin

3   Murano

11   Museo Vetro

Sant'Erasmo

San Michele

Ca' Savio

5   Cimitero di
San Michele

PUNTA SABBIONI

VENICE

GIUDECCA

Lido   S.M.ELISABETTA

1   The Lido

Lido di Venezia

Lido di Venezia Beaches

Golfo
di Venezia

Malamocco

Alberoni

BURANO, TORCELLO, SAN MICHELE, S. ERASMO,
AND MULTIPLE STOPS ON MURANO
ARE ALL REACHABLE BY VAPORETTTO
FROM FONDAMENTA NUOVE
IN VENICE PROPER

San Pietro in Volta

PELLESTRINA

0   10 mi

0   10 km

There are 118 islands in the Venetian Lagoon, between the Italian mainland and the Adriatic Sea—and they make the perfect stops for a convenient getaway from often-hectic Venice proper. Atmospheric Murano, Burano, and Torcello form the islands of the northern lagoon, while the Lido is Venice's barrier island, which serves as the lagoon's southern border.

The Venetian Lagoon formed about 6,000 to 7,000 years ago. In the 15th and 16th centuries, hydraulics projects stopped the lagoon from turning into a marsh, and draining programs since then have kept the islands livable. Each of the most visited islands has its own unique character—don't try to hit them all in one long day. If you have time, it's much more satisfying to appreciate each island's singular qualities by budgeting a full day for one or two—or even an overnight, as the islands seem much more magical after the day-trippers depart.

All of the Venetian islands can be reached by vaporetto from the Fondamenta Nove stop in Venice. Torcello is legendary for its beauty and sense of calm, and makes a wonderful destination for a picnic (be sure to pack a lunch). Otherwise, try to dine at Hemingway's fave Locanda Cipriani, where you may opt to spend the night in one of its cozy guest rooms. Burano, which has a storied history of lace production, is an island of fishing traditions and houses painted in a riot of colors—blue, yellow, pink, ocher, and dark red. For a more modern take, stroll across the bridge to Mazzorbo, the only Venetian island that still boasts working vineyards. You can sample the *vino*—or enjoy a deluxe Michelin-starred meal—at the island's Venissa restaurant. Murano is renowned for its glass, and you can tour a glass factory here, but be warned that you will be pressured to buy. Better to start at the Museo del Vetro (Glass Museum) to see what styles you like, then stroll the streets, popping into whatever stores strike your fancy. San Michele, a vaporetto stop on the way to Murano, is the cemetery island of Venice, the resting place of many international artists who have chosen to spend eternity in this beautiful city. Finally, the Lido, an 11 km (7-mile)-long barrier island, immortalized by Thomas Mann's *Death in Venice*, is home to Venice's beaches and the annual Venice Film Festival. It makes a lovely stop to beat the summer heat, relax on the sands, and have fun with the whole family.

Planning

Getting Here and Around

WATER BUSES

The only way to reach the Venetian islands is on the water. ACTV runs the water bus service. A single tourist ticket valid for 75 minutes costs €7.50. You may opt for a one-, two-, or three-day ticket if you choose to visit multiple islands. Water buses run 24 hours. Check routes and schedules on the ACTV website, or at individual vaporetto stations. Tickets are available at main vaporetto stops, on the AVM Venezia Official App, at tobacconists, and at some newspaper kiosks.

WATER TAXIS

Private water taxis (*motoscafi*) cost around €90 to the Lido and €100 or more per hour to other islands. Book through the Consorzio Motoscafi Venezia (☎ 041/2406712, weekdays 9 am to 6 pm; ☎ 041/5222303, weekends 6 pm to 9 am ⊕ www.motoscafivenezia.it).

The Lido

The Lido is Venice's barrier island, forming the southern border of the Venetian Lagoon and protecting Venice from the waters of the Adriatic. It forms the beach of Venice and is home to a series of bathing establishments, both public and private, some luxurious and elegant, some quite simple and catering to Venetian families and their children. Buses run the length of the island. Aside from the Jewish cemetery, the only other attractions are the many villas dating from the early 1900s, which display some interesting modernist architecture, and several art nouveau hotels.

TIMING

Allow an hour and a half from the time you arrive at the Santa Maria Elisabetta vaporetto stop (the main stop on the Lido) to arrive at and see the Jewish cemetery and to return to the vaporetto stop. If you plan on swimming or sunbathing, you may well want to spend the better part of a warm, sunny day on the Lido.

Sights

Antico Cimitero Ebraico (*Ancient Jewish Cemetery*)

CEMETERY | You might complete your circuit of Jewish Venice with a visit to the Antico Cimitero Ebraico, full of fascinating old tombstones half hidden by ivy and grass. The earliest grave dates from 1389; the cemetery remained in use until the late 18th century. You can book guided tours through the Jewish Museum of Venice. ⊠ *Via Cipro at San Nicolo, Lido* ☎ *041/715359 Jewish Museum* ⊕ *www.museoebraico.it* ☞ *€10 for guided tour* ☾ *Closed Sat.* Ⓜ *Vaporetto: Lido, San Nicolò.*

Beaches

Lido di Venezia Beaches

BEACH | **FAMILY** | Most hotels on the Lido have access to charming beach clubs with cabanas, striped umbrellas, and chaise longues—all of which are often available for nonguests to use for a fee. On either end of the long barrier island, the public beaches offer a more rustic but still delightful setting for nature lovers to dig their toes in the sand. **Amenities:** food and drink; lifeguards; showers; toilets. **Best for:** swimming; walking. ⊠ *Lido di Venezia, Lido* Ⓜ *Vaporetto: Lido.*

Restaurants

Glamy Bistro

$$$ | **ECLECTIC** | For a break from traditional Venetian cuisine, head to this charming eatery featuring two menus: one with innovative Italian dishes, and one with well-prepared sushi and sashimi. Michela Cafarchia, who started Glamy in the

Venice's barrier island, the Lido, is known for its beachfront.

garden of her family home, aims to use sustainable, local ingredients as much as possible. **Known for:** lovely garden seating; inventive fusion cuisine; excellent wine list. $ *Average main: €32* ⊠ *Via Sandro Gallo 111, Lido* ☎ *0320/8430999* ⊕ *www.glamybistrot.it* ⊗ *Closed Tues. No lunch* Ⓜ *Vaporetto: Lido.*

★ Ristorante Favorita

$$$ | **ITALIAN** | For an appealing selection of old-school Venetian recipes, this elegant restaurant on a peaceful side street—family-run since around 1950—more than delivers. Dishes are heavy on the seafood, and you can't go wrong with classics like spaghetti *allo scoglio* (with seafood) or *sarde e gamberi in saor* (sweet-and-sour sardines and shrimp), served up by the friendly staff. **Known for:** pretty outdoor setting; grilled local fish; good choice of wines. $ *Average main: €30* ⊠ *Via Francesco Duodo 33, Lido* ☎ *5261626* ⊗ *Closed Mon. No lunch Tues.–Thurs.* Ⓜ *Vaporetto: Lido.*

☕ Coffee and Quick Bites

★ Gelateria Da Titta

$ | **CAFÉ** | **FAMILY** | On the Lido, strategically located on the main drag between the vaporetto stop and the most central beaches, Titta is one of the oldest *gelaterie* (gelato shops) in Venice. Get your receipt at the *cassa* (register) for a cone to go, or enjoy one of the special combinations while lolling in a swinging chair under the trees that line the Gran Viale. **Known for:** ice caffè and ice *cioccolato* (chocolate); *gianduiotto* (chocolate and hazelnut) gelato, topped with cream and hazelnuts; many types of bruschette. $ *Average main: €8* ⊠ *Gran Viale Santa Maria Elisabetta 61, Lido* ☎ *041/4580007* ⊕ *da-tita.net* ⊗ *Closed Nov.–early Mar.* Ⓜ *Vaporetto: Lido.*

Pasticceria Maggion

$ | **BAKERY** | Since 1958, Venetians have been making the trip to the Lido even in bad weather for celebrated, custom-made fruit tarts (to be ordered one day ahead; no bar service). They also make pizzas, available by the slice, plus focaccia, pretzels, and other savory baked goods. **Known for:** traditional Venetian biscuits; savory pies; seasonal fruit tarts. $ *Average main: €5* ⊠ *Via Dardanelli 46, Lido* 📞 *041/5260836* ⊕ *pasticceria-maggion.weebly.com* ▭ *No credit cards* ⊘ *Closed Mon. and Tues.; closed 1–4 pm* Ⓜ *Vaporetto: Lido.*

🛏 Hotels

Hotel Excelsior Venice Lido Resort
$$$$ | **HOTEL** | **FAMILY** | Built in 1908, this grand hotel with Moorish decor has old-fashioned charm and loads of amenities—from a private beach with white cabanas and a seasonal bar and restaurant to a swimming pool, gym, and tennis courts (though, oddly, no spa). **Pros:** friendly, welcoming staff; lovely beachfront location; convenient water shuttle every 30 minutes to and from Venice proper. **Cons:** restaurants on the expensive side; could do with a refresh; can get very busy in summer and around the Venice Film Festival. $ *Rooms from: €610* ⊠ *Lungomare Marconi 41, Lido* 📞 *041/5260201* ⊕ *www.hotelexcelsior-venezia.com* ⇋ *196 rooms* ⦿ *No Meals* Ⓜ *Vaporetto: Lido.*

★ JW Marriott Venice Resort & Spa
$$$$ | **RESORT** | Once you get a taste of the resort's lush gardens, fabulous spa, and fantastic pools—all set on an exclusive island called Isole Delle Rose, a 20-minute boat ride from Venice—you may find yourself quickly settling in to *la dolce vita* (the sweet life). **Pros:** loads of amenities not found at hotels in Venice proper; relaxed vibe far from the Venice crowds; spacious rooms. **Cons:** not much Venetian style in rooms; getting to and from Venice can feel like a hassle; extra charge for spa. $ *Rooms from: €647* ⊠ *Isola delle Rose, Laguna di San Marco, Venezia Succursale 12, Venice* 📞 *041/8521300* ⊕ *www.jwvenice.com* ⊘ *Closed mid-Nov.–Feb.* ⇋ *266 rooms* ⦿ *Free Breakfast.*

🏃 Activities

BIKING
The flatness of the Lido makes it easy to ride a bike around the island, especially when you add a relaxing break at the beach.

Venice Bike Rental
BIKING | **FAMILY** | Rent bikes for adults and kids as well as tandem bikes, two-seater bikes, and four-seater bikes. ⊠ *Gran Viale Santa Maria Elisabetta 79A, Lido* 📞 *5261490* ⊕ *venicebikeren-tal.com* ⇌ *Bike rental from €10 per day* Ⓜ *Vaporetto: Lido.*

Islands of the Northern Lagoon

The perfect vacation from your Venetian vacation is an escape to Murano, Burano, and sleepy Torcello, the islands of the northern lagoon. If you have time to see only one, your choice should depend upon your tastes: Torcello is atmospheric and romantic and contains sights of major historical and artistic importance; Murano is the place to go to shop for glass and to visit the glass museum; and Burano is a fishing village awash with local color.

TIMING
Hitting all the sights on all the islands takes a busy, full day. If you limit yourself to Murano and San Michele, you can easily explore for an ample half day; the same goes for Burano and Torcello. In summer the express Vaporetto Line 7 will take you to Murano from San Zaccaria (the Jolanda landing) in 25 minutes; Line 3 will take you from Piazzale Roma to Murano via the Canale di Cannaregio in 21 minutes; otherwise, local Line 4.1 makes a 45-minute trip from San Zaccaria every 20 minutes, circling the east end of Venice, stopping at Fondamente Nove and San Michele on the way. To see

glassblowing, get off at Colonna; the Museo stop will put you near the Museo del Vetro.

Line 12 goes from Fondamente Nove direct to Murano and Burano every 30 minutes (from there, Torcello is a 5-minute ferry ride on Line 9); the full trip takes 45 minutes each way. To get to Burano and Torcello from Murano, pick up Line 12 at the Faro stop (Murano's lighthouse). Line 1 runs from San Marco to the Lido in about 20 minutes.

Torcello

Torcello offers ancient mosaics, greenery, breathing space, and picnic opportunities. Some people call this tiny island the most magical place in Venice. Nearly deserted today (except for the posh Locanda Cipriani, an inn and restaurant), the island still casts a spell, perhaps because, in the 10th century, this was Venice. In their flight from barbarians 1,500 years ago, the first Venetians landed here, prospering even after many left to found the city of Venice. By the 10th century, Torcello had a population of 10,000 and was more powerful than Venice itself. From the 12th century on, the lagoon around the island began silting up, and a malarial swamp developed. As malaria took its toll, Torcello was gradually abandoned and its palaces and houses were dismantled, their stones used for building materials in Venice. All that's left now is the hauntingly beautiful cathedral (built in 1008), containing exquisite Byzantine mosaics. The Virgin and the Apostles in the apse, as well as the spectacular *Last Judgment,* date from the 12th century, predating most of the mosaics in the Basilica di San Marco. There's also the graceful 11th- and 12th-century church of Santa Fosca.

TIMING
You can see Torcello's cathedral and the church of Santa Fosca easily in a half hour, but to avoid the hordes of tourists, come early in the day during the week or on a bright, mild day in winter. You will want to spend an hour or so appreciating the serene tranquility of the all-but-abandoned island and admiring the sights.

 Sights

★ Basilica di Santa Maria Assunta
CHURCH | The hallowed centerpiece of Torcello, Santa Maria Assunta was built in the 11th century, and the island's wealth at the time is evident in the church's high-quality mosaics. The mosaics show the gradually increasing cultural independence of Venice from Byzantium. The magnificent late-12th-century mosaic of the Last Judgment shows the transition from the stiffer Byzantine style on the left to the more fluid Venetian style on the right. The Virgin in the main apse dates possibly from about 1185 and is of a distinctly Byzantine type, with her right hand pointing to the Christ child held with her left arm. The depictions of the Twelve Apostles below her are possibly the oldest mosaics in the church and date from the early 12th century. Note that restoration of the mosaics is ongoing. The adjacent Santa Fosca church, built when the body of the saint arrived in 1011, is still used for religious services. ⌧ Torcello ☎ 041/730119 🎫 Santa Maria Assunta €5, Santa Fosca free Ⓜ Vaporetto: Torcello.

 Restaurants

Locanda Cipriani Restaurant
$$$ | VENETIAN | A nearly legendary restaurant—Hemingway came here often to eat, drink, and brood under the veranda's greenery—established by a nephew of Giuseppe Cipriani (the founder of Harry's Bar), this inn profits from its idyllic location on the island of Torcello. The food is not exceptional, especially considering the high prices, but dining here is more about getting lost in Venetian magic; the menu features pastas and lots of

seafood. **Known for:** a peaceful lunch choice when you want to get away from Venice; wonderful historic atmosphere; traditional Venetian cuisine, with a focus on seafood. ⓢ *Average main: €31* ⊠ *Piazza Santa Fosca 29, Torcello* ☎ *041/730150* ⊕ *www.locandacipriani.com* ⊗ *Closed Tues. and early Jan.–mid-Feb.* Ⓜ *Vaporetto: Torcello.*

Hotels

Locanda Cipriani

$$$ | **B&B/INN** | Founded by Giuseppe Cipriani in the late 1920s, this intimate *locanda* (inn) on the island of Torcello remains in the Cipriani family and retains the simple, classy character of the period. **Pros:** pure tranquility; charming ambience; real sense of history. **Cons:** breakfast could be better; some rooms on the small side; very isolated, yet Torcello is a delight. ⓢ *Rooms from: €293* ⊠ *Piazza Santa Fosca 29, Torcello* ☎ *041/730150* ⊕ *www. locandacipriani.com* ⊗ *Closed early Jan.– mid-Feb.* ⇌ *5 rooms* Ⓘ *Free Breakfast* Ⓜ *Vaporetto: Torcello.*

Activities

Hiring a private boat to sail around the lagoon lets you see hidden corners and avoid the crowds on the public boats.

BOATING
Classic Boats Venice

BOATING | **FAMILY** | Half-day or full-day private boat tours start in La Certosa before sailing to Torcello and back. You can also rent electric boats if you want to drive yourself. ⊠ *Isola della Certosa, Torcello* ☎ *5236720* ⊕ *www.classicboatsvenice. com* ⌕ *Electric boat rentals from €220 for 4 hrs.; boat tours with driver from €550* Ⓜ *Vaporetto: Certosa.*

Murano

In the 13th century the Republic, concerned about fire hazards and anxious to maintain control of its artisans' expertise, moved its glassworks to Murano, still renowned for its glass. As in Venice, bridges here link a number of small islands, which are dotted with houses that once were, and still largely are, workman's cottages. Many of them line Fondamenta dei Vetrai, the canalside walkway leading from the Colonna vaporetto landing.

To avoid being pressured to buy glass, take the regular vaporetto from Piazzale Roma or Fondamente Nove to Murano instead of succumbing to the hawkers offering you a "free" trip to Murano. They will take you to inferior glassmakers and will abandon you if you don't buy. If you do buy, rest assured that your taxi driver's commission will be added into the price you pay. Once on the island, "guides" herd new arrivals to factories, but you can avoid the hustle by just walking away.

Be aware that some of the glass sold as "Murano" is made in China or Eastern Europe. Even if a piece is, in fact, made on Murano, its origin does not ensure either its quality or its status as a good investment. If you are concerned with these issues, stick to pieces by those glassmakers with established reputations, most of whom have pieces displayed in the Murano Glass Museum or quality boutiques in and around Piazza San Marco.

TIMING

Murano has a few interesting churches, which can be seen without much investment of time, but its main sight is the glass museum. You will need about an hour to do the museum justice. But since Murano's main attractions are the glass shops and factories, your time commitment will depend essentially on how much you enjoy shopping and the size of your wallet.

👁 Sights

Basilica dei Santi Maria e Donato
CHURCH | Just past the glass museum, this is among the first churches founded by the lagoon's original inhabitants. The elaborate mosaic pavement includes the date 1140; its ship's-keel roof and Veneto-Byzantine columns add to the semblance of an ancient temple. ☒ Fondamenta Giustinian, Calle S. Donato 11, Murano ☎ 041/739056 Ⓜ Vaporetto: Murano Museo.

Chiesa di San Pietro Martire
CHURCH | You'll pass this church just before you reach Murano's Grand Canal (a little more than 800 feet from the landing). Reconstructed in 1511, it houses Giovanni Bellini's very beautiful and spectacular Madonna and Child with Doge Augostino Barbarigo and Veronese's St. Jerome. ☒ Fondamenta dei Vetrai, Murano ☎ 041/739704 Ⓜ Vaporetto: Murano Colonna, Murano Faro.

★ Museo del Vetro (Glass Museum)
ART MUSEUM | FAMILY | This compact yet informative museum displays glass items dating from the 3rd century to today. You'll learn all about techniques introduced through the ages (many of which are still in use), including 15th-century gold-leaf decoration, 16th-century filigree work that incorporated thin bands of white or colored glass into the crystal, and the 18th-century origins of Murano's iconic chandeliers. A visit here will help you to understand the provenance of the glass you'll see for sale—and may be tempted to buy—in shops around the island. ☒ Fondamenta Marco Giustinian 8, Murano ☎ 041/739586 ⊕ museovetro.visitmuve.it ☙ €11 ☙ Closed Mon.–Wed. Ⓜ Vaporetto: Murano Museo.

🍴 Restaurants

Acquastanca
$$$ | VENETIAN | Grab a seat among locals at this charming, intimate eatery—the perfect place to pop in for a lunchtime *primo* (first course) or to embark on a romantic evening. The name, referring to the tranquility of the lagoon at the turn of the tide, reflects this restaurant's approach to food and service, and you'll find such tempting seafood-based dishes as gnocchi with scallops and zucchini and curried scampi with black venere rice; tasteful decor sets the mood, with exposed brick, iron, and glass accents, and charming fish sculptures. **Known for:** relaxing atmosphere; focus on seafood dishes; light and fresh traditional food. ⑤ Average main: €26 ☒ Fondamenta Manin 48, Murano ☎ 041/3195125 ⊕ www.acquastanca.it ☙ Closed Sun. No dinner Tues.–Thurs. Ⓜ Vaporetto: Murano Colonna, Murano Faro.

Busa alla Torre da Lele
$$ | VENETIAN | If you're shopping for glass on Murano and want to sample some first-rate home cooking for lunch, you can't do better than stopping in this unpretentious trattoria in the island's central square. Friendly waiters will bring you ample portions of pasta, with freshly made seafood-based sauces, and a substantial variety of carefully grilled or baked fish. **Known for:** outdoor dining on a square; reliable lunch stop in Murano; tasty local fish and seafood. ⑤ Average main: €20 ☒ Campo Santo Stefano 3, Murano ☎ 041/739662 ☙ No dinner Ⓜ Vaporetto: Murano Colonna.

La Perla Ai Bisatei
$ | VENETIAN | FAMILY | A perennial favorite with locals (Murano and otherwise) and a welcome respite for travelers, La Perla offers a relaxed, local atmosphere and lots of delectably prepared standard Venetian fare. Don't even think of arriving

On a glass factory tour in Murano, you can often see glass being sculpted into art.

late in the lunch hour, or plan on waiting, as everyone else will have reserved or come early. **Known for:** lively lunchtime atmosphere; spaghetti *alle vongole* (with clams); catch of the day, grilled or fried. ⑤ *Average main: €11* ✉ *Campo San Bernardo 6, Murano* ☎ *041/739528* 🚫 *No credit cards* ⏰ *Closed Wed. and Aug.* Ⓜ *Vaporetto: Murano Venier.*

Trattoria Valmarana

$$ | **SEAFOOD** | The most upscale restaurant on Murano is housed in a palace on the *fondamenta* (walkway) across from the Museo del Vetro. Stucco walls and glass chandeliers complement well-appointed tables, and although the menu contains no surprises, the cuisine is more refined than at other places here. **Known for:** tables in the back garden; risotto of the day; spaghetti *allo scoglio* (with mussels, clams, prawns, and squid). ⑤ *Average main: €22* ✉ *Fondamenta Andrea Navagero 31, Murano*

☎ *041/739313* ⊕ *www.trattoriavalmarana. it* ⏰ *Closed 3 wks in Jan.* Ⓜ *Vaporetto: Murano Navagero.*

🛏 Hotels

★ Hyatt Centric Murano Venice

$$ | **HOTEL** | Befitting its location on Murano, this well-situated hotel is in a former glassmaking factory and has vitreous works of art throughout; it also has spacious, contemporary guest rooms with dark-wood floors, brown-and-cream color schemes, and good-size bathrooms with rain showers. **Pros:** easy walk to restaurants and shops; excellent breakfast buffet; vaporetto stop right outside the hotel, free airport transfers. **Cons:** gym is basic; most rooms have no views; extra charge for using wellness center. ⑤ *Rooms from: €153* ✉ *Riva Longa 49, Murano* ☎ *041/2731234* ⊕ *www.hyatt. com* *119 rooms* ❌ *No Meals* Ⓜ *Vaporetto: Murano Museo.*

Venice's Signature Crafts: Glass

Perhaps it's a matter of character that Venice, a city whose beauty depends so much upon the effects of shimmering, reflected light, also developed glass—a material that seems to capture light in solid form—as an artistic and expressive medium. There's not much in the way of a practical explanation for the affinity since the materials used to make glass, even from the earliest days, have not been found in the Venetian Lagoon. They've had to be imported, frequently with great difficulty and expense.

Glass production in the city dates back to the beginning of the Republic; evidence of a 7th- or 8th-century glass factory has been found on Torcello. Glass was already used as an artistic medium, employing techniques imported from Byzantine and Islamic glassmakers, by the 11th century. You can see surviving examples of early Venetian glass in the tiles of the mosaics of San Marco.

By 1295 the secrets of Venetian glassmaking were so highly prized that glassmakers were forbidden to leave the city. Venice succeeded in keeping the formulas of Venetian glass secret until the late 16th century, when some renegades started production in Bohemia. In 1291, to counter the risk of fire in Venice proper, the glass furnaces were moved to the then underpopulated island of Murano, which has remained the center of Venetian glassmaking to the present.

The fall of Damascus in 1400 and of Constantinople in 1435 sent waves of artisans to Venice, who added new techniques and styles to the repertoire of Venetian glass factories, but the most important innovation was developed by a native Venetian, Angelo Barovier. In the mid-15th century he discovered a way of making pure, transparent glass, *cristallo veneziano*. This allowed for the development of further decorative techniques, such as filigree glass, which became mainstays of Venetian glass production.

Glass studios such as Venini, Pauly, Moretti, and Berengo make up the premium line of Venetian glass production. These firms all have factories and showrooms on Murano, but they also have showrooms in Venice. Although their more elaborate pieces can cost thousands of dollars, you can take home a modest but lovely piece, such as a drinking glass, bearing one of their prestigious signatures for about $100, or even less.

On Murano you can visit a factory and watch Venetian glass being made, but among the premium manufacturers, only Berengo allows visitors to its factory, and they are quite dedicated to educating the public about glass. At minor factories, you'll generally get a demonstration of Venetian glassmaking.

Venice and Murano are full of shops selling glass, of varying quality. Some of it is made on the Venetian mainland, or even in Eastern Europe or China. Many minor producers on Murano have formed a consortium and identify their pieces with a sticker, which guarantees that the piece was made on Murano. The premium glass manufacturers, however, do not belong to the consortium—so the sticker guarantees only where the piece was made, not necessarily its quality or value.

Shopping

GLASS

Berengo Studio

GLASSWARE | In addition to contemporary fine-art glass, this high-end manufacturer gives tours of its Murano factory, something that most studios in this elite category do not do. ⊠ *Fondamenta dei Vetri 109/A, Murano* ☎ *041/739453* ⊕ *www.berengo.com* Ⓜ *Vaporetto: Murano Colonna, Murano Faro.*

Domus Vetri D'Arte

GLASSWARE | Vases, sculptures, objects, and jewelry from one of Murano's best glassworks are on offer. ⊠ *Fondamenta dei Vetri 82, Murano* ☎ *041/739215* Ⓜ *Vaporetto: Murano, Murano Faro.*

★ MaMa Salvadore Murano

GLASSWARE | To see more of glassmaking's artistic side, visit this gallery/shop that highlights works from international contemporary glass artists. ⊠ *Fondamenta da Mula 148, Murano* ☎ *0331/6224359* ⊕ *www.mamamurano.com* Ⓜ *Vaporetto: Murano.*

★ Salviati

GLASSWARE | One of the oldest and most prestigious Italian glassmakers (founded in 1859), Salviati partners with renowned international designers, including Tom Dixon, to create beautiful contemporary pieces. ⊠ *Fondamenta Radi 16, Murano* ☎ *041/5274085* ⊕ *www.salviati.com* Ⓜ *Vaporetto: Murano Museo, Murano Navagero.*

★ Simone Cenedese

GLASSWARE | This talented second-generation glass master produces intricately designed and often whimsical glass chandeliers and sculptures. ⊠ *Calle Bertolini 6, Murano* ☎ *041/5274455* ⊕ *simonecenedese.it* Ⓜ *Vaporetto: Murano Faro, Murano Colonna.*

JEWELRY

★ Davide Penso

JEWELRY & WATCHES | This Venice-born, Murano-based artist makes gorgeous glass necklaces, earrings, and bracelets using the lampwork technique, where he shapes colored glass rods over a flame. ⊠ *Fondamenta Riva Longa 48, Murano* ☎ *041/739819* ⊕ *www.davidepenso.info* Ⓜ *Vaporetto: Museo Murano.*

Activities

GLASS FACTORY TOURS

Though you'll find many tours to glass factories that include a boat trip from Venice, these often include hard sells for highly priced (and low-quality) glass products. You'll find a better selection and value if you travel to Murano yourself, by public boat, and sign up for a tour on your own.

★ Vetreria Artistica Colleoni Glass Factory Tour

SPECIAL-INTEREST TOURS | **FAMILY** | This guided tour of a glass factory includes a blowing and sculpting demonstration by a master glassmaker. Tours run many times each day; see the schedule and sign up online. ⊠ *Fondamenta San Giovanni dei Battuti 12, Murano* ☎ *5274872* ⊕ *www.colleoni.com* Ⓜ *Vaporetto: Murano Faro.*

Burano

Cheerfully painted houses in a riot of colors—blue, yellow, pink, ocher, and dark red—line the canals of this quiet village where lace making rescued a faltering fishing-based economy centuries ago. Visitors still love to shop here for "Venetian" lace, even though the vast majority of it is machine-made in Asia; visit the island's Museo del Merletto (Lace Museum) to discover the undeniable difference between the two. As you walk the 100

Burano is famous for its colorfully painted houses.

yards from the dock to Piazza Galuppi, the main square, you pass stall after stall of lace vendors. These good-natured vendors won't press you with a hard sell, but don't expect precise product information or great bargains—authentic, handmade Burano lace costs $1,000 to $2,000 for a 10-inch doily.

TIMING

The only official sight on Burano is the Lace Museum, which you should be able to see in a half hour. But the main reason for coming to Burano is simply to visit the charming, colorful houses. An hour meandering through the streets should suffice.

👁 Sights

Museo del Merletto (Lace Museum)

HISTORY MUSEUM | FAMILY | Home to the Burano Lace School from 1872 to 1970, the palace of Podestà of Torcello now houses a museum dedicated to the craft for which this island is known. Detailed explanations of the manufacturing process and Burano's distinctive history as a lace-making capital provide insight into displays that showcase everything from black Venetian Carnival capes to fingerless, elbow-length "mitten gloves" fashionable in 17th-century France. Portraits of Venice's aristocracy as well as embroidered silk and brocade gowns with lace embellishments provide greater societal context on the historical use of lace in European fashion. You can also watch interesting lace-making demonstrations. ⊠ *Piazza Galuppi 187, Burano* ☎ *041/730034* ⊕ *museomerletto. visitmuve.it* 🖃 *€6* ⊗ *Closed Mon.–Wed.* Ⓜ *Vaporetto: Burano.*

🍴 Restaurants

Trattoria Al Gatto Nero

$$$ | SEAFOOD | Around since 1965, Al Gatto Nero offers the best fish on Burano. No matter what you order, though, you'll savor the pride the owner and his family have in their lagoon, their island, and the quality of their *cucina* (maybe even more so when enjoying it on the picturesque fondamenta). **Known for:** *tagliolini* (thin spaghetti) with spider crab; the freshest fish and seafood around; risotto Burano-style, using local *ghiozzi* fish. $ *Average main: €33* ⊠ *Fondamenta della Giudecca 88, Burano* ☎ *041/730120* ⊕ *www.gattonero.com* ⊘ *Closed Mon., 1 wk in July, and 3 wks in Nov. No dinner Sun. or Wed.* Ⓜ *Vaporetto: Burano.*

★ **Venissa**

$$$$ | **MODERN ITALIAN** | Stroll across the bridge from Burano to the islet of Mazzorbo to see some of the Venetian islands' only working vineyards, amid which sits this charming restaurant where seasonal dishes incorporate vegetables, herbs, and flowers fresh from the garden and fish fresh from the lagoon, served in seven- to nine-course tasting menus (there's also a more casual osteria). To accompany your meal, pick out a local wine like the Dorona di Venezia, made with the island's native grape. **Known for:** perfect wine pairings; creative, sometimes avant-garde dishes; relaxed setting with tables overlooking the vines. $ *Average main: €140* ⊠ *Fondamenta Santa Caterina 3, Mazzorbo* ☎ *041/5272281* ⊕ *www.venissa.it* ⊘ *Closed Tues.–Wed. and Dec.–mid-Mar. No lunch* Ⓜ *Vaporetto: Mazzorbo.*

 Hotels

★ **Venissa Wine Resort Hotel**

$$ | **B&B/INN** | This laid-back contemporary guesthouse above Venissa's osteria is the perfect place to enjoy a food- and wine-centric getaway far from the hectic Venetian mainland. **Pros:** wonderful views; delicious breakfast made to order; spacious guest rooms. **Cons:** no wellness area; reception not staffed in the evenings; can hear noise from the osteria. $ *Rooms from: €200* ⊠ *Fondamenta Santa Caterina 3, Mazzorbo* ☎ *5272281* ⊕ *www.venissa.it* ⬎ *6 rooms* ◉ *Free Breakfast* Ⓜ *Vaporetto: Mazzorbo.*

 Shopping

★ **Emilia Burano**

FABRICS | This is not your grandmother's lace—these fourth-generation lace makers have updated their designs to produce exquisite bed linens, lampshades, sleepwear, and other items with lace trims and insets. There's also a small museum of antique lace and wedding garments from the 16th and 17th centuries. ⊠ *Piazza Galuppi 205, Burano* ☎ *041/735245* ⊕ *emiliaburano.it* Ⓜ *Vaporetto: Burano.*

Activities

KAYAKING

Explore the lagoon in a more intimate way by taking a kayak trip to Burano.

Venice Kayak

KAYAKING | These small-group guided kayaking tours on the Venice lagoon are perfect for experienced paddlers. Tours leave from La Certosa (just east of Venice) and pass by Sant'Erasmo and Mazzorbo before stopping in Burano. ⊠ *Isola della Certosa, Burano* ☎ *5236720* ⊕ *www.venicekayak.com* ⬎ *From €105 for full-day kayak tours* Ⓜ *Vaporetto: Certosa.*

San Michele

San Michele is the cemetery island of Venice, but unless you're interested in paying your respects to notables such as Ezra Pound and Igor Stravinsky, the main reason to make the crossing is to see the very beautiful church of San Michele in Isola by Renaissance architect Mauro Codussi. The cemetery itself, despite the illustrious people buried there, is really quite simple and indistinguishable from most other cemeteries in Italy. Vaporetto lines 4.1 or 4.2 from Fondamente Nove stop at San Michele during the hours it is open.

Did You Know?

San Michele is known
for its cemetery, where
you can come to pay your
respects to notables such
as Ezra Pound and Igor
Stravinsky.

TIMING

A half hour should suffice to see Codussi's church; how long you spend in the cemetery depends upon your degree of devotion to the memory of those buried there.

 Sights

★ Cimitero di San Michele (San Michele Cemetery)

CEMETERY | It's no surprise that serenity prevails on San Michele in Venice's northern lagoon. The city's island cemetery is surrounded by ocher brick walls and laced with cypress-lined pathways amid plots filled with thousands of graves; there's also a modern extension completed by British architect David Chipperfield in 2017. Among those who have made this distinctive island their final resting place are such international arts and science luminaries as Igor Stravinsky, Sergei Diaghilev, Ezra Pound, and the Austrian mathematician Christian Doppler (of the Doppler effect). You're welcome to explore the grounds if you dress respectfully and adhere to a solemn code of conduct. Photography and picnicking are not permitted. ⊠ *Isola di San Michele, San Michele* ☎ *041/7292841* 🎫 *Free* Ⓜ *Vaporetto: San Michele.*

San Michele in Isola

CHURCH | Tiny, cypress-lined San Michele is home to the first church designed by Mauro Codussi and the first example of Renaissance architecture in Venice; the gracefully elegant structure 'shows the profound influence of Florentine architects Alberti and Rossellino that would come to full fruition in Codussi's palaces on the Canale Grande. The church's dedication to St. Michael is singularly appropriate, since traditionally he holds the scales of the Last Judgment.

Next to the church is the somewhat later hexagonal Capella Emiliani (1528–1543), whose strangely shaped dome recalls those of Etruscan tombs. ⊠ *Isola San Michele, San Michele* ☎ *041/7292811* Ⓜ *Vaporetto: Cimitero.*

Chapter 10

SIDE TRIPS FROM VENICE

Updated by
Nick Bruno

👁 Sights	🍴 Restaurants	🛏 Hotels	💼 Shopping	🍸 Nightlife
★★★☆☆	★★★★★	★★★★☆	★★★☆☆	★★☆☆☆

WELCOME TO
SIDE TRIPS FROM VENICE

TOP REASONS TO GO

★ **Giotto's frescoes in the Cappella degli Scrovegni:** In this Padua chapel, Giotto's expressive and innovative frescoes foreshadowed the painting techniques of the Renaissance.

★ **Villa Barbaro in Maser:** Master architect Palladio's graceful creation meets Veronese's splendid frescoes in a onetime-only collaboration.

★ **Opera in Verona's ancient arena:** The performances may not be top-notch, but even serious opera fans can't resist the spectacle of these shows.

★ **Roman and early-Christian ruins at Aquileia:** Aquileia's ruins offer an image of the transition from pagan to Christian Rome and are almost entirely free of tourists.

1 Padua. A city of both high-rises and history, Padua is most noted for Giotto's frescoes in the Cappella degli Scrovegni.

2 Verona. Shakespeare placed Romeo, Juliet, and a couple of gentlemen in Verona—one of the oldest, best-preserved, and most beautiful cities in Italy.

3 Vicenza. This elegant art city, on the green plain reaching inland from Venice's lagoon, bears the signature of the great 16th-century architect Andrea Palladio, including several palazzi.

4 Udine. Friuli's compact and charming principal city has medieval and Renaissance splendors, including works by its favorite son, the 18th-century painter Tiepolo.

5 Aquileia. This sleepy little town's Roman and early-Christian remains offer an image of the transition from pagan to Christian Rome.

6 Trieste. The port city has a mixed Venetian-Austrian heritage and an important literary and political history that comes alive in belle epoque cafés and palaces built for Habsburg nobility.

EATING AND DRINKING WELL IN THE VENETO AND FRIULI–VENEZIA GIULIA

Pasta e fagioli

With the decisive seasonal changes of the Venetian Arc, it's little wonder that many restaurants shun printed menus. Elements from field and forest define much of the local cuisine, including white asparagus, herbs, chestnuts, radicchio, and wild mushrooms.

Restaurants here tend to cling to tradition, not only in the food they serve but in how they serve it. This means that from 3 in the afternoon until about 7:30 in the evening most places other than bars are closed tight, and on Sunday afternoon restaurants are packed with Italian families and friends indulging in a weekly ritual of lunching out. Meals are still sacred for most Italians in this region, so don't be surprised if you get disapproving looks when you gobble down a sandwich or a slice of pizza while seated on the church steps or a park bench. In many places it's actually illegal to do so. Likewise, your waiter will likely be very upset if you order just one course at a meal. If you want to dine lightly yet fit in with the locals, eat while standing at a bar.

THE BEST IN BEANS

Pasta e fagioli, a thick bean soup with pasta, served slightly warm or at room temperature, is made all over Italy. Folks in Veneto, though, take a special pride in their version. It features particularly fine beans that are grown around the village of Lamon, near Belluno.

Even when they're bought in the Veneto, the beans from Lamon cost more than double the next most expensive variety, but their rich and delicate taste is considered to be well worth the added expense. You never knew that bean soup could taste so good.

PASTA, RISOTTO, POLENTA

For *primi* (first courses), the Veneto dines on *bigoli* (thick whole-wheat pasta) generally served with an anchovy-onion sauce delicately flavored with cinnamon, and risotto flavored either with local fish, sausage, or vegetables. Polenta (corn meal gruel) is everywhere, whether it's a stiff porridge topped with Gorgonzola or stew, or a patty grilled alongside meat or fish, as in the photo below.

FISH

The catch of the day is always a good bet, whether sweet and succulent Adriatic shellfish, sea bream, bass, or John Dory, or freshwater fish from Lake Garda near Verona. A staple in the Veneto is *baccalà*, dried salt cod, soaked in water or milk, and then prepared in a different way in each city. In Vicenza, *baccalà alla vicentina*, pictured below, is cooked with onions, milk, and cheese, and is generally served with polenta.

MEAT

Because grazing land is scarce in the Veneto, beef is a rarity, but pork and veal are standards, while goose, duck, and guinea fowl are common poultry options. Lamb is available mostly in spring, when it's young and delicate. In Friuli–Venezia Giulia, menus show the influences of Austria-Hungary: you may find deer and hare on the menu, as well

Radicchio di Treviso

as Eastern European–style goulash. Throughout the Veneto an unusual treat is *nervetti*—cubes of gelatin from a cow's knee prepared with onions, parsley, olive oil, and lemon.

RADICCHIO DI TREVISO

In fall and winter be sure to try the radicchio di Treviso, pictured above, a red endive grown near that town but popular all over the region. Cultivation is very labor intensive, so it can be a bit expensive. It's best in a stew with chicken or veal, in a risotto, or just grilled or baked with a drizzle of olive oil and perhaps a little taleggio cheese from neighboring Lombardy.

WINE

Wine is excellent here: the Veneto produces more D.O.C. (Denominazione di Origine Controllata) wines than any other region in Italy. Amarone, the region's crowning achievement, is a robust and powerful red with an alcohol content as high as 16%. Valpolicella and Bardolino are other notable appellations. The best of the whites are Soave, sparkling Prosecco, and *pinot bianco* (pinot blanc). In Friuli–Venezia Giulia the local wines par excellence are *tocai friulano*, a dry, lively white made from the sauvignon vert grape, which has attained international stature, and piccolit, perhaps Italy's most highly prized dessert wine.

Baccalà

Much of the pleasure of exploring the Venetian Arc—the sweep of land curving from Verona to Trieste, encompassing the Veneto and Friuli–Venezia Giulia regions and spanning the River Adige to the Slovenian border—comes from discovering the variations on the Venetian theme that give a unique character to each of the towns.

Some of the cities outside Venice, such as Verona and Udine, have a solid medieval look. Padua, with its narrow arcaded streets, is romantic; Vicenza, ennobled by the architecture of Palladio, is elegant. Udine is a genteel, intricately sculpted city that's home to the first important frescoes by Gianbattista Tiepolo. Trieste shows off its past as a port of the Austro-Hungarian Empire in its Viennese-inspired coffeehouses and great palaces.

Wherever you go, the emblem of Venice, Saint Mark's winged lion, is emblazoned on palazzi or poised on pedestals, and the art, architecture, and way of life all in some way reflect Venetian splendor.

MAJOR REGIONS

The Venetian Arc is the sweep of land curving north and east from the River Adige to the Slovenian border. It's made up of two Italian regions, the Veneto and Friuli–Venezia Giulia, that were once controlled by Venice, and the culture is a mix of Venetian, Alpine, and central European sensibilities.

The **Veneto**, for centuries influenced by the city of Venice on the marshy Adriatic coast, is a prosperous region dotted by fortified cities with captivating history and undulating vineyards. Padua's alluring architecture, art, and canal network may reflect the Venetian influence as the closest terra firma dominion, but its ancient, pioneering university—famed for its humanist alumni—creates a beguiling buzz of cycling students, food markets, and commerce. With the cooling Dolomite Alpine waters of the Adige River snaking through its medieval, Roman, and Venetian heart, Verona combines splendor with intimacy. Perfectly formed and wealthy Vicenza is where the peerless Palladio put his harmonious architectural plans into bricks, mortar, and gleaming marble.

Heading northeast of the Veneto, the atmosphere of the **Friuli–Venezia Giulia** region derives from its fascinating mix of Italian, Slavic, and Central European influences. Venetian culture spread northward until it merged with northern European style evident in places like the medieval city of Udine. The old Austrian port of Trieste was, in the late 19th and early 20th centuries, an important center of Italian literature.

Planning

Planning Ahead

Reservations are required to see the Giotto frescoes in Padua's Cappella degli Scrovegni—though if there's space, you can "reserve" on the spot.

On the outskirts of Vicenza, Villa La Rotonda, one of star architect Palladio's masterpieces, is privately owned but open to the public some days (check for latest openings as the interiors are usually shut Monday through Thursday; hours for visiting the grounds are less restrictive).

Another important Palladian villa, Villa Barbaro near Maser, is open weekends and a couple of days during the week from April to October. From November to March, it's open only on weekends.

If you plan to take in an opera at the Arena di Verona, buy tickets as early as you can, since they sell out quickly. Also, book a room for the evening in Verona, as you are likely to miss the last train back to Venice.

⇨ *For details about Cappella degli Scrovegni, see Sights in the Padua section. For the villas, see Sights in Vicenza and Palladio Country. For the Arena di Verona, see Performing Arts in Verona.*

Making the Most of Your Time

Lined up in a row west of Venice are Padua, Vicenza, and Verona—three prosperous small cities that are each worth at least a day on a trip out of Venice. Verona has the greatest charm, and it's probably the best choice if you're going to visit only one of these cities, even though it also draws the biggest crowds of tourists.

East of Venice, the region of Friuli–Venezia Giulia is off the main tourist circuit, but you may be drawn by its caves and castles, its battle-worn hills, and its mix of Italian and central European culture. The port city of Trieste, famous for its elegant cafés, has quiet character that some people find dull and others find alluring.

Getting Here and Around

BUS

There are interurban and interregional connections throughout the Veneto and Friuli, handled by nearly a dozen private bus lines. To figure out which line will get you where, the best strategy is to get assistance from local tourist offices.

CAR

Padua, Vicenza, and Verona are on the highway (and train line) between Venice and Milan. Seeing them without a car isn't a problem; in fact, having a car can complicate matters. The cities sometimes limit automobile access, permitting only cars with plates ending in an even number on even days, odd on odd, or prohibiting cars altogether on weekends. There's no central source for information about these sporadic traffic restrictions; the best strategy is to check with your hotel before arrival for an update. You will need a car to get the most out of the hill country that makes up much of the Venetian Arc, and it will be particularly useful for visiting Aquileia, a rather interesting archaeological site with limited public transportation.

The A4, the primary route from Milan to Venice and Trieste, skirts Verona, Padua, and Udine along the way. Driving time, in normal traffic, from Venice to Padua is 30 minutes; Venice to Vicenza, 60 minutes, and to Verona 90 minutes. Heading east out of Venice, Aquileia is about 90 minutes, Udine about 90 minutes, and Trieste 120 minutes.

TRAIN

Trains on the main routes from Venice stop almost hourly in Verona, Vicenza, and Padua.

To the west of Venice, the main line running across the north of Italy stops at Padua (30 minutes from Venice), Vicenza (1 hour), and Verona (1½ hours); to the east is Trieste (2 hours).

Be sure to take express trains whenever possible—a local "milk run" that stops in every village along the way can take considerably longer. The fastest trains are the Eurostars, but reservations are obligatory and fares are much higher than on regular express trains.

TRAIN INFORMATION Trenitalia.
☎ 892021 ⊕ www.trenitalia.com.

Hotels

Rates tend to be higher in Padua and Verona; in Verona especially, seasonal rates vary widely and soar during trade fairs and the opera season. There are fewer good lodging choices in Vicenza, perhaps because overnighters are drawn to the better restaurant scenes in Verona and Padua. *Agriturismo* (farm stay) information is available at tourist offices and sometimes on their websites. Ask about weekend discounts, often available at hotels catering to business clients. Substantial savings can sometimes be had by booking through reservation services on the Internet.

Restaurant and hotel reviews have been shortened. For full information, visit Fodors.com. Prices in the dining reviews are the average cost of a main course at dinner, or, if dinner is not served, at lunch. Prices in the hotel reviews are the lowest cost of a standard double room in high season.

WHAT IT COSTS in Euros

	$	$$	$$$	$$$$
RESTAURANTS				
	under €15	€15–€24	€25–€35	over €35
HOTELS				
	under €125	€125–€200	€201–€300	over €300

Restaurants

Although the Veneto is not considered one of Italy's major culinary destinations, the region offers many opportunities for exciting gastronomic adventures. The fish offerings are among the most varied and freshest in Italy (and possibly Europe), and the vegetables from the islands in the Venetian Lagoon are considered a national treasure. Take a break from pasta and try the area's wonderful, creamy risottos and hearty polenta.

Padua

42 km (25 miles) west of Venice.

A romantic warren of arcaded streets, Padua has long been one of the major cultural centers of northern Italy. It has first-rate artistic monuments and, along with Bologna, is one of the few cities in the country where you can catch a glimpse of student life.

Its university, founded in 1222 and Italy's second oldest, attracted such cultural icons as Dante (1265–1321), Petrarch (1304–74), and Galileo Galilei (1564–1642), thus earning the city the sobriquet La Dotta (The Learned). Padua's Basilica di Sant'Antonio, begun around 1238, attracts droves of pilgrims, especially on his feast day, June 13. Three great artists—Giotto (1266–1337), Donatello (circa 1386–1466), and Mantegna (1431–1506)—left significant works in Padua, with Giotto's Scrovegni Chapel

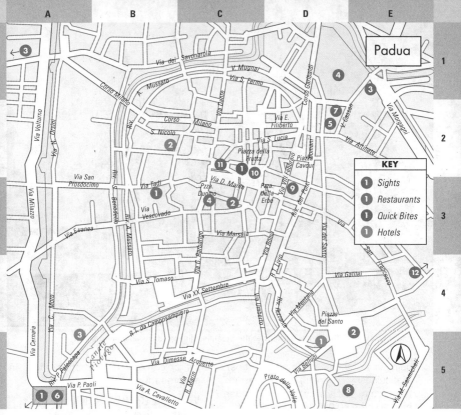

Padua

KEY

1	*Sights*
1	*Restaurants*
1	*Quick Bites*
1	*Hotels*

Padua's Basilica di Sant'Antonio combines the Byzantine, Romanesque, and Gothic styles.

being one of the best-known, and most meticulously preserved, works of art in the country. Today, a cycle-happy student body—some 60,000 strong—flavors every aspect of local culture. Don't be surprised if you spot a *laurea* (graduation) ceremony marked by laurel leaves, mocking lullabies, and X-rated caricatures.

GETTING HERE AND AROUND
The train trip between Venice and Padua is short, and regular bus service originates from Venice's Piazzale Roma. By car from Venice, Padua is on the Autostrada Torino–Trieste A4/E70. Take the San Carlo exit and follow Via Guido Reni to Via Tiziano Aspetti into town. Regular bus service connects Venice's Marco Polo airport with downtown Padua.

Padua is a walker's city. If you arrive by car, leave your vehicle in one of the parking lots on the outskirts or at your hotel. Unlimited bus service is included with the PadovaCard (€16 or €21, valid for 48 or 72 hours), which allows entry to all the city's principal sights (€1 extra for a Scrovegni Chapel reservation). It's

available at tourist information offices and at some museums and hotels.

VISITOR INFORMATION
Padua Tourism Office. ⊠ *Padova Railway Station, Piazzale Stazione, Padua* ☎ *049/5207415* ⊕ *www.turismopadova.it.*

Sights

Abano Terme
HOT SPRING | A very popular hot-springs spa town about 12 km (7 miles) southwest of Padua, Abano Terme lies at the foot of the Euganean Hills among hand-tilled vineyards. If a bit of pampering sounds better than traipsing through yet another church or castle, indulge yourself with a soak, a massage, stone therapy, a skin peel, or a series of mud treatments, which are especially recommended for joint aches. A good-value day pass (€35) is available at the central and well-equipped Hotel Antiche Terme Ariston Molino Buja (⊕ *aristonmolino.it*). For a longer stay check out the latest offers on the Abano spa hotel hub website (⊕ *www.abano.it*).

The nearest railway stop on the Bologna–Padua line is Terme Euganee–Montegrotto. Alternatively, you can board a train on the Milan–Venice line, disembark at Padua, and board an Abano-bound bus in front of the train station. The trip takes about half an hour. ⊠ *Abano Terme* ⊕ *Take the Padua West exit off A4, or the Terme Euganee exit off A13* ⊕ *www. abano.it; aristonmolino.it.*

★ Basilica di Sant'Antonio
(*Basilica del Santo*)

CHURCH | Thousands of faithful make the pilgrimage here each year to pray at the tomb of St. Anthony, while others come to admire works by the 15th-century Florentine master Donatello. His equestrian statue (1453) of the condottiere Erasmo da Narni, known as Gattamelata, in front of the church is one of the great masterpieces of Italian Renaissance sculpture. It was inspired by the ancient statue of Marcus Aurelius in Rome's Campidoglio. Donatello also sculpted the series of bronze reliefs in the imposing interior illustrating the miracles of St. Anthony, as well as the bronze statues of the Madonna and saints on the high altar.

The huge church, which combines elements of Byzantine, Romanesque, and Gothic styles, was probably begun around 1238, seven years after the death of the Portuguese-born saint. It underwent structural modifications into the mid-15th century. Masses are held in the basilica almost constantly, which makes it difficult to see these artworks. More accessible is the restored Cappella del Santo (housing the tomb of the saint), dating from the 16th century. Its walls are covered with impressive reliefs by important Renaissance sculptors.

The Museo Antoniano part of the basilica complex contains a Mantegna fresco and works by Tiepolo, Carpaccio, and Piazzetta. There's a collection of votive offerings in the Museo della Devozione, and a multimedia display introducing the life of the saint and the history of the basilica. ⊠ *Piazza del Santo, Padua* ☎ *049/8225652* ⊕ *www.basilicadelsanto. it* ☒ *Basilica free, museum complex €7* ⊘ *Museum complex closed Mon.*

Burchiello Excursion, Brenta Canal
BODY OF WATER | During the 16th century the Brenta was transformed into a mainland version of Venice's Grand Canal with the building of nearly 50 waterside villas. Back then, boating parties viewed them from *burchielli*—beautiful river barges. Today the Burchiello excursion boat makes full- and half-day tours along the Brenta in season, departing from Padua and Venice; tickets can also be bought at travel agencies. You visit three houses, including the Villas Pisani and Foscari, with a lunchtime break in Oriago (€23 or €30 extra). Note that most houses are on the left side coming from Venice, or the right from Padua. ⊠ *Via Porciglia 34, Padua* ☎ *049/8760233* ⊕ *www.ilburchiello.it* ☒ *€70 half day, €99 full day; lunch extra* ⊘ *Closed Mon. and Nov.–Feb.*

★ Cappella degli Scrovegni
(*The Arena Chapel*)

CHURCH | The spatial depth, emotional intensity, and naturalism of the frescoes illustrating the lives of Mary and Jesus in this world-famous chapel broke new ground in Western art. Enrico Scrovegni commissioned these frescoes to atone for the sins of his deceased father, Reginaldo, the usurer condemned to the Seventh Circle of the Inferno in Dante's *Divine Comedy*. Giotto and his assistants worked on the frescoes from 1303 to 1305, arranging them in tiers to be read from left to right. Opposite the altar is a *Last Judgment,* most likely designed and painted by Giotto's assistants.

■**TIP**→ **Mandatory timed-entry reservations (nonrefundable) should be made in advance at the ticket office, online, or by phone. Payments online or by phone by credit card must be made one day in advance. Reservations are necessary even if you have a PadovaCard.**

The Giotto frescoes at Padua's Cappella degli Scrovegni are some of northern Italy's greatest art treasures.

To preserve the artwork, doors are opened only every 15 minutes. A maximum of 25 visitors must spend 15 minutes in an acclimatization room before making a 15-minute chapel visit (20 minutes in certain months). Tickets should be picked up at least one hour before your reservation. It's sometimes possible to buy admission on the spot. A good place to get some background before visiting the chapel is the multimedia room. ⊠ *Piazza Eremitani 8, Padua* ☎ *049/2010020 reservations* ⊕ *www. cappelladegliscrovegni.it* ✉ *€14, includes Musei Civici and Palazzo Zuckermann.*

Chiesa degli Eremitani

CHURCH | This 13th-century church houses substantial fragments of Andrea Mantegna's frescoes (1448–50), which were damaged by Allied bombing in World War II. Despite their fragmentary condition, Mantegna's still beautiful and historically important depictions of the martyrdom of St. James and St. Christopher show the young artist's mastery of extremely complex problems of perspective. ⊠ *Piazza Eremitani, Padua* ☎ *049/8756410.*

Montegrotto Terme

HOT SPRING | At this spa town about 13 km (8 miles) southwest of Padua, you can luxuriate in thermal mineral pools. Montegrotto Terme has several hotels whose treatments vary from simple massage and thermal and mud baths to hydrokinetic therapy. Scuba enthusiasts head here for the world's deepest indoor pool, Y-40 Deep Joy. The nearest railway stop, on the Bologna–Padua line, is Terme Euganee–Montegrotto. Taxis are available outside the station. ⊠ *Montegrotto Terme* ⊹ *Terme Euganee exit off A13* ⊕ *www. visitabanomontegrotto.com.*

★ Musei Civici degli Eremitani (*Civic Museum*)

OTHER MUSEUM | Usually visited along with the neighboring Cappella degli Scrovegni, this former monastery houses a rich array of exhibits and has wonderful cloister gardens with a mix of ancient architectural fragments and modern sculpture. The Pinacoteca displays works of medieval

The Venetian Arc, Past and Present

Long before Venetians made their presence felt on the mainland in the 15th century, Ezzelino III da Romano (1194–1259) laid claim to Verona, Padua, and the surrounding lands and towns. He was the first of a series of brutal and aggressive rulers who dominated the cities of the region until the rise of Venetian rule. Because of Ezzelino's cruel and violent nature, Dante consigned his soul to Hell.

After Ezzelino was ousted, powerful families such as Padua's Carrara and Verona's della Scala (Scaligeri) vied throughout the 14th century to dominate these territories. Venetian rule ushered in a time of relative peace, when noble families from the lagoon and the mainland commissioned Palladio and other accomplished architects to design their palazzi and villas. This rich classical legacy, superimposed upon medieval castles and fortifications, is central to the identities of present-day Padua, Vicenza, and Verona.

The region remained under Venetian control until the Napoleonic invasion and the fall of the Venetian Republic in 1797. The Council of Vienna ceded it, along with Lombardy, to Austria in 1815. The region revolted against Austrian rule and joined the Italian Republic in 1866.

Friuli–Venezia Giulia has been marched through, fought over, hymned by patriots, and romanticized by writers that include James Joyce, Rainer Maria Rilke, Pier Paolo Passolini, and Jan Morris. The region has seen Fascists and Communists, Romans, Habsburgs, and Huns. It survived by forging sheltering alliances—Udine beneath the wings of San Marco (1420), Trieste choosing Duke Leopold of Austria (1382) over Venetian domination.

Some of World War I's fiercest fighting took place in Friuli–Venezia Giulia, where memorials and cemeteries commemorate hundreds of thousands who died before Italian troops arrived in 1918 and liberated Trieste from Austrian rule. Trieste, along with the whole of Venezia Giulia, was annexed to Italy in 1920. During World War II the Germans occupied the area and placed Trieste in an administrative zone along with parts of Slovenia. The only Nazi extermination camp on Italian soil, the Risiera di San Sabba, was in a suburb of Trieste. After the war, during a period of Cold War dispute, Trieste was governed by an allied military administration; it was officially reannexed to Italy in 1954, when Italy ceded the Istrian peninsula to the south to Yugoslavia. These arrangements were not finally ratified by Italy and Yugoslavia until 1975.

and modern masters, including some by Tintoretto, Veronese, and Tiepolo. Standouts are the *Giotto Crucifix*, which once hung in the Cappella degli Scrovegni, and the *Portrait of a Young Senator*, by Giovanni Bellini (1430–1516). Among the archaeological finds is an intriguing Egyptian section, while the Gabinetto Fotografico is an important collection of photographs. Set aside at least 60–90 minutes to appreciate the scope of this fabulous museum complex. ✉ *Piazza Eremitani 8, Padua* ☎ *049/8204551* 💶 *€10, €14 with Scrovegni Chapel and Palazzo Zuckermann; free with PadovaCard* ⊙ *Closed Mon.*

Orto Botanico (*Botanical Garden*)
GARDEN | The Venetian Republic ordered the creation of Padua's botanical garden in 1545 to supply the university with medicinal plants, and it retains its original layout. You can stroll the arboretum—still part of the university—and wander through hothouses and beds of plants that were introduced to Italy in this late-Renaissance garden. A St. Peter's palm, planted in 1585, inspired Goethe to write his 1790 essay, "The Metamorphosis of Plants." ⊠ *Via Orto Botanico 15, Padua* ☎ *049/8273939* ⊕ *www.ortobotanicopd.it* ✉ *€10 (€5 with PadovaCard)* ☉ *Closed Mon. May–Mar.*

★ **Palazzo del Bo**
CASTLE/PALACE | The University of Padua, founded in 1222, centers around this predominantly 16th-century palazzo with an 18th-century facade. It's named after the Osteria del Bo (*bo* means "ox"), an inn that once stood on the site. It's worth a visit to see the perfectly proportioned anatomy theater (1594), the beautiful Old Courtyard, and a hall with a lectern used by Galileo. You can enter only as part of a guided tour; weekend/public holiday tours allow access to other parts of the university; most guides speak English, but it is worth checking ahead by phone. ⊠ *Via 8 Febbraio, Padua* ☎ *049/8275111 university switchboard, 049/8273939* ⊕ *www.unipd.it* ✉ *€7; €12 extended tour weekends and public holidays.*

Palazzo della Ragione
CASTLE/PALACE | Also known as Il Salòne, the spectacular arcaded reception hall in Padua's original law courts is as notable for its grandeur—it's 85 feet high—as for its colorful setting, surrounded by shops, cafés, and open-air fruit and vegetable markets. Nicolò Miretto and Stefano da Ferrara, working from 1425 to 1440, painted the frescoes after Giotto's plan, which was destroyed by a fire in 1420. The stunning space hosts art shows, and an enormous wooden horse, crafted for a public tournament in 1466, commands

pride of place. It is patterned after the famous equestrian statue by Donatello in front of the Basilica di Sant'Antonio, and may, in fact, have been designed by Donatello himself in the last year of his life. ⊠ *Piazza della Ragione, Padua* ☎ *049/8205006* ✉ *€7 (free with Padova-Card)* ☉ *Closed Mon.*

Piazza dei Signori
PLAZA/SQUARE | Some fine examples of 15th- and 16th-century buildings line this square. On the west side, the **Palazzo del Capitanio** (facade constructed 1598–1605) has an impressive **Torre dell'Orologio,** with an astronomical clock dating from 1344 and a portal made by Falconetto in 1532 in the form of a Roman triumphal arch. The 12th-century **Battistero del Duomo** (Cathedral Baptistry), with frescoes by Giusto de' Menabuoi (1374–78), is a few steps away. ⊠ *Piazza dei Signori, Padua* ☎ *049/656914* ⊕ *www.battisteropadova.it* ✉ *Battistero €5 (free with PadovaCard).*

Villa Pisani
CASTLE/PALACE | FAMILY | Extensive grounds with rare trees, ornamental fountains, and garden follies surround this extraordinary palace in Stra, 13 km (8 miles) southeast of Padua. Built in 1721 for the Venetian doge Alvise Pisani, it recalls Versailles more than a Veneto villa. This was one of the last and grandest of many stately residences constructed along the Brenta River from the 16th to 18th centuries by wealthy Venetians for their villeggiatura escape from midsummer humidity. Gianbattista Tiepolo's (1696–1770) spectacular fresco on the ballroom ceiling, *The Apotheosis of the Pisani Family* (1761), alone is worth the visit. For a relaxing afternoon, explore the gorgeous park and maze. To get here from Padua, take the SITA bus, or from Venice or Padua, take AVTV Bus No. 53E. The villa is a five-minute walk from the bus stop in Stra. ■TIP➔ **Mussolini invited Hitler here for their first meeting, but they stayed only one night because of the mosquitoes, which continue to be a nuisance.**

If visiting on a late afternoon in summer, carry bug repellent. ⊠ *Via Doge Pisani 7, Stra* ☎ *049/502074* ⊕ *www.villapisani. beniculturali.it* ⊠ *€7.50, €4.50 park only* ⊗ *Closed Mon.*

⊕ Restaurants

★ Enoteca dei Tadi

$$ | ITALIAN | In this cozy and atmospheric cross between a wine bar and a restaurant, you can put together a fabulous, inexpensive dinner from various classic dishes from all over Italy. Portions are small, but prices are reasonable—just follow the local custom and order a selection, perhaps starting with fresh *burrata* (mozzarella's creamier cousin) with tomatoes, or a selection of prosciutti or salami. **Known for:** bountiful wine and grappa list; several kinds of lasagna; intimate and rustic setting. ⑤ *Average main: €22* ⊠ *Via dei Tadi 16, Padua* ☎ *049/8364099, 388/4083434 mobile* ⊕ *www.enotecadeitadi.it* ⊗ *Closed Mon., 2 wks in Jan., and 2 wks late June–July. No dinner Sun.*

L'Anfora

$$ | WINE BAR | This mix between a traditional *bacaro* (wine bar) and an osteria is a local institution, opened in 1922. Stand at the bar with a cross section of Padovano society, from construction workers to professors, and peruse the reasonably priced menu of simple *casalinga* (home-cooked dishes), plus salads and a selection of cheeses. **Known for:** very busy at lunchtime; atmospheric art-filled osteria with wood interior; no-nonsense traditional Veneto food. ⑤ *Average main: €19* ⊠ *Via Soncin 13, Padua* ☎ *049/656629* ⊕ *osteria-lanfora.eatbu.com* ⊗ *Closed Sun. (except in Dec.), 1 wk in Jan., and 1 wk in Aug.*

Le Calandre

$$$$ | MODERN ITALIAN | Traditional Veneto recipes are given a highly sophisticated and creative treatment here, and the whole theatrical tasting-menu experience and gorgeous table settings can seem by turns revelatory or overblown at this high-profile place. Owner-chef Massimiliano Alajmo's creative, miniscule-portion dishes, passion for design (bespoke lighting, carved wooden tables, and quirky plates), and first-class wine list make this an option for a pricey celebratory meal. **Known for:** reservations essential; theatrical, sensory dining experience; playful (or to some pretentious) touches. ⑤ *Average main: €150* ⊠ *Via Liguria 1, Sarmeola ✛ 7 km (4 miles) west of Padua* ☎ *049/630303* ⊕ *www.calandre.com* ⊗ *Closed Sun., Mon., and Jan. 1–20. No lunch Tues.*

Osteria dal Capo

$$ | VENETIAN | Located in the heart of what used to be Padua's Jewish ghetto, this friendly trattoria serves almost exclusively traditional Veneto dishes, and it does so with refinement and care. Everything from the well-crafted dishes to the unfussy ship's dining cabin–like decor and elegant plates reflect decades of Padovano hospitality. **Known for:** limited tables mean reservations essential; intimate and understated dining at decent prices; liver and onions with grilled polenta. ⑤ *Average main: €23* ⊠ *Via degli Obizzi 2, Padua* ☎ *049/663105* ⊕ *www.osteriadalcapo.it* ⊗ *Closed Sun. No lunch Mon.*

☕ Coffee and Quick Bites

Bar Romeo

$ | NORTHERN ITALIAN | Deep in the atmospheric Sotto Salone market, this busy bar does a fab selection of filled *tramezzini* (triangular sandwiches), panini, and other snacks. It's a great place to hear the local dialect and mingle with the market workers and shoppers any time of day; grab a breakfast caffè and brioche, a cheeky glass of Falanghina, or a bit later—after 11 am perhaps—an *apertivo* (aperitif) with snacks. **Known for:** superb selection of wine by the glass; good value sandwiches; friendly staff and Padovano vibe. ⑤ *Average main: €5* ⊠ *26 Sotto Salone, Padua* ☎ *340/556 0611.*

Bicycles line the streets of Padua.

 ## Hotels

Al Fagiano

$ | **HOTEL** | The refreshingly funky surroundings in this self-styled art hotel include sponge-painted walls, brush-painted chandeliers, and views of the spires and cupolas of the Basilica di Sant'Antonio. **Pros:** great for art lovers or those after a unique ambience; convenient location; relaxed, quirky, homey atmosphere. **Cons:** lots of stairs; some find the way-out-there (some risqué) art a bit much; not all rooms have views. $ *Rooms from: €99* ⊠ *Via Locatelli 45, Padua* ☎ *049/8750073* ⊕ *www.alfagiano. com* ⤳ *40 rooms* ⑩ *No Meals.*

Albergo Verdi

$ | **HOTEL** | One of the best-situated hotels in the city provides understated modern rooms and public areas that tend toward the minimalist without being severe, while the intimate breakfast room with stylish Eames Eiffel chairs and adjoining terrace is a tranquil place to start the day. **Pros:** 24-hour bar service; excellent location close to Piazza dei Signori; attentive staff. **Cons:** few views; student noise in piazza-facing rooms; steep stairs and small elevator. $ *Rooms from: €90* ⊠ *Via Dondi dell'Orologio 7, Padua* ☎ *049/8364163* ⊕ *www.albergoverdipa-dova.it* ⤳ *14 rooms* ⑩ *Free Breakfast.*

Methis Hotel & Spa

$ | **HOTEL** | Four floors of sleekly designed guest rooms reflect nature's elements at this modern spa hotel: there are gentle earth tones and fiery red in the Classic rooms; watery, cool blues in Superior rooms; and airy white in the top-floor suites. **Pros:** gym, sauna, Turkish bath, and spa treatments; better views of canal across road from front rooms; superb canal walks nearby. **Cons:** public spaces lack some character; 15-minute walk from major sights and restaurants; tired decor and unkempt corners. $ *Rooms from: €120* ⊠ *Riviera Paleocapa 70, Padua* ☎ *049/8725555* ⊕ *www.methishotel.it* ⤳ *59 rooms* ⑩ *Free Breakfast.*

Ⓨ Nightlife

CAFÉS AND WINE BARS
★ Caffè Pedrocchi

CAFÉS | No visit to Padua is complete without taking time to sit in this historic café and iconic Padovano venue, patronized by luminaries like the French novelist Stendhal in 1831. Nearly 200 years later, it remains central to the city's social life. The café was built in the Egyptian Revival style, and it's now famed for its innovative aperitivi and signature mint coffee. The accomplished, innovative restaurant serves breakfast, lunch, and dinner. The grand salons and terrace provide a backdrop for the occasional jazz, swing, and cover bands. ✉ *Piazzetta Pedrocchi, Padua* ☎ *049/8781231* ⊕ *www.caffepedrocchi.it.*

🛍 Shopping

★ Mercato Sotto il Salone

FOOD | Under the Salone there's an impressive food market where shops sell choice salami and cured meats, local cheeses, wines, coffee, and tea. With the adjacent Piazza delle Erbe fruit and vegetable market, you can pick up all the makings of a fine picnic. On weekends and public holidays, the piazza is often filled with fabulous street food, as well as wine and beer stalls. ✉ *Piazza della Ragione, Padua* ⊕ *mercatosottoilsalone.it.*

Zotti Antiquariato

ANTIQUES & COLLECTIBLES | Owned by antiques dealer Pietro Maria Zotti—who has worked for more than 40 years in the trade—this always-changing shop has fascinating finds from Venetian artworks to stylish midcentury furniture, plus lots of smaller, more affordable items, including books, prints, jewelry, militaria, and coins. ✉ *Selciato San Nicolò 5, Padua* ☎ *338/2930830* ⊕ *www.zottiantiquariato.it.*

Cocktail Hour Ⓨ on Padua's Piazzas

One of Padua's greatest traditions is the outdoor en masse consumption of aperitifs: a spritz mixing Aperol or Campari with soda water and wine, Prosecco (sparkling wine), or wine. It all happens in Piazza delle Erbe and Piazza delle Frutta. Several bars there provide drinks in plastic cups, so you can take them outside and mingle among the crowds. The ritual, practiced primarily by students, begins at 6 or so, at which hour you can also pick up a snack from one of the outdoor vendors.

🏃 Activities

HelloVeneto Tours

WALKING TOURS | **FAMILY** | HelloVeneto runs numerous tours around the region, including a Giotto-theme walk and a Gardens and Castles excursion that explores Villa Barbarigo and Castello del Catajo. ✉ *Via Martiri d'Ungheria 60, Padua* ⟐ *Abano Terme* ☎ *0444/886737* ⊕ *www.helloveneto.it* 💶 *from €90.*

Verona

114 km (71 miles) west of Venice, 60 km (37 miles) west of Vicenza.

On the banks of the fast-flowing River Adige, enchanting Verona has timeless monuments, a picturesque town center, and a romantic reputation as the setting of Shakespeare's *Romeo and Juliet*. With its lively Venetian air and proximity to Lake Garda, it attracts hordes of tourists, especially Germans and Austrians. Tourism peaks during summer's renowned season of open-air opera in the arena and during spring's Vinitaly, one of the world's most important wine expos. For five days you can sample the wines of more than 3,000 wineries from dozens of countries.

Verona grew to power and prosperity within the Roman Empire as a result of its key commercial and military position in northern Italy. With its Roman arena, theater, and city gates, it has the most significant monuments of Roman antiquity north of Rome. After the fall of the empire, the city continued to flourish under the guidance of barbarian kings, such as Theodoric, Alboin, Pepin, and Berenger I, reaching its cultural and artistic peak in the 13th and 14th centuries under the della Scala (Scaligero) dynasty. (Look for the *scala*, or ladder, emblem all over town.) In 1404 Verona traded its independence for security and placed itself under the control of Venice. (The other recurring architectural motif is the lion of St. Mark, a symbol of Venetian rule.)

If you're going to visit more than one or two sights, it's worth purchasing a VeronaCard, available at museums, churches, and tobacconists for €20 (for 24 hours) or €25 (48 hours). It buys a single admission to most of the city's significant museums and churches, plus you can ride free on city buses. If you're mostly interested in churches, a €6 cumulative ticket is sold at Verona's major houses of worship and gains you entry to the Duomo, San Fermo Maggiore, San Zeno Maggiore, and Sant'Anastasia. Note that Verona's churches strictly enforce their dress code: no sleeveless shirts, shorts, or short skirts.

GETTING HERE AND AROUND

Verona is midway between Venice and Milan. Several trains per hour depart from any point on the Milan–Venice line. By car, from Venice, take the Autostrada Trieste–Torino A4/E70 to the SS12 and follow it north into town.

VISITOR INFORMATION

Verona Tourism Office (IAT Verona).
⊠ *Via degli Alpini 9, Piazza Bra, Verona* ☎ *045/8068680* ⊕ *www.veronatouristoffice.it/en.*

 # Sights

In addition to ancient Verona's famous Roman theater and arena, two of its city gates (Porta dei Leoni and Porta dei Borsari) and a beautiful triumphal arch (Arco dei Gavi) have survived. These graceful and elegant portals provide an idea of the high aesthetic standards of their time. Look, too, beyond the main sights of the Città Antica (historic center): take time to wander the streets, and be sure not to miss out on the many leafy stretches of the riverside Lungadige. Away from the crowds there's a wealth of varied architecture from ancient Rome to the Fascist era to the contemporary, as well as tranquil spots for feeding the ducks.

Arche Scaligere

TOMB | On a little square off Piazza dei Signori are the fantastically sculpted Gothic tombs of the della Scala family, who ruled Verona during the late Middle Ages. The 19th-century English traveler and critic John Ruskin described the tombs as graceful places where people who have fallen asleep live. The tomb of Cangrande I (1291–1329) hangs over the portal of the adjacent church and is the work of the Maestro di Sant'Anastasia. The tomb of Mastino II, begun in 1345, has an elaborate baldachin, originally painted and gilded, and is surrounded by an iron grillwork fence and topped by an equestrian statue. The latest and most elaborate tomb is that of Cansignorio (1375), the work principally of Bonino da Campione. The major tombs are all visible from the street. ⊠ *Via Arche Scaligere, Verona.*

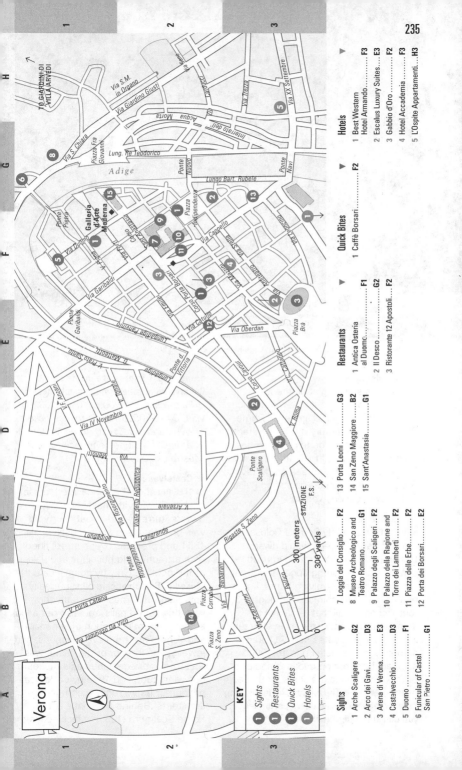

Verona

KEY

- 1 Sights
- 1 Restaurants
- 1 Quick Bites
- 1 Hotels

► Sights

1 Arche Scaligere G2
2 Arco dei Gavi D3
3 Arena di Verona E3
4 Castelvecchio D3
5 Duomo F1
6 Funicular of Castel
San Pietro G1
7 Loggia del Consiglio F2
8 Museo Archeologico and
Teatro Romano G1
9 Palazzo degli Scaligeri ... F2
10 Palazzo della Ragione and
Torre dei Lamberti F2
11 Piazza delle Erbe F2
12 Porta dei Borsari E2
13 Porta Leoni G3
14 San Zeno Maggiore B2
15 Sant'Anastasia G1

► Restaurants

1 Antica Osteria
al Duomo F1
2 Il Desco G2
3 Ristorante 12 Apostoli ... F2

► Quick Bites

1 Caffè Borsari F2

► Hotels

1 Best Western
Hotel Armando F3
2 Escalus Luxury Suites E3
3 Gabbio d'Oro F2
4 Hotel Accademia F3
5 L'Ospite Appartamenti ...H3

The ruins of the Arco dei Gavi lie on the Adige River in Verona.

★ Arco dei Gavi

RUINS | This stunning structure is simpler and less imposing, but also more graceful, than the triumphal arches in Rome. Built in the 1st century by the architect Lucius Vitruvius Cerdo to celebrate the accomplishments of the patrician Gavia family, it was highly esteemed by several Renaissance architects, including Palladio. ⊠ *Corso Cavour, Verona.*

Arena di Verona

RUINS | FAMILY | Only Rome's Colosseum and Capua's arena would dwarf this amphitheater, built for gymnastic competitions, choreographed sacrificial rites, and games involving hunts, fights, battles, and wild animals. Although four arches are all that remain of the arena's outer arcade, the main structure is complete and dates from AD 30. In summer, you can join up to 16,000 for spectacular opera productions and pop or rock concerts (extra costs for these events). ■TIP→ **The opera's the main thing here: when there is no opera performance, you can still enter the interior, but the arena is less impressive inside than the Colosseum or other Roman amphitheaters.** ⊠ *Piazza Bra 5, Verona* ☎ *045/8003204 visit, 045/8005151 performance tickets* ⊕ *www.arena.it* ✉ *€10 (free with VeronaCard); €11 includes entrance to nearby Museo Lapidario Maffeiano.*

★ Castelvecchio

CASTLE/PALACE | This crenellated, russet brick building with massive walls, towers, turrets, and a vast courtyard was built for Cangrande II della Scala in 1354 and presides over a street lined with attractive old buildings and palaces of the nobility. Only by going inside the **Museo di Castelvecchio** can you really appreciate this massive castle complex with its vaulted halls. You also get a look at a significant collection of Venetian and Veneto art, medieval weapons, and jewelry. The interior of the castle was restored and redesigned as a museum between 1958 and 1975 by Carlo Scarpa, one of Italy's most accomplished architects. Behind the castle is the Ponte Scaligero (1355), which spans the

River Adige. ✉ *Corso Castelvecchio 2, Verona* ☎ *045/8062611* ⊕ *museodicastelvecchio.comune.verona.it* 🎟 *€6 (free with VeronaCard)* ⊘ *Closed Mon.*

Duomo

CHURCH | The present church was begun in the 12th century in the Romanesque style; its later additions are mostly Gothic. On pilasters guarding the main entrance are 12th-century carvings thought to represent Oliver and Roland, two of Charlemagne's knights and heroes of several medieval epic poems. Inside, Titian's *Assumption* (1532) graces the first chapel on the left. ✉ *Via Duomo, Verona* ☎ *045/592813* ⊕ *www.chieseverona.it* 🎟 *€3 (free with Church Cumulative Ticket or VeronaCard).*

★ Funicular of Castel San Pietro

VIEWPOINT | Opened in 2017, this funicular ride ascends 500 feet from near the Teatro Romano up to a panoramic terrace in just 90 seconds, affording fabulous Veronese views. For the adventurous, there's scope for long walks around the parkland paths and quiet lanes crisscrossing the elevated city walls. ✉ *Via Fontanelle S. Stefano, Verona* ☎ *342/8966695* ⊕ *www.funicolarediverona.it* 🎟 *€2.50 round-trip, €1.50 one way.*

Loggia del Consiglio

GOVERNMENT BUILDING | This graceful structure on the north flank of Piazza dei Signori was finished in 1492 and built to house city council meetings. Although the city was already under Venetian rule, Verona still had a certain degree of autonomy, which was expressed by the splendor of the loggia. Very strangely for a Renaissance building of this quality, its architect remains unknown, but it's the finest surviving example of late-15th-century architecture in Verona. The building is not open to the public, but the exterior is worth a visit. ✉ *Piazza dei Signori, Verona.*

Museo Archeologico and Teatro Romano

HISTORY MUSEUM | The archaeological holdings of this museum in a 15th-century former monastery consist largely of the donated collections of Veronese citizens proud of their city's classical past. You'll find few blockbusters here, but there are some noteworthy pieces (especially among the bronzes), and it is interesting to see what cultured Veronese collected between the 17th and 19th centuries. The museum complex includes the Teatro Romano, Verona's 1st-century theater, which is open to visitors. ✉ *Rigaste del Redentore 2, Verona* ☎ *045/8000360* ⊕ *museoarcheologico.comune.verona.it* 🎟 *€4.50 (free with VeronaCard)* ⊘ *Closed Mon.*

Palazzo degli Scaligeri

(*Palazzo di Cangrande*)
CASTLE/PALACE | The della Scala family ruled Verona from this stronghold built (over Roman ruins) at the end of the 13th century and then inhabited by Cangrande I. At that time Verona controlled the mainland Veneto from Treviso and Lombardy to Mantua and Brescia, hence the building's alternative name as a seat of Domini di Terraferma (Venetian administration): Palazzo del Podestà. The portal facing Piazza dei Signori was added in 1533 by the accomplished Renaissance architect Michele Sanmicheli. You have to admire the palazzo from the outside, as it's not open to the public. ✉ *Piazza dei Signori, Verona.*

★ Palazzo della Ragione and Torre dei Lamberti

VIEWPOINT | An elegant 15th-century pink-marble staircase leads up from the *mercato vecchio* (old market) courtyard to the magistrates' chambers in this 12th-century palace, built at the intersection of the main streets of the ancient Roman city. The interior now houses exhibitions of art from the **Galleria d'Arte Moderna Achille Forti.** You can get the highest view in town from atop the attached 270-foot-high Romanesque

Opera productions at the Arena di Verona often include larger-than-life sets.

Torre dei Lamberti. About 50 years after a lightning strike in 1403 knocked its top off, it was rebuilt and extended to its current height. ⊠ *Piazza dei Signori, Verona* ☎ *045/9273027* ⊕ *torredeilamberti.it* ⛝ *Gallery and tower €8 (free with VeronaCard); €4 gallery only; €6 tower only* ⊘ *Gallery closed Mon.*

Piazza delle Erbe

PLAZA/SQUARE | Frescoed buildings surround this medieval square, where a busy Roman forum once stood; during the week it's still bustling, as vendors sell produce and trinkets, much as they have been doing for generations. Eyes are drawn to the often sun-sparkling Madonna Verona fountain (1368) and its Roman statue (the body is from AD 380, with medieval additions). ⊠ *Verona.*

★ Porta dei Borsari

RUINS | As its elegant decoration suggests, this is the main entrance to ancient Verona—dating, in its present state, from the 1st century. It's at the beginning of the narrow, pedestrianized Corso Porta Borsari, now a smart shopping street leading to Piazza delle Erbe. ⊠ *Corso Porta Borsari, Verona.*

Porta dei Leoni

RUINS | The oldest of Verona's elegant and graceful Roman portals, the Porta dei Leoni (on Via Leoni, just a short walk from Piazza delle Erbe) dates from the 1st century BC, but its original earth-and-brick structure was sheathed in local marble during the early imperial era. It has become the focus of a campaign against violence—there are often flowers and messages by the monument—in memory of the murder of a young Veronese here in 2009. ⊠ *Via Leoni, Verona.*

★ San Zeno Maggiore

CHURCH | One of Italy's finest Romanesque churches is filled with treasures, including a rose window by the 13th-century sculptor Brioloto that represents a wheel of fortune, with six of the spokes formed by statues depicting the rising and falling fortunes of mankind. The 12th-century porch is the work of Maestro Niccolò; it's flanked by marble reliefs by Niccolò and Maestro Gugliel-mo depicting scenes from the Old and New Testaments and from the legend of Theodoric. The bronze doors date from the 11th and 12th centuries; some were probably imported from Saxony, and some are from Veronese workshops. They combine allegorical representations with scenes from the lives of saints.

Inside, look for the 12th-century statue of San Zeno to the left of the main altar. In modern times it has been dubbed the "Laughing San Zeno" because of a misinterpretation of its conventional Romanesque grin. A famous *Madonna and Saints* triptych by Andrea Mantegna (1431–1506) hangs over the main altar, and a peaceful cloister (1120–38) lies to the left of the nave. The detached bell tower was finished in 1173. ⊠ *Piazza San Zeno, Verona* ☎ *045/592813* ⊕ *www. chieseverona.it* 🎫 *€3 (free with Church Cumulative Ticket or VeronaCard).*

Sant'Anastasia

CHURCH | Verona's largest church, begun in 1290 but only consecrated in 1471, is a fine example of Gothic brickwork and has a grand doorway with elaborately carved biblical scenes. The main reason for visiting this church, however, is *St. George and the Princess* (dated 1434, but perhaps earlier) by Pisanello (1377–1455). It's above the Pellegrini Chapel off the main altar. As you come in, look also for the *gobbi* (hunchbacks) supporting the holy-water basins. ⊠ *Piazza Sant'Ana-stasia, Verona* ☎ *045/592813* ⊕ *www. chieseverona.it* 🎫 *€3 (free with Church Cumulative Ticket or VeronaCard).*

Vinitaly

FESTIVALS | This widely attended interna-tional wine and spirits event takes place in Verona over four days in April. ⊠ *Fiera di Verona, Viale del Lavoro 8, Verona* ☎ *045/8298111* ⊕ *www.vinitaly.com.*

 Restaurants

★ Antica Osteria al Duomo

$$ | NORTHERN ITALIAN | This side-street eatery, lined with old wood paneling and decked out with musical instruments, serves traditional Veronese classics, like *bigoli* (thick whole-wheat spaghetti) with donkey ragù and *pastissada con polenta* (horsemeat stew with polenta). Don't be deterred by the unconventional meats—they're tender and delicious, and this is probably the best place in town to sample them. **Known for:** rustic courtyard; blackboard menu, bar, and wooden interiors; occasional live music. ⑤ *Average main: €20* ⊠ *Via Duomo 7/A, Verona* ☎ *045/8004505* ⊕ *alduomooste-ria.altervista.org* ⊙ *Closed Sun. except in Dec. and during wine fair.*

★ Il Desco

$$$$ | MODERN ITALIAN | Opened in 1981 by Elia Rizzo, the nationally renowned fine-dining Desco cuisine is now crafted by talented son Matteo. True to Ital-ian and Rizzo culinary traditions, he preserves natural flavors through careful ingredient selection, adding daring com-binations inspired by stints in kitchens around the world. **Known for:** pricey tasting menus; inventive, colorful plates of food; elegant, arty surroundings fit for a modern opera. ⑤ *Average main: €95* ⊠ *Via Dietro San Sebastiano 7, Verona* ☎ *045/595358* ⊕ *www.ristoranteildesco. it* ⊙ *Closed Sun. and Mon. (open for dinner Mon. in Dec.).*

Ristorante 12 Apostoli

$$$$ | NORTHERN ITALIAN | Run by the Gioco family for over a century, 12 Apostoli offers a fine-dining experience amid gorgeous frescoes and dramatically lit place settings. Near Piazza delle Erbe, this historic palazzo setting stands on the foundations of a Roman temple: you can view architectural fragments and a model in the wine cellar. **Known for:** innovative tasting menus; slow and sumptuous dining; elegant, atmospheric rooms

Castelvecchio is a celebrated landmark in Verona.

and cantina. $ *Average main: €120* ✉ *Vicolo Corticella San Março 3, Verona* ☎ *045/596999* ⊕ *www.12apostoli.com* ⊗ *Closed Sun. dinner and Mon.*

☕ Coffee and Quick Bites

★ Caffè Borsari

$ | **NORTHERN ITALIAN** | This bustling café-bar is famed for its excellent creamy coffee and freshly made brioche—pre-COVID, it was cheek-by-jowl *al banco* (at the counter/bar), but for now the Veronese patrons must spill outside. The narrow space on the charming Corso Borsari cobbles is packed with coffee- and tea-making pots and cups, as are its walls with colorful gifts and oddities according to the time of year. **Known for:** fab staff may decorate your *schiuma* (froth); indulgent hot chocolate; selection of coffee, tea, candies, and chocolates to take away. $ *Average main: €4* ✉ *Corso Portoni Borsari 15, Verona* ☎ *045/8031313.*

🛏 Hotels

Book hotels months in advance for spring's Vinitaly, usually the second week in April, and for opera season. Verona hotels are also very busy during the January, May, and September gold fairs in neighboring Vicenza. Hotels jack up prices considerably at all these times.

Best Western Hotel Armando

$$ | **HOTEL** | In a residential area a few minutes' walk from the Arena, this contemporary Best Western hotel offers respite from the busy city as well as easier parking. **Pros:** large rooms for Italy; free Wi-Fi; good breakfast. **Cons:** noise from neighboring restaurant; simple room decor; no parking valet. $ *Rooms from: €130* ✉ *Via Dietro Pallone 1, Verona* ☎ *045/8000206* ⊕ *www.hotelarmando. it* ⊗ *Closed 2 wks late Dec.–early Jan.* ⤴ *28 rooms* ⦿ *Free Breakfast.*

Escalus Luxury Suites

$$$ | HOTEL | FAMILY | Near the Arena and Verona's marble-paved main shopping street, Via Mazzini, these suites and mini-apartments offer contemporary minimalist style in muted colors; the larger ones have handy kitchenettes, and all have swank bathrooms. **Pros:** large showers; chic location near sights and shopping; family-friendly Glamour Deluxe Suite with balcony. **Cons:** constant street noise from Via Mazzini; checkout is before 11 am; minimalist decor not to everyone's taste. $ *Rooms from: €275* ⊠ *Vicolo Tre Marchetti 12, Verona* ☎ *045/8036754* ⊕ *www.escalusverona. com* ⤳ *6 suites* ⦿ *Free Breakfast.*

Gabbia d'Oro

$$$$ | HOTEL | Occupying a historic building off Piazza delle Erbe in the ancient heart of Verona, this hotel is a romantic fantasia of ornamentation, rich fabrics, and period-style furniture. **Pros:** romantic atmosphere; central location; great breakfast. **Cons:** small bathrooms; some very small rooms, especially considering the price; some guests may find the decor overly ornate, even stuffy. $ *Rooms from: €375* ⊠ *Corso Porta Borsari 4/a, Verona* ☎ *045/8003060* ⊕ *www. hotelgabbiadoro.it* ⤳ *27 rooms* ⦿ *Free Breakfast.*

Hotel Accademia

$$$ | HOTEL | The Palladian facade of columns and arches here hint at the well-proportioned interior layout: expect an elegant contemporary take on art deco in public spaces and immaculate if impersonal traditional-style decor in guest rooms. **Pros:** rooftop solarium; central location; good fitness room. **Cons:** some may find the decor lacking; expensive parking; service can be patchy. $ *Rooms from: €286* ⊠ *Via Scala 12, Verona* ☎ *045/596222* ⊕ *www.hotelaccademiaverona.it* ⤳ *96 rooms* ⦿ *Free Breakfast.*

★ L'Ospite Appartamenti

$ | APARTMENT | Friendly and energetic Federica has transformed this three-story property, owned by her family (of De Rossi patisserie fame), into some of the most stylish contemporary apartments—and one of the best values—in Verona, complete with kitchenettes. **Pros:** immaculately clean; great location in the Veronetta near the university and the Adige River; helpful host offers tips and some cooking courses. **Cons:** on a busy road; narrow pavement outside; books up early. $ *Rooms from: €95* ⊠ *Via Venti Settembre 3, Verona* ☎ *045/8036994, 329/4262524 (mobile)* ⊕ *www.lospite. com* ☽ *Closed early Jan.* ⤳ *6 apartments* ⦿ *No Meals.*

⬢ Performing Arts

★ Arena di Verona Opera Festival

OPERA | Milan's La Scala and Naples' San Carlo offer performances more likely to attract serious opera fans, but neither offers a greater spectacle than the Arena di Verona. During the venue's summer season (June to August), as many as 16,000 attendees sit on the original stone terraces or in modern cushioned stalls. Most of the operas presented are big and splashy, like *Aida* or *Turandot,* demanding huge choruses, lots of color and movement, and, if possible, camels, horses, or elephants. Order tickets by phone or through the arena website. If you book a spot on the cheaper terraces, be sure to take or rent a cushion—four hours on a 2,000-year-old stone bench can be an ordeal. ⊠ *Box office, Via Dietro Anfiteatro 6/b, Verona* ☎ *045/8005151* ⊕ *www.arena.it* 🎫 *From €35 (for general admission).*

🛍 Shopping

ANTIQUES
Sant'Anastasia
ANTIQUES & COLLECTIBLES | The area around the Gothic church of Sant'Anastasia has a smattering of antiques shops, some catering to serious collectors. Head to San Zeno on the first Sunday of the month for the Mercato dell'Antiquariato fair on the piazza. ✉ *Corso Sant'Anastasia, Verona*.

BOOKS AND PRINTS
Libreria del Novecento
BOOKS | All bibliophiles should make a beeline to this small bookshop with its fascinating selection of second-hand volumes spanning many subjects. Have a rummage to unearth paperbacks with alluringly designed covers, collectibles, first editions, and intriguing art books. They also have a selection of vinyl records and CDs. ✉ *Via Santa Maria in Chiavica 3/A, Verona* ☎ *045/8008108* ⊕ *www.libreriadelnovecento.it*.

★ Museo Conte–Antica Tipografia
ART GALLERIES | Look out for the striking Fascism-era signage typography above the door—TIPOGRAFIA—and enter Verona's oldest printing press, opened in 1750 and run by the Conte family since the '30s. Marvel at the well-oiled working machinery, tools and rows of printing blocks before perusing their striking, colorful prints and stationery. Since 2000 it's become a nonprofit cultural association. ✉ *Via Santa Maria in Chiavica 3, Verona* ☎ *045/8003392*.

FOOD AND WINE
De Rossi
FOOD | Opened in 1947, De Rossi is a Veronese institution producing oven-hot bread, cakes, pastries, biscotti, and other specialities like fresh pasta. ✉ *Corso Porta Borsari 3, Verona* ☎ *045/8002489* ⊕ *www.derossi.it*.

🏃 Activities

★ Adige Rafting
RAFTING | FAMILY | Briefed by expert guides and issued with paddles and life jackets, the adventurous can set off on a *gommone* (dinghy) from the Chievo (eastern) area of town and navigate the cool waters of the Adige, finishing up at the picnic area of Boschetto. Along the 8-km (5-mile) stretch of river there are wonderful water-level views of Verona's architectural and natural riches. The trip takes around three hours, with two hours spent on the water, including a fun race along the way. ✉ *Centro Sportivo Bottagisio, Via del Perloso 14/A, Verona* ☎ *347/8892498* ⊕ *adigerafting.it* 💶 *€25*.

Vicenza

74 km (46 miles) west of Venice, 43 km (27 miles) west of Padua.

A visit to Vicenza is a must for any student or fan of architecture. This elegant, prosperous city bears the distinctive signature of the 16th-century architect Andrea Palladio, whose name has been given to the "Palladian" style of architecture. He emphasized the principles of order and harmony using the classical style of architecture established by Renaissance architects, such as Brunelleschi, Alberti, and Sansovino. He used these principles and classical motifs not only for public buildings but also for private dwellings. His elegant villas and palaces were influential in propagating classical architecture in Europe, especially in Britain, and later in America—most notably at Thomas Jefferson's Monticello.

In the mid-16th century Palladio was commissioned to rebuild much of Vicenza, which had been greatly damaged during wars waged against Venice by the League of Cambrai (1505), an alliance of the papacy, France, the Holy Roman

Continued on page 248

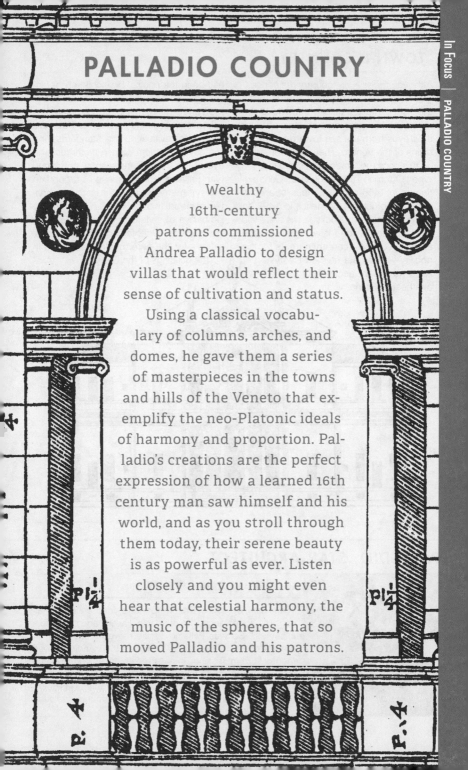

PALLADIO COUNTRY

Wealthy 16th-century patrons commissioned Andrea Palladio to design villas that would reflect their sense of cultivation and status. Using a classical vocabulary of columns, arches, and domes, he gave them a series of masterpieces in the towns and hills of the Veneto that exemplify the neo-Platonic ideals of harmony and proportion. Palladio's creations are the perfect expression of how a learned 16th century man saw himself and his world, and as you stroll through them today, their serene beauty is as powerful as ever. Listen closely and you might even hear that celestial harmony, the music of the spheres, that so moved Palladio and his patrons.

TOWN & COUNTRY

Although the villa, or "country residence," was still a relatively new phenomenon in the 16th century, it quickly became all the rage once the great lords of Venice turned their eyes from the sea toward the fertile plains of the Veneto. They were forced to do this once their trade routes had faltered when Ottoman Turks conquered Constantinople in 1456 and Columbus opened a path to the riches of America in 1492. In no time, canals were built, farms were laid out, and the fashion for *villeggiatura*—the attraction of idyllic country retreats for the nobility—became a favored lifestyle.

As a means of escaping an overheated Rome, villas had been the original brainchild of the ancient emperors and it was no accident that the Venetian lords wished to emulate this palatial style of country residence. Palladio's method of evaluating the standards, and standbys, of ancient Roman life through the eye of the Italian Renaissance, combined with Palladio's innate sense of proportion and symmetry, became the lasting foundation of his art. In turn, Palladio threw out the jambalaya of styles prevalent in Venetian architecture—Oriental, Gothic, and Renaissance—for the pure, noble lines found in the buildings of the Caesars.

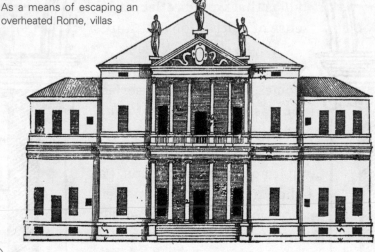

PALLADIO, STAR ARCHITECT

ANDREA PALLADIO (1508–1580)

"Face dark, eyes fiery. Dress rich. His appearance that of a genius." So was Palladio described by his wealthy mentor, Count Trissino. Trissino encouraged the young student to trade in his birth name, Andrea di Pietro della Gondola, for the elegant Palladio. He did, and it proved a wise move indeed. Born in Padua in 1508, Andrea moved to nearby Vicenza in 1524 and was quickly taken up by the city's power elite. He experienced a profound revelation

THE OLD BECOMES NEW

La Malcontenta

Studying ancient Rome with the eyes of an explorer, Palladio employed a style that linked old with new—but often did so in unexpected ways. Just take a look at Villa Foscari, nicknamed "**La Malcontenta**" (✉ *Mira* ☎ *041/5470012* ⊕ *www. lamalcontenta.com €10.* ⊙ *Open Apr.– Oct. daily; from Venice, take an ACTV bus from Piazzale Roma to Mira or opt for a boat ride up on the Burchiello).* Shaded by weeping willows and mirrored by the Brenta Canal, "The Sad Lady" was built for Nicolò and Alvise Foscari and is the quintessence of Palladian poetry. Inspired by the grandeur of Roman public buildings, Palladio applied the ancient motif of a temple facade to a domestic dwelling, topped off by a pediment, a construct most associated with religious structures. Inside, he used the technique of vaulting seen in ancient Roman baths, with giant windows and immense white walls ready-made for the colorful frescoes painted by Zelotti. No one knows for certain the origin of the villa's nickname—some say it came from a Venetian owner's wife who was exiled there due to her scandalous behavior. Regardless of the name, it's hard today to associate such a beautiful, graceful villa with anything but harmony and contentment.

on his first trip, in 1541, to Rome, where he sensed the harmony of the ancient ruins and saw the elements of classicism that were working their way into contemporary architecture. This experience led to his spectacular conversion of the Vicenza's Palazzo della Ragione (1545) into a basilica recalling the great meeting halls of antiquity. In years to come, after relocating to Venice, he created some memorable churches, such as S. Giorgio Maggiore (1564). Despite these varied projects, Palladio's unassailable position as one of the world's greatest architects is tied to the countryside villas, which he spread across the Veneto plains like a firmament of stars. Nothing else in the Veneto illuminates more clearly the idyllic beauty of the region than these elegant residences, their stonework now nicely mellowed and suntanned after five centuries.

VICENZA, CITY OF PALLADIO

Palazzo della Ragione

La Rotonda

To see Palladio's pageant of palaces, head for Vicenza. His **Palazzo della Ragione**, or "Basilica," marks the city's heart, the Piazza dei Signori. This building rocketed young Palladio from an unknown to an architectural star. Across the way is his redbrick **Loggia dei Capitaniato**.

One block past the Loggia is Vicenza's main street, appropriately named Corso Andrea Palladio. Just off this street is the Contrà Porti, where you'll find the **Palazzo Barbaran da Porto** (1570) at No. 11, with its fabulously rich facade erupting with Ionic and Corinthian pillars. Today this hosts the Palladio Museum and Centro (☎ 0444/323014, ⊕ www.palladiomuseum.org; 🎫 Museum €8 ⊘ Wed.-Sun.), a study center which mounts impressive temporary exhibitions. A few steps away, on the Contrà San Gaetano Thiene, is the Palazzo Thiene (1542-58), designed by Giulio Romano and completed by Palladio.

Doubling back to Contrà Porti 21, you find the **Palazzo Iseppo da Porto** (1544), the first palazzo where you can see the neoclassical effects of young Palladio's trip to Rome. Following the Contrà Reale, you come to Corso Fogazzaro 16 and the **Palazzo Valmarana Braga** (1565). Its gigantic pilasters were a first for domestic architecture.

Returning to the Corso Palladio, head left to the opposite end of the Corso, about five blocks, to the Piazza Mattoti and **Palazzo Chiericati** (1550). This was practically a suburban area in the 16th century, and for the palazzo Palladio combined elements of urban and rural design. The pedestal raising the building and the steps leading to the entrance—unknown in urban palaces—were to protect from floods and to keep cows from wandering in the front door. (⇨ *For opening times and details, see Sights in the Vicenza section of this chapter*).

Across the Corso Palladio is Palladio's last and one of his most spectacular works, the **Teatro Olimpico** (1580). By careful study of ancient ruins and architectural texts, he reconstructed a Roman theater with archaeological precision. Palladio died before it was completed, but he left clear plans for the project. (⇨ *For opening times and details, see Sights in the Vicenza section of this chapter.*)

Although it's on the outskirts of town, the **Villa Almerico Capra**, better known as **La Rotonda** (1566), is an indispensable part of any visit to Vicenza. It's the iconic Palladian building, the purest expression of his aesthetic. (⇨ *For opening times, details, and a discussion of the villa, see Sights in the Vicenza section of this chapter.*)

A MAGNIFICENT COLLABORATION

Villa Barbaro

At the **Villa Barbaro** (1554) near the town of Maser in the province of Treviso, 48 km (30 miles) northeast of Vicenza, you can see the results of a one-time collaboration between two of the greatest artists of their age.

Palladio was the architect, and Paolo Veronese decorated the interior with an amazing cycle of trompe l'oeil frescoes—walls dissolve into landscapes, and illusions of courtiers and servants enter rooms and smile down from balustrades.

Legend has it a feud developed between Palladio and Veronese, with Palladio feeling the illusionistic frescoes detracted from his architecture; but there is practically nothing to support the idea of such a rift.

It's also noteworthy that Palladio for the first time connected the two lateral granaries to the main villa. This was a working farm, and Palladio thus created an architectural unity by connecting with graceful arcades the working parts of the estate to the living quarters, bringing together the Renaissance dichotomy of the active and the contemplative life.

🎫 €9 ⏱ Open Apr.–Oct. Tues., Weds., Sat. and Sun.; Nov.–early Dec. and mid-Feb.–Mar. weekends; or group visits by appointment; Closed Dec. 24–Jan. 1.

ALONG THE BRENTA CANAL

During the 16th century the Brenta was transformed into a landlocked version of Venice's Grand Canal with the building of nearly 50 waterside villas.

Back then, boating parties viewed them in burchielli—beautiful boats. Today, the Burchiello excursion boat (✉ Via Orlandini 3, Padua, ☎ 049/8760233, ⊕ www. ilburchiello.it) makes full- and half-day tours along the Brenta, from March to November, departing from Padua and Venice Tues.–Sun., running in both directions; tickets are €55–€95 and can also be bought at travel agencies. You visit three houses, including the Villas Pisani and Foscari, with a lunchtime break in Oriago (€30 extra). Note that most houses are on the left side coming from Venice, or the right from Padua.

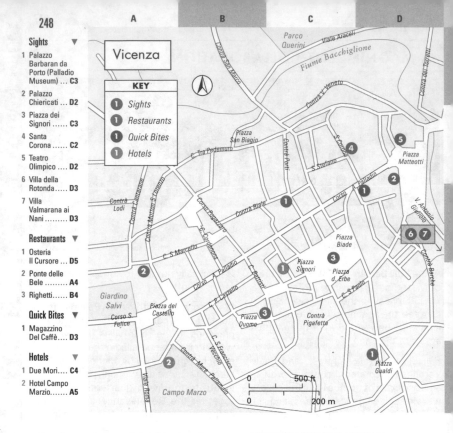

Empire, and several neighboring city-states. He made his name with the renovation of the Basilica, begun in 1549 in the heart of Vicenza, and then embarked on a series of lordly buildings, all of which adhere to the same classicism and principles of harmony.

GETTING HERE AND AROUND

Vicenza is midway between Padua and Verona; several trains leave from Venice every hour. By car, take the Autostrada Brescia–Padova/Torino–Trieste A4/E70 to SP247 North directly into Vicenza.

VISITOR INFORMATION

Vicenza Tourism Office. ⊠ *Piazza Giacomo Matteotti 12, Vicenza* ☎ *0444/320854* ⊕ *www.vicenzae.org.*

◉ Sights

Palazzo Barbaran da Porto (Palladio Museum)

CASTLE/PALACE | Palladio executed this beautiful city palace for the Vicentine noble Montano Barbarano between 1570 and 1575. The noble patron, however, did not make things easy for Palladio; the architect had to incorporate at least two pre-existing medieval houses, with irregularly shaped rooms, into his classical, harmonious plan. It also had to support the great hall of the *piano nobile* (moving floor) above the fragile walls of the original medieval structure. The wonder of it is that this palazzo is one of Palladio's most harmonious constructions; the viewer has little indication that this is actually a transformation of a medieval structure. The palazzo also contains a museum dedicated to Palladio and is the seat of a center for Palladian studies. ⊠ *Contrà Porti 11, Vicenza* 🕾 *0444/323014* ⊕ *www.palladiomuseum. org* 🖾 *€8; €20 Vicenza Card, includes Palazzo Chiericati and Teatro Olimpico, plus others* ☉ *Closed Mon. and Tues.*

Palazzo Chiericati

CASTLE/PALACE | This imposing Palladian palazzo (1550) would be worthy of a visit even if it didn't house Vicenza's **Museo Civico.** Because of the ample space surrounding the building, Palladio combined elements of an urban palazzo with those he used in his country villas. The museum's important Venetian holdings include significant paintings by Cima, Tiepolo, Piazetta, and Tintoretto, but its main attraction is an extensive collection of rarely found works by painters from the Vicenza area, among them Jacopo Bassano (1515–92) and the eccentric and innovative Francesco Maffei (1605–60), whose work foreshadowed important currents of Venetian painting of subsequent generations. ⊠ *Piazza Matteotti, Vicenza* 🕾 *0444/222811* ⊕ *www.museicivicivicenza.it* 🖾 *€7; €20 Vicenza Card, includes Palazzo Barbaran da Porto and Teatro Olimpico, plus others* ☉ *Closed Mon.*

Piazza dei Signori

PLAZA/SQUARE | At the heart of Vicenza, this square contains the **Palazzo della Ragione** (1549), the project with which Palladio made his name by successfully modernizing a medieval building, grafting a graceful two-story exterior loggia onto the existing Gothic structure. Commonly known as Palladio's basilica, the palazzo served as a courthouse and public meeting hall (the original Roman meaning of the term *basilica*) and is now open only when it houses exhibits. The main point of interest, though, is the loggia, is visible

from the piazza. Take a look also at the **Loggia del Capitaniato,** opposite, which Palladio designed but never completed. ⊠ *Vicenza.*

Santa Corona

CHURCH | An exceptionally fine *Baptism of Christ* (1502), a work of Giovanni Bellini's maturity, hangs over the altar on the left, just in front of the transept of this church. Santa Corona also houses the elegantly simple Valmarana chapel, designed by Palladio. ⊠ *Contrà S. Corona, Vicenza* 🕾 *0444/320854* 🖾 *€3 (free with Vicenza Card)* ☉ *Closed Mon.*

★ Teatro Olimpico

PERFORMANCE VENUE | Palladio's last, perhaps most famous work was begun in 1580 and completed in 1585, after his death, by Vincenzo Scamozzi (1552–1616). Based closely on the model of ancient Roman theaters, it represents an important development in theater and stage design and is noteworthy for its acoustics and the cunning use of perspective in Scamozzi's permanent backdrop. The anterooms are frescoed with images of important figures in Venetian history. One of the few Renaissance theaters still standing, it can be visited (with guided tours) during the day and is used for concerts, operas, and other performances. ⊠ *Ticket office, Piazza Matteotti 12, Vicenza* 🕾 *0444/964380* ⊕ *www.teatrolimpicovicenza.it* 🖾 *€11; €20 Vicenza Card, includes Palazzo Barbaran da Porto and Palazzo Chiericati, plus others* ☉ *Closed Mon.*

★ Villa La Rotonda (*Villa Almerico Capra*)

HISTORIC HOME | Commissioned in 1556 as a suburban residence for Paolo Almerico, this beautiful Palladian villa is the purest expression of Palladio's architectural theory and aesthetic. More a villa-temple than a residence, it contradicts the rational utilitarianism of Renaissance architecture and demonstrates the priority Palladio gave to the architectural symbolism of celestial harmony over practical considerations. A visit to view the interior can

The Teatro Olimpico is a stunning place to catch a concert or opera in Vicenza.

be difficult to schedule—the villa remains privately owned, and visiting hours are limited and constantly change—but this is a worthwhile stop, if only to see how Palladio's harmonious arrangement of smallish interconnected rooms around a central domed space paid little attention to the practicalities of living. The interior decoration, mainly later Baroque stuccowork, contains some allegorical frescoes in the cupola by Palladio's contemporary, Alessandro Maganza.

Even without a peek inside, experiencing the exterior and the grounds is a must for any visit to Vicenza. The villa is a 20-minute walk from town or a cab (€12) or bus ride (#8) from Vicenza's Piazza Roma. Private tours are by appointment; see their website for the latest visiting details. ✉ *Via della Rotonda, Vicenza* ☎ *0444/321793* ⊕ *www.villalarotonda. it* ✉ *€10 villa and grounds, €5 grounds only* ⊙ *Interior closed Mon.–Thurs. late March.–late Nov.*

★ **Villa Valmarana ai Nani**

HISTORIC HOME | Inside this 17th- to 18th-century country house, named for the statues of dwarfs adorning the garden, is a series of frescoes executed in 1757 by Gianbattista Tiepolo depicting scenes from classical mythology, the *Iliad*, Tasso's *Jerusalem Delivered*, and Ariosto's *Orlando furioso* (The Frenzy of Orlando). They include his *Sacrifice of Iphigenia*, a major masterpiece of 18th-century painting. The neighboring *foresteria* (guesthouse) is also part of the museum; it contains frescoes showing 18th-century life at its most charming and scenes of chinoiserie popular in the 18th century, by Tiepolo's son Giandomenico (1727–1804). The garden dwarfs are probably taken from designs by Giandomenico. You can reach the villa on foot by following the same path that leads to Palladio's Villa La Rotonda. ✉ *Via dei Nani 2/8, Vicenza* ☎ *0444/321803* ⊕ *www. villavalmarana.com* ✉ *€11.*

🍴 Restaurants

★ Osteria Il Cursore

$$ | NORTHERN ITALIAN | This cozy 19th-century *locale storico* (historic hostelry) is steeped in Vicentina atmosphere, from the bar serving local wines and *sopressa* (premium salami) to the intimate dark-wood restaurant serving hearty classics. Grab a table out back for a sit-down meal of robust dishes like *bigoli* (thick, egg-enriched spaghetti) with duck, spaghetti with *baccalà* (cod), and, in spring, *risi e bisi* (rice with peas). **Known for:** quality wine and cold cuts; buzzy atmosphere, especially on Vicenza soccer match days; great value pasta. $ *Average main: €16* ✉ *Stradella Pozzetto 10, Vicenza* ☎ *0444/323504* ⊕ *www.osteriacursore.it* ⊗ *Closed Tues.*

Ponte delle Bele

$$ | NORTHERN ITALIAN | Many of Vicenza's wealthier residents spend at least part of the summer in the Alps to escape the heat, and the dishes of this popular and friendly trattoria reflect the hearty Alpine influences on local cuisine. The house specialty, *stinco di maiale al forno* (roast pork shank), is wonderfully fragrant, with herbs and aromatic vegetables. **Known for:** unfussy, relaxed atmosphere and kitschy Alpine decor; mountain cheeses and cold cuts; hearty Vicentina classics, including baccalà served with polenta. $ *Average main: €15* ✉ *Contrà Ponte delle Bele 5, Vicenza* ☎ *0444/320647* ⊕ *www.pontedellebele.it* ⊗ *Closed Sun. and 2 wks in Aug.*

Righetti

$ | ITALIAN | Vicentini of all generations gravitate to this popular self-service cafeteria for classic dishes that don't put a dent in your wallet. Expect hearty helpings of fare such as *orzo e fagioli* (barley and bean soup) and *baccalà alla vicentina* (stockfish Vicenza style). **Known for:** entertaining local atmosphere; classic dishes; very popular, especially for lunch. $ *Average main: €12* ✉ *Piazza Duomo 3, Vicenza* ☎ *0444/543135* ⊕ *www.selfrighetti.it* ⊗ *Closed weekends and 1 wk in Jan. and Aug.*

☕ Coffee and Quick Bites

Magazzino del Caffè

$ | NORTHERN ITALIAN | Il Magazzino is a great spot to grab a snack any time of day, as this well-run, modern place covers all the bases, from caffè and brioche breakfast fixes, to brunch panini and plates of pasta or risotto with a glass of wine later. Check out their fab selection of brioche pastries with novel fruit and nutty fillings, as well as heaped salads. **Known for:** aperitivi with stuzzichini snacks; friendly, youthful staff; tempting biscuits and gelato. $ *Average main: €10* ✉ *Corso Palladio 152, Vicenza* ☎ *0444/212774.*

🛏 Hotels

During annual gold fairs in January, March, and September, it may be quite difficult to find lodging. If you're coming then, be sure to reserve well in advance and expect to pay higher rates.

★ Due Mori

$ | HOTEL | The public areas and guest rooms at one of the oldest (1883) hotels in the city, just off Piazza dei Signori, are filled with turn-of-the-20th-century antiques, and regulars favor the place because the high ceilings in the main building make it feel light and airy. **Pros:** free Wi-Fi; comfortable, tastefully furnished rooms in central location; rate same year-round. **Cons:** no help with luggage; no AC, although ceiling fans minimize the need for it; no TVs in rooms. $ *Rooms from: €90* ✉ *Contrà Do Rode 24, Vicenza* ☎ *0444/321886* ⊕ *www.albergoduemori.it* ⊗ *Closed 2 wks in early Aug. and 2 wks in late Dec.* ⇥ *30 rooms* ❍| *No Meals.*

Hotel Campo Marzio

$$ | HOTEL | Rooms at this comfortable full-service hotel—a five-minute walk from the train station and right in front of the city walls—are ample in size, with a mix of contemporary and traditional accents. **Pros:** free bike hire; set back from the street, so it's quiet and bright; great location. **Cons:** breakfast room a tad uninspiring; businesslike exterior; no in-room tea- or coffee-making facilities. ⑤ *Rooms from: €140* ✉ *Viale Roma 21, Vicenza* ☎ *0444/5457000* ⊕ *www. hotelcampomarzio.com* 🛏 *36 rooms* 🍽 *Free Breakfast.*

 Activities

Palladian Routes

CULTURAL TOURS | FAMILY | Based in the handsome Palazzo Valmarana Braga, this company offers a wealth of tours around the province of Vicenza. The most popular excursion is their two-day Vicenza and Odyssey around the lake by e-bike tour. Visit their office to pick up your bike with GPS and be guided by a narration app via smartphone around gorgeous landscapes, three villas, and the verdant shores of Lago di Fimon. ✉ *Palazzo Valmarana Braga, Corso Fogazzaro 16, Vicenza* ☎ *0444/1270212* ⊕ *www.palladianroutes.com* 🎟 *from €45 for eBike rental; €59 e-bike tour.*

Udine

127 km (79 miles) northeast of Venice.

The main reason for devoting some time to Udine is to see works by Gianbattista Tiepolo (1696–1770), one of the greatest European painters of the 18th century.

Udine's hilltop castle has art and archaeology museums as well as wonderful views.

Distributed in several palaces and churches around town, this is the largest assembly of his art outside Venice. In fact, Udine calls itself "la città di Tiepolo."

The largest city on the Friuli side of the region, Udine has a provincial, genteel atmosphere and lots of charm. The city sometimes seems completely unaffected by tourism, and things are still done the way they were decades ago. In the medieval and Renaissance historical center of town, you'll find unevenly spaced streets with appealing wine bars and open-air cafés. Friulani are proud of their culture, with many restaurants featuring local cuisine, and street signs and announcements written in both Italian and Friulano (Furlan), which, although it is classified as a dialect, is really a separate language from Italian.

Commanding a view from the Alpine foothills to the Adriatic Sea, Udine stands on a mound that, according to legend, was erected so Attila the Hun could watch the burning of Aquileia, an important Roman center to the south.

Although the legend is unlikely (Attila burned Aquileia about 500 years before the first historical mention of Udine), the view from Udine's castle across the alluvial plane down to the sea is impressive. In the Middle Ages Udine flourished, thanks to its favorable trade location and the right granted by the local patriarch to hold regular markets.

GETTING HERE AND AROUND

There's frequent train service from both Venice and Trieste; the trip takes about two hours from Venice, and a little over an hour from Trieste. By car from Venice, take the SR11 to the E55 and head east. Take the E55 (it eventually becomes the Autostrada Alpe Adria) to SS13 (Viale Venezia) east into Udine. Driving from Trieste, take the SS202 to the E70, which becomes the A4. Turn onto the E55 north, which is the same road you would take coming from Venice. Driving times are 1½ to 2 hours from Venice and 1 hour from Trieste.

VISITOR INFORMATION

The tourist office sells the FVG (Friuli Venezia Giulia) Card, which includes admission to most museums in Udine and other important sites in the region. Its price ranges from €25 (for 48 hours) up to €39 (for one week).

Udine Tourism Office. ⊠ *Piazza I Maggio 7, Udine* ☎ *0432/295972* ⊕ *www.turismofvg.it.*

Sights

★ Castello and Musei Civici

CASTLE/PALACE | The hilltop castle (construction began in 1517) has panoramic views extending to Monte Nero (7,360 feet) in neighboring Slovenia, but head inside to see Udine's civic museums of art and archaeology, with myriad collections that can detain you for hours. On the ground floor are the Museo del Risorgimento (tracing the history of Italian unification) and Museo Archeologico; the third floor is the Museo della Fotografia, with fascinating 19th- and 20th-century images of the Friuli. Particularly worthwhile is the national and regional art collection in the Galleria d'Arte Antica, which has canvases by Venetians Vittore Carpaccio (circa 1460–1525) and Gianbattista Tiepolo, the recently restored (2020) *Il San Francesco Riceve le Stimmate* (St. Francis Receiving the Stigmata) by Caravaggio, and carefully selected works by lesser known but still interesting Veneto and Friuli artists. ■TIP→ **The museum's small collection of drawings includes several by Tiepolo; some find his drawings even more moving than his paintings.** ⊠ *Via Lionello 1, Udine* ☎ *0432/1272591* ⊕ *www.civicimuseiudine.it* ☑ *€8, €10 Unico ticket also includes Casa Cavazzini and Museo Etnografico del Friuli, (free with FVG Card)* ☉ *Closed Mon.*

Duomo

CHURCH | A few steps from the Piazza della Libertà is Udine's 1335 Duomo, with some significant works by Tiepolo. Its Cappella del Santissimo has important early frescoes by Tiepolo, and the Cappella della Trinità has a Tiepolo altarpiece. There is also a beautiful late Tiepolo *Resurrection* (1751) in an altar by the sculptor Giuseppe Toretti. Ask the Duomo's attendant to let you into the adjacent **Chiesa della Purità** to see more important late paintings by Tiepolo. ⊠ *Piazza del Duomo 1, Udine* ☎ *0432/505302* ⊕ *www.cattedraleudine.it* ☑ *Free.*

★ Museo d'Arte Moderna e Contemporanea–Casa Cavazzini

ART GALLERY | Udine's fine civic collection of modern and contemporary art is housed in the handsome and part-modernized 16th-century Casa Cavazzini, which retains some ornate apartment interiors. The first and second floors display the permanent collection: first-floor highlights include bold sculptural works by the three Udinese brothers Dino, Mirko, and Afro Basaldella, with a backdrop of 14th-century frescoes discovered during the 2012 refurbishing. There are also fine works by Giorgio Morandi, Renato Guttuso, and Carlo Carrà. Up a floor is the Collezione Astaldi, spanning the 1920s through the 1960s, and Collezione FRIAM, with '60s and '70s works. Worth seeking out are Giorgio de Chirico's *I Gladiatori* (1931) and pieces by 20th-century American icons Willem de Kooning, Roy Lichtenstein, and Sol LeWitt. Entry to themed temporary exhibitions costs extra. ⊠ *Via Cavour 14, Udine* ☎ *0432/1273772* ⊕ *www.civicimuseiudine.it* ☑ *€5 (€12 temporary shows), €10 Unico ticket also includes Castello and Museo Etnografico del Friuli (free with FVG Card)* ☉ *Closed Mon.*

★ Museo Diocesano e Gallerie del Tiepolo

CASTLE/PALACE | The handsome Palazzo Patriarcale o Arcivescovile contains several rooms of frescoes by the young Gianbattista Tiepolo, painted from 1726 to 1732, which comprise the most important collection of early works by Italy's most brilliant 18th-century painter. The Galleria del Tiepolo (1727)

Tiepolo's frescoes can be seen in Udine's Palazzo Patriarcale o Arcivescovile.

contains superlative Tiepolo frescoes depicting the stories of Abraham, Isaac, and Jacob. The *Judgment of Solomon* (1729) graces the Pink Room. There are also beautiful and important Tiepolo frescoes in the staircase, throne room, and palatine chapel of this palazzo. Even in these early works we can see the Venetian master's skill in creating an illusion of depth, not only through linear perspective, but also through subtle gradations in the intensity of the colors, with the stronger colors coming forward and the paler ones receding into space. Tiepolo was one of the first artists to use this method of representing space and depth, which reflected the scientific discoveries of perception and optics in the 17th century.

The Museo Diocesano here features sculptures from Friuli churches from the 13th through 18th centuries; and don't miss the magnificent library, the Biblioteca Arcivescovile Delfiniana. ⊠ *Piazza Patriarcato 1, Udine* ☎ *0432/25003* ⊕ *www.musdioc-tiepolo.it* ☛ *€8, includes Museo Diocesano (free with FVG Card)* ☉ *Closed Tues.*

Piazza della Libertà

PLAZA/SQUARE | Udine was conquered by the Venetians in 1420, so there is a distinctly Venetian stamp on the architecture of the historic center, most noticeably here, in the large main square. The Loggia del Leonello, begun in 1428, dominates the square and houses the municipal government. Its similarity to the facade of Venice's Palazzo Ducale (finished in 1424) is clear, but there is no evidence that it is an imitation of that palace. It's more likely a product of the same architectural fashion. Opposite stands the Renaissance Porticato di San Giovanni (1533–35) and the Torre dell'Orologio, a 1527 clock tower with naked *mori* (Moors), who strike the hours on the top. ⊠ *Udine.*

Restaurants

★ Hostaria alla Tavernetta

$$$ | FRIULIAN | The trusty Hostaria (open since 1954) has rustic fireside dining downstairs and more elegantly decorated rooms upstairs, where there's also an intimate terrace under the Duomo. It's a great place for sampling regional specialties such as *orzotto* (barley prepared like risotto), delicious *cjalzòns* (ravioli from the Carnia), and seasonal meat dishes, accompanied by a fabulous wine list. **Known for:** superb local Collio wine, grappa, and regional selections; rustic yet sophisticated atmosphere; Friulian ingredients and traditions. ⑤ *Average main: €25 ⊠ Via di Prampero 2, Udine ☎ 0432/501066 ⊕ www.allatavernetta. com ⊗ Closed Sun. and Mon. No lunch Sat.*

★ Vitello d'Oro

$$$ | ITALIAN | Udine's very chic landmark restaurant is the one reserved most by locals for special occasions, and the menu features the freshest meat and fish in sophisticated dishes served with moodily lit culinary stagecraft. You might start with an antipasto of assorted raw shellfish, including the impossibly sweet Adriatic scampi, followed by the fresh fish of the day. **Known for:** large terrace popular in summer; multicourse tasting menu; seafood served raw and cooked. ⑤ *Average main: €26 ⊠ Via Valvason 4, Udine ☎ 0432/508982 ⊕ www.vitello-doro.com ⊗ Closed Tues. No lunch Wed. and Thurs.*

🖵 Coffee and Quick Bites

★ Grosmi Caffè

$ | NORTHERN ITALIAN | Under the porticoes of gorgeous Piazza Matteoti, with its vibrant student and dialect-speaking locals, Grosmi is a reliable choice for excellent coffee, pastries, and people-watching. Although the brioche filled with chocolate, custard, or fruit jam are staples, some opt for a cheeky small cake or macaroon to accompany their caffeine fix. **Known for:** brioche, pastries, and cakes; tables on the piazza; selection of imported blends. ⑤ *Average main: €5 ⊠ Piazza Giacomo Matteotti 9, Udine ☎ 0432/506411 ⊕ biquadrocaffe.it.*

🛏 Hotels

Hotel Clocchiatti Next

$ | HOTEL | You have two smart and contrasting choices here: the 19th-century villa, with canopy beds and Alpine-style wood ceilings and paneling; and the "Next Wing," with rich colors and spare furnishings in starkly angular rooms. **Pros:** a tranquil Zen-garden haven; stylish, individually decorated rooms; excellent breakfast for €10 extra. **Cons:** small bathrooms; 10-minute drive from town center; no restaurant. ⑤ *Rooms from: €120 ⊠ Via Cividale 29, Udine ☎ 0432/505047 ⊕ www.hotelclocchiatti.it �’ 27 rooms ⦿l No Meals.*

Hotel Ristorante Allegria

$$ | HOTEL | Renovation of this 15th-century building took a decidedly minimalist approach: the breakfast room, lounges, and guest rooms feature plenty of light wood, mood lighting, and sleek, angular design. **Pros:** well-appointed, neutral-hue rooms; easy walking distance to the center; easy access, secure garage. **Cons:** AC can be unreliable; fee for parking; rooms may be too minimalist for some. ⑤ *Rooms from: €160 ⊠ Via Grazzano 18, Udine ☎ 0432/201116 ⊕ www. hotelallegria.it �’ 21 rooms ⦿l Free Breakfast.*

Activities

L'Ippovia del Cormor

BIKING | L'Ippovia del Cormor is a 26-km (16-mile) path that allows walkers, cyclists, and horseback riders to immerse themselves in the rural hamlets north of Udine, including Tricesimo, Colloredo di Monte Albano, Cassacco, and Treppo Grande. The path rises and ends at Buja, where the source of the river Cormor bubbles with numerous streams, including the Rio Gelato, and is surrounded by the mountain peaks. Contact Cussigh Bike for suitably robust wheels to hire. ⊠ *Via del Lavoro, Feletto Umberto—Tavagnacco, Udine* ☎ *040/9828570 Cussigh Bike* ⊕ *www.cussighbike.it.*

Aquileia

123 km (77 miles) east of Venice, 42 km (25 miles) south of Udine.

This sleepy little town is refreshingly free of the tourists that you might expect at such a culturally historic place. In the time of Emperor Augustus, it was Italy's fourth most important city (after Rome, Milan, and Capua), as well as the principal northern Adriatic port of Italy and the beginning of Roman routes north. Aquileia's Roman and early-Christian remains offer an image of the transition from pagan to Christian Rome.

GETTING HERE AND AROUND
Getting to Aquileia by public transportation is difficult but not impossible. There's frequent train service from Venice and Trieste to Cervignano di Friuli, which is 8 km (5 miles) away from Aquileia by taxi (about €25) or infrequent bus service. (Ask the newsstand attendant or the railroad ticket teller for assistance.) By car from Venice or Trieste, take Autostrada A4 (Venezia–Trieste) to the Palmanova exit and continue 17 km (11 miles) to Aquileia. From Udine, take Autostrada A23 to the Palmanova exit.

VISITOR INFORMATION
Aquileia Infopoint. ⊠ *Via Giulia Augusta 11, Aquileia* ☎ *0431/919491* ⊕ *www.turismofvg.it.*

 Sights

Aquileia Archaeological Site
RUINS | Roman remains of the forum, houses, cemetery, and port are surrounded by cypresses here, and the little stream was once an important waterway extending to Grado. Unfortunately, many of the excavations of Roman Aquileia could not be left exposed, because of the extremely high water table under the site, and had to be reburied after archaeological studies had been conducted; nevertheless, what remains above ground, along with the monuments in the archaeological museum, gives an idea of the grandeur of this ancient city. The area is well signposted. ⊠ *Near basilica, Aquileia* ☞ *Free.*

★ Basilica
CHURCH | The highlight here is the spectacular 3rd- to 4th-century mosaic covering the entire floor of the basilica and the adjacent crypt, which make up one of the most important early-Christian monuments. Theodore, the basilica's first bishop, built two parallel basilicas (now the north and the south halls) on the site of a Gnostic chapel in the 4th century. These were joined by a third hall, forming a "U." The complex later accumulated the Romanesque portico and Gothic bell tower. The mosaic floor of the basilica is the remains of the floor of Theodore's south hall.

In his north hall, Theodore retained much of the floor of the earlier Gnostic chapel, whose mosaics represent the ascent of the soul, through the realm of the planets and constellations, to God, who is represented as a ram. (The ram, at the head of the zodiac, is the Gnostic generative force.) This integration of Gnosticism into a Christian church is interesting, since Gnosticism had been branded a heresy by early church fathers.

The 4th-century mosaics of the south hall (the present-day nave) represent the story of Jonah as prefiguring the salvation offered by the Church. Down a flight of steps, the Cripta degli Affreschi contains 12th-century frescoes. ⊠ *Piazza Capitolo*

1, Aquileia ☎ 0431/919719 ⊕ www.
fondazioneaquileia.it ☒ €3 basilica and
Cripta degli Affreschi, €5 with Cripta degli
Scavi; €2 campanile; €10 whole complex;
all sites free with FGV Card ⊘ Campanile
closed Oct.–Mar.

Museo Archeologico

OTHER MUSEUM | The museum's wealth
of material from Roman times includes
portrait busts from the Republican era,
semiprecious gems, amber—including
preserved flies—and goldwork, and a fine
glass collection. Beautiful pre-Christian
mosaics are from the floors of Roman
houses and palaces. ✉ Via Roma 1, Aquileia ☎ 0431/91016 ⊕ www.museoarche-
ologicoaquileia.beniculturali.it ☒ €7 (free
with FGV card) ⊘ Closed Mon.

Museo Paleocristiano

HISTORY MUSEUM | What started out as
an early-Christian 4th-century suburban
basilica was transformed in the 9th
century into a monastery and then a
farmhouse. Now it's a museum: some
of the fragments of 4th-century mosaics
preserved here are even more delicate
than those in the main basilica. ✉ Local-
ità Monastero, Aquileia ☎ 0431/91016
⊕ www.museoarcheologicoaquileia.
beniculturali.it ☒ Free ⊘ Closed Mon.

Trieste

*163 km (101 miles) east of Venice, 77
miles (48 km) east of Aquileia.*

Trieste is Italy's only truly cosmopolitan city.
In a country—perhaps even in a conti-
nent—where the amalgamation of cultures
has frequently proved difficult, Trieste
stands out as one of the few authentic
melting pots. Not only do Italian, Slavic, and
central European cultures meet here, they
actually merge to create a unique Triestino
culture. To discover this culture, visiting
Trieste's coffeehouses, local eateries, and
piazzas is probably more important than
visiting its churches and museums, interesting though they are.

Trieste is built along a fringe of coastline
where the rugged Karst Plateau tumbles
abruptly into the beautiful Adriatic. It was
the only port of the Austro-Hungarian
Empire and, therefore, a major industrial
and financial center. In the early years of
the 20th century, Trieste and its surround-
ings also became famous by their asso-
ciation with some of the most important
names of Italian literature, such as Italo
Svevo, and Irish and German writers.
James Joyce drew inspiration from the
city's multiethnic population, and Rainer
Maria Rilke was inspired by the coast to
the west.

The city has lost its importance as a port
and a center of finance, but perhaps
because of its multicultural nature, at the
juncture of Latin, Slavic, and Germanic
Europe, it's never fully lost its role as an
intellectual center. In recent years the
city has become a center for science
and technology. The streets hold a mix
of monumental neoclassical and art nouveau architecture, built by the Austrians
during Trieste's days of glory, granting an
air of melancholy stateliness to a city that
lives as much in the past as the present.

Italian revolutionaries of the 1800s rallied
their battle cry around Trieste, because of
what they believed was foreign occupation of their motherland. After World War
II the sliver of land including Trieste and a
small part of Istria became an independent, neutral state that was officially recognized in a 1947 peace treaty. Although
it was actually occupied by British and
American troops for its nine years of
existence, the Free Territory of Trieste
issued its own currency and stamps. In
1954 a Memorandum of Understanding
was signed in London, giving civil administration of Trieste to Italy.

GETTING HERE AND AROUND

Trains to Trieste depart regularly from
Venice, Udine, and other major Italian
cities. By car, it's the eastern terminus
of the Autostrada Torino–Trieste (E70).
The city is served by Trieste–Friuli Venezia

Giulia Airport, which receives flights from major Italian airports and some European cities. The airport is 33 km (20½ miles) from the city; transfers into Trieste are by taxi or APT coach No. 51.

VISITOR INFORMATION

Trieste Infopoint. ✉ *Via dell'Orologio 1, Piazza Unità d'Italia, Trieste* ☎ *040/3478312* ⊕ *www.turismofvg.it.*

 # Sights

Castello di Duino

CASTLE/PALACE | This 14th-century castle, the property of the Princes of Thurn and Taxis, contains a collection of antique furnishings and an amazing Palladian circular staircase, but the main attractions are the surrounding gardens and the spectacular views. In 1912 Rainer Maria Rilke wrote much of his masterpiece, the *Duino Elegies,* here. The easy path along the seacoast from the castle toward Trieste has gorgeous views that rival those of the Amalfi Coast and the Cinque Terre. For more spectacular clifftop views, visit the ruins of the nearby 11th-century Castelvecchio. ✉ *Frazione Duino 32, 12 km (7½ miles) from Trieste, Duino* ⊕ *Take Bus No. 44 or 51 from the Trieste train station to Duino* ☎ *040/208120* ⊕ *www.castellodiduino.it* 🎟 *€10; €12 Castello di Duino & Castello Vecchio* 🕐 *Closed Tues.; closed weekdays Jan.–mid-Mar., Nov., and Dec.*

Castello di San Giusto

CASTLE/PALACE | This hilltop castle, built between 1470 and 1630, was constructed on the ruins of the Roman town of Tergeste. Given the excellent view, it's no surprise that 15th-century Venetians turned the castle into a shipping observation point; the structure was further enlarged by Trieste's subsequent rulers, the Habsburgs. The castle also contains the Civic Museum, which has a collection of furnishings, tapestries, and weaponry, as well as Roman artifacts in the atmospheric Lapidario Tergestino. ✉ *Piazza della Cattedrale 3, Trieste* ☎ *040/309362* ⊕ *www.castellodisangiustotrieste.it* 🎟 *€5*

includes all complex museums 🕐 *Closed Mon. during winter months.*

Cattedrale di San Giusto

CHURCH | Dating from the 14th century and occupying the site of an ancient Roman forum, the cathedral contains remnants of at least three previous buildings, the earliest a hall dating from the 5th century. A section of the original floor mosaic still remains, incorporated into the floor of the present church. In the 9th and 11th centuries two adjacent churches were built—the Church of the Assumption and the Church of San Giusto. The beautiful apse mosaics of these churches, done in the 12th and 13th centuries by a Venetian artist, still remain in the apses of the side aisles of the present church. The mosaics in the main apse date from 1932. In the 14th century the two churches were joined and a Romanesque Gothic facade was attached, ornamented with fragments of Roman monuments taken from the forum. The jambs of the main doorway are the most conspicuous Roman element. ✉ *Piazza della Cattedrale 2, Trieste* ☎ *040/2600892* ⊕ *www.sangiustomartire.it.*

Grotta Gigante

CAVE | More than 300 feet high, 900 feet long, and 200 feet wide, this gigantic cave is filled with spectacular stalactites and stalagmites. The required tour takes 50 minutes. Bring a sweater to ward off the year-round chill and be willing (and able) to descend 500 steps and then climb back up. To get here you can take Bus No. 42, which leaves every 30 minutes from the Piazza Oberdan; a more scenic route is to take the tram uphill from Piazza Oberdan to Opicina, where you connect with Bus No. 42. ✉ *Trieste* ⊕ *10 km (6 miles) north of Trieste* ☎ *040/327312* 🎟 *€13* 🕐 *Closed Mon. in Sept.–May.*

★ Miramare

CASTLE/PALACE | FAMILY | A 19th-century castle on the Gulf of Trieste, this is nothing less than a major expression

of the culture of the decaying Austrian Habsburg monarchy: nowhere else—not even in Vienna—can you savor the decadent opulence of the last years of the empire. Maximilian of Habsburg, brother of Emperor Franz Josef and the retired commander of the Austrian Navy, built the seafront extravaganza between 1856 and 1860, complete with a throne room under a wooden ceiling shaped like a ship's keel. The rooms are generally furnished with copies of medieval, Renaissance, and French period furniture, and the walls are covered in red damask. In 1864 Maximilian became emperor of Mexico at the initiative of Napoléon III. He was executed three years later by a Mexican firing squad.

During the last years of the Habsburg reign, Miramare became one of the favorite residences of Franz Josef's wife, the Empress Elizabeth (Sissi). The castle was later owned by Duke Amedeo of Aosta. Changing exhibitions in the revamped Sala Progetti showcase the impressive museum archive. Tours in English are available by reservation. Surrounding the castle is a 54-acre park. To get here from central Trieste, take Bus No. 36 from Piazza Oberdan; it runs every half hour. ⊠ *Viale Miramare, off SS14, Trieste* ✛ *7 km (4½ miles) NW of Trieste* ☎ *040/224143* ⊕ *www.castello-miramare. it* ⊠ *€10.*

Museo d'Antichità J. J. Winckelmann
HISTORY MUSEUM | On the hill near the Castello, this eclectic collection showcases statues from the Roman theater, mosaics, and a wealth of artifacts from Egypt, Greece, and Rome. There's also an assortment of glass and manuscripts. The Orto Lapidario (Lapidary Garden) has classical statuary, pottery, and a small Corinthian temple. The collection was renamed in 2018 after the pioneering art historian and Hellenist J. J. Winckelmann, who was murdered in Trieste in 1768. ⊠ *Via Cattedrale 1, Trieste* ☎ *040/310500* ⊕ *museoantichitawinckelmann.it* ⊠ *Free* ⊙ *Closed Mon.*

★ Museo Revoltella–Galleria d'Arte Moderna
ART MUSEUM | Housed in three magnificent buildings and partly remodeled by influential Italian architect Carlo Scarpa, the Revoltella provides a stimulating survey of 19th- and 20th-century art and decoration. Building on the bequeathment of the grand palazzo and art of Triestino collector-industrialist Pasquale Revoltella (1795–1869), the institution has continued to add important artworks from the Venice Biennale by the likes of Carrà, Mascherini, Morandi, de Chirico, Manzù, Fontana, and Burri. In contrast, a gorgeous cochlear staircase connects the three floors of the museum: its history and 1850–60 cityscapes are on the ground floor; 19th-century classical statuary, portraits, and historic scenes take up the first; while the third preserves opulent *saloni.* ⊠ *Via Diaz 27, Trieste* ☎ *040/6754350* ⊕ *museorevoltella.it* ⊠ *Free* ⊙ *Closed Tues.*

Piazza della Borsa
PLAZA/SQUARE | A statue of Habsburg emperor Leopold I looks out over this square, which contains Trieste's original stock exchange, the Borsa Vecchia (1805), an attractive neoclassical building now serving as the chamber of commerce. It sits at the end of the Canal Grande, dug in the 18th century by the Austrian empress Maria Theresa as a first step in the expansion of what was then a small fishing village of 7,000 into the port of her empire. ⊠ *Trieste.*

Piazza Unità d'Italia
PLAZA/SQUARE | The imposing square, ringed by grandiose facades, was set out as a plaza open to the sea, like Venice's Piazza San Marco, in the late Middle Ages. It underwent countless changes through the centuries, and its present size and architecture are essentially products of late-19th- and early-20th-century Austria. It was given its current name

The top floor of the Museo Revoltella–Galleria d'Arte Moderna is strikingly modern compared to many of the region's historic palaces.

in 1955, when Trieste was finally given to Italy. On the inland side of the piazza, note the facade of the **Palazzo Comunale** (Town Hall), designed by the Triestino architect Giuseppe Bruni in 1875. It was from this building's balcony in 1938 that Mussolini proclaimed the infamous racial laws, depriving Italian Jews of most of their rights. The sidewalk cafés on this vast seaside piazza are popular meeting places in the summer months. ✉ *Trieste.*

Risiera di San Sabba

HISTORIC SIGHT | In September 1943 the Nazi occupation established Italy's only concentration camp in this rice-processing factory outside Trieste. In April 1944 a crematorium was put into operation. The Nazis destroyed much of the evidence of their atrocities before their retreat, but a good deal of the horror of the place is still perceivable in the reconstructed museum (1975). The site, an Italian national monument since 1965, receives more than 100,000 visitors per year. ✉ *Via Giovanni Palatucci 5, Trieste* ⊹ *Take municipal Bus No. 8 or 10; off the Autostrada A4, take exit Valmaura/Stadio/*

Cimitero ☎ *040/826202* ⊕ *www.risieras-ansabba.it* ✉ *Free.*

San Silvestro

CHURCH | This small Romanesque gem, dating from the 9th to the 12th centuries, is the oldest church in Trieste that's still in use and in approximately its original form. Its interior walls have some fragmentary remains of Romanesque frescoes. The church was deconsecrated under the secularizing reforms of the Austrian emperor Josef II in 1785 and was later sold to the Swiss Evangelical community; it then became, and is still, the Reformed Evangelical and Waldensian Church of Trieste. ✉ *Piazza San Silvestro 1, Trieste* ☎ *040/632770* ⊕ *triestevangelica.org.*

Teatro Romano

RUINS | The ruins of this 1st-century amphitheater, near the Via Giuseppe Mazzini opposite the city's *questura* (police station), were discovered during 1938 demolition work. Its statues are now displayed at the Museo Civico, and the space is used for summer plays and concerts. ✉ *Via del Teatro Romano, Trieste.*

🍴 Restaurants

Al Bagatto

$$$ | SEAFOOD | At this warm and sophisticated seafood place, going strong since 1966 near Piazza Unità d'Italia, you'll find exquisite dishes that honor the traditions of the Mancussi family. Although now run by the Leonardi family, Roberto Mancussi's culinary ethos remains: integrating nouvelle ingredients without overshadowing the freshness of whatever local fish he bought in the market that morning. **Known for:** novel culinary experience; freshest seafood beautifully prepared; more than 300 wine labels and spirits. ⑤ *Average main: €28 ⊠ Via Luigi Cadorna 7, Trieste ☎ 040/301771 ⊕ www. albagatto.it* ⊙ *Closed Sun. No lunch Mon.*

Buffet da Siora Rosa

$$ | NORTHERN ITALIAN | FAMILY | Serving delicious and generous portions of traditional Triestino buffet fare, such as boiled pork and sausages with savory sauerkraut, Siora Rosa is a bit more comfortable than many buffets. In addition to ample seating in the simple dining room, there are tables outside for when the weather is good. **Known for:** meat dishes galore; well-loved Trieste institution (opened 1921); chatty locals speaking in dialect. ⑤ *Average main: €19 ⊠ Piazza Hortis 3, Trieste ☎ 040/301460 ⊕ buffet-siorarosa.it* ⊙ *Closed Sun. and Mon.*

Mare alla Voliga

$$ | SEAFOOD | Hidden halfway up the hill to the Castello di San Giusto, in what the Triestini call Zità Vecia (Old City), this informal little restaurant specializes in simply prepared seafood. Amid white-washed wooden walls and nautical ephemera, you can sample the freshest catches—bluefish, sardines, mackerel, mussels, and squid—accompanied by salad, potatoes, polenta, and house wine. **Known for:** beach-hut decor and atmosphere; tasty fish and seafood; locals packed in like sarde. ⑤ *Average main: €16 ⊠ Via della Fornace 1, Trieste ☎ 040/309606 ⊕ www.allavoliga.it* ⊙ *Closed Mon. and Tues.*

★ Suban

$$ | NORTHERN ITALIAN | An easy trip just outside town, this landmark trattoria—serving Triestino food with Slovene, Hungarian, and Austrian accents—has been in business since 1865. Sit by the dining room fire or relax on a huge terrace with a pergola, watching the sun set as you tuck into rich soups and roasts spiced with rosemary, thyme, and sweet paprika. ■TIP→ **Portions tend to be small, so if you're hungry, order both a first and second course, as well as an antipasto. Known for:** warm hospitality; smallish portions; *jota carsolina* (a rich soup of cabbage, potatoes, and beans). ⑤ *Average main: €24 ⊠ Via Comici 2, Trieste ⊹ Take Bus No. 35 from Piazza Oberdan ☎ 040/54368 ⊕ www.suban.it* ⊙ *Closed Tues. and 2 wks in early Jan.*

☕ Coffee and Quick Bites

★ Da Pepi

$ | NORTHERN ITALIAN | A Triestino institution, this is the oldest and most esteemed of the many "buffet" restaurants serving pork and sausages around town, with a wood-paneled interior and seating outside. It specializes in *bollito di maiale*, a dish of boiled pork and pork sausages accompanied by delicately flavored sauerkraut, mustard, and grated horseradish. **Known for:** good for a snack on the hoof; porky platter La Caldaia Da Pepi; *panino porzina* (pork shoulder with mustard and *kren* [horseradish]). ⑤ *Average main: €14 ⊠ Via Cassa di Risparmio 3, Trieste ☎ 040/366858 ⊕ www. buffetdapepi.it* ⊙ *Closed Sun. and last 2 wks in July.*

Hotels

★ Duchi d'Aosta

$$$ | HOTEL | Bang smack in regal Piazza Unità d'Italia, this grand dame of a hotel is beautifully furnished in Venetian Renaissance style, with dark-wood antiques, rich carpets, and plush fabrics. **Pros:** sumptuous breakfast; outstanding indoor pool and spa on grand scale; lots of charm paired with modern convenience. **Cons:** restaurant overpriced; rooms overlooking the piazza can be very expensive; expensive and inconvenient parking. $ *Rooms from: €270* ⊠ *Piazza Unità d'Italia 2/1, Trieste* ☎ *040/7600011* ⊕ *www.grandhotelduchidaosta.com* ⇨ *55 rooms* ○ *Free Breakfast.*

Hotel Riviera & Maximilian's

$$$ | HOTEL | Set on gorgeous, verdant grounds with stunning sea views, this clifftop hotel—a villa with a modern annex—offers a mix of traditional and minimalist rooms, many with private balconies. **Pros:** superb views of the Golfo di Trieste; spa facilities; area for swimming in sea. **Cons:** small spa; rooms on the small side; far from town. $ *Rooms from: €252* ⊠ *Strada Costiera 22, 7 km (4½ miles) north of Trieste, Trieste* ☎ *040/224551* ⊕ *www.hotelrivieraemaximilian.com* ⇨ *67 rooms* ○ *Free Breakfast.*

★ L'Albero Nascosto Hotel Residence

$$ | B&B/INN | There's plenty of architectural character mixed with contemporary, artsy warmth in the guest rooms of this central 18th-century building, while the nearby annex offers five spacious apartments. **Pros:** great tea and coffee; very central; spacious and simple but tasteful rooms. **Cons:** street noise can be a problem (if noise sensitive, ask for a room in the back); no elevator; tricky parking nearby. $ *Rooms from: €155* ⊠ *Via Felice Venezian 18, Trieste* ☎ *040/300188* ⊕ *www.alberonascosto.it* ⇨ *10 rooms* ○ *Free Breakfast.*

Victoria Hotel Letterario

$ | HOTEL | The former home of James Joyce is a real gem of a hotel—with stylish, unfussy traditional decor and a just-out-of-town location that's convenient for both local sightseeing and trips into the Karst mountains. **Pros:** wellness center and spa; large, pleasant, light-filled rooms; excellent two-bedroom apartments for longer stays. **Cons:** a bit removed and a stroll into town; parking fee; some rooms suffer from traffic noise. $ *Rooms from: €121* ⊠ *Alfredo Oriani 2, Trieste* ☎ *040/362415* ⊕ *www.hotelvictoriatrieste.com* ⇨ *44 rooms* ○ *No Meals.*

▼ Nightlife

Trieste is justly famous for its coffee. The elegant civility of Trieste plays out beautifully in a caffè culture combining the refinement of Vienna with the passion of Italy. In Trieste, as elsewhere in Italy, ask for a caffè and you'll get a thimbleful of high-octane espresso. Your cappuccino here will come in the Viennese fashion, with a dollop of whipped cream. Many cafés are part of a *torrefazione* (roasting shop), so you can sample a cup and then buy beans to take with you.

Antico Caffè San Marco

CAFÉS | Few cafés in Italy can rival Antico Caffè San Marco for its historic and cultured atmosphere. Founded in 1914, it was largely destroyed in World War I and rebuilt in the 1920s, then restored several more times, but some of the original art nouveau interior remains. It became a meeting place for local intellectuals and was the haunt of the Triestino writers Italo Svevo and Umberto Saba. It remains open until midnight on Friday and Saturday, and light meals are available. ⊠ *Via Battisti 18, Trieste* ☎ *040/2035357* ⊕ *www.caffesanmarco.com.*

Caffè degli Specchi

CAFÉS | For a great view of the great piazza, you can't do better than this café, whose many mirrors make for engaging people-watching. Originally opened in 1839, it was taken over by the British Navy after World War II, and Triestini were not allowed in unless accompanied by someone British. Because of its location, the café—which stays open late—is heavily frequented by tourists. It's now owned by the Segafredo Zanetti coffee company, and some feel it has lost its local character. ⊠ *Piazza Unità d'Italia 7, Trieste* ☎ *040/368033* ⊕ *www.caffespecchi.it.*

Caffè Tommaseo

CAFÉS | Founded in 1830, this classic café is a comfortable place to linger, especially on weekend evenings and at lunchtime (11–1:30) on Sunday, when there's live music. Although you can still have just a coffee, Tommaseo has evolved into a restaurant, with an extensive menu. It's open nightly until 10:30. ⊠ *Piazza Tommaseo 4/C, Trieste* ☎ *040/362666* ⊕ *www.caffetommaseo.it.*

 Performing Arts

Teatro Verdi

OPERA | Trieste's main opera house, built under Austrian rule in 1801, is of interest to aficionados of fine architecture as well as music lovers. Gian Antonio Selva, the architect of Venice's Teatro La Fenice, designed the interior, and Matteo Pertsch, responsible for Milan's Teatro alla Scala, designed the facade. You'll have to attend a performance to view Teatro Verdi's interior; guided tours aren't conducted for individuals. ■ **TIP→ Opera season runs from October through May, with a brief operetta festival in July and August.** ⊠ *Piazza Verdi 1, Trieste* ☎ *040/6722298* ⊕ *www.teatroverdi-trieste.com.*

🛍 Shopping

Trieste has some 50 local dealers in jewelry, antiques, and bric-a-brac; the city's old center hosts an antiques and collectibles market on the third Sunday (Mercatino dell'Usato e dell'Antiquariato in Largo Granatieri) and fourth Saturday (Mercato dei Tritoni in Piazza Vittorio Veneto) of each month, and there's a large antiques fair, **Trieste Antiqua,** at the end of October. Trieste's busy shopping street, **Corso Italia,** is off Piazza della Borsa.

Katastrofa

ANTIQUES & COLLECTIBLES | Head to this bonkers emporium for an entertaining and eye-popping perusal of 20th-century antiques and ephemera, from vintage stereo equipment and funky furniture to quirky artworks and designer handbags. ⊠ *Via Armando Diaz 4, Trieste* ☎ *335/8298432 cell.*

Rigatteria

ANTIQUES & COLLECTIBLES | Opened in 1981, the fascinating Rigatteria is crammed with antiques, paintings, and a cornucopia of printed matter, including books, newspapers, and magazines, many documenting Triestina life over the decades. ⊠ *Via Malcanton 12, Trieste* ☎ *040/630866* ⊕ *www.rigatteria.com.*

Activities

Arawak Sailing Club

BOATING | **FAMILY** | Renowned for its fierce Bora breeze and the largest sailing regatta in the world, Barcolana, Trieste is the perfect spot for boating adventures. Arawak Sailing Club rents all sorts of craft, from skippered yachts and catamarans to kayaks and motorboats. They also run a number of courses, including beginner sailing lessons and more advanced instruction. ⊠ *Via della Geppa 19, Trieste* ☎ *040/2654315* ⊕ *www.arawak.it.*

Photo Credits

Front Cover: Harald Laschitz/Getty Images/EyeEm [Description: Rear View of Man Standing on Footbridge Over Canal by Church of San Giorgio Maggiore]. **Back cover, from left to right:** Boris Stroujko, Dieter Meyer, Vishnevetskiy/Shutterstock **Spine:** shahramazizi **Interior, from left to right:** AlexAnton/Shutterstock (1) Adisa/Shutterstock (2) Mapics/Dreamstime.com (5) **Chapter 1: Experience Venice:** Catarina Belova/Shutterstock (6) Irina Demenkova/Shutterstock (8) Sailorr/Shutterstock (9) Marion Meyer/Dreamstime (9) Royal Gondola/Venice (10) Jeanette Teare/Shutterstock (10) Bissun/Shutterstock (10) GenOMart/Shutterstock (10) Adisa/Shutterstock (11) Photogolfer/Dreamstime (11) Ufficio stampa/Venice (12) Monysasi/Dreamstime (12) Taverna La Fenice/Venice (12) Elena Odareeva/Dreamstime (12) Sepy67/Dreamstime (13) CastecoDesign/Shutterstock (13) Romangorielov/Dreamstime (14) Waku/Shutterstock (14) Tomas Marek/Shutterstock (15) Marion Meyer/ Dreamstime (20) Matteo De Fina/Peggy Guggenheim Collection, Venice (20) Joao Segatti/Dreamstime (20) Chrisdorney/Shutterstock (21) Photogolfer/Dreamstime (21) Igor Dutina/Shutterstock (22) Fivetonine/Shutterstock (22) Bulgnn/iStockphoto (22) Jackmalipan/Dreamstime (22) Martin Rettenberger/Shutterstock (23) Alexander Prokopenko/Shutterstock (23) Malkovstock/iStockphoto (23) Oxana Denezhkina/Shutterstock (23) EQRoy/Shutterstock (24) Stockcube/Dreamstime (24) M.bonotto/Shutterstock (24) EQRoy/Shutterstock (25) Fedecandoniphoto/Dreamstime (25) AndrewSoundarajan/iStockphoto (26) AndreaAstes/iStockphoto (26) Robert Zehetmayer/Dreamstime (26) LizCoughlan/Shutterstock (26) Venezia, Palazzo Ducale (27) Mapics/Dreamstime.com (31) Alexey Arkhipov/Shutterstock (32) Agiampiccolo/Dreamstime.com (33) Paul D'Innocenzo2007 (33) minnystock/Dreamstime.com (34) Steve Allen/Brand X Pictures (35) Jaro68/Shutterstock (35) EQRoy/Shutterstock (36) Corbis RF (37) Walencienne/Shutterstock (37) **Chapter 3: San Marco:** RuslanKaln/iStockphoto (69) Viacheslav Lopatin/iStockphoto (77) Catarina Belova/Shutterstock (80) Olaf Unger/Shutterstock (82) Lybid/Shutterstock (82) Zvonimir Atletic/Shutterstock (82) 2019 ArTono/Shutterstock (82) Zoltan Tarlacz/Shutterstock (82) SvetlanaSF/Shutterstock (83) Don Mammoser/Shutterstock (83) Viacheslav Lopatin/Shutterstock (84) ArTono/Shutterstock (84) Viacheslav Lopatin/Shutterstock (84) Evgeny Shmulev/Shutterstock (85) Marco Rubino/Shutterstock (86) ilozavr/Shutterstock (86) Minnystock/Dreamstime (87) Image Professionals GmbH / Alamy Stock Photo (88) Elena Odareeva/Shutterstock (90) Peter B Nyren/Flickr (93) fivetonine/Shutterstock (94) Anna Yordanova/Shutterstock (98) **Chapter 4: Dorsoduro:** Givaga/Shutterstock (101) FooTToo/Shutterstock (106) agefotostock/Alamy Stock Photo (108) Alexandr Medvedkov/Shutterstock (110) Mark Longair/Flickr (115) REDA (118) Advencap/Flickr (123) Blickwinkel2511/Shutterstock (124) **Chapter 5: San Polo and Santa Croce:** Antanovich1985/Dreamstime (127) Mihail Ivanov/Dreamstime (133) Courtesy of Vela Spa (143) Walencienne/iStockphoto (145) Maigi/Dreamstime (146) **Chapter 6: Cannaregio:** Igor Abramovych/Dreamstime (151) Scaliger/Dreamstime (154) Bortnikau/Dreamstime.com (156) Matthias Scholz/Alamy Stock Photo (163) Bpaties/Flickr (164) REDA (166) **Chapter 7: Castello:** RossHelen/Shutterstock (171) Cezary Wojtkowski/Shutterstock (179) LorenzoP/Alamy Stock Photo (180) Seventyoneplace/Flickr (182) Leklek73/Dreamstime (184) Thomas Smith/Dreamstime (187) **Chapter 8: San Giorgio Maggiore and the Giudecca:** Vitalyedush/Dreamstime (189) Pani Garmyder/Shutterstock (193) Minhbao/Dreamstime (194) **Chapter 9: Islands of the Lagoon:** Inguskruklitis/Dreamstime (199) Zefart/Dreamstime (204) Arkantostock/Dreamstime (208) Martina Lanotte/Shutterstock (210) Adisa/Shutterstock (213) Mail50777/Dreamstime.com (215) **Chapter 10: Side Trips from Venice:** Dmitry Ometsinsky/Dreamstime (217) Photology1971/Shutterstock (220) ChiccoDodiFC/Shutterstock (221) Visionsi/Shutterstock (221) Sven Hansche/Shutterstock (226) Andrea La Corte(Andrews71)/Dreamstime (228) Ekaterina Spirina(Kattsspi)/Dreamstime (232) Xbrchx/Shutterstock (236) Yang Zhang(Zy1224)/Dreamstime (238) Marco Rubino/Shutterstock (240) ArTono/Shutterstock (244) Massimo Parisi/Shutterstock (245) Aliaksandr Antanovich/Shutterstock (246) Giancarlo Peruzzi/Shutterstock (246) Boerescu/Shutterstock (247) Marcobrivio.photo/Shutterstock (250) Marco Lissoni/Shutterstock (253) Peewam/Dreamstime.com (255) Freesurf69/Dreamstime (260) Freesurf69/Dreamstime (263) **About Our Writers:** All photos are courtesy of the writers.

*Every effort has been made to trace the copyright holders, and we apologize in advance for any accidental errors. We would be happy to apply the corrections in the following edition of this publication.

Fodor's VENICE

Publisher: Stephen Horowitz, *General Manager*

Editorial: Douglas Stallings, *Editorial Director*; Jill Fergus, Amanda Sadlowski, *Senior Editors*; Kayla Becker, Alexis Kelly, *Editors*; Angelique Kennedy-Chavannes, *Assistant Editor*

Design: Tina Malaney, *Director of Design and Production*; Jessica Gonzalez, *Graphic Designer*

Production: Jennifer DePrima, *Editorial Production Manager*; Elyse Rozelle, *Senior Production Editor*; Monica White, *Production Editor*

Maps: Rebecca Baer, *Senior Map Editor*; Mark Stroud (Moon Street Cartography), David Lindroth, *Cartographers*

Photography: Viviane Teles, *Senior Photo Editor*; Namrata Aggarwal, Payal Gupta, Ashok Kumar, *Photo Editors*; Eddie Aldrete, *Photo Production Intern*

Business and Operations: Chuck Hoover, *Chief Marketing Officer*; Robert Ames, *Group General Manager*; Devin Duckworth, *Director of Print Publishing*

Public Relations and Marketing: Joe Ewaskiw, *Senior Director of Communications and Public Relations*

Fodors.com: Jeremy Tarr, *Editorial Director*; Rachael Levitt, *Managing Editor*

Technology: Jon Atkinson, *Director of Technology*; Rudresh Teotia, *Lead Developer*

Writers: Nick Bruno, Liz Humphreys, Erla Zwingle

Editor: Kayla Becker

Production Editor: Monica White

2nd Edition

ISBN 978-1-64097-430-2

ISSN 2330-0620

SPECIAL SALES

This book is available at special discounts for bulk purchases for sales promotions or premiums. For more information, e-mail SpecialMarkets@fodors.com.

PRINTED IN CANADA

10 9 8 7 6 5 4 3 2 1

About Our Writers

 Nick Bruno is an Italy specialist and frequent Fodor's contributor. As well as authoring and updating books and features, he makes radio packages for the BBC. A lifelong interest in history and Italian language has led to a project researching his paternal Italian family during the Il Ventennio Fascista period. Nick updated the Experience, Travel Smart, Cannaregio, Castello, San Giorgio Maggiore and the Giudecca, and Side Trips from Venice chapters. Follow him on Instagram and Twitter @nickjgbruno and at barbruno.com.

 Liz Humphreys is a transplant to Europe from New York City, where she spent a decade in editorial positions for media companies including Condé Nast and Time Inc. Since then she's written and edited for publications including *Condé Nast Traveler*, *Michelin Green Guides*, *Time Out*, *Forbes Travel*, and *Rough Guides*. Liz updated the San Marco and Islands of the Lagoon chapters. Follow Liz on Instagram @winederlust_wanderings.

 Erla Zwingle has been a major contributor to *National Geographic* since 1982 and wrote their guidebook to Venice, as well as writing for scores of other publications including *Smithsonian*, *Esquire*, *Edutopia*, and *Craftsmanship Quarterly*. She lives in Venice and writes a blog about daily life there called "Venice: I am not making this up." She updated the Dorsoduro and San Polo and Santa Croce chapters of this guide.